The Modern Regime, Volume I

Hippolyte A. Taine

The Modern Regime, Volume 1 [Napoleon]
The Origins of Contemporary France, Volume 5
by Hippolyte A. Taine

Contents:

PREFACE

BOOK FIRST.　　　　Napoleon Bonaparte.

　　Chapter I　.Historical Importance of his Character and　Genius.

　　Chapter II.　His Ideas, Passions and Intelligence.

BOOK SECOND.　　Formation and Character of the New State.

　　Chapter I.　The Institution of Government.

　　Chapter II.　Use and Abuse of Government Services.

　　Chapter III　.The New Government Organization.

BOOK THIRD.　　　Object and Merits of the System.

　　Chapter I.　Recovery of Social Order.

　　Chapter II.　Taxation and Conscription.

　　Chapter III.　Ambition and Self-esteem.

BOOK FOURTH.　　Defect and Effects of the System.

　　Chapter I.　Local Society.

　　Chapter II　.Local society since 1830.

PREFACE

The following third and last part of the Origins of Contemporary France is to consist of two volumes. After the present volume, the second is to treat of the Church, the School and the Family, describe the modern milieu and note the facilities and obstacles which a society like our own encounters in this new milieu: here, the past and the present meet, and the work already done is continued by the work which is going on under our eyes. - -The undertaking is hazardous and more difficult than with the two preceding parts. For the Ancient Régime and the Revolution are henceforth complete and finished periods; we have seen the end of both and are thus able to comprehend their entire course. On the contrary, the end of the ulterior period is still wanting; the great institutions which date from the Consulate and the Empire, either consolidation or dissolution, have not yet reached their historic term: since 1800, the social order of things, notwithstanding eight changes of political form, has remained almost intact. Our children or grandchildren will know whether it will finally succeed or miscarry; witnesses of the denouement, they will have fuller light by which to judge of the entire drama. Thus far four acts only have been played; of the fifth act, we have simply a presentiment. - On the other hand, by dint of living under this social system, we have become accustomed to it; it no longer excites our wonder; however artificial it may be it seems to us natural. We can scarcely conceive of another that is healthier; and what is much worse, it is repugnant to us to do so. For, such a conception would soon lead to comparisons and hence to a judgment and, on many points, to an unfavorable judgment, one which would be a censure, not only of our institutions but of ourselves. The machine of the year VIII, applied to us for three generations, has permanently shaped and fixed us as we are, for better or for worse. If, for a century, it sustains us, it represses us for a century. We have contracted the infirmities it imports - stoppage of development, instability of internal balance, disorders of the intellect and of the will, fixed ideas and ideas that are false. These ideas are ours; therefore we hold on to them, or, rather, they have taken hold of us. To get rid of them, to impose the necessary recoil on our mind, to transport us to a distance and place us at a critical point of view, where we can study ourselves, our ideas and our institutions as scientific objects, requires a great effort on our part, many precautions, and long reflection. - Hence, the delays of this study; the reader will pardon them on considering that an ordinary opinion, caught on the wing, on such a subject, does not suffice. In any event, when one presents an opinion on such a subject one is bound to believe it. I can believe in my own only when it has become precise and seems to me proven.

Menthon Saint-Bernard, September, 1890.

BOOK FIRST. NAPOLEON BONAPARTE.

CHAPTER I. Historical Importance of his Character and Genius.

If you want to comprehend a building, you have to imagine the circumstances, I mean the difficulties and the means, the kind and quality of its available materials, the moment, the opportunity, and the urgency of the demand for it. But, still more important, we must consider the genius and taste of the architect, especially whether he is the proprietor, whether he built it to live in himself, and, once installed in it, whether he took pains to adapt it to how own way of living, to his own necessities, to his own use. - Such is the social edifice erected by Napoleon Bonaparte, its architect, proprietor, and principal occupant from 1799 to 1814. It is he who has made modern France; never was an individual character so profoundly stamped on any collective work, so that, to comprehend the work, we must first study the character of the Man. [2]

I. Napoleon's Past and Personality.

He is of another race and another century. - Origin of his paternal family. - Transplanted to Corsica. - His maternal family. - Laetitia Ramolino. - Persistence of Corsican souvenirs in Napoleon's mind. - His youthful sentiments regarding Corsica and France. - Indications found in his early compositions and in his style. - Current monarchical or democratic ideas have no hold on him. - His impressions of the 20th of June and 10th of August after the 31st of May. - His associations with Robespierre and Barras without committing himself. - His sentiments and the side he takes Vendémiaire 13th. - The great Condottière. - His character and conduct in Italy. - Description of him morally and physically in 1798. - The early and sudden ascendancy which he exerts. Analogous in spirit and character to his Italian ancestors of the XVth century.

Disproportionate in all things, but, stranger still, he is not only out of the common run, but there is no standard of measurement for him; through his temperament, instincts, faculties, imagination, passions, and moral constitution he seems cast in a special mould, composed of another metal than that which enters into the composition of his fellows and contemporaries. Evidently he is not a Frenchman, nor a man of the eighteenth century; he belongs to another race and another epoch. [3] We detect in him, at the first glance, the foreigner, the Italian, [4] and something more, apart and beyond these, surpassing all similitude or analogy. -Italian he was through blood and lineage; first, through his paternal family, which is Tuscan, [5] and which we can follow down from the twelfth century, at Florence, then at San Miniato; next at Sarzana, a small, backward, remote town in the state of Genoa, where, from father to son, it vegetates obscurely in provincial isolation, through a long line of notaries and municipal syndics. "My origin, " says Napoleon himself, [6] " has made all Italians regard me as a compatriot. . .. When the question of the marriage of my sister Pauline with Prince Borghése came up there was but one voice in Rome and in Tuscany, in that family, and with all its connections: 'It will do, ' said all of them, 'it's amongst ourselves, it is one of our own families... '" When the Pope later hesitated about coming to Paris to crown Napoleon, "the Italian party in the Conclave prevailed against the Austrian party by supporting political arguments with the following slight tribute to national amour propre: 'After all we are imposing an Italian family on the barbarians, to govern them. We are revenging ourselves on the Gauls. '" Significant words, which will one day throw light upon the depths of the Italian nature, the eldest daughter of modern civilization, imbued with her right of primogeniture, persisting in her grudge against the transalpines, the rancorous inheritor of Roman pride and of antique patriotism. [7]

From Sarzana, a Bonaparte emigrates to Corsica, where he establishes himself and lives after 1529. The following year Florence is taken and subjugated for good. Henceforth, in Tuscany, under Alexander de Medici, then under Cosmo I. and his successors, in all Italy under Spanish rule, municipal independence, private feuds, the great exploits of political adventures and successful usurpations, the system of ephemeral principalities, based on force and fraud, all give way to permanent repression, monarchical discipline, external order, and a certain species of public tranquility. Thus, just at the time when the energy and ambition, the vigorous and free sap of the Middle Ages begins to run down and then dry up in the shriveled trunk, [8] a small detached branch takes root in an island, not less Italian but almost barbarous, amidst institutions, customs, and passions belonging to the primitive medieval epoch, [9] and in a social atmosphere sufficiently rude for the maintenance of all its vigor and harshness. - Grafted, moreover, by frequent marriages, on the wild stock of the island, Napoleon, on the maternal side, through his grandmother and mother, is wholly indigenous. His grandmother, a Pietra-Santa, belonged to Sarténe, [10] a Corsican canton par excellence where, in 1800, hereditary vendettas still maintained the system of the eleventh century; where the permanent strife of inimical families was suspended only by truces; where, in many villages, nobody stirred out of doors except in armed bodies, and where the houses were crenellated like fortresses. His mother, Laetitia Ramolini, from whom, in character and in will, he derived much more than from his father, [11] is a primitive soul on which Civilization has taken no hold. She is simple, all of a piece, unsuited to the refinements, charms, and graces of a worldly life; indifferent to comforts, without literary culture, as parsimonious as any peasant woman, but as energetic as the leader of a band. She is powerful, physically and spiritually, accustomed to danger, ready in desperate resolutions. She is, in short, a "rural Cornelia, " who conceived and gave birth to her son amidst the risks of battle and of defeat, in the thickest of the French invasion, amidst mountain rides on horseback, nocturnal surprises, and volleys of musketry. [12]

"Losses, privations, and fatigue, " says Napoleon, "she endured all and braved all. Hers was a man's head on a woman's shoulders. "

Thus fashioned and brought into the world, he felt that, from first to the last, he was of his people and country.

"Everything was better there, " said he, at Saint Helena, [13] "even the very smell of the soil, which he could have detected with his eyes shut; nowhere had he found the same thing. He imagined himself there again in early infancy, and lived over again the days of his youth, amidst precipices, traversing lofty peaks, deep valleys, and narrow defiles, enjoying the honors and pleasures of hospitality, " treated everywhere as a brother and compatriot, " without any accident or insult ever suggesting to him that his confidence was not well grounded. " At Bocognano, [14] where his mother, pregnant with him, had taken refuge, "where hatred and vengeance extended to the seventh degree of relationship, and where the dowry of a young girl was estimated by the number of her Cousins, I was feasted and made welcome, and everybody would have died for me. " Forced to become a Frenchman, transplanted to France, educated at the expense of the king in a French school, he became rigid in his insular patriotism, and loudly extolled Paoli, the liberator, against whom his relations had declared themselves. "Paoli, " said he, at the dinner table, [15]" was a great man. He loved his country. My father was his adjutant, and never will I forgive him for having aided in the union of Corsica with France. He should have followed her fortunes and have succumbed only with her. " Throughout his youth he is at heart anti-French, morose, "bitter, liking very few and very little liked, brooding over resentment, " like a vanquished man, always moody and compelled to work against the grain. At Brienne, he keeps aloof from his comrades, takes no part in their sports, shuts himself in the library, and opens himself up only to Bourrienne in explosions of hatred: "I will do you Frenchmen all the harm I can! - "Corsican by nation and character, " wrote his professor of history in the Military Academy, "he will go far if circumstances favor him."[16] - Leaving the Academy, and in garrison at Valence and Auxonne, he remains always hostile, denationalized; his old bitterness returns, and, addressing his letters to Paoli, he says: "I was born when our country perished. Thirty thousand Frenchmen vomited on our shores, drowning the throne of liberty in floods of blood -such was the odious spectacle on which my eyes first opened! The groans of the dying, the shrieks of the oppressed, tears of despair, surrounded my cradle from my birth. .. I will blacken those who betrayed the common cause with the brush of infamy. . .. vile, sordid souls corrupted by gain! "[17] A little later, his letter to Buttafuoco, deputy in the Constituent Assembly and principal agent in the annexation to France, is one long strain of renewed, concentrated hatred, which, after at first trying to restrain it within the bounds of cold sarcasm, ends in boiling over, like red- hot lava, in a torrent of scorching invective. - From the age of fifteen, at the Academy and afterwards in his regiment, he finds refuge in imagination in the past of his island; [18] he recounts its history, his mind dwells upon it for many years, and he dedicates his work to Paoli. Unable to get it published, he abridges it, and dedicates the abridgment to Abbé Raynal, recapitulating in a strained style, with warm, vibrating sympathy, the annals of his small community, its revolts and deliverances, its heroic and sanguinary outbreaks, its public and domestic tragedies, ambuscades, betrayals, revenges, loves, and murders, - in short, a history similar to that of the Scottish highlanders, while the style, still more than the sympathies, denotes the foreigner. Undoubtedly, in this work, as in other youthful writings, he follows as well as he can the authors in vogue - Rousseau, and especially Raynal; he gives a schoolboy imitation of their tirades, their sentimental declamation, and their humanitarian grandiloquence. But these borrowed clothes, which incommode him, do not fit him; they are too tight, and the cloth is too fine; they require too much circumspection in walking; he does not know how to put them on, and they rip at every seam. Not only has he never learned how to spell, but he does not know the true meaning, connections, and relations of words, the propriety or impropriety of phrases, the exact significance of imagery; [19] he strides on impetuously athwart a pell-mell of incongruities, incoherencies, Italianisms, and barbarisms, undoubtedly stumbling along through awkwardness and inexperience, but also through excess of ardor and of heat; [20] his jerking, eruptive thought, overcharged with passion, indicates the depth and temperature of its source. Already, at the Academy, the professor of belles-lettres[21] notes down that "in the strange and incorrect grandeur of his amplifications he seems to see granite fused in a volcano. " However original in mind and in sensibility, ill-adapted as he is to the society around him, different from his comrades, it is clear beforehand that the current ideas which take such hold on them will obtain no hold on him.

Of the two dominant and opposite ideas which clash with each other, it might be supposed that he would lean either to one or to the other, although accepting neither. - Pensioner of the king, who supported him at Brienne, and afterwards in the Military Academy; who also supported his sister at Saint-Cyr; who, for twenty years, is the benefactor of his family; to whom, at this very time, he addresses entreating or grateful letters over his mother's signature - he does not regard him as his born general; it does not enter his mind to take sides and draw his sword in his patron's behalf; ' in vain is he a gentleman, to whom, d'Hozier has certified; reared in a school of noble cadets, he has no noble or monarchical traditions. [22] - Poor and tormented by ambition, a reader of Rousseau, patronized by Raynal, and tacking together sentences of philosophic fustian about equality, if he speaks the jargon of the day, it is without any belief in it. The phrases in vogue form a decent, academical drapery for his ideas, or serve him as a red cap for the club; he is not bewildered by democratic illusions, and entertains no other feeling than disgust for the revolution and the sovereignty of the populace. - At Paris, in April, 1792, when the struggle between the monarchists and the revolutionaries is at its height, he tries to find "some successful speculation, "[23] and thinks he will hire and sublet houses at a profit. On the 20th of June he witnesses, only as a matter of curiosity, the invasion of the Tuileries, and, on seeing the king at a window place the red cap on his head, exclaims, so as to be heard, " Che Caglione! " Immediately after this: "How could they let that rabble enter! Mow down four or five hundred of them with cannons and the rest would run away. " On August 10, when the tocsin sounds, he regards the people and the king with equal contempt; he rushes to a friend's house on the Carrousel and there, still as a looker-on, views at his ease all the occurrences of the day. [24] Finally, the chateau is forced and he strolls through the Tuileries, looks in at the neighboring cafés, and that is all: he is not disposed to take sides, he has no Jacobin or royalist inclination. His features, even, are so calm "as to provoke many hostile and distrustful stares, as someone who is unknown and suspicious. " - Similarly, after the 31st of May and the 2nd of June, his "Souper de Beaucaire" shows that if he condemns the departmental insurrection it is mainly because he deems it futile: on the side of the insurgents, a defeated army, no position tenable, no cavalry, raw artillerymen, Marseilles reduced to its own troops, full of hostile sans-culottes and so besieged, taken and pillaged. Chances are against it: "Let the impoverished regions, the inhabitants of Vivaris, of the Cevennes, of Corsica, fight to the last extremity, but if you lose a battle and the fruit of a thousand years of fatigue, hardship, economy, and happiness become the soldier's prey. "[25] Here was something with which the Girondists could be converted! - None of the political or social convictions which then exercised such control over men's minds have any hold on him. Before the 9th of Thermidor he seemed to be a "republican montagnard, " and we follow him for months in Provence. "the favorite and confidential adviser of young Robespierre, " "admirer" of the elder Robespierre, [26] intimate at Nice with Charlotte Robespierre. After the 9th of Thermidor has passed, he frees himself with bombast from this compromising friendship: "I thought him sincere, " says he of the younger Robespierre, in a letter intended to be shown, "but were he my father and had aimed at tyranny, I would have stabbed him myself. " On returning to Paris, after having knocked at several doors, he takes Barras for a patron. Barras, the most brazen of the corrupt, Barras, who has overthrown and contrived the death of his two former protectors. [27] Among the contending parties and fanaticisms which succeed each other he keeps cool and free to dispose of himself as he pleases, indifferent to every cause and concerning himself only with his own interests. - On the evening of the 12th of Vendémiaire, on leaving the Feydeau theatre, and noticing the preparations of the sectionists, [28] he said to Junot:

"Ah, if the sections put me in command, I would guarantee to place them in
    the Tuileries in two hours and have all those Convention rascals driven out! "

Five hours later, summoned by Barras and the Conventionalists, he takes "three minutes" to make up his mind, and, instead of "blowing up the representatives, " he mows down the Parisians. Like a good condottière, he does not commit himself, considers the first that offers and then the one who offers the most, only to back out afterwards, and finally, seizing the opportunity, to grab everything. - He will more and more become a true condottière, that is to say, leader of a band, increasingly independent, pretending to submit under the pretext of the public good, looking out only for his own interest, self-centered, general on his own account and for his own advantage in his Italian campaign before and after the 18th of Fructidor. [29] He is, however, a condottière of the first class, already aspiring to the loftiest summits, "with no stopping-place but the throne or the scaffold, "[30] "determined[31] to master France, and through France Europe. Without distraction, sleeping only three hours during the night, " he plays with ideas, men, religions, and governments, exploiting people with incomparable dexterity and brutality. He is, in the choice of means as of ends, a superior artist, inexhaustible in glamour, seductions, corruption, and intimidation, fascinating, and yet more terrible than any wild beast suddenly released among a herd of browsing cattle. The expression is not too strong and was uttered by an eye-witness, almost at this very date, a friend and a competent diplomat: "You know that, while I am very fond of the dear general, I call him to myself the little tiger, so as to properly characterize his figure, tenacity, and courage, the rapidity of his movements, and all that he has in him which maybe fairly regarded in that sense. "[32]

At this very date, previous to official adulation and the adoption of a recognized type, we see him face to face in two portraits drawn from life, one physical, by a truthful painter, Guérin, and the other moral, by a superior woman, Madame de Staël, who to the best European culture added tact and worldly perspicacity. Both portraits agree so perfectly that each seems to interpret and complete the other. "I saw him for the first time, "[33] says Madame de Staël, "on his return to France after the treaty of Campo-Formio. After recovering from the first excitement of admiration there succeeded to this a decided sentiment of fear. " And yet, "at this time he had no power, for it was even then supposed that the Directory looked upon him with a good deal of suspicion. " People regarded him sympathetically, and were even prepossessed in his favor;

"thus the fear he inspired was simply due to the singular effect of his person on almost all who approached him. I had met men worthy of respect and had likewise met men of ferocious character; but nothing in the impression which Bonaparte produced on me reminded me of either. I soon found, in the various opportunities I had of meeting him during his stay in Paris, that his character was not to be described in terms commonly employed; he was neither mild nor)violent, nor gentle nor cruel, like certain personages one happens to know. A being like him, wholly unlike anybody else, could neither feel nor excite sympathy; he was both more and less than a man; his figure, intellect, and language bore the imprint of a foreign nationality . . .. far from being reassured on seeing Bonaparte oftener, he intimidated me more and more every day. I had a confused impression that he was not to be influenced by any emotion of sympathy or affection. He regards a human being as a fact, an object, and not as a fellow-creature. He neither hates nor loves, he exists for himself alone; the rest of humanity are so many ciphers. The force of his will consists in the imperturbable calculation of his egoism. He is a skillful player who has the human species for an antagonist, and whom he proposes to checkmate. .. Every time that I heard him talk I was struck with his superiority; it bore no resemblance to that of men informed and cultivated through study and social intercourse, such as we find in France and England. His conversation indicated the tact of circumstances, like that of the hunter in pursuit of his prey. His spirit seemed a cold, keen sword-blade, which freezes while it wounds. I felt a profound irony in his mind, which nothing great or beautiful could escape, not even his own fame, for he despised the nation whose suffrages he sought. .. "
- "With him, everything was means or aims; spontaneity, whether for good or for evil, was entirely absent. "

No law, no ideal and abstract rule, existed for him;

"he examined things only with reference to their immediate usefulness; a general principle was repugnant to him, either as so much nonsense or as an enemy. "

Now, if we contemplate Guérin's portrait, [34] we see a spare body, whose narrow shoulders under the uniform wrinkled by sudden movements, the neck swathed in its high twisted cravat, the temples covered by long, smooth, straight hair, exposing only the mask, the hard features intensified through strong contrasts of light and shade, the cheeks hollow up to the inner angle of the eye, the projecting cheek-bones, the massive, protuberant jaw, the sinuous, mobile lips, pressed together as if attentive, the large, clear eyes, deeply sunk under the broad, arched eyebrows, the fixed, oblique look, as penetrating as a rapier, and the two creases which extend from the base of the nose to the brow, as if in a frown of suppressed anger and determined will. Add to this the accounts of his contemporaries[35] who saw or heard the curt accent or the sharp, abrupt gesture, the interrogating, imperious, absolute tone of voice, and we comprehend how, the moment they accosted him, they felt the dominating hand which seizes them, presses them down, holds them firmly and never relaxes its grasp.

Already, at the receptions of the Directory, when conversing with men, or even with ladies, he puts questions "which prove the superiority of the questioner to those who have to answer them. "[36] "Are you married? " says he to this one, and "How many children have you? "to another. To that one, "When did you come here? " or, again, "When are you going away? He places himself in front of a French lady, well- known for her beauty and wit and the vivacity of her opinions, "like the stiffest of German generals, and says: 'Madame, I don't like women who meddle with politics! '" Equality, ease, familiarity and companionship, vanish at his approach. Eighteen months before this, on his appointment as commander-in-chief of the army in Italy, Admiral Decrès, who had known him well at Paris, [37] learns that he is to pass through Toulon: "I at once propose to my comrades to introduce them, venturing to do so on my acquaintance with him in Paris. Full of eagerness and joy, I start off. The door opens and I am about to press forwards, " he afterwards wrote, "when the attitude, the look, and the tone of voice suffice to arrest me. And yet there was nothing offensive about him; still, this was enough. I never tried after that to overstep the line thus imposed on me. " A few days later, at Albenga, [38] certain generals of division, and among them Augereau, a vulgar, heroic old soldier, vain of his tall figure and courage, arrive at headquarters, not well disposed toward the little parvenu sent out to them from Paris. Recalling the description of him which had been given to them, Augereau is abusive and insubordinate beforehand: one of Barras' favorites, the Vendémiaire general, a street general, "not yet tried out on the field of battle, [39] hasn't a friend, considered a loner because he is the only one who can thinks for himself, looking peaky, said to be a mathematician and a dreamer! " They enter, and Bonaparte keeps them waiting. At last he appears, with his sword and belt on, explains the disposition of the forces, gives them his orders, and dismisses them. Augereau has remained silent; It is only when he gets out of doors does he recover himself and fall back on his accustomed oaths. He admits to Massena that "that little bastard of a general frightened him. " He cannot "comprehend the ascendancy which made him feel crushed right away. "[40]

Extraordinary and superior, made for command[41] and for conquest, singular and of an unique species, is the feeling of all his contemporaries. Those who are most familiar with the histories of other nations, Madame de Staël and, after her, Stendhal, go back to the right sources to comprehend him, to the "petty Italian tyrants of the fourteenth and fifteenth centuries, " to Castruccio-Castracani, to the Braccio of Mantua, to the Piccinino, the Malatestas of Rimini, and the Sforzas of Milan. In their opinion, however, it is only a chance analogy, a psychological resemblance. Really, however, and)historically it is a positive relationship. He is a descendant of the great Italians, the men of action of the year 1400, the military adventurers, usurpers, and founders of governments lasting their life- time. He inherits in direct affiliation their blood and inward organization, mental and moral. [42] A bud, collected in their forest, before the age of refinement, impoverishment, and decay, has been transported into a similar and remote nursery, where a tragic and militant régime is permanently established. There the primitive germ is preserved intact and transmitted from one generation to another, renewed and invigorated by interbreeding. Finally, at the last stage of its growth, it springs out of the ground and develops magnificently, blooming the same as ever, and producing the same fruit as on the original stem. Modern cultivation and French gardening have pruned away but very few of its branches and blunted a few of its thorns: its original texture, inmost substance, and spontaneous development have not changed. The soil of France and of Europe, however, broken up by revolutionary tempests, is more favorable to its roots than the worn-out fields of the Middle Ages and there it grows by itself, without being subject, like its Italian ancestors, to rivalry with its own species; nothing checks the growth; it may absorb all the juices of the ground, all the air and sunshine of the region, and become the Colossus which the ancient plants, equally deep-rooted and certainly as absorbent, but born in a less friable soil and more crowded together, could not provide.

II. The Leader and Statesman

Intelligence during the Italian Renaissance and at the present day. - Integrity of Bonaparte's mental machinery. - Flexibility, force, and tenacity of his attention. - Another difference between Napoleon's intellect and that of his contemporaries. - He thinks objects and not words. - His antipathy to Ideology. - Little or no literary or philosophical education. - Self-taught through direct observation and technical instruction. - His fondness for details. - His inward vision of physical objects and places. - His mental portrayal of positions, distances, and quantities.

"The human plant, " said Alfieri, "is in no country born more vigorous than in Italy"; and never, in Italy, was it so vigorous as from 1300 to 1500, from the contemporaries of Dante down to those of Michael Angelo, Caesar Borgia, Julius II., and Macchiavelli. [43] The first distinguishing mark of a man of those times is the soundness of his mental instrument. Nowadays, after three hundred years of service, ours has lost somewhat of its moral fiber, sharpness, and versatility: usually the compulsory specialization has caused it to become lop- sided making it unfit for other purposes. What's more, the increase in ready-made ideas and clichés and acquired methods incrusts it and reduces its scope to a sort of routine. Finally, it is exhausted by an excess of intellectual activity and diminished by the continuity of sedentary habits. It is just the opposite with those impulsive minds of uncorrupted blood and of a new stock. - Roederer, a competent and independent judge, who, at the beginning of the consular government, sees Bonaparte daily at the meetings of the Council of State, and who notes down every evening the impressions of the day, is carried away with admiration: [44]

"Punctual at every sitting, prolonging the session five or six hours, discussing before and afterwards the subjects brought forward, always returning to two questions, 'Can that be justified? [45]' 'Is that useful? ' examining each question in itself, in these two respects, after having subjected it to a most exact and sharp analysis; next, consulting the best authorities, the pasts, experience, and obtaining information about bygone jurisprudence, the laws of Louis XIV. and of Frederick the Great. . .. Never did the council adjourn without its members knowing more than the day before; if not through knowledge derived from him, at least through the researches he obliged them to make. Never did the members of the Senate and the

Legislative Corps, or of the tribunals, pay their respects to him without being rewarded for their homage by valuable instructions. He cannot be surrounded by public men without being the statesman, all forming for him a council of state. "

"What characterizes him above them all, " is not alone the penetration and universality of his comprehension, but likewise and especially "the force, flexibility, and constancy of his attention. He can work eighteen hours at a stretch, on one or on several subjects. I never saw him tired. I never found his mind lacking in inspiration, even when weary in body, nor when violently exercised, nor when angry. I never saw him diverted from one matter by another, turning from that under discussion to one he had just finished or was about to take up. The news, good or bad, he received from Egypt, did not divert his mind from the civil code, nor the civil code from the combinations which the safety of Egypt required. Never did a man more wholly devote himself to the work in hand, nor better devote his time to what he had to do. Never did a mind more inflexibly set aside the occupation or thought which did not come at the right day or hour, never was one more ardent in seeking it, more alert in its pursuit, more capable of fixing it when the time came to take it up. "

He himself said later on: [46]

"Various subjects and affairs are stowed away in my brain as in a chest of drawers. When I want to take up any special business I shut one drawer and open another. None of them ever get mixed, and never does this incommode me or fatigue me. If I feel sleepy I shut all the drawers and go to sleep. "

Never has brain so disciplined and under such control been seen, one so ready at all times for any task, so capable of immediate and absolute concentration. Its flexibility[47] is wonderful, "in the instant application of every faculty and energy, and bringing them all to bear at once on any object that concerns him, on a mite as well as on an elephant, on any given individual as well as on an enemy's army. . .. When specially occupied, other things do not exist for him; it is a sort of chase from which nothing diverts him. " And this hot pursuit, which nothing arrests save capture, this tenacious hunt, this headlong course by one to whom the goal is never other than a fresh starting-point, is the spontaneous gait, the natural, even pace which his mind prefers.

"I am always at work, " says he to Roederer. [48] "I meditate a great deal. If I seem always equal to the occasion, ready to face what comes, it is because I have thought the matter over a long time before undertaking it. I have anticipated whatever might happen. It is no spirit which suddenly reveals to me what I ought to do or say in any unlooked-for circumstance, but my own reflection, my own meditation. . .. I work all the time, at dinner, in the theatre. I wake up at night in order to resume my work. I got up last night at two o'clock. I stretched myself on my couch before the fire to examine the army reports sent to me by the Minister of War. I found twenty mistakes in them, and made notes which I have this morning sent to the minister, who is now engaged with his clerks in rectifying them."

His associates weaken and sink under the burden imposed on them and which he supports without feeling the weight. When Consul, [49] "he sometimes presides at special meetings of the section of the interior from ten o'clock in the evening until five o'clock in the morning. . .. Often, at Saint-Cloud, he keeps the counselors of state from nine o'clock in the morning until five in the evening, with fifteen minutes' intermission, and seems no more fatigued at the close of the session than when it began. " During the night sessions "many of the members succumb through weariness, while the Minister of War falls asleep"; he gives them a shake and wakes them up, "Come, come, citizens, let us bestir ourselves, it is only two o'clock and we must earn the money the French people pay us. " Consul or Emperor, [50] "he demands of each minister an account of the smallest details: It is not rare to see them leaving the council room overcome with fatigue, due to the long interrogatories to which he has subjected them; he appears not to have noticed, and talks about the day's work simply as a relaxation which has scarcely given his mind exercise. " And what is worse, "it often happens that on returning home they find a dozen of his letters requiring immediate response, for which the whole night scarcely suffices. " The quantity of facts he is able to retain and store away, the quantity of ideas he elaborates and produces, seems to surpass human capacity, and this insatiable, inexhaustible, unmovable brain thus keeps on working uninterruptedly for thirty years.

Through another result of the same mental organization, Napoleon's brain is never unproductive; that's today our great danger. - During the past three hundred years we have more and more lost sight of the exact and direct meaning of things. Subject to the constraints of a conservative, complex, and extended educational system we study

* the symbols of objects rather than on the objects themselves;
* instead of the ground itself, a map of it;
* instead of animals struggling for existence, [51] nomenclatures and classifications, or, at best, stuffed specimens displayed in a museum;
* instead of persons who feel and act, statistics, codes, histories, literatures, and philosophies;

in short, printed words. Even worse, abstract terms, which from century to century have become more abstract and therefore further removed from experience, more difficult to understand, less adaptable and more deceptive, especially in all that relates to human life and society. Here, due to the growth of government, to the multiplication of services, to the entanglement of interests, the object, indefinitely enlarged and complex, now eludes our grasp. Our vague, incomplete, incorrect idea of it badly corresponds with it, or does not correspond at all. In nine minds out of ten, or perhaps ninety- nine out of a hundred, it is but little more than a word. The others, if they desire some significant indication of what society actually is beyond the teachings of books, require ten or fifteen years of close observation and study to re-think the phrases with which these have filled their memory, to interpret them anew, to make clear their meaning, to get at and verify their sense, to substitute for the more or less empty and indefinite term the fullness and precision of a personal impression. We have seen how ideas of Society, State, Government, Sovereignty, Rights, Liberty, the most important of all ideas, were, at the close of the eighteenth century, curtailed and falsified; how, in most minds, simple verbal reasoning combined them together in dogmas and axioms; what an offspring these metaphysical simulacra gave birth to, how many lifeless and grotesque abortions, how many monstrous and destructive chimeras. There is no place for any of these fanciful dreams in the mind of Bonaparte; they cannot arise in it, nor find access to it; his aversion to the unsubstantial phantoms of political abstraction extends beyond disdain, even to disgust. [52] That which was then called ideology, is his particular bugbear; he loathes it not alone through calculation, but still more through an instinctive demand for what is real, as a practical man and statesman, always keeping in mind, like the great Catherine, "that he is operating, not on paper, but on the human hide, which is ticklish. " Every idea entertained by him had its origin in his personal observation, and he used his own personal observations to control them.

If books are useful to him it is to suggest questions, which he never answers but through his own experience. He has read only a little, and hastily; [53] his classical education is rudimentary; in the way of Latin, he remained in the lower class. The instruction he got at the Military Academy as well as at Brienne was below mediocrity, while, after Brienne, it is stated that "for the languages and belles- lettres, he had no taste. " Next to this, the literature of elegance and refinement, the philosophy of the closet and drawing-room, with which his contemporaries are imbued, glided over his intellect as over a hard rock. None but mathematical truths and positive notions about geography and history found their way into his mind and deeply impressed it. Everything else, as with his predecessors of the fifteenth century, comes to him through the original, direct action of his faculties in contact with men and things, through his prompt and sure tact, his indefatigable and minute attention, his indefinitely repeated and rectified divinations during long hours of solitude and silence. Practice, and not speculation, is the source of his instruction, the same as with a mechanic brought up amongst machinery.

"There is nothing relating to warfare that I cannot make myself. If nobody knows how to make gunpowder, I do. I can construct gun-carriages. If cannon must be cast, I will see that it is done properly. If tactical details must be taught, I will teach them. "[54]

This is why he is competent right from the beginning, general in the artillery, major-general, diplomatist, financier and administrator of all kinds. Thanks to this fertile apprenticeship, beginning with the Consulate, he shows officials and veteran ministers who send in their reports to him what to do.

"I am a more experienced administrator than they, [55] when one has been obliged to extract from his brains the ways and means with which to feed, maintain, control, and move with the same spirit and will two or three hundred thousand men, a long distance from their country, one has soon discovered the secrets of administration. "

In each of the human machines he builds and manipulates, he perceives right away all the parts, each in its proper place and function, the motors, the transmissions, the wheels, the composite action, the speed which ensues, the final result, the complete effect, the net product. Never is he content with a superficial and summary inspection; he penetrates into obscure corners and to the lowest depths "through the technical precision of his questions, " with the lucidity of a specialist, and in this way, borrowing an expression from the philosophers, with him the concept should be adequate to its purpose.

Hence his eagerness for details, for these form the body and substance of the concept; the hand that has not grasped these, or lets them go, retains only the shell, an envelope. With respect to these his curiosity is "insatiable. "[57] In each ministerial department he knows more than the ministers, and in each bureau he knows as much as the clerks. "On his table[58] lie reports of the positions of his forces on land and on water. He has furnished the plans of these, and fresh ones are issued every month"; such is the daily reading he likes best.

"I have my reports on positions always at hand; my memory for an Alexandrine is not good, but I never forget a syllable of my reports on positions. I shall find them in my room this evening, and I shall not go to bed until I have read them. "

He always knows "his position" on land and at sea better than is known in the War and Navy departments; better even than his staff-officers the number, size, and qualities of his ships in or out of port, the present and future state of vessels under construction, the composition and strength of their crews, the formation, organization, staff of officers, material, stations, and enlistments, past and to come, of each army corps and of each regiment. It is the same in the financial and diplomatic services, in every branch of the administration, laic or ecclesiastical, in the physical order and in the moral order. His topographical memory and his geographical conception of countries, places, ground, and obstacles culminate in an inward vision which he evokes at will, and which, years afterwards, revives as fresh as on the first day. His calculation of distances, marches, and maneuvers is so rigid a mathematical operation that, frequently, at a distance of two or four hundred leagues, his military foresight, calculated two or four months ahead, turns out correct, almost on the day named, and precisely on the spot designated. [60] Add to this one other faculty, and the rarest of all. For, if things turn out as he foresaw they would, it is because, as with great chess-players, he has accurately measured not alone the mechanical moves of the pieces, but the character and talent of his adversary, "sounded his draft of water, " and divined his probable mistakes. He has added the calculation of physical quantities and probabilities to the calculation of moral quantities and probabilities, thus showing himself as great a psychologist as he is an accomplished strategist. In fact, no one has surpassed him in the art of judging the condition and motives of an individual or of a group of people, the real motives, permanent or temporary, which drive or curb men in general or this or that man in particular, the incentives to be employed, the kind and degree of pressure to be employed. This central faculty rules all the others, and in the art of mastering Man his genius is found supreme.

III. His acute Understanding of Others.

His psychological faculty and way of getting at the thought and feeling of others. - His self-analysis. - How he imagines a general situation by selecting a particular case, imagining the invisible interior by deducting from the visible exterior. - Originality and superiority of his style and discourse. - His adaptation of these to his hearers and to circumstances. - His notation and calculation of serviceable motives.

No faculty is more precious for a political engineer; for the forces he acts upon are never other than human passions. But how, except through divination, can these passions, which grow out of the deepest sentiments, be reached? How, save by conjecture, can forces be estimated which seem to defy all measurement? On this dark and uncertain ground, where one has to grope one's way, Napoleon moves with almost absolute certainty; he moves promptly. First of all, he studies himself; indeed, to find one's way into another's soul requires, preliminarily, that one should dive deep into one's own. [61]

"I have always delighted in analysis, " said he, one day, "and should I ever fall seriously in love I would take my sentiment to pieces. Why and How are such important questions one cannot put them to one's self too often. "

"It is certain, " writes an observer, "that he, of all men, is the one who has most meditated on the why which controls human actions."

His method, that of the experimental sciences, consists in testing every hypothesis or deduction by some positive fact, observed by him under definite conditions; a physical force being ascertained and accurately measured through the deviation of a needle, or through the rise and fall of a fluid, this or that invisible moral force can likewise be ascertained and approximately measured through some emotional sign, some decisive manifestation, consisting of a certain word, tone, or gesture. It is these words, tones, and gestures which he dwells on; he detects inward sentiments by the outward expression; he figures to himself the internal by the external, by some facial appearance, some telling attitude, some brief and topical scene, by such specimen and shortcuts, so well chosen and detailed that they provide a summary of the innumerable series of analogous cases. In this way, the vague, fleeting object is suddenly arrested, brought to bear, and then gauged and weighed, like some impalpable gas collected and kept in a graduated transparent glass tube. - Accordingly, at the Council of State, while the others, either jurists or administrators, see abstractions, articles of the law and precedents, he sees people as they are - the Frenchman, the Italian, the German; that of the peasant, the workman, the bourgeois, the noble, the returned émigré, [62] the soldier, the officer and the functionary - everywhere the individual man as he is, the man who plows, manufactures, fights, marries, brings forth children, toils, enjoys himself, and dies. - Nothing is more striking than the contrast between the dull, grave arguments advanced by the wise official editor, and Napoleon's own words caught on the wing, at the moment, vibrating and teeming with illustrations and imagery. [63] Apropos of divorce, the principle of which he wishes to maintain:

"Consult, now, national manners and customs. Adultery is no phenomenon; it is common enough - une affaire de canapé . .. There must be some curb on women who commit adultery for trinkets, poetry, Apollo, and the muses, etc. "

But if divorce be allowed for incompatibility of temper you undermine marriage; the fragility of the bond will be apparent the moment the obligation is contracted;

"it is just as if a man said to himself, 'I am going to marry until I feel different. ' "

Nullity of marriage must not be too often allowed; once a marriage is made it is a serious matter to undo it.

"Suppose that, in marrying my cousin just arrived from the Indies, I wed an adventuress. She bears me children, and I then discover she is not my cousin - is that marriage valid? Does not public morality demand that it should be so considered? There has been a mutual exchange of hearts, of transpiration. "

On the right of children to be supported and fed although of age, he says:

"Will you allow a father to drive a girl of fifteen out of his house? A father worth 60,000 francs a year might say to his son, 'You are stout and fat; go and turn plowman. ' The children of a rich father, or of one in good circumstances, are always entitled to the paternal porridge. Strike out their right to be fed, and you compel children to murder their parents. "

As to adoption :

"You regard this as law-makers and not as statesmen. It is not a civil contract nor a judicial contract. The analysis (of the jurist) leads to vicious results. Man is governed by imagination only; without imagination he is a brute. It is not for five cents a day, simply to distinguish himself, that a man consents to be killed; if you want to electrify him touch his heart. A notary, who is paid a fee of twelve francs for his services, cannot do that. It requires some other process, a legislative act. Adoption, what is that? An imitation by which society tries to counterfeit nature. It is a new kind of sacrament. . .. Society ordains that the bones and blood of one being shall be changed into the bones and blood of another. It is the greatest of all legal acts. It gives the sentiments of a son to one who never had them, and reciprocally those of a parent. Where ought this to originate? From on high, like a clap of thunder! "

All his expressions are bright flashes one after another. [64] Nobody, since Voltaire and Galiani, has launched forth such a profusion of them; on society, laws, government, France and the French, some penetrate and explain, like those of Montesquieu, as if with a flash of lightening. He does not hammer them out laboriously, but they burst forth, the outpourings of his intellect, its natural, involuntary, constant action. And what adds to their value is that, outside of councils and private conversations, he abstains from them, employing them only in the service of thought; at other times he subordinates them to the end he has in view, which is always their practical effect. Ordinarily, he writes and speaks in a different language, in a language suited to his audience; he dispenses with the oddities, the irregular improvisations and imagination, the outbursts of genius and inspiration. He retains and uses merely those which are intended to impress the personage whom he wishes to dazzle with a great idea of himself, such as Pius VII., or the Emperor Alexander. In this case, his conversational tone is that of a caressing, expansive, amiable familiarity; he is then before the footlights, and when he acts he can play all parts, tragedy or comedy, with the same life and spirit whether he fulminates, insinuates, or even affects simplicity. When he is with his generals, ministers, and principal performers, he falls back on the concise, positive, technical business style; any other would be harmful. The keen mind only reveals itself through the brevity and imperious strength and rudeness of the accent. For his armies and the common run of men, he has his proclamations and bulletins, that is to say, sonorous phrases composed for effect, a statement of facts purposely simplified and falsified, [65] in short, an excellent effervescent wine, good for exciting enthusiasm, and an equally excellent narcotic for maintaining credulity, [66] a sort of popular mixture to be distributed just at the proper time, and whose ingredients are so well proportioned that the public drinks it with delight, and becomes at once intoxicated. - His style on every occasion, whether affected or spontaneous, shows his wonderful knowledge of the masses and of individuals; except in two or three cases, on one exalted domain, of which he always remains ignorant, he has ever hit the mark, applying the appropriate lever, giving just the push, weight, and degree of impulsion which best accomplishes his purpose. A series of brief, accurate memoranda, corrected daily, enables him to frame for himself a sort of psychological tablet whereon he notes down and sums up, in almost numerical valuation, the mental and moral dispositions, characters, faculties, passions, and aptitudes, the strong or weak points, of the innumerable human beings, near or remote, on whom he operates.

IV. His Wonderful Memory.

His Three Atlases. - Their scale and completeness.

Let us try for a moment to show the range and contents of this intellect; we may have to go back to Caesar to his equal; but, for lack of documents, we have nothing of Caesar but general features - a summary outline. Of Napoleon we have, besides the perfect outline, the features in detail. Read his correspondence, day by day, then chapter by chapter; [67] for example, in 1806, after the battle of Austerlitz, or, still better, in 1809, after his return from Spain, up to the peace of Vienna; whatever our technical shortcomings may be, we shall find that his mind, in its comprehensiveness and amplitude, largely surpasses all known or even credible proportions.

He has mentally within him three principal atlases, always at hand, each composed of "about twenty note-books, " each distinct and each regularly posted up. -

1. The first one is military, forming a vast collection of topographical charts as minute as those of an general staff, with detailed plans of every stronghold, also specific indications and the local distribution of all forces on sea and on land - crews, regiments, batteries, arsenals, storehouses, present and future resources in supplies of men, horses, vehicles, arms, munitions, food, and clothing.

2. The second, which is civil, resembles the heavy, thick volumes published every year, in which we now read the state of the budget, and comprehend, first, the innumerable items of ordinary and extraordinary receipt and expenditure, internal taxes, foreign contributions, the products of the domains in France and out of France, the fiscal services, pensions, public works, and the rest; next, all administrative statistics, the hierarchy of functions and of functionaries, senators, deputies, ministers, prefects, bishops, professors, judges, and those under their orders, each where he resides, with his rank, jurisdiction, and salary.

3. The third is a vast biographical and moral dictionary, in which, as in the pigeon-holes of the Chief of Police, each notable personage and local group, each professional or social body, and even each population, has its label, along with a brief note on its situation, needs, and antecedents, and, therefore, its demonstrated character,

eventual disposition, and probable conduct. Each label, card, or strip of paper has its summary; all these partial summaries, methodically classified, terminate in totals, and the totals of the three atlases, combined together, thus furnish their possessor with an estimate of his disposable forces.

Now, in 1809, however full these atlases, they are clearly imprinted on Napoleon's mind he knows not only the total and the partial summaries, but also the slightest details; he reads them readily and at every hour; he comprehends in a mass, and in all particulars, the various nations he governs directly, or through some one else; that is to say, 60,000,000 men, the different countries he has conquered or overrun, consisting of 70,000 square leagues. At first, France increased by the addition of Belgium and Piedmont; next Spain, from which he is just returned, and where he has placed his brother Joseph; southern Italy, where, after Joseph, he has placed Murat; central Italy, where he occupies Rome; northern Italy, where Eugène is his delegate; Dalmatia and Istria, which he has joined to his empire; Austria, which he invades for the second time; the Confederation of the Rhine, which he has made and which he directs; Westphalia and Holland, where his brothers are only his lieutenants; Prussia, which he has subdued and mutilated and which he oppresses, and the strongholds of which he still retains; and, add a last mental tableau, that which represents the northern seas, the Atlantic and the Mediterranean, all the fleets of the continent at sea and in port from Dantzic to Flessingen and Bayonne, from Cadiz to Toulon and Gaëta, from Tarentum to Venice, Corfu, and Constantinople. [69] - On the psychological and moral atlas, besides a primitive gap which he will never fill up, because this is a characteristic trait, there are some estimates which are wrong, especially with regard to the Pope and to Catholic conscience. In like manner he rates the energy of national sentiment in Spain and Germany too low. He rates too high his own prestige in France and in the countries annexed to her, the balance of confidence and zeal on which he may rely. But these errors are rather the product of his will than of his intelligence, he recognizes them at intervals; if he has illusions it is because he fabricates them; left to himself his good sense would rest infallible, it is only his passions which blurred the lucidity of his intellect. - As to the other two atlases, the topographical and the military, they are as complete and as exact as ever; No matter how much the realities they contain will swell and daily become ever more complex, they continue to correspond to it in their fullness and precision, trait for trait.

V. His Imagination and its Excesses.

His constructive imagination. - His projects and dreams. - Manifestation of the master faculty and its excesses.

But this multitude of information and observations form only the smallest portion of the mental population swarming in this immense brain; for, on his idea of the real, germinate and swarm his concepts of the possible; without these concepts there would be no way to handle and transform things, and that he did handle and transform them we all know. Before acting, he has decided on his plan, and if this plan is adopted, it is one among several others, [70] after examining, comparing, and giving it the preference; he has accordingly thought over all the others. Behind each combination adopted by him we detect those he has rejected; there are dozens of them behind each of his decisions, each maneuver effected, each treaty signed, each decree promulgated, each order issued, and I venture to say, behind almost every improvised action or word spoken. For calculation enters into everything he does, even into his apparent expansiveness, also into his outbursts when in earnest; if he gives way to these, it is on purpose, foreseeing the effect, with a view to intimidate or to dazzle. He turns everything in others as well as in himself to account - his passion, his vehemence, his weaknesses, his talkativeness, he exploits it all for the advancement of the edifice he is constructing. [71] Certainly among his diverse faculties, however great, that of the constructive imagination is the most powerful. At the very beginning we feel its heat and boiling intensity beneath the coolness and rigidity of his technical and positive instructions.

"When I plan a battle, " said he to Roederer, "no man is more spineless than I am. I over exaggerate to myself all the dangers and all the evils that are possible under the circumstances. I am in a state of truly painful agitation. But this does not prevent me from appearing quite composed to people around me; I am like a woman giving birth to a child. [72]

Passionately, in the throes of the creator, he is thus absorbed with his coming creation; he already anticipates and enjoys living in his imaginary edifice. "General, " said Madame de Clermont-Tonnerre to him, one day, "you are building behind a scaffolding which you will take down when you have done with it. " "Yes, Madame, that's it, " replied Bonaparte; "you are right. I am always living two years in advance. "[73] His response came with "incredible vivacity, " as if a sudden inspiration, that of a soul stirred in its innermost fiber. - Here as well, the power, the speed, fertility, play, and abundance of his thought seem unlimited. What he has accomplished is astonishing, but what he has undertaken is more so; and whatever he may have undertaken is far surpassed by what he has imagined. However vigorous his practical faculty, his poetical faculty is stronger; it is even too vigorous for a statesman; its grandeur is exaggerated into enormity, and its enormity degenerates into madness. In Italy, after the 18th of Fructidor, he said to Bourrienne:

"Europe is a molehill; never have there been great empires and great revolutions, except in the Orient, with its 600,000,000 inhabitants."[74]

The following year at Saint-Jean d'Acre, on the eve of the last assault, he added

"If I succeed I shall find in the town the pasha's treasure and arms for 300,000 men. I stir up and arm all Syria. . .. I march on Damascus and Aleppo; as I advance in the country my army will increase with the discontented. I proclaim to the people the abolition of slavery, and of the tyrannical government of the pashas. I reach Constantinople with armed masses. I overthrow the Turkish Empire; I found in the East a new and grand empire, which fixes my place with posterity, and perhaps I return to Paris by the way of Adrianople, or by Vienna, after having annihilated the house of Austria. " [75]

Become consul, and then emperor, he often referred to this happy period, when, "rid of the restraints of a troublesome civilization, " he could imagine at will and construct at pleasure. [76]

"I created a religion; I saw myself on the road to Asia, mounted on an elephant, with a turban on my head, and in my hand a new Koran, which I composed to suit myself. "

Confined to Europe, he thinks, after 1804, that he will reorganize Charlemagne's empire.

"The French Empire will become the mother country of other sovereignties. .. I mean that every king in Europe shall build a grand palace at Paris for his own use; on the coronation of the Emperor of the French these kings will come and occupy it; they will grace this imposing ceremony with their presence, and honor it with their salutations. "[77] The Pope will come; he came to the first one; he must necessarily return to Paris, and fix himself there permanently. Where could the Holy See be better off than in the new capital of Christianity, under Napoleon, heir to Charlemagne, and temporal sovereign of the Sovereign Pontiff? Through the temporal the emperor will control the spiritual, [78] and through the Pope, consciences. "

In November, 1811, unusually excited, he says to De Pradt:

"In five years I shall be master of the world; only Russia will remain, but I will crush her. [79] . .. Paris will extend out to St. Cloud. "

To render Paris the physical capital of Europe is, through his own confession, "one of his constant dreams. "

"At times, " he says, [80]"I would like to see her a city of two, three, four millions of inhabitants, something fabulous, colossal, unknown down to our day, and its public establishments adequate to its population. . .. Archimedes proposed to lift the world if he could be allowed to place his lever; for myself, I would have changed it wherever I could have been allowed to exercise my energy, perseverance, and budgets. "

At all events, he believes so; for however lofty and badly supported the next story of his structure may be, he has always ready a new story, loftier and more unsteady, to put above it. A few months before launching himself, with all Europe at his back, against Russia, he said to Narbonne: [81]

"After all, my dear sir, this long road is the road to India. Alexander started as far off as Moscow to reach the Ganges; this has occurred to me since St. Jean d'Acre. . .. To reach England to- day I need the extremity of Europe, from which to take Asia in the rear. . ... Suppose Moscow taken, Russia subdued, the czar reconciled, or dead through some court conspiracy, perhaps another and dependent throne, and tell me whether it is not possible for a French army, with its auxiliaries, setting out from Tiflis, to get as far as the Ganges, where it needs only a thrust of the French sword to bring down the whole of that grand commercial scaffolding throughout India. It would be the most gigantic expedition, I admit, but practicable in the nineteenth century. Through it France, at one stroke, would secure the independence of the West and the freedom of the seas. "

While uttering this his eyes shone with strange brilliancy, and he accumulates subjects, weighing obstacles, means, and chances: the inspiration is under full headway, and he gives himself up to it. The master faculty finds itself suddenly free, and it takes flight; the artist, [82] locked up in politics, has escaped from his sheath; he is creating out of the ideal and the impossible. We take him for what he is, a posthumous brother of Dante and Michael Angelo. In the clear outlines of his vision, in the intensity, coherency, and inward logic of his dreams, in the profundity of his meditations, in the superhuman grandeur of his conceptions, he is, indeed, their fellow and their equal. His genius is of the same stature and the same structure; he is one of the three sovereign minds of the Italian Renaissance. Only, while the first two operated on paper and on marble, the latter operates on the living being, on the sensitive and suffering flesh of humanity.

Notes:

[2] The main authority is, of course, the "correspondance de l'Empereur Napoléon I., " in thirty-two-volumes. This correspondance, " unfortunately, is still incomplete, while, after the sixth volume, it must not be forgotten that much of it has been purposely stricken out. "In general, " say the editors (XVI.), "we have been governed simply by this plain rule, that we were required to publish only what the Emperor himself would have given to the public had he survived himself, and, anticipating the verdict of time, exposed to posterity his own personality and system. " - The savant who has the most carefully examined this correspondence, entire in the French archives, estimates that it comprises about 80,000 pieces, of which 30,000 have been published in the collection referred to; passages in 20,000 of the others have been stricken out on account of previous publication, and about 30,000 more, through considerations of propriety or policy. For example, but little more than one-half of the letters from Napoleon to Bigot de Préameneu on ecclesiastical matters have been published; many of these omitted letters, all important and characteristic, may be found in "L'Église romaine et le Premier Empire, " by M. d'Haussonville. The above-mentioned savant estimates the number of important letters not yet published at 2,000.

[3] "Mémorial de Sainte Hélène, " by Las Casas (May 29, 1816). —- "In Corsica, Paoli, on a horseback excursion, explained the positions to him, the places where liberty found resistance or triumphed. Estimating the character of Napoleon by what he saw of it through personal observation, Paoli said to him, "Oh, Napoleon, there is nothing modern in you, you belong wholly to Plutarch! " — Antonomarchi, "Mémoires, " Oct. 25, 1819. The same account, slightly different, is there given: "Oh. Napoleon, " said Paoli to me, "you do not belong to this century; you talk like one of Plutarch's characters. Courage, you will take flight yet! "

[4] De Ségur, "Histoire et Mémoires, " I., 150. (Narrative by Pontécoulant, member of the committee in the war, June, 1795.) "Boissy d'Anglas told him that he had seen the evening before a little Italian, pale, slender, and puny, but singularly audacious in his views and in the vigor of his expressions. - The next day, Bonaparte calls on Pontécoulant, "Attitude rigid through a morbid pride, poor exterior, long visage, hollow and bronzed. . .. He is just from the army and talks like one who knows what he is talking about. "

[5] Coston, "Biographie des premières années de Napoléon Buonaparte, " 2 vols. (1840), passim. - Yung, " Bonaparte et son Temps, " I., 300, 302. (Pièces généalogiques.) - King Joseph, "Mémoires, " I., 109, 111. (On the various branches and distinguished men of the Bonaparte family.) - Miot de Melito, "Mémoires, " II., 30. (Documents on the Bonaparte family, collected on the spot by the author in 1801.)

[6] "Mémorial, " May 6, 1816. - Miot de Melito, II., 30. (On the Bonapartes of San Miniato): "The last offshoot of this branch was a canon then still living in this same town of San Miniato, and visited by Bonaparte in the year IV, when he came to Florence. "

[7] "Correspondance de l'Empereur Napoléon I. " (Letter of Bonaparte, Sept. 29, 1797, in relation to Italy): "A people at bottom inimical to the French through the prejudices, character, and customs of centuries. "

[8] Miot de Melito, I., 126, (1796): "Florence, for two centuries and a half, had lost that antique energy which, in the stormy times of the Republic, distinguished this city. Indolence was the dominant spirit of all classes. .. Almost everywhere I saw only men lulled to rest by the charms of the most exquisite climate, occupied solely with the

details of a monotonous existence, and tranquilly vegetating under its beneficent sky. " - (On Milan, in 1796, cf. Stendhal, introduction to the "Chartreuse de Parme. ")

[9] "Miot de Melito, I., 131: "Having just left one of the most civilized cities in Italy, it was not without some emotion that I found myself suddenly transported to a country (Corsica) which, in its savage aspect, its rugged mountains, and its inhabitants uniformly dressed in coarse brown cloth, contrasted so strongly with the rich and smiling landscape of Tuscany, and with the comfort, I should almost say elegance, of costume worn by the happy cultivators of that fertile soil. "

[10] Miot de Melito, II., 30: "Of a not very important family of Sartène. " - II., 143. (On the canton of Sartène and the Vendettas of 1796). - Coston, I., 4: "The family of Madame Laetitia, sprung from the counts of Cotalto, came originally from Italy. "

[11] His father, Charles Bonaparte, weak and even frivolous, "too fond of pleasure to care about his children, " and to see to his affairs, tolerably learned and an indifferent head of a family, died at the age of thirty-nine of a cancer in the stomach, which seems to be the only bequest he made to his son Napoleon. - His mother, on the contrary, serious, authoritative, the true head of a family, was, said Napoleon, "hard in her affections she punished and rewarded without distinction, good or bad; she made us all feel it. " - On becoming head of the household, "she was too parsimonious-even ridiculously so. This was due to excess of foresight on her part; she had known want, and her terrible sufferings were never out of her mind. . .. Paoli had tried persuasion with her before resorting to force. . .. Madame replied heroically, as a Cornelia would have done. . .. From 12 to 15,000 peasants poured down from the mountains of Ajaccio; our house was pillaged and burnt, our vines destroyed, and our flocks. . .. In other respects, this woman, from whom it would have been so difficult to extract five francs, would have given up everything to secure my return from Elba, and after Waterloo she offered me all she possessed to restore my affairs. " (" Mémorial, " May 29, 1816, and "Mémoires d'Antonomarchi, " Nov. 18, 1819. - On the ideas and ways of Bonaparte's mother, read her "Conversation" in "Journal et Mémoires, " vol. IV., by Stanislas Girardin.) Duchesse d'Abrantès, " Mémoires, " II., 318, 369. "Avaricious out of all reason except on a few grave occasions. . .. No knowledge whatever of the usages of

society. . ... very ignorant, not alone of our literature, but of her own." - Stendhal, "Vie de Napoleon": "The character of her son is to be explained by the perfectly Italian character of Madame Laetitia. "

[12] The French conquest is effected by armed force between July 30, 1768, and May 22, 1769. The Bonaparte family submitted May 23, 1769, and Napoleon was born on the following 15th of August.

[13] Antonomarchi, "Mémoires, " October 4, 1819. "Mémorial, " May 29, 1816.

[14] Miot de Melito, II., 33: "The day I arrived at Bocognano two men lost their lives through private vengeance. About eight years before this one of the inhabitants of the canton had killed a neighbor, the father of two children. . ... On reaching the age of sixteen or seventeen years these children left the country in order to dog the steps of the murderer, who kept on the watch, not daring to go far from his village. . ... Finding him playing cards under a tree, they fired at and killed him, and besides this accidentally shot another man who was asleep a few paces off. The relatives on both sides pronounced the act justifiable and according to rule. " Ibid., I., 143: "On reaching Bastia from Ajaccio the two principal families of the place, the Peraldi and the Visuldi, fired at each other, in disputing over the honor of entertaining me.

[15] Bourrienne, " Mémoires, " I., 18, 19.

[16] De Ségur, "Histoire et Mémoires, " I,, 74.

[17] Yung, I., 195. (Letter of Bonaparte to Paoli, June 12, 1789); I., 250 (Letter of Bonaparte to Buttafuoco, January 23 1790).

[18] Yung, I., 107 (Letter of Napoleon to his father, Sept. 12, 1784); I., 163 (Letter of Napoleon to Abbé Raynal, July, 1786); I., 197 (Letter of Napoleon to Paoli, June 12, 1789). The three letters on the history of Corsica are dedicated to Abbé Raynal in a letter of June 24, 1790, and may be found in Yung, I., 434.

[19] Read especially his essay "On the Truths and Sentiments most important to inculcate on Men for their Welfare" (a subject proposed by the Academy of Lyons in 1790). Some bold men driven by genius. . ... Perfection grows out of reason as fruit out of a tree. . ... Reason's eyes guard man from the precipice of the passions. .. The spectacle of

the strength of virtue was what the Lacedaemonians principally felt. . .. Must men then be lucky in the means by which they are led on to happiness? . . .. My rights (to property) are renewed along with my transpiration, circulate in my blood, are written on my nerves, on my heart. . .. Proclaim to the rich -your wealth is your misfortune, withdrawn within the latitude of your senses. . .. Let the enemies of nature at thy voice keep silence and swallow their rabid serpents' tongues. . .. The wretched shun the society of men, the tapestry of gayety turns to mourning. . .. Such, gentlemen, are the Sentiments which, in animal relations, mankind should have taught it for its welfare. "

[20] Yung, I., 252 (Letter to Buttafuoco). "Dripping with the blood of his brethren, sullied by every species of crime, he presents himself with confidence under his vest of a general, the sole reward of his criminalities. " - I., 192 (Letter to the Corsican Intendant, April 2, 1879). "Cultivation is what ruins us" - See various manuscript letters, copied by Yung, for innumerable and gross mistakes in French. - Miot de Melito, I., 84 (July, 1796). "He spoke curtly and, at this time, very incorrectly. " - Madame de Rémusat, I., 104. "Whatever language he spoke it never seemed familiar to him; he appeared to force himself in expressing his ideas. "- Notes par le Comte Chaptal (unpublished), councillor of state and afterwards minister of the interior under the Consulate: "At this time, Bonaparte did not blush at the slight knowledge of administrative details which he possessed; he asked a good many questions and demanded definitions and the meaning of the commonest words in use. As it very often happened with him not to clearly comprehend words which he heard for the first time, he always repeated these afterwards as he understood them; for example, he constantly used section for session, armistice for amnesty, fulminating point for culminating point, rentes voyagères for 'rentes viagères, ' etc. "

[21] De Ségur, I., 174

[22] Cf. the "Mémoires" of Marshal Marmont, I., 15, for the ordinary sentiments of the young nobility. "In 1792 I had a sentiment for the person of the king, difficult to define, of which I recovered the trace, and to some extent the power, twenty-two years later; a sentiment of devotion almost religious in character, an innate respect as if due to a being of a superior order. The word King then possessed a magic, a force, which nothing had changed in pure and honest breasts. . .. This religion of royalty still existed in the mass of the nation,, and

especially amongst the well-born, who, sufficiently remote from power, were rather struck with its brilliancy than with its imperfections. . ... This love became a sort of worship. "

[23] Bourrienne, "Mémoires, ' I. 27. - Ségur, I. 445. In 1795, at Paris, Bonaparte, being out of military employment, enters upon several commercial speculations, amongst which is a bookstore, which does not succeed. (Stated by Sebastiani and many others.)

[24] "Mémorial, " Aug. 3, 1816.

[25] Bourrienne, I., 171. (Original text of the "Souper de Beaucaire. ")

[26] Yung, II., 430, 431. (Words of Charlotte Robespierre.) Bonaparte as a souvenir of his acquaintance with her, granted her a pension, under the consulate, of 3600 francs. - Ibid. (Letter of Tilly, chargé d'affaires at Genoa, to Buchot, commissioner of foreign affairs.) Cf. in the "Mémorial, " Napoleon's favorable judgment of Robespierre.

[27] Yung, II., 455. (Letter from Bonaparte to Tilly, Aug. 7, 1794.) Ibid., III., 120. (Memoirs of Lucien.) "Barras takes care of Josephine's dowry, which is the command of the army in Italy. " Ibid., II., 477. (Grading of general officers, notes by Schérer on Bonaparte.) "He knows all about artillery, but is rather too ambitious, and too intriguing for promotion. "

[28] De Ségur, I., 162. - La Fayette, "Mémoires, " II., 215. "Mémorial" (note dictated by Napoleon). He states the reasons for and against, and adds, speaking of himself: "These sentiments, twenty-five years of age, confidence in his strength, his destiny, determined him. " Bourrienne, I., 51: " It is certain that he has always bemoaned that day; he has often said to me that he would give years of his life to efface that page of his history. "

[29] "Mémorial, " I., Sept 6, 1815. " It is only after Lodi that the idea came to me that I might, after all, become a decisive actor on our political stage. Then the first spark of lofty ambition gleamed out. " On his aim and conduct in the Italian campaign of Sybel, "Histoire de l'Europe pendant la Révolution Française" (Dosquet translation), vol. IV., books II. and III., especially pp. 182, 199, 334, 335, 406, 420, 475, 489.

[30] Yung, III., 213. (Letter of M. de Sucy, August 4, 1797.)

[31] Ibid., III., 214. (Report of d'Entraigues to M. de Mowikinoff, Sept., 1797.) "If there was any king in France which was not himself, he would like to have been his creator, with his rights at the end of his sword, this sword never to be parted with, so that he might plunge it in the king's bosom if he ever ceased to be submissive to him. " - Miot de Melito, I., 154. (Bonaparte to Montebello, before Miot and Melzi, June, 1797.) Ibid, I., 184. (Bonaparte to Miot, Nov. 18, 1797, at Turin.)

[32] D'Haussonville, "L'Église Romaine et la Premier Empire, " I., 405. (Words of M. Cacault, signer of the Treaty of Tolentino, and French Secretary of Legation at Rome, at the commencement of negotiations for the Concordat.) M. Cacaut says that he used this expression, "After the scenes of Tolentino and of Leghorn, and the fright of Manfredini, and Matéi threatened, and so many other vivacities. "

[33] Madame de Staël, "Considérations sur la Révolution Française, " 3rd part, ch. XXVI., and 4th part, ch. XVIII.

[34] Portrait of Bonaparte in the "Cabinet des Etampes, " "drawn by Guérin, engraved by Fiesinger, deposited in the National Library, Vendémiaire 29, year VII. "

[35] Madame de Rémusat, "Mémoires, " I., 104. - Miot de Melito, I., 84.

[36] Madame de Staël, "Considerations, " etc., 3rd part, ch. XXV. - Madame de Rémusat, II., 77.

[37] Stendhal, "Mémoires sur Napoléon, " narration of Admiral Decrès. - Same narration in the "Mémorial. "

[38] De Ségur, I., 193.

[39] Roederer, "Oeuvres complétes, " II., 560. (Conversations with General Lasalle in 1809, and Lasalle's judgment on the débuts of Napoleon).

[40] Another instance of this commanding influence is found in the case of General Vandamme, an old revolutionary soldier still more brutal and energetic than Augereau. In 1815, Vandamme said to Marshal d'Ornano, one day, on ascending the staircase of the

Tuileries together: "My dear fellow, that devil of a man (speaking of the Emperor) fascinates me in a way I cannot account for. I, who don't fear either God or the devil, when I approach him I tremble like a child. He would make me dash through the eye of a needle into the fire! " ("Le Général Vandamme, " by du Casse, II., 385).

[41] Roederer, III., 356. (Napoleon himself says, February 11, 1809): "I, military! I am so, because I was born so; it is my habit, my very existence. Wherever I have been I have always had command. I commanded at twenty-three, at the siege of Toulon; I commanded at Paris in Vendémiaire; I won over the soldiers in Italy the moment I presented myself. I was born for that. "

[42] Observe the various features of the same mental and moral structure among different members of the family. (Speaking of his brothers and sisters in the "Memorial" Napoleon says): "What family as numerous presents such a splendid group? " - "Souvenirs", by PASQUIER (Etienne-Dennis, duc), chancelier de France. in VI volumes, Librarie Plon, Paris 1893. Vol. I. (This author, a young magistrate under Louis XVI., a high functionary under the Empire, an important political personage under the restoration and the July monarchy, is probably the best informed and most judicious of eye-witnesses during the first half of our century.): "Their vices and virtues surpass ordinary proportions and have a physiognomy of their own. But what especially distinguishes them is a stubborn will, and inflexible resolution. . .. All possessed the instinct of their greatness. " They readily accepted "the highest positions; they even got to believing that their elevation was inevitable. . .. Nothing in the incredible good fortune of Joseph astonished him; often in January, 1814, I heard him say over and over again that if his brother had not meddled with his affairs after the second entry into Madrid, he would still be on the throne of Spain. As to determined obstinacy we have only to refer to the resignation of Louis, the retirement of Lucien, and the resistances of Fesch; they alone could stem the will of Napoleon and sometimes break a lance with him. -Passion, sensuality, the habit of considering themselves outside of rules, and self-confidence combined with talent, super abound among the women, as in the fifteenth century. Elisa, in Tuscany, had a vigorous brain, was high spirited and a genuine sovereign, notwithstanding the disorders of her private life, in which even appearances were not sufficiently maintained. " Caroline at Naples, "without being more scrupulous than her sisters, " better observed the proprieties; none of the others so much resembled the Emperor; "with her, all tastes

succumbed to ambition"; it was she who advised and prevailed upon her husband, Murat, to desert Napoleon in 1814. As to Pauline, the most beautiful woman of her epoch, "no wife, since that of the Emperor Claude, surpassed her in the use she dared make of her charms; nothing could stop her, not even a malady attributed to the strain of this life-style and for which we have so often seen her borne in a litter. " - Jerome, " in spite of the uncommon boldness of his debaucheries, maintained his ascendancy over his wife to the last. " - On the "pressing efforts and attempts" of Joseph on Maria Louise in 1814, Chancelier Pasquier, after Savary's papers and the evidence of M. de Saint-Aignan, gives extraordinary details. - "Mes souvenirs sur Napoléon, 346, by the count Chaptal: "Every member of this numerous family (Jér'me, Louis, Joseph, the Bonaparte sisters) mounted thrones as if they had recovered so much property. "

[43] Burkhardt, "Die Renaissance in Italien, " passim. - Stendhal, "Histoire de la peinture en Italie"(introduction), and" Rome, Naples, et Florence, " passim. - " Notes par le Comte Chaptal": When these notes are published, many details will be found in them in support of the judgment expressed in this and the following chapters. The psychology of Napoleon as here given is largely confirmed by them.

[44] Roederer, III, 380 (1802).

[45] Napoleon uses the French word just which means both fair, justifiable, pertinent, correct, and in music true.

[46] "Mémorial. "

[47] De Pradt, "Histoire de l'Ambassade dans la grande-duché de Varsovie en 1812, " preface, p. X, and 5.

[48] Roederer, III., 544 (February 24, 1809). Cf. Meneval, "Napoléon et Marie-Louise, souvenirs historiques, " I., 210-213.

[49] Pelet de la Lozère, " Opinions de Napoléon au conseil d'état, ", Roederer, III., 380.

[50] Mollien, "Mémoires, " I., 379; II., 230. -Roederer, III., 434. "He is at the head of all things. He governs, administrates, negotiates, works eighteen hours a day, with the clearest and best organized head; he has governed more in three years than kings in a hundred years. " - Lavalette, "Mémoires, " II., 75. (The words of Napoleon's

secretary on Napoleon's labor in Paris, after Leipsic) "He retires at eleven, but gets up at three o'clock in the morning, and until the evening there is not a moment he does not devote to work. It is time this stopped, for he will be used up, and myself before he is. "- Gaudin, Duc de Gaëte, "Mémoires, " III. (supplement). Account of an evening in which, from eight o'clock to three in the morning, Napoleon examines with Gaudin his general budget, during seven consecutive hours, without stopping a minute. -Sir Neil Campbell, "Napoléon at Fontainebleau and at Elbe, ". "Journal de Sir Neil Campbell a' l'ile d'Elbe": I never saw any man, in any station in life, so personally active and so persistent in his activity. He seems to take pleasure in perpetual motion and in seeing those who accompany him completely tired out, which frequently happened in my case when I accompanied him. .. Yesterday, after having been on his legs from eight in the morning to three in the afternoon, visiting the frigates and transports, even to going down to the lower compartments among the horses, he rode on horseback for three hours, and, as he afterwards said to me, to rest himself. "

[51] The starting-point of the great discoveries of Darwin is the physical, detailed description he made in his study of animals and plants, as living; during the whole course of life, through so many difficulties and subject to a fierce competition. This study is wholly lacking in the ordinary zoologist or botanist, whose mind is busy only with anatomical preparations or collections of plants. In every science, the difficulty lies in describing in a nutshell, using significant examples, the real object, just as it exists before us, and its true history. Claude Bernard one day remarked to me, "We shall know physiology when we are able to follow step by step a molecule of carbon or azote in the body of a dog, give its history, and describe its passage from its entrance to its exit. "

[52] Thibaudeau, "Mémoires sur le Consulat, " 204. (Apropos of the tribunate): "They consist of a dozen or fifteen metaphysicians who ought to be flung into the water; they crawl all over me like vermin.

[53] Madame de Rémusat, I., 115: "He is really ignorant, having read very little and always hastily. " - Stendhal, "Mémoires sur Napoleon": " His education was very defective. . .. He knew nothing of the great principles discovered within the past one hundred years," and just those which concern man or society. "For example, he had not read Montesquieu as this writer ought to be read, that is to say, in a way to accept or decidedly reject each of the thirty-one

books of the 'Esprit des lois. ' He had not thus read Bayle's Dictionary nor the Essay on the Wealth of Nations by Adam Smith. This ignorance of the Emperor's was not perceptible in conversation, and first, because he led in conversation, and next because with Italian finesse no question put by him, or careless supposition thrown out, ever betrayed that ignorance. " - Bourrienne. I., 19, 21: At Brienne, "unfortunately for us, the monks to whom the education of youth was confided knew nothing, and were too poor to pay good foreign teachers. . .. It is inconceivable how any capable man ever graduated from this educational institution. " - Yung, I., 125 (Notes made by him on Bonaparte, when he left the Military Academy): "Very fond of the abstract sciences, indifferent to others, well grounded in mathematics and geography. "

[54] Roederer, III., 544 (March 6, 1809), 26, 563 (Jan. 23, 1811, and Nov. 12, 1813).

[55] Mollien, I., 348 (a short time before the rupture of the peace of Amiens), III., 16: "It was at the end of January, 1809, that he wanted a full report of the financial situation on the 31st of December, 1808 . . .. This report was to be ready in two days. " - III., 34: "A complete balance sheet of the public treasury for the first six months of 1812 was under Napoleon's eyes at Witebsk, the 11th of August, eleven days after the close of these first six months. What is truly wonderful is, that amidst so many different occupations and preoccupations . . .. he could preserve such an accurate run of the proceedings and methods of the administrative branches about which he wanted to know at any moment. Nobody had any excuse for not answering him, for each was questioned in his own terms; it is that singular aptitude of the head of the State, and the technical precision of his questions, which alone explains how he could maintain such a remarkable ensemble in an administrative system of which the smallest threads centered in himself. "

[57] An expression of Mollien.

[58] Meneval, I., 210, 213. - Roederer, III., 537, 545 (February and March, 1889): Words of Napoleon: "At this moment it was nearly midnight. " - Ibid., IV., 55 (November, 1809). Read the admirable examination of Roederer by Napoleon on the Kingdom of Naples. His queries form a vast systematic and concise network, embracing the entire subject, leaving no physical or moral data, no useful circumstance not seized upon. - Ségur, II., 231: M. De Ségur, ordered

to inspect every part of the coast-line, had sent in his report: "'I have seen your reports, ' said the First Consul to me, 'and they are exact. Nevertheless, you forgot at Osten two cannon out of the four. ' - And he pointed out the place, 'a roadway behind the town. ' I went out overwhelmed with astonishment that among thousands of cannon distributed among the mounted batteries or light artillery on the coast, two pieces should not have escaped his recollection. " - "Correspondance, " letter to King Joseph, August 6, 1806: "The admirable condition of my armies is due to this, that I give attention to them every day for an hour or two, and, when the monthly reports come in, to the state of my troops and fleets, all forming about twenty large volumes. I leave every other occupation to read them over in detail, to see what difference there is between one month and another. I take more pleasure in reading those than any young girl does in a novel. " - Cadet de Gassicourt, "Voyage en Autriche"(1809). On his reviews at Schoenbrunn and his verification of the contents of a pontoon-wagon, taken as an example.

[60] Bourrienne, II., 116; IV., 238: "He had not a good memory for proper names, words, and dates, but it was prodigious for facts and localities. I remember that, on the way from Paris to Toulon, he called my attention to ten places suitable for giving battle. . .. It was a souvenir of his youthful travels, and he described to me the lay of the ground, designating the positions he would have taken even before we were on the spot. " March 17, 1800, puncturing a card with a pin, he shows Bourrienne the place where he intends to beat Mélas, at San Juliano. "Four months after this I found myself at San Juliano with his portfolio and dispatches, and, that very evening, at Torre-di-Gafolo, a league off, I wrote the bulletin of the battle under his dictation" (of Marengo). -De Ségur, II., 30 (Narrative of M. Daru to M. De Ségur Aug. 13, 1805, at the headquarters of La Manche, Napoleon dictates to M. Daru the complete plan of the campaign against Austria): "Order of marches, their duration, places of convergence or meeting of the columns, attacks in full force, the various movements and mistakes of the enemy, all, in this rapid dictation, was foreseen two months beforehand and at a distance of two hundred leagues. . .. The battle-field, the victories, and even the very days on which we were to enter Munich and Vienna were then announced and written down as it all turned out. . .. Daru saw these oracles fulfilled on the designated days up to our entry into Munich; if there were any differences of time and not of results between Munich and Vienna, they were all in our favor. " -M. de La Vallette, "Mémoires, " II. (He was postmaster-general): "It often happened to

me that I was not as certain as he was of distances and of many details in my administration on which he was able to set me straight. " - On returning from the camp at Bologna, Napoleon encounters a squad of soldiers who had got lost, asks what regiment they belong to, calculates the day they left, the road they took, what distance they should have marched. and then tells them, "You will find your battalion at such a halting place. " - At this time, "the army numbered 200,000 men. "

[61] Madame de Rémusat, I., 103, 268.

[62] Thibaudeau, p. 25, I (on the Jacobin survivors): "They are nothing but common artisans, painters, etc., with lively imaginations, a little better instructed than the people, living amongst the people and exercising influence over them. " - Madame de Rémusat, I., 271 (on the royalist party): "It is very easy to deceive that party because its starting-point is not what it is, but what it would like to have. " - I., 337: "The Bourbons will never see anything except through the Oeil de Boeuf. " - Thibaudeau, p. 46: "Insurrections and emigrations are skin diseases; terrorism is an internal malady. " Ibid., 75: "What now keeps the spirit of the army up is the idea soldiers have that they occupy the places of former nobles. "

[63] Thibaudeau(Both texts are given in separate columns.) And passim, for instance, p. 84, the following portrayal of the decadal system of worship under the Republic: "It was imagined that citizens could be got together in churches, to freeze with cold and hear, read, and study laws, in which there was already but little fun for those who executed them. " Another example of the way in which his ideas expressed themselves through imagery (Pelet de la Lozère, p. 242): "I am not satisfied with the customs regulations on the Alps. They show no life. We don't hear the rattle of crown pieces pouring into the public treasury. " To appreciate the vividness of Napoleon's expressions and thought the reader must consult, especially, the five or six long conversations, noted on the very evening of the day they occurred by Roederer; the two or three conversations likewise noted by Miot de Melito; the scenes narrated by Beugnot; the notes of Pelet de la Lozère and by Stanislas de Girardin, and nearly the entire volume by Thibaudeau.

[64] Pelet de la Lozère, 63, 64. (On the physiological differences between the English and the French.) - Madame de Rémusat, I., 273,

392: "You, Frenchmen, are not in earnest about anything, except, perhaps, equality, and even here you would gladly give this up if you were sure of being the foremost. . ... The hope of advancement in the world should be cherished by everybody. . ... Keep your vanity always alive The severity of the republican government would have worried you to death. What started the Revolution? Vanity. What will end it? Vanity, again. Liberty is merely a pretext. " - III., 153 "Liberty is the craving of a small and privileged class by nature, with faculties superior to the common run of men; this class, therefore, may be put under restraint with impunity; equality, on the contrary, catches the multitude. " - Thibaudeau, 99: "What do I care for the opinions and cackle of the drawing-room? I never heed it. I pay attention only to what rude peasants say. " His estimates of certain situations are masterpieces of picturesque concision. "Why did I stop and sign the preliminaries of Leoben? Because I played vingt-et-un and was satisfied with twenty. " His insight into (dramatic) character is that of the most sagacious critic. "The 'Mahomet' of Voltaire is neither a prophet nor an Arab, only an impostor graduated out of the École Polytechnique. " - " Madame de Genlis tries to define virtue as if she were the discoverer of it. " - (On Madame de Staël): "This woman teaches people to think who never took to it, or have forgotten how. " - (On Chateaubriand, one of whose relations had just been shot): "He will write a few pathetic pages and read them aloud in the faubourg Saint-Germain; pretty women will shed tears, and that will console him. " - (On Abbé Delille): "He is wit in its dotage. " - (On Pasquier and Molé): "I make the most of one, and made the other. " - Madame de Rémusat, II., 389, 391, 394, 399, 402; III., 67.

[65] Bourrienne, II., 281, 342: "It pained me to write official statements under his dictation, of which each was an imposture. " He always answered: "My dear sir, you are a simpleton - you understand nothing! " - Madame de Rémusat, II., 205, 209.

[66] See especially the campaign bulletins for 1807, so insulting to the king and queen of Prussia, but, owing to that fact, so well calculated to excite the contemptuous laughter and jeers of the soldiers.

[67] In "La Correspondance de Napoleon, " published in thirty-two volumes, the letters are arranged under dates. - In his '"Correspondance avec Eugène, vice-roi d'Italie, " they are arranged under chapters; also with Joseph, King of Naples and afterwards King of Spain. It is easy to select other chapters not less instructive:

one on foreign affairs (letters to M. de Champagny, M de Talleyrand, and M. de Bassano); another on the finances (letters to M. Gaudin and to M. Mollien); another on the navy (letters to Admiral Decrès); another on military administration (letters to General Clarke); another on the affairs of the Church (letters to M. Portalis and to M. Bigot de Préameneu); another on the Police (letters to Fouché), etc. - Finally, by dividing and distributing his letters according as they relate to this or that grand enterprise, especially to this or that military campaign, a third classification could be made. - In this way we can form a concept of the vastness of his positive knowledge, also of the scope of his intellect and talents. Cf. especially the following letters to Prince Eugène, June II, 1806 (on the supplies and expenses of the Italian army); June 1st and 18th, 1806 (on the occupation of Dalmatia, and on the military situation, offensive and defensive). To Gen. Dejean, April 28, 1806 (on the war supplies); June 27, 1806 (on the fortifications of Peschiera) July 20, 1806 (on the fortifications of Wesel and of Juliers). - "Mes souvenirs sur Napoleon", p. 353 by the Count Chaptal: "One day, the Emperor said to me that he would like to organize a military school at Fontainebleau; he then explained to me the principal features of the establishment, and ordered me to draw up the necessary articles and bring them to him the next day. I worked all night and they were ready at the appointed hour. He read them over and pronounced them correct, but not complete. He bade me take a seat and then dictated to me for two or three hours a plan which consisted of five hundred and seventeen articles. Nothing more perfect, in my opinion, ever issued from a man's brain. - At another time, the Empress Josephine was to take the waters at Aix-la-Chapelle, and the Emperor summoned me. 'The Empress, ' said he, 'is to leave to-morrow morning. She is a good-natured, easy-going woman and must have her route and behavior marked out for her. Write it down. ' He then dictated instructions to me on twenty-one large sheets of paper, in which everything she was to say and to do was designated, even the questions and replies she was to make to the authorities on the way. "

[69] Cf. in the "Correspondance" the letters dated at Schoenbrunn near Vienna, during August and September, 1809, and especially:

the great number of letters and orders relating to the English expeditions to Walcheren; the letters to chief-judge Régnier and to the arch-chancellor Cambacérès on expropriations for public benefit (Aug. 21, Sept. 7 and 29); the letters and orders to M. de Champagny to treat with Austria (Aug. 19, and Sept. 10, 15, 18, 22, and 23); the letters to Admirable Decrès, to despatch naval expeditions to the colonies (Aug. 17 and Sept. 26); the letter to Mollien on the budget of expenditure (Aug. 8); the letter to Clarke on the statement of guns in store throughout the empire (Sept. 14). Other letters, ordering the preparation of two treatises on military art (Oct. 1), two works on the history and encroachments of the Holy See (Oct. 3), prohibiting conferences at Saint-Sulpice (Sept. 15), and forbidding priests to preach outside the churches (Sept. 24). - From Schoenbrunn, he watches the details of public works in France and Italy; for instance, the letters to M. le Montalivet (Sept. 30), to send an auditor post to Parma, to have a dyke repaired at once, and (Oct. 8) to hasten the building of several bridges and quays at Lyons.

[70] He says himself; "I always transpose my theme in many ways. "

[71] Madame de Rémusat, I., 117, 120. "1 heard M. de Talleyrand exclaim one day, some what out of humor, 'This devil of a man misleads you in all directions. Even his passions escape you, for he finds some way to counterfeit them, although they really exist. '" - For example, immediately prior to the violent confrontation with Lord Whitworth, which was to put an end to the treaty of Amiens, he was chatting and amusing himself with the women and the infant Napoleon, his nephew, in the gayest and most unconcerned manner: "He is suddenly told that the company had assembled. His countenance changes like that of an actor when the scene shifts. He seems to turn pale at will and his features contract"; he rises, steps up precipitately to the English ambassador, and fulminates for two hours before two hundred persons. (Hansard's Parliamentary History, vol. XXVI, dispatches of Lord Whitworth, pp. 1798, 1302, 1310.) - "He often observes that the politician should calculate every advantage that could be gained by his defects. " One day, after an explosion he says to Abbé de Pradt: "You thought me angry! you are mistaken. Anger with me never mounts higher than here (pointing to his neck). "

[72] Roederer, III. (The first days of Brumaire, year VIII.)

[73] Bourrienne, III., 114.

[74] Bourrienne, II., 228. (Conversation with Bourrienne in the park at Passeriano.)

[75] Ibid., II., 331. (Written down by Bourrienne the same evening.)

[76] Madame de Rémusat, I., 274. - De Ségur, II., 459. (Napoleon's own words on the eve of the battle of Austerlitz): "Yes, if I had taken Acre, I would have assumed the turban, I would have put the army in loose breeches; I would no longer have exposed it, except at the last extremity; I would have made it my sacred battalion, my immortals. It is with Arabs, Greeks, and Armenians that I would have ended the war against the Turks. Instead of one battle in Moravia I would have gained a battle of Issus; I would have made myself emperor of the East, and returned to Paris by the way of Constantinople. " - De Pradt, p. 19 (Napoleon's own words at Mayence, September, 1804): "Since two hundred years there is nothing more to do in Europe; it is only in the East that things can be carried out on a grand scale. "

[77] Madame de Rémusat, I., 407. - Miot de Melito, II., 214 (a few weeks after his coronation): "There will be no repose in Europe until it is under one head, under an Emperor, whose officers would be kings, who would distribute kingdoms to his lieutenants, who would make one of them King of Italy, another King of Bavaria, here a landmann of Switzerland, and here a stadtholder of Holland, etc. "

[78] "Correspondance de Napoleon I., " vol. XXX., 550, 558. (Memoirs dictated by Napoleon at Saint Hélène.) - Miot de Melito, II., 290. - D'Hausonvillc, "l'Église Romaine et le Premier Empire, " passiM. -" Mémorial. " "Paris would become the capital of the Christian world, and I would have governed the religious world as well as the political world. "

[79] De Pradt, 23.

[80] "Mémoires et Mémorial. " "It was essential that Paris should become the unique capital, not to be compared with other capitals. The masterpieces of science and of art, the museums, all that had illustrated past centuries, were to be collected there. Napoleon regretted that he could not transport St. Peter's to Paris; the meanness of Notre Dame dissatisfied him. "

[81] Villemain, "Souvenir contemporaines, " I., 175. Napoleon's statement to M. de Narbonne early in March, 1812, and repeated by him to Villemain an hour afterwards. The wording is at second hand and merely a very good imitation, while the ideas are substantially Napoleon's. Cf. his fantasies about Italy and the Mediterranean, equally exaggerated ("Correspondence, " XXX., 548), and an

admirable improvisation on Spain and the colonies at Bayonne. - De Pradt. "Mémoires sur les revolutions d'Espagne, " p. 130: "Therefore Napoleon talked, or rather poetised; he Ossianized for a long time . .. like a man full of a sentiment which oppressed him, in an animated, picturesque style, and with the impetuosity, imagery, and originality which were familiar to him, . .. on the vast throne of Mexico and Peru, on the greatness of the sovereigns who should possess them . . .. and on the results which these great foundations would have on the universe. I had often heard him, but under no circumstances had I ever heard him develop such a wealth and compass of imagination. Whether it was the richness of his subject, or whether his faculties had become excited by the scene he conjured up, and all the chords of the instrument vibrated at once, he was sublime. "

[82] Roederer, III., 541 (February 2, 1809): "I love power. But I love it as an artist. . .. I love it as a musician loves his violin, for the tones, chords, and harmonies he can get out of it. "

CHAPTER II. His Ideas, Passions and Intelligence.

I. Intense Passions.

Personality and character during the Italian Renaissance and during the present time. - Intensity of the passions in Bonaparte. - His excessive touchiness. - His immediate violence. - His impatience, rapidity, and need of talking. - His temperament, tension, and faults.

On taking a near view of the contemporaries of Dante and Michael Angelo, we find that they differ from us more in character than in intellect. [1] With us, three hundred years of police and of courts of justice, of social discipline and peaceful habits, of hereditary civilization, have diminished the force and violence of the passions natural to Man. In Italy, in the Renaissance epoch, they were still intact; human emotions at that time were keener and more profound than at the present day; the appetites were ardent and more unbridled; man's will was more impetuous and more tenacious; whatever motive inspired, whether pride, ambition, jealousy, hatred, love, envy, or sensuality, the inward spring strained with an energy and relaxed with a violence that has now disappeared. All these energies reappear in this great survivor of the fifteenth century; in him the play of the nervous machine is the same as with his Italian ancestors; never was there, even with the Malatestas and the Borgias, a more sensitive and more impulsive intellect, one capable of such electric shocks and explosions, in which the roar and flashes of tempest lasted longer and of which the effects were more irresistible. In his mind no idea remains speculative and pure; none is a simple transcript of the real, or a simple picture of the possible; each is an internal eruption, which suddenly and spontaneously spends itself in action; each darts forth to its goal and would reach it without stopping were it not kept back and restrained by force[2] Sometimes, the eruption is so sudden, that the restraint does not come soon enough. One day, in Egypt, [3] on entertaining a number of French ladies at dinner, he has one of them, who was very pretty and whose husband he had just sent off to France, placed alongside of him; suddenly, as if accidentally, he overturns a pitcher of water on her, and, under the pretence of enabling her to rearrange her wet dress, he leads her into another room where he remains with her a long time, too long, while the other guests seated at the table wait quietly and exchange glances. Another day, at Paris, toward the epoch of the Concordat, [4] he says to Senator Volney: "France wants a religion. "

Volney replies in a frank, sententious way, "France wants the Bourbons. " Whereupon he gives Volney a kick in the stomach and he falls unconscious; on being moved to a friend's house, he remains there ill in bed for several days. - No man is more irritable, so soon in a passion; and all the more because he purposely gives way to his irritation; for, doing this just at the right moment, and especially before witnesses, it strikes terror; it enables him to extort concessions and maintain obedience. His explosions of anger, half-calculated, half-involuntary, serve him quite as much as they relieve him, in public as well as in private, with strangers as with intimates, before constituted bodies, with the Pope, with cardinals, with ambassadors, with Talleyrand, with Beugnot, with anybody that comes along, [5] whenever he wishes to set an example or "keep the people around him on the alert. " The public and the army regard him as impassible; but, apart from the battles in which he wears a mask of bronze, apart from the official ceremonies in which he assumes a necessarily dignified air, impression and expression with him are almost always confounded, the inward overflowing in the outward, the action, like a blow, getting the better of him. At Saint Cloud, caught by Josephine in the arms of another woman, he runs after the unlucky interrupter in such a way that "she barely has time to escape"; [6] and again, that evening, keeping up his fury so as to put her down completely, "he treats her in the most outrageous manner, smashing every piece of furniture that comes in his way. " A little before the Empire, Talleyrand, a great mystifier, tells Berthier that the First Consul wanted to assume the title of king. Berthier, in eager haste, crosses the drawing-room full of company, accosts the master of the house and, with a beaming smile, "congratulates him. "[7] At the word king, Bonaparte's eyes flash. Grasping Berthier by the throat, he pushes him back against the wall, exclaiming, "You fool! who told you to come here and stir up my bile in this way? Another time don't come on such errands. " - Such is the first impulse, the instinctive action, to pounce on people and seize them by the throat; we divine under each sentence, and on every page he writes, outbursts and assaults of this description, the physiognomy and intonation of a man who rushes forward and knocks people down. Accordingly, when dictating in his cabinet, "he strides up and down the room, " and, " if excited, " which is often the case, " his language consists of violent imprecations, and even of oaths, which are suppressed in what is written. "[8] But these are not always suppressed, for those who have seen the original minutes of his correspondence on ecclesiastical affairs find dozens of them, the b..., the p... and the swearwords of the coarsest kind. [9]

Never was there such impatient touchiness. "When dressing himself,
[10] he throws on the floor or into the fire any part of his attire which
does not suit him. . .. On gala-days and on grand ceremonial
occasions his valets are obliged to agree together when they shall
seize the right moment to put some thing on him. .. He tears off or
breaks whatever causes him the slightest discomfort, while the poor
valet who has been the means of it meets with a violent and positive
proof of his anger. No thought was ever more carried away by its
own speed. "His handwriting, when he tries to write, "is a mass of
disconnected and undecipherable signs; [11] the words lack one-half
of their letters. " On reading it over himself, he cannot tell what it
means. At last, he becomes almost incapable of producing a
handwritten letter, while his signature is a mere scrawl. He
accordingly dictates, but so fast that his secretaries can scarcely keep
pace with him: on their first attempt the perspiration flows freely
and they succeed in noting down only the half of what he says.
Bourrienne, de Meneval, and Maret invent a stenography of their
own, for he never repeats any of his phrases; so much the worse for
the pen if it lags behind, and so much the better if a volley of
exclamations or of oaths gives it a chance to catch up. - Never did
speech flow and overflow in such torrents, often without either
discretion or prudence, even when the outburst is neither useful nor
creditable the reason is that both spirit and intellect are charged to
excess subject to this inward pressure the improvisator and polemic,
under full headway, [12] take the place of the man of business and
the statesman.

"With him, " says a good observer, [13] "talking is a prime necessity,
and, assuredly, among the prerogatives of high rank, he ranks first
that of speaking without interruption. "

Even at the Council of State he allows himself to run on, forgetting
the business on hand; he starts off right and left with some
digression or demonstration, some invective or other, for two or
three hours at a stretch, [14] insisting over and over again, bent on
convincing or prevailing, and ending in demanding of the others if
he is not right, "and, in this case, never failing to find that all have
yielded to the force of his arguments. " On reflection, he knows the
value of an assent thus obtained, and, pointing to his chair, he
observes:

"It must be admitted that it is easy to be brilliant when one is in that
seat! "

Nevertheless he has enjoyed his intellectual exercise and given way to his passion, which controls him far more than he controls it.

"My nerves are very irritable, " he said of himself, "and when in this state were my pulse not always regular I should risk going crazy."[15]

The tension of accumulated impressions is often too great, and it ends in a physical break-down. Strangely enough in so great a warrior and with such a statesman, "it is not infrequent, when excited, to see him shed tears. " He who has looked upon thousands of dying men, and who has had thousands of men slaughtered, "sobs, " after Wagram and after Bautzen, [16] at the couch of a dying comrade. "I saw him, " says his valet, "weep while eating his breakfast, after coming from Marshal Lannes's bedside; big tears rolled down his cheeks and fell on his plate. " It is not alone the physical sensation, the sight of a bleeding, mangled body, which thus moves him acutely and deeply; for a word, a simple idea, stings and penetrates almost as far. Before the emotion of Dandolo, who pleads for Venice his country, which is sold to Austria, he is agitated and his eyes moisten. [17] Speaking of the capitulation of Baylen, at a full meeting of the Council of State, [18] his voice trembles, and "he gives way to his grief, his eyes even filling with tears. " In 1806, setting out for the army and on taking leave of Josephine, he has a nervous attack which is so severe as to bring on vomiting. [19] "We had to make him sit down, " says an eye- witness, "and swallow some orange water; he shed tears, and this lasted a quarter of an hour. " The same nervous and stomachic crisis came on in 1808, on deciding on the divorce; he tosses about a whole night, and laments like a woman; he melts, and embraces Josephine; he is weaker than she is: "My poor Josephine, I can never leave you! " Folding her in his arms, he declares that she shall not quit him; he abandons himself wholly to the sensation of the moment; she must undress at once, sleep alongside of him, and he weeps over her; "literally, " she says, " he soaked the bed with his tears. " - Evidently, in such an organism, however powerful the superimposed regulator, there is a risk of the equilibrium being destroyed. He is aware of this, for he knows himself well; he is afraid of his own nervous sensibility, the same as of an easily frightened horse; at critical moments, at Berezina, he refuses to receive the bad news which might excite this, and, on the informer's insisting on it, he asks him again, [20] "Why, sir, do you want to disturb me? " - Nevertheless, in spite of his precautions, he is twice taken unawares, at times when the peril was alarming and of a new kind; he, so clear headed and so cool under fire, the boldest of military heroes and the most audacious of political adventurers, quails twice in a parliamentary storm and again in a popular crisis. On the 18th of Brumaire, in the Corps Législatif, "he turned pale, trembled, and seemed to lose his head at the shouts of outlawry . . .. they had to drag him out . . .. they even thought for a moment that he was going to faint. "[21] After the abdication at Fontainebleau, on encountering the rage and imprecations which greeted him in Provence, he seemed for some days to be morally shattered; the animal instincts assert their supremacy; he is afraid and makes no attempt at concealment. [22] After borrowing the uniform of an Austrian colonel, the helmet of a Prussian quartermaster, and the cloak of the Russian quartermaster, he still considers that he is not sufficiently disguised. In the inn at Calade, "he starts and changes color at the slightest noise"; the commissaries, who repeatedly enter his room, "find him always in tears. " "He wearies them with his anxieties and irresolution"; he says that the French government would like to have him assassinated on the road, refuses to eat for fear of poison, and thinks that he might escape by jumping out of the window. And yet he gives vent to his feelings and lets his tongue run on about himself without stopping, concerning his past, his character, unreservedly, indelicately, trivially; like a cynic and one who is half-crazy; his ideas run loose and crowd each other like the anarchical gatherings of a tumultuous mob; he does not recover his mastery of them until he reaches Fréjus, the end of his journey, where he feels himself safe and protected from any highway assault; then only do they return within ordinary limits and fall back in regular line under the control of the sovereign intellect which, after sinking for a time, revives and resumes its ascendancy. - There is nothing in him so extraordinary as this almost perpetual domination of the lucid, calculating reason; his willpower is still more formidable than his intelligence; before it can obtain the mastery of others it must be master at home. To measure its power, it does not suffice to note its fascinations; to enumerate the millions of souls it captivates, to estimate the vastness of the obstacles it overcomes: we must again, and especially, represent to ourselves the energy and depth of the passions it keeps in check and urges on like a team of prancing, rearing horses - it is the driver who, bracing his arms, constantly restrains the almost ungovernable steeds, who controls their excitement, who regulates their bounds, who takes advantage even of their viciousness to guide his noisy vehicle over precipices as it rushes on with thundering speed. If the pure ideas of the reasoning brain thus maintain their daily supremacy it is due to the vital flow which nourishes them; their roots are deep in his heart and temperament, and those roots which give them their vigorous sap constitute a primordial instinct more powerful than intellect, more powerful even than his will, the instinct which leads him to center everything on himself, in other words egoism. [23]

II. Will and Egoism.

Bonaparte's dominant passion. - His lucid, calculating mind. - Source and power of the Will. - Early evidences of an active, absorbing egoism. - His education derived from the lessons of things. - In Corsica. - In France during the Revolution. - In Italy. - In Egypt. - His idea of Society and of Right. - Maturing after the 18th of Brumaire. - His idea of Man. - It conforms to his character

It is egoism, not a passive, but an active and intrusive egoism, proportional to the energy and extension of his faculties developed by his education and circumstances, exaggerated by his success and his omnipotence to such a degree that a monstrous colossal I has been erected in society. It expands unceasingly the circle of a tenacious and rapacious grasp, which regards all resistance as offensive, which all independence annoys, and which, on the boundless domain it assigns to itself, is intolerant of anybody that does not become either an appendix or a tool. - The germ of this absorbing personality is already apparent in the youth and even in the infant.

"Character: dominating, imperious, and stubborn, "

says the record at Brienne. [24] And the notes of the Military Academy add; [25]

"Extremely inclined to egoism, " - "proud, ambitious, aspiring in all directions, fond of solitude, "

undoubtedly because he is not master in a group of equals and is ill at ease when he cannot rule.

"I lived apart from my comrades, " he says at a later date. [26] - "I had selected a little corner in the playgrounds, where I used to go and sit down and indulge my fancies. When my comrades were disposed to drive me out of this corner I defended it with all my might. My instinct already told me that my will should prevail against other wills, and that whatever pleased me ought to belong to me. "

Referring to his early years under the paternal roof at Corsica, he depicts himself as a little mischievous savage, rebelling against every sort of restraint, and without any conscience. [27] " I respected nothing and feared nobody; I beat one and scratched another; I made everybody afraid of me. I beat my brother Joseph; I bit him and complained of him almost before he knew what he was about. " A clever trick, and one which he was not slow to repeat. His talent for improvising useful falsehoods is innate; later on, at maturity, he is proud of this; he makes it the index and measure of "political superiority, " and "delights in calling to mind one of his uncles who, in his infancy, prognosticated to him that he would govern the world because he was fond of lying. "[28]

Remark this observation of the uncles - it sums up the experiences of a man of his time and of his country; it is what social life in Corsica inculcated; morals and manners there adapted themselves to each other through an unfailing connection. The moral law, indeed, is such because similar customs prevail in all countries and at all times where the police is powerless, where justice cannot be obtained, where public interests are in the hands of whoever can lay hold of them, where private warfare is pitiless and not repressed, where every man goes armed, where every sort of weapon is fair, and where dissimulation, fraud, and trickery, as well as gun or poniard, are allowed, which was the case in Corsica in the eighteenth century, as in Italy in the fifteenth century. - Hence the early impressions of Bonaparte similar to those of the Borgias and of Macchiavelli; hence, in his case, that first stratum of half-thought which, later on, serves as the basis of complete thought; hence, the whole foundation of his future mental edifice and of the conceptions he subsequently entertains of human society. Afterwards, on leaving the French schools and every time he returns to them and spends any time in them, the same impressions, often renewed, intensify in his mind the same final conclusion. In this country, report the French commissioners, [29] "the people have no idea of principle in the abstract, " nor of social interest or justice. "Justice does not exist; one hundred and thirty assassinations have occurred in ten years. . ... The institution of juries has deprived the country of all the means for punishing crime; never do the strongest proofs, the clearest evidence, lead a jury composed of men of the same party, or of the same family as the accused, to convict him; and, if the accused is of the opposite party, the juries likewise acquit him, so as not to incur the risk of revenge, slow perhaps but always sure. " - "Public spirit is unknown. " There is no social body, except any number of small parties hostile to each other. . ... One is not a Corsican without belonging to some family, and consequently attached to some party;

he who would serve none, would be detested by all. . ... All the leaders have the same end in view, that of getting money no matter by what means, and their first care is to surround themselves with creatures entirely devoted to them and to whom they give all the offices. . ... The elections are held under arms, and all with violence. . .. The victorious party uses its authority to avenge itself on their opponents, and multiplies vexations and outrages. . ... The leaders form aristocratic leagues with each other. . ... and mutually tolerate abuses. They impose no assessment or collection (of taxes) to curry favor with electors through party spirit and relationships. . .. Customs-duties serve simply to compensate friends and relatives. . ... Salaries never reach those for whom they are intended. The rural districts are uninhabitable for lack of security. The peasants carry guns even when at the plow. One cannot take a step without an escort; a detachment of five or six men is often sent to carry a letter from one post-office to another. "

Interpret this general statement by the thousands of facts of which it is the summary; imagine these little daily occurrences narrated with all their material accompaniments, and with sympathetic or angry comments by interested neighbors, and we have the moral lessons taught to young Bonaparte. [30] At table, the child has listened to the conversation of his elders, and at a word uttered, for instance, by his uncle, or at a physiognomic expression, a sign of approbation, a shrug of the shoulders, he has divined that the ordinary march of society is not that of peace but of war; he sees by what ruses one maintains one's-self, by what acts of violence one makes ones way, by what sort of help one mounts upward. Left to himself the rest of the day, to the nurse Ilaria, or to Saveria the housekeeper, or to the common people amongst whom he strays at will, he listens to the conversation of sailors or of shepherds assembled on the public square, and their simple exclamations, their frank admiration of well- planned ambuscades and lucky surprises, impress more profoundly on him, often repeated with so much energy, the lessons which he has already learned at home. These are the lessons taught by things. At this tender age they sink deep, especially when the disposition is favorable, and in this case the heart sanctions them beforehand, because education finds its confederate in instinct. Accordingly, at the outbreak of the Revolution, on revisiting Corsica, he takes life at once as he finds it there, a combat with any sort of weapon, and, on this small arena, he acts unscrupulously, going farther than anybody. [31] If he respects justice and law, it is only in words, and even here ironically; in his eyes, law is a term of the code, justice a book term, while might makes right.

A second blow of the coining-press gives another impression of the same stamp on this character already so decided, while French anarchy forces maxims into the mind of the young man, already traced in the child's mind by Corsican anarchy; the lessons of things provided by a society going to pieces are the same as those of a society which is not yet formed. - His sharp eyes, at a very early period, see through the flourish of theory and the parade of phrases; they detect the real foundation of the Revolution, namely, the sovereignty of unbridled passions and the conquest of the majority by the minority; conquering or conquered, a choice must be made between these two extreme conditions; there is no middle course. After the 9th of Thermidor, the last veils are torn away, and the instincts of license and domination, the ambitions of individuals, fully display themselves. There is no concern for public interests or for the rights of the people; it is clear that the rulers form a band, that France is their prey, and that they intend to hold on to it for and against everybody, by every possible means, including bayonets. Under this civil régime, a clean sweep of the broom at the center makes it necessary to be on the side of numbers. - In the armies, especially in the army of Italy, republican faith and patriotic abnegation, since the territory became free, have given way to natural appetites and military passions. [32] Barefoot, in rags, with four ounces of bread a day, paid in assignats which are not accepted in the markets, both officers and men desire above all things to be relieved of their misery; "the poor fellows, after three years of longing on the summits of the Alps, reach the promised land, and want to enjoy it. "[33] Another spur consists in the pride which is stimulated by the imagination and by success; add to this the necessity for finding an outlet for their energy, the steam and high pressure of youth; nearly all are very young men, who regard life, in Gallic or French fashion, as a party of pleasure and as a duel. But to feel brave and to prove that one is so, to face bullets for amusement and defiantly, to abandon a successful adventure for a battle and a battle for a ball, to enjoy ones-self and take risks to excess, without dissimulating, and with no other object than the sensation of the moment, [34] to revel in excitement through emulation and danger, is no longer self-devotion, but giving one's-self up to one's fancies; and, for all who are not harebrained, to give one's- self up to one's fancies means to make one's way, obtain promotion, pillage so as to become rich, like Massena, and conquer so as to become powerful, like Bonaparte. - All this is understood between the general and his army from the very first, [35] and, after one year's experience, the understanding is perfect. One moral is derived from their common acts, vague in the army, precise in the general; what the army only half sees, he sees clearly; if he urges his comrades on, it is because they follow their own inclination. He simply has a start on them, and is quicker to make up his mind that the world is a grand banquet, free to the first-comer, but at which, to be well served, one must have long arms, be the first to get helped, and let the rest take what is left.

So natural does this seem to him, he says so openly and to men who are not his intimates; to Miot, a diplomat, and to Melzi a foreigner:

"Do you suppose, says he to them, [36] after the preliminaries of Leoben, "that to make great men out of Directory lawyers, the Carnots' and the Barras, I triumph in Italy? Do you suppose also that it is for the establishment of a republic? What an idea! A republic of thirty million men! With our customs, our vices, how is that possible? It is a delusion which the French are infatuated with and which will vanish along with so many others. What they want is glory, the gratification of vanity - they know nothing about liberty. Look at the army! Our successes just obtained, our triumphs have already brought out the true character of the French soldier. I am all for him. Let the Directory deprive me of the command and it will see if it is master. The nation needs a chief, one who is famous though his exploits, and not theories of government, phrases and speeches by ideologists, which Frenchmen do not comprehend. . .. As to your country, Monsieur de Melzi, it has still fewer elements of republicanism than France, and much less ceremony is essential with it than with any other. .. In other respects, I have no idea of coming to terms so promptly with Austria. It is not for my interest to make peace. You see what I am, what I can do in Italy. If peace is brought about, if I am no longer at the head of this army which has become attached to me, I must give up this power, this high position I have reached, and go and pay court to lawyers in the Luxembourg. I should not like to quit Italy for France except to play a part there similar to that which I play here, and the time for that has not yet come - the pear is not ripe. "

To wait until the pear is ripe, but not to allow anybody else to gather it, is the true motive of his political fealty and of his Jacobin proclamations: "A party in favor of the Bourbons is raising its head; I have no desire to help it along. One of these days I shall weaken the republican party, but I shall do it for my own advantage and not for that of the old dynasty. Meanwhile, it is necessary to march with the Republicans, " along with the worst, and' the scoundrels about to purge the Five Hundred, the Ancients, and the Directory itself, and then re-establish in France the Reign of Terror. - In effect, he contributes to the 18th of Fructidor, and, the blow struck, he explains very clearly why he took part in it:

"Do not believe[37] I did it in conformity with the ideas entertained by those with whom I acted. I did - not want a return of the Bourbons, and especially if brought back by Moreau's army and by Pichegru. .. Finally, I will not take the part of Monk, I will not play it, and I will not have others play it. . .. As for myself, my dear Miot, I declare to you that I can no longer obey; I have tasted command and I cannot give it up. My mind is made up. If I cannot be master I will leave France. "

There is no middle course for him between the two alter natives. On returning to Paris he thinks of "overthrowing the Directory, [38] dissolving the councils and of making himself dictator"; but, having satisfied himself that there was but little chance of succeeding, "he postpones his design" and falls back on the second course. "This is the only motive of his expedition into Egypt. "[39] - That, in the actual condition of France and of Europe, the expedition is opposed to public interests, that France deprives itself of its best army and offers its best fleet to almost certain destruction, is of little consequence provided, in this vast and gratuitous adventure, Bonaparte finds the employment he wants, a large field of action and famous victories which, like the blasts of a trumpet, will swell beyond the seas and renew his prestige: in his eyes, the fleet, the army, France, and humanity exist only for him and are created only for his service. - If, in confirmation of this persuasion, another lesson in things is still necessary, it will be furnished by Egypt. Here, absolute sovereign, free of any restraint, contending with an inferior order of humanity, he acts the sultan and accustoms himself to playing the part. [40] His last scruples towards the human species disappear; "I became disgusted with Rousseau"; he is to say, later on, "After seeing the Orient: the savage man is a dog, "[41] and, in the civilized man, the savage is just beneath the skin; if the intellect has become somewhat polished, there is no change in his instincts. A master is as necessary to one as to the other - a magician who subjugates his imagination, disciplines him, keeps him from biting without occasion, ties him up, cares for him, and takes him out hunting. He is born to obey, does not deserve any better lot, and has no other right.

Become consul and afterward emperor, he applies the theory on a grand scale, and, in his hands, experience daily furnishes fresh verifications of the theory. At his first nod the French prostrate themselves obediently, and there remain, as in a natural position; the lower class, the peasants and the soldiers, with animal fidelity, and the upper class, the dignitaries and the functionaries, with Byzantine servility. - The republicans, on their side, make no resistance; on the contrary, among these he has found his best governing instruments - senators, deputies, state councilors, judges, and administrators of every grade. [42] He has at once detected behind their sermonizing on liberty and equality, their despotic instincts, their craving for command, for leadership, even as subordinates; and, in addition to this, with most of them, the appetite for money or for sensual pleasures. The difference between the delegate of the Committee of Public Safety and the minister, prefect, or subprefect under the Empire is small; it is the same person in two costumes: at first in the carmagnole, and later in the embroidered coat. If a rude, poor puritan, like Cambon or Baudot, refuses to don the official uniform, if two or three Jacobin generals, like Lecourbe and Delmas, grumble at the coronation parade, Napoleon, who knows their mental grasp, regards them as ignoramuses, limited to and rigid inside a fixed idea. - As to the cultivated and intelligent liberals of 1789, he consigns them with a word to the place where they belong; they are "ideologists"; in other words, their pretended knowledge is mere drawing-room prejudice and the imagination of the study. "Lafayette is a political ninny, " the eternal "dupe of men and of things. "[43] With Lafayette and some others, one embarrassing detail remains namely:

* impartiality and generosity,
* constant care for the common good,
* respect for others,
* the authority of conscience,
* loyalty,
* and good faith.

In short, noble and pure motives.

Napoleon does not accept the denial thus given to his theory; when he talks with people, he questions their moral nobleness. "General

Dumas, "[44] said he, abruptly, to Mathieu Dumas, "you were one of the imbeciles who believed in liberty? " "Yes, sire, and I was and am still one of that class. " "And you, like the rest, took part in the Revolution through ambition? " "No, sire, I should have calculated badly, for I am now precisely where I stood in 1790. "

"You were not sufficiently aware of the motives which prompted you; you cannot be different from other people; it is all personal interest. Now, take Massena. He has glory and honors enough; but he is not content. He wants to be a prince, like Murat and like Bernadotte. He would risk being shot to-morrow to be a prince. That is the incentive of Frenchmen. " -

His system is based on this. The most competent witnesses, and those who were most familiar with him certify to his fixed idea on this point.

"His opinions on men, " writes M. de Metternich, [45] "centered on one idea, which, unfortunately for him, had acquired in his mind the force of an axiom; he was persuaded that no man who was induced to appear on the public stage, or who was merely engaged in the active pursuits of life, governed himself, or was governed, otherwise than by his interest. "

According to him, Man is held through his egoistic passions, fear, cupidity, sensuality, self-esteem, and emulation; these are the mainsprings when he is not under excitement, when he reasons. Moreover, it is not difficult to turn the brain of man; for he is imaginative, credulous, and subject to being carried away; stimulate his pride or vanity, provide him with an extreme and false opinion of himself and of his fellow-men, and you can start him off head downward wherever you please. [46] - None of these motives is entitled to much respect, and beings thus fashioned form the natural material for an absolute government, the mass of clay awaiting the potter's hand to shape it. If parts of this mass are obdurate, the potter has only to crush and pound them and mix them thoroughly.

Such is the final conception on which Napoleon has anchored himself, and into which he sinks deeper and deeper, no matter how directly and violently he may be contradicted by palpable facts. Nothing will dislodge him; neither the stubborn energy of the English, nor the inflexible gentleness of the Pope, nor the declared insurrection of the Spaniards, nor the mute insurrection of the

Germans, nor the resistance of Catholic consciences, nor the gradual disaffection of the French; the reason is, that his conception is imposed on him by his character; [47] he sees man as he needs to see him.

III. Napoleon's Dominant Passion: Power.

His mastery of the will of others. - Degree of submission required by him. - His mode of appreciating others and of profiting by them. - Tone of command and of conversation.

We at last confront his dominant passion, the inward abyss into which instinct, education, reflection, and theory have plunged him, and which is to engulf the proud edifice of his fortune - I mean, his ambition. It is the prime motor of his soul and the permanent substance of his will, so profound that he no longer distinguishes between it and himself, and of which he is sometimes unconscious.

"I, " said he to Roederer, [48] "I have no ambition, " and then, recollecting himself, he adds, with his ordinary lucidity, "or, if I have any, it is so natural to me, so innate, so intimately associated with my existence, that it is like the blood which flows in my veins and the atmosphere I breathe. " -

Still more profoundly, he likens it to that unconscious, savage, and irresistible emotion which vibrates the soul from one end to the other, to this universal thrill moving all living beings, animal or moral, to those keen and terrible tremors which we call the passion of love.

"I have but one passion, [49] one mistress, and that is France. I sleep with her. She has never been false to me. She lavishes her blood and treasures on me. If I need 500,000 men, she gives them to me. "

Let no one come between him and her. Let Joseph, in relation to the coronation, abstain from claiming his place, even secondary and prospective, in the new empire; let him not put forth his fraternal rights. [50] "It is to wound me in the most tender spot. " This he does, and, "Nothing can efface that from my souvenirs. It is as if he had told an impassioned lover that he had slept with his mistress, or merely that he hoped to succeed with her. My mistress is power. I have worked too hard to obtain her, to let her be ravished from me, or even suffer anybody to covet her. " This ambition, as avid as it is jealous, which becomes exasperated at the very idea of a rival, feels hampered by the mere idea of setting a limit to it; however vast the acquired power, he would like to have it still more vast; on quitting the most copious banquet, he still remains insatiate. On the day after the coronation he said to Decrés: [51]

"I come too late, there is no longer anything great to accomplish. I admit that my career is brilliant and that I have made my way successfully. But what a difference alongside of antiquity! Take Alexander! After having conquered Asia, and proclaimed himself to the people as the son of Jupiter, with the exception of Olympias, who knew what all this meant, and Aristotle, and a few Athenian pedants, the entire Orient believed him. Very well, should I now declare that I was the son of God Almighty, and proclaim that I am going to worship him under this title, every market woman would hoot at me as I walked along the streets. People nowadays know too much. Nothing is left to do. "

And yet, even on this secluded, elevated domain, and which twenty centuries of civilization keeps inaccessible, he still encroaches, and to the utmost, in a roundabout way, by laying his hand on the Church, and next on the Pope; here, as elsewhere, he takes all he can get. Nothing in his eyes, is more natural; he has a right to it, because he is the only capable one.

"My Italian people[52] must know me well enough not to forget that there is more in my little finger than in all their brains put together. "

Alongside of him, they are children, "minors, " the French also, and likewise the rest of mankind. A diplomat, who often saw him and studied him under all as aspects, sums up his character in one conclusive phrase:

"He considered himself an isolated being in this world, made to govern and direct all minds as he pleased. "[53]

Hence, whoever has anything to do with him, must abandon his independence and become his tool of government.

"That terrible man, " often exclaimed Decrés[54] "has subjugated us all! He holds all our imaginations in his hands, now of steel and now of velvet, but whether one or the other during the day nobody knows, and there is no way to escape from them whatever they seize on they never let go! "

Independence of any kind, even eventual and merely possible, puts him in a bad mood; intellectual or moral superiority is of this order, and he gradually gets rid of it; [55] toward the end he no longer tolerates alongside of him any but subject or captive spirits. His principal servants are machines or fanatics, a devout worshipper, like Maret, a gendarme, like Savary, [56] ready to do his bidding. From the outset, he has reduced his ministers to the condition of clerks; for he is administrator as well as ruler, and in each department he watches details as closely as the entire mass. Accordingly, he requires simply for head of departments active pen pushers, mute executors, docile and special hands, no need for honest and independent advisers.

"I should not know what to do with them, " he said, "if they were not to a certain extent mediocre in mind and character. "

As to his generals, he admits himself that "he likes to award fame only to those who cannot stand it. " In any event, "he must be sole master in making or unmaking reputations, " according to his personal requirements. Too brilliant a soldier would become too important; a subordinate should never be tempted to be less submissive. To this end he studies what he will omit in his bulletins, what alterations and what changes shall be made in them.

"It is convenient to keep silent about certain victories, or to convert the defeat of this or that marshal into a success. Sometimes a general learns by a bulletin of an action that he was never in and of a speech that he never made. "

If he complains, he is notified to keep still, or by way of recompense he is allowed to pillage, levy contributions, and enrich himself. On becoming duke or hereditary prince, with half a million or a million of revenue from his estate, he is not less held in subjection, for the creator has taken precautions against his own creations.

"There are men, "[57] he said, "who I have made independent, but I know well where to find them and keep them from being ungrateful."

In effect, if he has endowed them magnificently it is with domains assigned to them in conquered countries, which insures their fortune being his fortune. Besides, in order that they may not enjoy any pecuniary stability, he expressly encourages them and all his grand dignitaries to make extravagant outlays; thus, through their financial embarrassments be holds them in a leash. "We have seen most of his marshals, constantly pressed by their creditors, come to him for assistance, which he has given as he fancied, or as he found it for his interest to attach some one to him. "[58]

Thus, beyond the universal ascendancy which his power and genius have conferred on him, he craves a personal, supplementary, and irresistible hold on everybody. Consequently, [59]"he carefully cultivates all the bad passions . . .. he is glad to find the bad side in a man, so as to get him in his power"; the thirst for money in Savary, the Jacobin defects of Fouché, the vanity and sensuality of Cambacérès, the careless cynicism and "the easy immorality" of Talleyrand, the "dry bluntness " of Duroc, the courtier-like insipidity of Maret, "the silliness" of Berthier; he brings this out, diverts himself with it, and profits by it. "Where he sees no vice, he encourages weaknesses, and, in default of anything better, he provokes fear, so that he may be ever and continually the strongest. . .. He dreads ties of affection, and strives to alienate people from each other. . .. He sells his favors only by arousing anxiety; he thinks that the best way to attach individuals to him is to compromise them, and often, even, to ruin them in public opinion. " - " If Caulaincourt is compromised, " said he, after the murder of the Duc d'Enghien, "it is no great matter, he will serve me all the better. "

Once that the creature is in his clutches, let him not imagine that he can escape or withhold anything of his own accord; all that he has belongs to him. Zeal and success in the performance of duty, punctual obedience within limits previously designated, is not enough; behind the functionary he claims the man. "All that may well be, " he replies, to whatever may be said in praise of him, [60] "but he does not belong to me as I would like. " It is devotion which he exacts, and, by devotion, he means the irrevocable and complete surrender "of the entire person, in all his sentiments and opinions. " According to him, writes a witness, "one must abandon every old habit, even the most trifling, and be governed by one thought alone,. that of his will and interests. "[61] For greater security, his servitors ought to extinguish in themselves the critical sense. "What he fears the most is that, close to him or far off, the faculty of judging should be applied or even preserved. "

"His idea is a marble groove, " out of which no mind should diverge. [62] Especially as no two minds could think of diverging at the same time, and on the same side, their concurrence, even when passive, their common understanding, even if kept to themselves, their whispers, almost inaudible, constitute a league, a faction, and, if they are functionaries, "a conspiracy. " On his return from Spain he declares, with a terrible explosion of wrath and threats, [63] "that the ministers and high dignitaries whom he has created must stop expressing their opinions and thoughts freely, that they cannot be otherwise than his organs, that treason has already begun when they begin to doubt, and that it is under full headway when, from doubt, they proceed to dissent. " If, against his constant encroachments, they strive to preserve a last refuge, if they refuse to abandon their conscience to him, their faith as Catholics or their honor as honest men, he is surprised and gets irritated. In reply to the Bishop of Ghent, who, in the most respectful manner, excuses himself for not taking a second oath that is against his conscience, he rudely turns his back, and says, "Very well, sir, your conscience is a blockhead! "[64] Portalis, director of the publishing office, [65] having received a papal brief from his cousin, the Abbé d'Astros, respected a confidential communication; he simply recommended his cousin to keep this document secret, and declared that, if it were made public, he would prohibit its circulation; by way of extra precaution he notified the prefect of police. But he did not specially denounce his cousin, have the man arrested and the document seized. On the strength of this, the Emperor, in full council of state, apostrophizes him to his face, and, "with one of those looks which go straight through one, "[66] declares that he has committed "the vilest of perfidies"; he bestows on him for half an hour a hailstorm of reproaches and insults, and then orders him out of the room as if a lackey who had been guilty of a theft. Whether he keeps within his function or not, the functionary must be content to do whatever is demanded of him, and readily anticipate every commission. If his scruples arrest him, if he alleges personal obligations, if he had rather not fail in delicacy, or even in common loyalty, he incurs the risk of offending or losing the favor of the master, which is the case with M. de Rémusat, [67] who is unwilling to become his spy, reporter, and denunciator for the Faubourg Saint-Germain, who does not offer, at Vienna, to pump out of Madame d'André the address of her husband so that M. d'André may be taken and immediately shot. Savary, who was the negotiator for his being given up, kept constantly telling M. de Rémusat, "You are going against your interest - I must say that I do not comprehend you! " And yet Savary, himself minister of the police, executor of most important services, head manager of the murder of the Duc d'Enghien and of the ambuscade at Bayonne, counterfeiter of Austrian bank-notes for the campaign of 1809 and of Russian banknotes for that of 1812, [68] Savary ends in getting weary; he is charged with too many dirty jobs; however hardened his conscience it has a tender spot; he discovers at last that he has scruples. It is with great repugnance that, in February, 1814, he executes the order to have a small infernal machine prepared, moving by clock-work, so as to blow up the Bourbons on their return into France. [69] "Ah, " said he, giving himself a blow on the forehead, "it must be admitted that the Emperor is sometimes hard to serve! "

If he exacts so much from the human creature, it is because, in playing the game he has to play, he must absorb everything; in the situation in which be has placed himself, caution is unnecessary. "Is a statesman, " said he, "made to have feeling? Is he not wholly an eccentric personage, always alone by himself, he on one side and the world on the other? "[70]

In this duel without truce or mercy, people interest him only whilst they are useful to him; their value depends on what he can make out of them; his sole business is to squeeze them, to extract to the last drop whatever is available in them.

"I find very little satisfaction in useless sentiments, " said he again, [71] "and Berthier is so mediocre that I do not know why I waste my time on him. And yet when I am not set against him, I am not sure that I do not like him. "

He goes no further. According to him, this indifference is necessary in a statesman. The glass he looks through is that of his own policy; [72] he must take care that it does not magnify or diminish objects. - Therefore, outside of explosions of nervous sensibility, "he has no consideration for men other than that of a foreman for his workmen,"[73] or, more precisely, for his tools; once the tool is worn out, little does he care whether it rusts away in a corner or is cast aside on a heap of scrap-iron. "Portalis, Minister of Justice, [74] enters his room one day with a downcast look and his eyes filled with tears. 'What's the matter with you, Portalis? ' inquired Napoleon, 'are you ill? 'No, sire, but very wretched. The poor Archbishop of Tours, my old schoolmate . .. ' 'Eh, well, what has happened to him? ' 'Alas, sire, he has just died. ' 'What do I care? he was no longer good for anything. '" Owning and making the most of men and of things, of bodies and of souls, using and abusing them at discretion, even to exhaustion, without being responsible to any one, he reaches that point after a few years where he can say as glibly and more despotically than Louis XIV. himself,

"My armies, my fleets, my cardinals, my councils, my senate, my populations, my empire. "[75]

Addressing army corps about to rush into battle:

"Soldiers, I need your lives, and you owe them to me. "

He says to General Dorsenne and to the grenadiers of the guard: [76]

"I hear that you complain that you want to return to Paris, to your mistresses. Undeceive yourselves. I shall keep you under arms until you are eighty. You were born to the bivouac, and you shall die there. "

How he treats his brothers and relations who have become kings; how he reins them in; how he applies the spur and the whip and makes them trot and jump fences and ditches, may be found in his correspondence; every stray impulse to take the lead, even when justified by an unforeseen urgency and with the most evident good intention, is suppressed as a deviation, is arrested with a brusque roughness which strains the loins and weakens the knees of the delinquent. The amiable Prince Eugene, so obedient and so loyal, [77] is thus warned:

"If you want orders or advice from His Majesty in the alteration of the ceiling of your room you should wait till you get them; were Milan burning and you asked orders for putting out the fire, you should let Milan burn until you got them. .. His Majesty is displeased, and very much displeased, with you; you must never attempt to do his work. Never does he like this, and he will never forgive it. "

This enables us to judge of his tone with subalterns. The French battalions are refused admission into certain places in Holland: [78]

"Announce to the King of Holland, that if his ministers have acted on their own responsibility, I will have them arrested and all their heads cut off. "

He says to M. de Ségur, member of the Academy commission which had just approved M. de Chateaubriand's discourse: [79]

"You, and M. de Fontaines, as state councillor and grand master, I ought to put in Vincennes. . .. Tell the second class of the Institute that I will have no political subjects treated at its meetings. . . .. If it disobeys, I will break it up like a bad club.

Even when not angry or scolding, [80] when the claws are drawn in, one feels the clutch. He says to Beugnot, whom he has just berated, scandalously and unjustly, - conscious of having done him injustice and with a view to produce an effect on the bystanders, -

"Well, you great imbecile, you have got back your brains? "

On this, Beugnot, tall as a drum-major, bows very low, while the smaller man, raising his hand, seizes him by the ear, "a heady mark of favor, " says Beugnot, a sign of familiarity and of returning good humor. And better yet, the master deigns to lecture Beugnot on his personal tastes, on his regrets, on his wish to return to France: What would he like? To be his minister in Paris? "Judging by what he saw of me the other day I should not be there very long; I might die of worry before the end of the month. " He has already killed Portalis, Cretet, and almost Treilhard, even though he had led a hard life: he could no longer urinate, nor the others either. The same thing would have happened to Beignot, if not worse. . . .

" Stay here . . .. after which you will be old, or rather we all shall be old, and I will send you to the Senate to drivel at your ease. "

Evidently, [81 the nearer one is to his person the more disagreeable life becomes. [82] "Admirably served, promptly obeyed to the minute, he still delights in keeping everybody around him in terror concerning the details of all that goes on in his palace. " Has any difficult task been accomplished? He expresses no thanks, never or scarcely ever praises, and, which happens but once, in the case of M. de Champagny, Minister of Foreign Affairs, who is praised for having finished the treaty of Vienna in one night, and with unexpected advantages; [83] this time, the Emperor has thought aloud, is taken by surprise; "ordinarily, he manifests approbation only by his silence. " - When M. de Rémusat, prefect of the palace, has arranged "one of those magnificent fêtes in which all the arts minister to his enjoyment, " economically, correctly, with splendor and success, his wife never asks her husband[84] if the Emperor is satisfied, but whether he has scolded more or less.

"His leading general principle, which he applies in every way, in great things as well as in small ones, is that a man's zeal depends upon his anxiety. "

How insupportable the constraint he exercises, with what crushing weight his absolutism bears down on the most tried devotion and on the most pliable characters, with what excess he tramples on and wounds the best dispositions, up to what point he represses and stifles the respiration of the human being, he knows as well as anybody. He was heard to say,

"The lucky man is he who hides away from me in the depths of some province. "

And, another day, having asked M. de Ségur what people would say of him after his death, the latter enlarged on the regrets which would be universally expressed. "Not at all, " replied the Emperor; and then, drawing in his breath in a significant manner indicative of universal relief, he replied,

"They'll say, 'Whew! '"[85]

IV. His Bad Manners.

His bearings in Society. - His deportment toward Women. - His disdain of Politeness.

There are very few monarchs, even absolute, who persistently, arid from morning to night, maintain a despotic attitude. Generally, and especially in France, the sovereign makes two divisions of his time, one for business and the other for social duties, and, in the latter case, while always head of the State, he is also head of his house: for he welcomes visitors, entertains his guests, and, that his guests may not be robots, he tries to put them at their ease. - That was the case with Louis XIV. [86] - polite to everybody, always affable with men, and sometimes gracious, always courteous with women, and some times gallant, carefully avoiding brusqueness, ostentation, and sarcasms, never allowing himself to use an offensive word, never making people feel their inferiority and dependence, but, on the contrary, encouraging them to express opinions, and even to converse, tolerating in conversation a semblance of equality, smiling at a repartee, playfully telling a story - such was his drawing-room constitution. The drawing-room as well as every human society needs one, and a liberal one; otherwise life dies out. Accordingly, the observance of this constitution in by-gone society is known by the phrase savoir-vivre, and, more rigidly than anybody else, Louis XIV. submitted himself to this code of proprieties. Traditionally, and through education, he had consideration for others, at least for the people around him; his courtiers becoming his guests without ceasing to be his subjects.

There is nothing of this sort with Napoleon. He preserves nothing of the etiquette he borrows from the old court but its rigid discipline and its pompous parade. "The ceremonial system, " says an eyewitness, "was carried out as if it had been regulated by the tap of a drum; everything was done, in a certain sense, 'double-quick. '[87] . .. This air of precipitation, this constant anxiety which it inspires, " puts an end to all comfort, all ease, all entertainment, all agreeable intercourse; there is no common bond but that of command and obedience. " The few individuals he singles out, Savary, Duroc, Maret, keep silent and simply transmit orders. . .. We did not appear to them, in doing what we were ordered to do, and we did not appear to ourselves, other than veritable machines, all resembling, or but little short of it, the elegant gilded arm-chairs with which the palaces of Saint-Cloud and the Tuileries had just been embellished. "

For a machine to work well it is important that the machinist should overhaul it frequently, which this one never fails to do, especially after a long absence. Whilst he is on his way from Tilsit, "everybody anxiously examines his conscience to ascertain what he has done that this rigid master will find fault with on his return. Whether spouse, family, or grand dignitary, each is more or less disturbed; while the Empress, who knows him better than any one, naively says, 'As the Emperor is so happy it is certain that he will do a deal of scolding! '"[88] Actually, he has scarcely arrived when he gives a rude and vigorous wrench of the bolt; and then, "satisfied at having excited terror all around, he appears to have forgotten what has passed and resumes the usual tenor of his life. " "Through calculation as well as from taste, [89] he never ceases to be a monarch"; hence, "a mute, frigid court . . .. more dismal than dignified; every face wears an expression of uneasiness . .. a silence both dull and constrained. " At Fontainebleau, "amidst splendors and pleasures, " there is no real enjoyment nor anything agreeable, not even for himself. "I pity you, " said M. de Talleyrand to M. de Rémusat, "you have to amuse the unamusable. " At the theatre he is abstracted or yawns. Applause is prohibited; the court, sitting out "the file of eternal tragedies, is mortally bored . . .. the young ladies fall asleep, people leave the theatre, gloomy and discontented. " - There is the same constraint in the drawing-room. "He did not know how to appear at ease, and I believe that he never wanted anybody else to be so, afraid of the slightest approach to familiarity, and inspiring each with a fear of saying something offensive to his neighbor before witnesses. . .. During the quadrille, he moves around amongst the rows of ladies, addressing them with some trifling or disagreeable remark, " and never does he accost them otherwise than "awkwardly and ill at his ease. " At bottom, he distrusts them and is ill-disposed toward them. [90] It is because "the power they have acquired in society seems to him an intolerable usurpation. - "Never did he utter to a woman a graceful or even a well-turned compliment, although the effort to find one was often apparent on his face and in the tone of his voice. . .. He talks to them only of their toilet, of which he declares himself a severe and minute judge, and on which he indulges in not very delicate jests; or again, on the number of their children, demanding of them in rude language whether they nurse them themselves; or again, lecturing them on their social relations. "[91] Hence, "there is not one who does not rejoice when he moves off. "[92] He would often amuse himself by putting them out of countenance, scandalizing and bantering them to their faces, driving them into a corner the same as a colonel worries his canteen women. "Yes, ladies, you furnish the good people of the Faubourg Saint-Germain with something to talk about. It is said, Madame A..., that you are intimate with Monsieur B..., and you Madame C...., with Monsieur D. " On any intrigue chancing to appear in the police reports, "he loses no time in informing the husband of what is going on. " - He is no less indiscreet in relation to his own affairs; [93] when it is over he divulges the fact and gives the name; furthermore, he informs Josephine in detail and will not listen to any reproach: "I have a right to answer all your objections with an eternal I! "

This term, indeed, answers to everything, and he explains it by adding: "I stand apart from other men. I accept nobody's conditions, " nor any species of obligation, no code whatever, not even the common code of outward civility, which, diminishing or dissimulating primitive brutality, allows men to associate together without clashing. He does not comprehend it, and he repudiates it. "I have little liking, "[94] he says, "for that vague, leveling word propriety (convenances), which you people fling out every chance you get. It is an invention of fools who want to pass for clever men; a kind of social muzzle which annoys the strong and is useful only to the mediocre. .. Ah, good taste! Another classic expression which I do not accept. " "It is your personal enemy"; says Talleyrand to him, one day, "if you could have shot it away with bullets, it would have disappeared long ago! " - It is because good taste is the highest attainment of civilization, the innermost vestment which drapes human nudity, which best fits the person, the last garment retained after the others have been cast off, and which delicate tissue continues to hamper Napoleon; he throws it off instinctively, because it interferes with his natural behavior, with the uncurbed, dominating, savage ways of the vanquisher who knocks down his adversary and treats him as he pleases.

V. His Policy.

His tone and bearing towards Sovereigns. - His Policy. - His means and ends. - After Sovereigns he sets populations against him. - Final opinion of Europe.

Such behavior render social intercourse impossible, especially among the independent and armed personages known as nations or States. This is why they are outlawed in politics and in diplomacy and every head of a State or representative of a country, carefully and on principle, abstains from them, at least with those on his own level. He is bound to treat these as his equals, humor them, and, accordingly, not to give way to the irritation of the moment or to personal feeling; in short, to exercise self-control and measure his words. To this is due the tone of manifestos, protocols, dispatches, and other public documents the formal language of legations, so cold, dry, and elaborated, those expressions purposely attenuated and smoothed down, those long phrases apparently spun out mechanically and always after the same pattern, a sort of soft wadding or international buffer interposed between contestants to lessen the shocks of collision. The reciprocal irritations between States are already too great; there are ever too many unavoidable and regrettable encounters, too many causes of conflict, the consequences of which are too serious; it is unnecessary to add to the wounds of interest the wounds of imagination and of pride; and above all, it is unnecessary to amplify these without reason, at the risk of increasing the obstacles of to-day and the resentments of to-morrow. - With Napoleon it is just the opposite: his attitude, even at peaceful interviews, remains aggressive and militant; purposely or in-voluntarily, he raises his hand and the blow is felt to be coming, while, in the meantime, he insults. In his correspondence with sovereigns, in his official proclamations, in his deliberations with ambassadors, and even at public audiences, [95] he provokes, threatens, and defies. [96] He treats his adversary with a lofty air, insults him often to his face, and charges him with the most disgraceful imputations. [97] He divulges the secrets of his private life, of his closet, and of his bed; he defames or calumniates his ministers, his court, and his wife; [98] he purposely stabs him in the most sensitive part. He tells one that he is a dupe, a betrayed husband; another that he is an abettor of assassination; he assumes the air of a judge condemning a criminal, or the tone of a superior reprimanding an inferior, or, at best, that of a teacher taking a scholar to task. With a smile of pity, he points out mistakes, weak points, and incapacity, and shows him beforehand that he must be defeated. On receiving the envoy of the Emperor Alexander at Wilna, [99] be says to him:

"Russia does not want this war; none of the European powers are in favor of it; England herself does not want it, for she foresees the harm it will do to Russia, and even, perhaps, the greatest. .. I know as well as yourself, and perhaps even better, how many troops you have. Your infantry in all amounts to 120,000 men and your cavalry to about 60,000 or 70,000; I have three times as many. . .. The Emperor Alexander is badly advised. How can he tolerate such vile people around him - an Armfeld, an intriguing, depraved, rascally fellow, a ruined debauchee, who is known only by his crimes and who is the enemy of Russia; a Stein, driven from his country like an outcast, a miscreant with a price on his head; a Bennigsen, who, it is said, has some military talent, of which I know nothing, but whose hands are steeped in blood? [100] . . .. Let him surround himself with the Russians and I will say nothing. . .. Have you no Russian gentlemen among you who are certainly more attached to him than these mercenaries? Does he imagine that they are fond of him personally? Let him put Armfeld in command in Finland and I have nothing to say; but to have him about his person, for shame ! . . .. What a superb perspective opened out to the Emperor Alexander at Tilsit, and especially at Erfurt! . . .. He has spoilt the finest reign Russia ever saw. . .. How can he admit to his society such men as a Stein, an Armfeld, a Vinzingerode? Say to the Emperor Alexander, that as he gathers around him my personal enemies it means a desire to insult me personally, and, consequently, that I must do the same to him. I will drive all his Baden, Wurtemburg, and Weimar relations out of Germany. Let him provide a refuge for them in Russia! "

Note what he means by - personal insult[101], how he intends to avenge himself by reprisals of the worst kind, to what excess he carries his interference, how he enters the cabinets of foreign sovereigns, forcibly entering and breaking, to drive out their councilors and control their meetings: like the Roman senate with an Antiochus or a Prusias, like an English Resident with the King of Oude or of Lahore. With others as at home, he cannot help but act as a master. The aspiration for universal dominion is in his very nature; it may be modified, kept in check, but never can it be completely stifled. "[102]

It declares itself on the organization of the Consulate. It explains why the peace of Amiens could not last; apart from the diplomatic discussions and behind his alleged grievances, his character, his exactions, his avowed plans, and the use he intends making of his forces form the real and true causes of the rupture. In comprehensible sometimes even in explicit terms, he tells the English: Expel the Bourbons from your island and close the mouths of your journalists. If this is against your constitution so much the worse for it, or so much the worse for you. "There are general principles of international law to which the (special) laws of states must give way. "[103] Change your fundamental laws. Suppress the freedom of the press and the right of asylum on your soil, the same as I have done. "I have a very poor opinion of a government which is not strong enough to interdict things objectionable to foreign governments. "[104] As to mine, my interference with my neighbors, my late acquisitions of territory, that does not concern you: "I suppose that you want to talk about Piedmont and Switzerland? These are trifles"[105] "Europe recognizes that Holland, Italy, and Switzerland are at the disposition of France. [106] On the other hand, Spain submits to me and through her I hold Portugal. Thus, from Amsterdam to Bordeaux, from Lisbon to Cadiz and Genoa, from Leghorn to Naples and to Tarentum, I can close every port to you; no treaty of commerce between us. Any treaty that I might grant to you would be trifling: for each million of merchandise that you would send into France a million of French merchandise would be exported; [107] in other words, you would be subject to an open or concealed continental blockade, which would cause you as much distress in peace as if you were at war. " My eyes are nevertheless fixed on Egypt; "six thousand Frenchmen would now suffice to re-conquer it"; [108] forcibly, or otherwise, I shall return there; opportunities will not be lacking, and I shall be on the watch for them; "sooner or later she will belong to France, either through the dissolution of the Ottoman empire, or through some arrangement with the Porte. "[109] Evacuate Malta so that the Mediterranean may become a French lake; I must rule on sea as on land, and dispose of the Orient as of the Occident. In sum, "with my France, England must naturally end in becoming simply an appendix: nature has made her one of our islands, the same as Oleron or Corsica. "[110] Naturally, with such a perspective before them, the English keep Malta and recommence the war. He has anticipated such an occurrence, and his resolution is taken; at a glance, he perceives and measures the path this will open to him; with his usual clear-sightedness he has comprehended, and he announces that the

English resistance "forces him to conquer Europe. . .. "[111] - "The First Consul is only thirty-three and has thus far destroyed only the second-class governments. Who knows how much time he will require to again change the face of Europe and resurrect the Western Roman Empire? "

To subjugate the Continent in order to form a coalition against England, such, henceforth, are his means, which are as violent as the end in view, while the means, like the end, are given by his character. Too imperious and too impatient to wait or to manage others, he is incapable of yielding to their will except through constraint, and his collaborators are to him nothing more than subjects under the name of allies. - Later, at St. Helena, with his indestructible imaginative energy and power of illusion, he plays on the public with his humanitarian illusions. [112] But, as he himself avows, the accomplishment of his retrospective dream required beforehand the entire submission of all Europe; a liberal sovereign and pacificator, "a crowned Washington, yes, " he used to say, "but I could not reasonably attain this point, except through a universal dictatorship, which I aimed at. "[113] In vain does common sense demonstrate to him that such an enterprise inevitably rallies the Continent to the side of England, and that his means divert him from the end. In vain is it repeatedly represented to him that he needs one sure great ally on the Continent; [114] that to obtain this he must conciliate Austria; that he must not drive her to despair, but rather win her over and compensate her on the side of the Orient; place her in permanent conflict with Russia, and attach her to the new French Empire by a community of vital interests. In vain does he, after Tilsit, make a bargain of this kind with Russia. This bargain cannot hold, because in this arrangement Napoleon, as usual with him, always encroaching, threatening, and attacking, wants to reduce Alexander to the role of a subordinate and a dupe. [115] No clear-sighted witness can doubt this. In 1809, a diplomat writes: "The French system, which is now triumphant, is directed against the whole body of great states, "[116] not alone against England, Prussia, and Austria, but against Russia, against every power capable of maintaining its independence; for, if she remains independent, she may become hostile, and as a precautionary step Napoleon crushes in her a probable enemy.

All the more so because this course once entered upon he cannot stop; at the same time his character and the situation in which he has placed himself impels him on while his past hurries him along to his future. [117] At the moment of the rupture of the treaty of Amiens he is already so strong and so aggressive that his neighbors are obliged, for their own security, to form an alliance with England; this leads him to break down all the old monarchies that are still intact, to conquer Naples, to mutilate Austria the first time, to dismember and cut up Prussia, to mutilate Austria the second time, to manufacture kingdoms for his brothers at Naples, in Holland and in Westphalia. — At this same date, all the ports of his empire are closed against the English, which leads him to close against them all the ports of the Continent, to organize against them the continental blockade, to proclaim against them an European crusade, to prevent the neutrality of sovereigns like the Pope, of lukewarm subalterns like his brother Louis, of doubtful collaborators or inadequate, like the Braganzas of Portugal and the Bourbons of Spain, and therefore to get hold of Portugal, Spain, the Pontifical States, and Holland, and next of the Hanseatic towns and the duchy of Oldenburg, to extending along the entire coast, from the mouths of the Cattaro and Trieste to Hamburg and Dantzic, his cordon of military chiefs, prefects, and custom- houses, a sort of net of which he draws the meshes tighter and tighter every day, even stifling not alone his home consumer, but the producer and the merchant. [118] - And all this sometimes by a simple decree, with no other alleged motive than his interest, his convenience, or his pleasure, [119] brusquely and arbitrarily, in violation of international law, humanity, and hospitality. It would take volumes to describe his abuses of power, the tissue of brutalities and knaveries, [120] the oppression of the ally and despoiling of the vanquished, the military brigandage exercised over populations in time of war, and by the systematic exactions practiced on them in times of peace. [121]

Accordingly, after 1808, these populations rise against him. He has so deeply injured them in their interests, and hurt their feelings to such an extent, [122] he has so trodden them down, ransomed, and forced them into his service. He has destroyed, apart from French lives, so many Spanish, Italian, Austrian, Prussian, Swiss, Bavarian, Saxon, and Dutch lives, he has slain so many men as enemies, he has enlisted such numbers at home, and slain so many under his own banners as auxiliaries, that nations are still more hostile to him than sovereigns. Unquestionably, nobody can live together with such a character; his genius is too vast, too baneful, and all the more because it is so vast. War will last as long as he reigns; it is in vain to reduce him, to confine him at home, to drive him back within the ancient frontiers of France; no barrier will restrain him; no treaty will bind him; peace with him will never be other than a truce; he will use it simply to recover himself, and, as soon as he has done this, he will begin again; [123] he is in his very essence anti-social. The mind of Europe in this respect is made up definitely and unshakably. One petty detail alone shows how unanimous and profound this conviction was. On the 7th of March the news reached Vienna that he had escaped from the island of Elba, without its being yet known where he would land. M. de Metternich[124] brings the news to the Emperor of Austria before eight o'clock in the morning, who says to him, "Lose no time in finding the King of Prussia and the Emperor of Russia, and tell them that I am ready to order my army to march at once for France. " At a quarter past eight M. de Metternich is with the Czar, and at half-past eight, with the King of Prussia; both of them reply instantly in the same manner. "At nine o'clock, " says M. de Metternich, "I was back. At ten o'clock aids flew in every direction countermanding army orders. . .. Thus was war declared in less than an hour. "

VI. Fundamental Defaults of his System.

Inward principle of his outward deportment. - He subordinates the
State to him instead of subordinating himself to the State. - Effect of
this. - His work merely a life-interest. - It is ephemeral. - Injurious. -
The number of lives it cost. - The mutilation of France. - Vice of
construction in his European edifice. - Analogous vice in his French
edifice.

Other heads of states have similarly passed their lives in doing
violence to mankind; but it was for something that was likely to last,
and for a national interest. What they deemed the public good was
not a phantom of the brain, a chimerical poem due to a caprice of the
imagination, to personal passions, to their own peculiar ambition
and pride. Outside of themselves and the coinage of their brain a real
and substantial object of prime importance existed, namely, the
State, the great body of society, the vast organism which lasts
indefinitely through the long series of interlinked and responsible
generations. If they drew blood from the passing generation it was
for the benefit of coming generations, to preserve them from civil
war or from foreign domination. [125] They have acted generally like
able surgeons, if not through virtue, at least through dynastic
sentiment and family traditions; having practiced from father to son,
they had acquired the professional conscience; their first and only
aim was the safety and health of their patient. It is for this reason
that they have not recklessly undertaken extravagant, bloody, and
over-risky operations; rarely have they given way to temptation
through a desire to display their skill, through the need of dazzling
and astonishing the world, through the novelty, keenness, and
success of their saws and scalpels. They felt that a longer and
superior existence to their own was imposed upon them; they looked
beyond them-selves as far as their sight would reach, and so took
measures that the State after them might do without them, live on
intact, remain independent, vigorous, and respected athwart the
vicissitudes of European conflict and the uncertain problems of
coming history. Such, under the ancient régime, was what were
called reasons of state; these had prevailed in the councils of princes
for eight hundred years; along with unavoidable failures and after
temporary deviations, these had become for the time being and
remained the preponderating motive. Undoubtedly they excused or
authorized many breaches of faith, many outrages, and, to come to
the word, many crimes; but, in the political order of things,

especially in the management of external affairs, they furnished a governing and a salutary principle. Under its constant influence thirty monarchs had labored, and it is thus that, province after province, they had solidly and enduringly built up France, by ways and means beyond the reach of individuals but available to the heads of States.

Now, this principle is lacking with their improvised successor. On the throne as in the camp, whether general, consul, or emperor, he remains the military adventurer, and cares only for his own advancement. Owing to the great defect in the education of both conscience and sentiments, instead of subordinating himself to the State, he subordinates the State to him; he does not look beyond his own brief physical existence to the nation which is to survive him. Consequently, he sacrifices the future to the present, and his work is not to be enduring. After him the deluge! Little does he care who utters this terrible phrase; and worse still, he earnestly wishes, from the bottom of his heart that everybody should utter it.

"My brother, " said Joseph, in 1803, [126] "desires that the necessity of his existence should be so strongly felt, and the benefit of this considered so great, that nobody could look beyond it without shuddering. He knows, and be feels it, that he reigns through this idea rather than through force or gratitude. If to-morrow, or on any day, it could be said, 'Here is a tranquil, established order of things, here is a known successor; Bonaparte might die without fear of change or disturbance, ' my brother would no longer think himself secure. . .. Such is the principle which governs him. "

In vain do years glide by, never does he think of putting France in a way to subsist without him; on the contrary, he jeopardizes lasting acquisitions by exaggerated annexations, and it is evident from the very first day that the Empire will end with the Emperor. In 1805, the five per cents being at eighty francs, his Minister of the Finances, Gaudin, observes to him that this is a reasonable rate. [127] "No complaint can now be made, since these funds are an annuity on Your Majesty's life. " - "What do you mean by that? " - "I mean that the Empire has become so great as to be ungovernable without you. " - "If my successor is a fool so much the worse for him! " - "Yes, but so much the worse for France! " Two years later, M. de Metternich, by way of a political summing up, expresses his general opinion: "It is remarkable that Napoleon, constantly disturbing and modifying the relations of all Europe, has not yet taken a single step toward ensuring the maintenance of his successors. "[128] In 1809, adds the same diplomat: [129] "His death will be the signal for a new and frightful upheaval; so many divided elements all tend to combine. Deposed sovereigns will be recalled by former subjects; new princes will have new crowns to defend. A veritable civil war will rage for half a century over the vast empire of the continent the day when the arms of iron which held the reins are turned into dust. " In 1811, "everybody is convinced[130] that on the disappearance of Napoleon, the master in whose hands all power is concentrated, the first inevitable consequence will be a revolution. " At home, in France, at this same date, his own servitors begin to comprehend that his empire is not merely a life-interest and will not last after he is gone, but that the Empire is ephemeral and will not last during his life; for he is constantly raising his edifice higher and higher, while all that his building gains in elevation it loses in stability. "The Emperor is crazy, " said Decrees to Marmont, [131]"completely crazy. He will ruin us all, numerous as we are, and all will end in some frightful catastrophe. " In effect, he is pushing France on to the abyss, forcibly and by deceiving her, through a breach of trust which willfully, and by his fault, grows worse and worse just as his own interests, as he comprehends these, diverge from those of the public from year to year.

At the treaty of Luneville and before the rupture of the peace of Amiens, [132] this variance was already considerable. It becomes manifest at the treaty of Presbourg and still more evident at the treaty of Tilsit. It is glaring in 1808, after the deposition of the Spanish Bourbons; it becomes scandalous and monstrous in 1812, when the war with Russia took place. Napoleon himself admits that this war is against the interests of France and yet he undertakes it. [133] Later, at St. Helena, he falls into a melting mood over "the French people whom he loved so dearly. "[134] The truth is, he loves it as a rider loves his horse; as he makes it rear and prance and show off its paces, when he flatters and caresses it; it is not for the advantage of the animal but for his own purposes, on account of its usefulness to him; to be spurred on until exhausted, to jump ditches growing wider and wider, and leap fences growing higher and higher; one ditch more, and still another fence, the last obstacle which seems to be the last, succeeded by others, while, in any event, the horse remains forcibly and for ever, what it already is, namely, a beast of burden and broken down. - For, on this Russian expedition, instead of frightful disasters, let us imagine a brilliant success, a victory at Smolensk equal to that of Friedland, a treaty of Moscow more advantageous than that of Tilsit, and the Czar brought to heel. As a result the Czar is probably strangled or dethroned, a patriotic insurrection will take place in Russia as in Spain, two lasting wars, at the two extremities of the Continent, against religious fanaticism, more irreconcilable than positive interests, and against a scattered barbarism more indomitable than a concentrated civilization. At best, a European empire secretly mined by European resistance; an exterior France forcibly superposed on the enslaved Continent; [135] French residents and commanders at St. Petersburg and Riga as at Dantzic, Hamburg, Amsterdam, Lisbon, Barcelona, and Trieste. Every able-bodied Frenchman that can be employed from Cadiz to Moscow in maintaining and administering the conquest. All the able-bodied youth annually seized by the conscription, and, if they have escaped this, seized again by decrees. [136] The entire male population thus devoted to works of constraint, nothing else in prospect for either the cultivated or the uncultivated, no military or civil career other than a prolonged guard duty, threatened and threatening, as soldier, customs-inspector, or gendarme, as prefect, sub-prefect, or commissioner of police, that is to say, as subaltern henchman and bully restraining subjects and raising contributions, confiscating and burning merchandise, seizing grumblers, and making the refractory toe the mark. [137] In 1810, one hundred and sixty thousand of the refractory were already condemned by name, and, moreover, penalties were imposed on their families to the amount of one hundred and seventy millions of francs In 1811 and 1812 the roving columns which tracked fugitives gathered sixty thousand of them, and drove them along the coast from the Adour to the Niemen; on reaching the frontier, they were en-rolled in the grand army; but they desert the very first month, they and their chained companions, at the rate of four or five thousand a day. [138] Should England be conquered, garrisons would have to be maintained there, and of soldiers equally zealous. Such is the dark future which this system opens to the French, even with the best of good luck. It turns out that the luck is bad, and at the end of 1812 the grand army is freezing in the snow; Napoleon's horse has let him tumble. Fortunately, the animal has simply foundered; "His Majesty's health was never better"; [139] nothing has happened to the rider; he gets up on his legs, and what concerns him at this moment is not the sufferings of his broken-down steed, but his own mishap; his reputation as a horseman is compromised; the effect on the public, the hooting of the audience, is what troubles him, the comedy of a perilous leap, announced with such a flourish of trumpets and ending in such a disgraceful fall. On reaching Warsaw[140] he says to himself, ten times over:

"There is only a step from the sublime to the ridiculous. "

The following year, at Dresden, he exposes still more foolishly, openly, and nakedly his master passion, the motives which determine him, the immensity and ferocity of his pitiless pride.

"What do they want of me? " said he to M. de Metternich. [141] " Do they want me to dishonor myself? Never! I can die, but never will I yield an inch of territory! Your sovereigns, born to the throne, may be beaten twenty times over and yet return to their capitals: I cannot do this, because I am a parvenu soldier. My domination will not survive the day when I shall have ceased to be strong, and, consequently, feared. "

In effect, his despotism in France is founded on his European omnipotence; if he does not remain master of the Continent, " he must settle with the corps législatif. [142] Rather than descend to an inferior position, rather than be a constitutional monarch, controlled by parliamentary chambers, he plays double or quits, and will risk losing everything.

"I have seen your soldiers, " says Metternich to him, "they are children. When this army of boys is gone, what will you do then? "

At these words, which touch his heart, he grows pale, his features contract, and his rage overcomes him; like a wounded man who has made a false step and exposes himself, he says violently to Metternich:

"You are not a soldier You do not know the impulses of a soldier's breast! I have grown up on the battle-field, and a man like me does not give a damn for the lives of a million men! "[143]

His imperial pipe-dreams has devoured many more. Between 1804 and 1815 he has had slaughtered 1,700,000 Frenchmen, born within the boundaries of ancient France, [144] to which must be added, probably, 2,000,000 men born outside of these limits, and slain for him, under the title of allies, or slain by him under the title of enemies. All that the poor, enthusiastic, and credulous Gauls have gained by entrusting their public welfare to him is two invasions; all that he bequeaths to them as a reward for their devotion, after this prodigious waste of their blood and the blood of others, is a France shorn of fifteen departments acquired by the republic, deprived of Savoy, of the left bank of the Rhine and of Belgium, despoiled of the northeast angle by which it completed its boundaries, fortified its most vulnerable point, and, using the words of Vauban, "made its field square, " separated from 4,000,000 new Frenchmen which it had assimilated after twenty years of life in common, and, worse still, thrown back within the frontiers of 1789, alone, diminished in the midst of its aggrandized neighbors, suspected by all Europe, and lastingly surrounded by a threatening circle of distrust and rancor.

Such is the political work of Napoleon, the work of egoism served by genius. In his European structure as in his French structure this sovereign egoism has introduced a vice of construction. This fundamental vice is manifest at the outset in the European edifice, and, at the expiration of fifteen years, it brings about a sudden downfall: in the French edifice it is equally serious but not so apparent; only at the end of half a century, or even a whole century, is it to be made clearly visible; but its gradual and slow effects will be equally pernicious and they are no less sure.

Notes:

[1] See my "Philosophy of Art" for texts and facts, Part II., ch. VI. - Other analogies, which are too long for development here, may be found, especially in all that concerns the imagination and love. "He was disposed to accept the marvelous, presentiments, and even certain mysterious communications between beings. . .. I have seen him excited by the rustling of the wind, speak enthusiastically of the roar of the sea, and sometimes inclined to believe in nocturnal apparitions; in short, leaning to certain superstitions. " (Madame de Rémusat, I., 102, and III., 164.) - Meneval (III., 114) notes his "crossing himself involuntarily on the occurrence of some great danger, on the discovery of some important fact. " During the consulate, in the evening, in a circle of ladies, he sometimes improvised and declaimed tragic "tales, " Italian fashion, quite worthy of the story-tellers of the XVth and XVIth centuries. (Bourrienne, VI., 387, gives one of his improvisations. Cf. Madame de Rémusat, I., 102.) - As to love, his letters to Josephine during the Italian campaign form one of the best examples of Italian passion and "in most piquant contrast with the temperate and graceful elegance of his predecessor M. de Beauharnais. " (Madame de

Rémusat, I., 143). - His other amours, simply physical, are too difficult to deal with; I have gathered some details orally on this subject which are almost from first hands and perfectly authentic. It is sufficient to cite one text already published: "According to Josephine, he had no moral principle whatever; did he not seduce his sisters one after the other? " - "I am not a man like other men, he said of himself, "and moral laws and those of propriety do not apply to me. " (Madame de Rémusat, I., 204, 206.) - Note again (II., 350) his proposals to Corvisart. - Such are everywhere the sentiments, customs, and morality of the great Italian personages of about the year 1500.

[2] De Pradt, "Histoire de l'ambassade dans le grand-duché de Varsovie, " p. 96. "with the Emperor, desire springs out of his imagination; his idea becomes passion the moment it comes into his head. "

[3] Bourrienne, II., 298. - De Ségur, I., 426.

[4] Bodin, "Recherches sur l'Anjou, " II., 325. - " Souvenirs d'un nonagénaire, " by Besnard. - Sainte-Beuve, "Causeries du Lundi, " article on Volney. - Miot de Melito, I., 297. He wanted to adopt Louis's son, and make him King of Italy. Louis refused, alleging that this marked favor would give new life to the reports spread about at one time in relation to this child. " Thereupon, Napoleon, exasperated, "seized Prince Louis by the waist and pushed him violently out of the room. " - " Mémorial, " Oct. 10, 1816. Napoleon relates that at the last conference of Campo-Fermio, to put an end to the resistance of the Austrian plenipotentiary, he suddenly arose, seized a set of porcelain on a stand near him and dashed it to the floor, exclaiming, "Thus will I shatter your monarchy before a month is over! " (Bourrienne questions this story.)

[5] Varnhagen von Ense, "Ausgewahlte Schriften, " III., 77 (Public reception of July 22, 1810). Napoleon first speaks to the Austrian Ambassador and next to the Russian Ambassador with a constrained air, forcing himself to be polite, in which he cannot persist. "Treating with I do not know what unknown personage, he interrogated him, reprimanded him, threatened him, and kept him for a sufficiently long time in a state of painful dismay. Those who stood near by and who could not help feeling a dismayed, stated later that there had been nothing to provoke such fury, that the Emperor had only sought an opportunity to vent his ill-humor; that he did it purposely

on some poor devil so as to inspire fear in others and to put down in advance any tendency to opposition. Cf. Beugnot, "Mémoires, " I., 380, 386, 387. - This mixture of anger and calculation likewise explains his conduct at Sainte Helena with Sir Hudson Lowe, his unbridled diatribes and insults bestowed on the governor like so many slaps in the face. (W. Forsyth, "History of the Captivity of Napoleon at Saint Helena, from the letters and journals of Sir Hudson Lowe, " III., 306.)

[6] Madame de Rémusat, II., 46.

[7] "Les Cahiers de Coignat. " 191. "At Posen, already, I saw him mount his horse in such a fury as to land on the other side and then give his groom a cut of the whip. "

[8] Madame de Rémusat, I., 222.

[9] Especially the letters addressed to Cardinal Consalvi and to the Préfet of Montenotte (I am indebted to M. d'Haussonville for this information). - Besides, he is lavish of the same expressions in conversation. On a tour through Normandy, he sends for the bishop of Séez and thus publicly addresses him: "Instead of merging the parties, you distinguish between constitutionalists and non-constitutionalists. Miserable fool! You are a poor subject, - hand in your resignation at once! " - To the grand-vicars he says, "Which of you governs your bishop - who is at best a fool? " - As M. Legallois is pointed out to him, who had of late been absent. "Fuck, where were you then? " "With my family. " "With a bishop who is merely a damned fool, why are you so often away, etc.? " (D'Haussonville, VI., 176, and Roederer, vol. III.)

[10] Madame de Rémusat - I., 101; II., 338.

[11] Ibid., I., 224. - M. de Meneval, I., 112, 347; III., 120: " On account of the extraordinary event of his marriage, he sent a handwritten letter to his future father-in-law (the Emperor of Austria). It was a grand affair for him. Finally, after a great effort, he succeeded in penning a letter that was readable. " - Meneval, nevertheless, was obliged "to correct the defective letters without letting the corrections be too plainly seen. "

[12] For example, at Bayonne and at Warsaw (De Pradt); the outrageous and never-to-be forgotten scene which, on his return

from Spain, occurred with Talleyrand - ("Souvenirs", by PASQUIER Etienne-Dennis, duc, Chancelier de France. Librarie Plon, Paris 1893. I., 357); - The gratuitous insult of M. de Metternich, in 1813, the last word of their interview ("Souvenirs du feu duc de Broglie, " I., 230). Cf. his not less gratuitous and hazardous confidential communications to Miot de Melito, in 1797, and his five conversations with Sir Hudson Lowe, immediately recorded by a witness, Major Gorrequer. (W. Forsyth, I., 147, 161, 200.)

[13] De Pradt, preface X

[14] Pelet de la Lozére, - Mollien, "Mémoires, " II., 222. - "Souvenirs du feu duc de Broglie, " I., 66, 69.

[15] "Madame de Rémusat, " I., 121: I have it from Corvisart that the pulsations of his arteries are fewer than is usual with men. He never experienced what is commonly called giddiness. " With him, the nervous apparatus is perfect in all its functions, incomparable for receiving, recording, registering, combining, and reflecting, but other organs suffer a reaction and are very sensitive. " (De Ségur, VI., 15 and 16, note of Drs. Yvan and Mestivier, his physicians.) "To preserve the equilibrium it was necessary with him that the skin should always fulfill its functions; as soon as the tissues were affected by any moral or atmospheric cause . . .. irritation, cough, ischuria. " Hence his need of frequent prolonged and very hot baths. "The spasm was generally shared by the stomach and the bladder. If in the stomach, he had a nervous cough which exhausted his moral and physical energies. " Such was the case between the eve of the battle of Moscow and the morning after his entry into Moscow: "a constant dry cough, difficult and intermittent breathing; the pulse sluggish, weak, and irregular; the urine thick and sedimentary, drop by drop and painful; the lower part of the legs and the feet extremely oedematous. " Already, in 1806, at Warsaw, "after violent convulsions in the stomach, " he declared to the Count de Loban, "that he bore within him the germs of a premature death, and that he would die of the same disease as his father's. " (De Ségur, VI., 82.) After the victory of Dresden, having eaten a ragout containing garlic, he is seized with such violent gripings as to make him think he was poisoned, and he makes a retrograde movement, which causes the loss of Vandamme's division, and, consequently, the ruin of 1813. "Souvenirs", by Pasquier, Etienne-Dennis, duc, chancelier de France. Librarie Plon, Paris 1893, (narrative of Daru, an eye-witness.) - This susceptibility of the nerves and stomach is hereditary with him and

shows itself in early youth. "One day, at Brienne, obliged to drop on his knees, as a punishment, on the sill of the refectory, he is seized with sudden vomiting and a violent nervous attack. " De Segur, I., 71. - It is well known that he died of a cancer in the stomach, like his father Charles Bonaparte. His grandfather Joseph Bonaparte, his uncle Fesch, his brother Lucien, and his sister Caroline died of the same, or of an analogous disease.

[16] Meneval, I., 269. Constant, "Mémoires, " V., 62. De Ségur, VI., 114, 117.

[17] Marshal Marmont, "Mémoires, " I., 306. Bourrienne, II., 119: "When off the political field he was sensitive, kind, open to pity. "

[18] Pelet de la Lozére, p. 7. De Champagny, " Souvenirs, " p. 103. At first, the emotion was much stronger. "He had the fatal news for nearly three hours; he had given vent to his despair alone by himself. He summoned me . . .. plaintive cries involuntarily escaped him. "

[19] Madame de Rémusat, I., 121, 342; II., 50; III., 61, 294, 312.

[20] De Ségur, V., 348.

[21] Yung, II., 329, 331. (Narrated by Lucien, and report to Louis XVIII.)

[22] "Nouvelle relation de l'Itinéraire de Napoléon, de Fontainebleau à l'Ile de l'Elbe, " by Count Waldberg-Truchsees, Prussian commissioner (1885), pp. 22, 24, 25, 26, 30, 32, 34, 37. - The violent scenes, probably, of the abdication and the attempt at Fontainebleau to poison himself had already disturbed his balance. On reaching Elba, he says to the Austrian commissioner, Koller, "As to you, my dear general, I have let you see my bare rump. " - Cf. in "Madame de Rémusat, " I., 108, one of his confessions to Talleyrand: he crudely points out in himself the distance between natural instinct and studied courage. - Here and elsewhere, we obtain a glimpse of the actor and even of the Italian buffoon; M. de Pradt called him "Jupiter Scapin. " Read his reflections before M. de Pradt, on his return from Russia, in which he appears in the light of a comedian who, having played badly and failed in his part, retires behind the scenes, runs down the piece, and criticize the imperfections of the audience. (De Pradt,)

[23] The reader may find his comprehension of the author's meaning strengthened by the following translation of a passage from his essay on Jouffroy (Philosophes classiques du XIXth Siécle, " 3rd ed.):

"What is a man, master of himself? He is one who, dying with thirst, refrains from swallowing a cooling draft, merely moistening his lips: who insulted in public, remains calm in calculating his most appropriate revenge; who in battle, his nerves excited by a charge, plans a difficult maneuver, thinks it out, and writes it down with a lead-pencil while balls are whistling around him, and sends it to his colonels. In other words, it is a man in whom the deliberate and abstract idea of the greatest good is stronger than all other ideas and sensations. The conception of the greatest good once attained, every dislike, every species of indolence, every fear, every seduction, every agitation, are found weak. The tendency which arise from the idea of the greatest good constantly dominates all others and determines all actions. " TR.

[24] Bourrienne, I. 21.

[25] Yung, 1., 125.

[26] Madame de Rémusat, I., 267. - Yung, II., 109. On his return to Corsica he takes upon himself the government of the whole family. "Nobody could discuss with him, says his brother Lucien; he took offence at the slightest observation and got in a passion at the slightest resistance. Joseph (the eldest) dared not even reply to his brother. "

[27] Mémorial, August 27-31, 1815.

[28] "Madame de Rémusat, " I., 105. - Never was there an abler and more persevering sophist, more persuasive, more eloquent, in order to make it appear that he was right. Hence his dictations at St. Helena; his proclamations, messages, and diplomatic correspondence; his ascendancy in talking as great as through his arms, over his subject and over his adversaries; also his posthumous ascendancy over posterity. He is as great a lawyer as he is a captain and administrator. The peculiarity of this disposition is never submitting to truth, but always to speak or write with reference to an audience, to plead a cause. Through this talent one creates phantoms which dupe the audience; on the other hand, as the author himself

forms part of the audience, he ends in not along leading others into error but likewise himself, which is the case with Napoleon.

[29] Yung, II., 111. (Report by Volney, Corsican commissioner, 1791. - II., 287. (Mémorial, giving a true account of the political and military state of Corsica in December, 1790.) - II., 270. (Dispatch of the representative Lacombe Saint-Michel, Sept. 10, 1793.) - Miot de Melito I., 131, and following pages. (He is peace commissioner in Corsica in 1797 and 1801.)

[30] Miot de Melito, II., 2. "The partisans of the First consul's family . .. regarded me simply as the instrument of their passions, of use only to rid them of their enemies, so as to center all favors on their protégés. "

[31] Yung., I., 220. (Manifest of October -31, 1789.) - I., 265. (Loan on the seminary funds obtained by force, June 23, 1790.) - I., 267, 269. (Arrest of M. de la Jaille and other officers; plan for taking the citadel of Ajaccio.) - II., 115. (letter to Paoli, February 17, 1792.) "Laws are like the statues of certain divinities - veiled on certain occasions. " - II., 125. (Election of Bonaparte as lieutenant-colonel of a battalion of volunteers, April1, 1792.) The evening before he had Murati, one of the three departmental commissioners, carried off by an armed band from the house of the Peraldi, his adversaries, where he lodged. Murati, seized unawares, is brought back by force and locked up in Bonaparte's house, who gravely says to him "I wanted you to be free, entirely at liberty; you were not so with the Peraldi. " - His Corsican biographer (Nasica, "Mémoires sur la jeunesse et l'enfance de Napoléon, ") considers this a very praiseworthy action

[32] Cf. on this point, the Memoirs of Marshal Marmont, I., 180, 196; the Memoirs of Stendhal, on Napoleon; the Report of d'Antraigues (Yung, III., 170, 171); the "Mercure Britannique" of Mallet-Dupan, and the first chapter of "La Chartreuse de Parme, " by Stendhal.

[33] "Correspondance de Napoléon, " I. (Letter of Napoleon to the Directory, April 26, 1796.) - Proclamation of the same date: "You have made forced marches barefoot, bivouacked without brandy, and often without bread. "

[34] Stendhal, "Vie de Napoléon, " p. 151. "The commonest officers were crazy with delight at having white linen and fine new boots. All were fond of music; many walked a league in the rain to secure a

seat in the La Scala Theatre. . ... In the sad plight in which the army found itself before Castiglione and Arcole, everybody, except the knowing officers, was disposed to attempt the impossible so as not to quit Italy. " - " Marmont, " I., 296: "We were all of us very young, . .. all aglow with strength and health, and enthusiastic for glory. . ... This variety of our occupations and pleasures, this excessive employment of body and mind gave value to existence, and made time pass with extraordinary rapidity. "

[35] "Correspondance de Napoléon, " I. Proclamation of March 27, 1796: ' Soldiers, you are naked and poorly fed. The government is vastly indebted to you; it has nothing to give you. . ... I am going to lead you to the most fertile plains in the world; rich provinces, large cities will be in your power; you will then obtain honor, glory, and wealth. " - Proclamation of April 26, 1796: - "Friends, I guarantee that conquest to you! " - Cf. in Marmont's memoirs the way in which Bonaparte plays the part of tempter in offering Marmont, who refuses, an opportunity to rob a treasury chest.

[36] Miot de Melito, I., 154. (June, 1797, in the gardens of Montebello.) "Such are substantially the most remarkable expressions in this long discourse which I have recorded and preserved. "

[37] Miot de Melito, I. 184. (Conversation with Bonaparte, November 18, 1797, at Turin.) "I remained an hour with the general tête-à-tête. I shall relate the conversation exactly as it occurred, according to my notes, made at the time. "

[38] Mathieu Dumas, " Mémoires, " III., 156. "It is certain that he thought of it from this moment and seriously studied the obstacles, means, and chances of success. " (Mathieu Dumas cites the testimony of Desaix, who was engaged in the enterprise): "It seems that all was ready, when Bonaparte judged that things were not yet ripe, nor the means sufficient. " - Hence his departure. "He wanted to get out of the way of the rule and caprices of these contemptible dictators, while the latter wanted to get rid of him because his military fame and influence in the army were obnoxious to them.

[39] Larevellière-Lepaux (one of the five directors on duty), "Mémoires, " II., 340. "All that is truly grand in this enterprise, as well as all that is bold and extravagant, either in its conception or execution, belongs wholly to Bonaparte. The idea of it never

occurred to the Directory nor to any of its members. . .. His ambition and his pride could not endure the alternative of no longer being prominent or of accepting a post which, however eminent, would have always subjected him to the orders of the Directory. "

[40] Madame de Rémusat, I., 142. "Josephine laid great stress on the Egyptian expedition as the cause of his change of temper and of the daily despotism which made her suffer so much. "- "Mes souvenirs sur Napoleon, " 325 by the count Chaptal. (Bonaparte's own words to the poet Lemercier who might have accompanied him to the Middle East and there would have learned many things about human nature): "You would have seen a country where the sovereign takes no account of the lives of his subjects, and where the subject himself takes no account of his own life. You would have got rid of your philanthropic 'notions. "

[41] Roederer, III., 461 (Jan. 12, 1803)

[42] Cf. "The Revolution, " Vol. p. 773. (Note I., on the situation, in 1806, of the Conventionalists who had survived the revolution.) For instance, Fouché is minister; Jeanbon-Saint-André, prefect; Drouet (de Varennes), sub-prefect; Chépy (of Grenoble), commissary-general of the police at Brest; 131 regicides are functionaries, among whom we find twenty one prefects and forty-two magistrates. - Occasionally, a chance document that has been preserved allows one to catch "the man in the act. " ("Bulletins hebdomadaires de la censure, 1810 and 1814, " published by M. Thurot, in the Revue Critique, 1871): "Seizure of 240 copies of an indecent work printed for account of M. Palloy, the author. This Palloy enjoyed some celebrity during the Revolution, being one of the famous patriots of the Faubourg Saint-Antoine. The constituent Assembly had conceded to him the ownership of the site of the Bastille, of which he distributed its stones among all the communes. He is a bon vivant, who took it into his head to write out in a very bad style the filthy story of his amours with a prostitute of the Palais-Royal. He was quite willing that the book should be seized on condition that he might retain a few copies of his jovial production. He professes high admiration for, and strong attachment to His Majesty's person, and expresses his sentiments piquantly, in the style of 1789. "
[43] Mémorial, " June 12, 1816.

[44] Mathieu Dumas, III., 363 (July 4, 1809, a few days before Wagram). - Madame de Rémusat, " I., 105: "I have never heard him

express any admiration or comprehension of a noble action. " - I.,
179: On Augustus's clemency and his saying, "Let us be friends,
Cinna, " the following is his interpretation of it: "I understand this
action simply as the feint of a tyrant, and approve as calculation
what I find puerile as sentiment. "- "Notes par le Comte Chaptal":
"He believed neither in virtue nor in probity, often calling these two
words nothing but abstractions; this is what rendered him so
distrustful and so immoral. . .. He never experienced a generous
sentiment; this is why he was so cold in company, and why he never
had a friend. He regarded men as so much counterfeit coin or as
mere instruments. "

[45] M. de Metternich, "Mémoires, " I., 241. - "Madame de Rémusat,"
I., 93: "That man has been so harmful (si assommateur de toute
vertu...) to all virtue. " - Madame de Staël, "Considerations sur la
Revolution Française, " 4th part, ch. 18. (Napoleon's conduct with M.
de Melzi, to destroy him in public opinion in Milan, in 1805.)

[46] Madame de Rémusat, I., 106; II., 247, 336: "His means for
governing man were all derived from those which tend to debase
him. . .. He tolerated virtue only when he could cover it with
ridicule. "

[47] Nearly all his false calculations are due to this defect, combined
with an excess of constructive imagination. - Cf. De Pradt, p. 94:
"The Emperor is all system, all illusion, as one cannot fail to be when
one is all imagination. Whoever has watched his course has noticed
his creating for himself an imaginary Spain, an imaginary
Catholicism, an imaginary England, an imaginary financial state, an
imaginary noblesse, and still more an imaginary France, and, in late
times, an imaginary congress. "

[48] Roederer, III., 495. (March 8, 1804.)

[49] Ibid., III., 537 (February 11, 1809.)

[50] Roederer, III., 514. (November 4, 1804.)

[51] Marmont, II., 242.

[52] Correspondance de Napoléon, " I. (Letter to Prince Eugéne,
April 14, 1806.)

[53] M. de Metternich, I., 284.

[54] Mollien, III., 427.

[55] "Notes par le Comte Chaptal": During the Consulate, "his opinion not being yet formed on many points, he allowed discussion and it was then possible to enlighten him and enforce an opinion once expressed in his presence. But, from the moment that he possessed ideas of his own, either true or false, on administrative subjects, he consulted no one; . .. he treated everybody who differed from him in opinion contemptuously, tried to make them appear ridiculous, and often exclaimed, giving his forehead a slap, that here was an instrument far more useful than the counsels of men who were commonly supposed to be instructed and experienced. .. For four years, he sought to gather around him the able men of both parties. After this, the choice of his agents began to be indifferent to him. Regarding himself as strong enough to rule and carry on the administration himself, the talents and character of those who stood in his way were discarded. What he wanted was valets and not councillors. .. The ministers were simply head-clerks of the bureaus. The Council of State served only to give form to the decrees emanating from him; he ruled even in petty details. Everybody around him was timid and passive; his will was regarded as that of an oracle and executed without reflection. . .. Self-isolated from other men, having concentrated in his own hands all powers and all action, thoroughly convinced that another's light and experience could be of no use to him, he thought that arms and hands were all that he required. "

[56] "Souvenirs", by Pasquier (Etienne-Dennis, duc), chancelier de France. In VI volumes, Librarie Plon, Paris 1893. Vol I. chap. IX. and X. pp. 225-268. (Admirable portraiture of his principal agents, Cambacérès, Talleyrand, Maret, Cretet, Real, etc.) Lacuée, director of the conscription, is a perfect type of the imperial functionary. Having received the broad ribbon of the Legion d'Honneur, he exclaimed, at the height of his enthusiasm: "what will not France become under such a man? To what degree of happiness and glory will it not ascend, always provided the conscription furnishes him with 200,000 men a year! And, indeed, that will not be difficult, considering the extent of the empire. " - And likewise with Merlin de Douai: "I never knew a man less endowed with the sentiment of the just and the unjust; everything seems to him right and good, as the consequences of a legal text. He was even endowed with a kind of satanic smile

which involuntarily rose to his lips . ... every time the opportunity occurred, when, in applying his odious science, he reached the conclusion that severity is necessary or some condemnation. " The same with Defermon, in fiscal matters

[57] Madame de Rémusat, II., 278; II., 175.

[58] Ibid., III., 275, II., 45. (Apropos of Savary, his most intimate agent.): "He is a man who must be constantly corrupted. "

[59] Ibid., I., 109; II., 247; III., 366.

[60] "Madame de Rémusat, " II., 142, 167, 245. (Napoleon's own words.) "If I ordered Savary to rid himself of his wife and children, I am sure he would not hesitate. " - Marmont, II., 194: "We were at Vienna in 1809. Davoust said, speaking of his own and Maret's devotion: "If the Emperor should say to us both, 'My political interests require the destruction of Paris without any one escaping, ' Maret would keep the secret, I am sure; but nevertheless he could not help letting it be known by getting his own family out. I, rather than reveal it1 would leave my wife and children there. " (These are bravado expressions, wordy exaggerations, but significant.)

[61] Madame de Rémusat, II., 379.

[62] Souvenirs du feu duc de Broglie, " I., 230. (Words of Maret, at Dresden, in 1813; he probably repeats one of Napoleon's figures.)

[63] Mollien, II., 9.

[64] D'Haussonville, "L'Église Romaine et le premier Empire, "VI., 190, and passim.

[65] Ibid., III., 460-473. - Cf. on the same scene, "Souvenirs", by Pasquier (Etienne-Dennis, duc), Chancelier de France. (He was both witness and actor.)

[66] An expression of Cambacérès. M. de Lavalette, II., 154.

[67] Madame de Rémusat, III. 184

[68] "Souvenirs", by Pasquier, Librarie Plon, Paris 1893. -, I., 521. Details of the manufacture of counterfeit money, by order of Savary,

in an isolated building on the plain of Montrouge. - Metternich, II., 358. (Words of Napoleon to M. de Metternich): "I had 300 millions of banknotes of the Bank of Vienna all ready and was going to flood you with them. " Ibid., Correspondence of M. de Metternich with M. de Champagny on this subject (June, 1810).

[69] "Souvenirs", by Pasquier, Librarie Plon, Paris 1893. - Vol. II. p. 196.

[70] Madame de Rémusat, II., 335.

[71] Madame de Rémusat, I., 231.

[72] Ibid., 335.

[73] M. de Metternich, I., 284. "One of those to whom he seemed the most attached was Duroc. 'He loves me the same as a dog loves his master, ' is the phrase he made use of in speaking of him to me. He compared Berthier's sentiment for his person to that of a child's nurse. Far from being opposed to his theory of the motives influencing men these sentiments were its natural consequence whenever he came across sentiments to which he could not apply the theory of calculation based on cold interest, he sought the cause of it in a kind of instinct. "

[74] Beugnot, "Mémoires, " II., 59.

[75] "Mémorial. " "If I had returned victorious from Moscow, I would have brought the Pope not to regret temporal power: I would have converted him into an idol. .. I would have directed the religious world as well as the political world. .. My councils would have represented Christianity, and the Pope would have only been president of them. "

[76] De Ségur, III., 312. (In Spain, 1809.)

[77] "Mémoires du Prince Eugène. " (Letters of Napoleon, August, 1806.)

[78] Letter of Napoleon to Fouché, March 3, 1810. (Left out in the "Correspondance de Napoléon I., " and published by M. Thiers in "Histoire du Consulat et de l'Empire, XII., p. 115.

[79] De Ségur, III., 459.

[80] Words of Napoleon to Marmont, who, after three months in the hospital, returns to him in Spain with a broken arm and his hand in a black sling: "You hold on to that rag then? " Sainte-Beuve, who loves the truth as it really is, quotes the words as they came, which Marmont dared not reproduce. (Causeries du Lundi, VI., 16.) - "Souvenirs", by Pasquier, Librarie Plon, Paris 1893: "M. de Champagny having been dismissed and replaced, a courageous friend defended him and insisted on his merit: "You are right, " said the Emperor, "he had some when I took him; but by cramming him too full, I have made him stupid. "

[81] Beugnot, I., 456, 464

[82] Mme. de Rémusat, II., 272.

[83] M. de Champagny, "Souvenirs, " 117.

[84] Madame de Rémusat, I., 125.

[85] De Ségur, III., 456.

[86] "The Ancient Regime, " p. 125. - "Œuvres de Louis XIV., " 191: "If there is any peculiar characteristic of this monarchy, it is the free and easy access of the subjects to the king; it an egalité de justice between both, and which, so to say, maintains both in a genial and honest companionship, in spite of the almost infinite distance in birth, rank, and power. This agreeable society, which enables persons of the Court to associate familiarly with us, impresses them and charms them more than one can tell. "

[87] Madame de Rémusat, II., 32, 39.

[88] Madame de Rémusat, III., 169.

[89] Ibid., II., 32, 223, 240, 259; III., 169.

[90] Ibid., I., 112, II., 77.
[91] M. de Metternich, I., 286. - "It would be difficult to imagine any greater awkwardness than that of Napoleon in a drawing-room. - Varnhagen von Ense, "Ausgewählte Schriften, " III., 177. (Audience of July 10, 1810): "I never heard a harsher voice, one so inflexible.

When he smiled, it was only with the mouth and a portion of the cheeks; the brow and eyes remained immovably sombre, . .. This compound of a smile with seriousness had in it something terrible and frightful. " - On one occasion, at St. Cloud, Varnhagen heard him exclaim over and over again, twenty times, before a group of ladies, "How hot! "

[92] Mme. de Rémusat, II., 77, 169. - Thibaudeau, " Mémoires sur le Consulat, " p. 18: "He sometimes pays them left-handed compliments on their toilet or adventures, which was his way of censuring morals. " - "Mes souvenirs sur Napoléon, " 322 by le Comte Chaptal: "At a fête, in the H'tel de Ville, he exclaimed to Madame — —, who had just given her name to him: 'Good God, they told me you were pretty! ' To some old persons: 'You haven't long to live! To another lady: 'It is a fine time for you, now your husband is on his campaigns! ' In general, the tone of Bonaparte was that of an ill-bred lieutenant. He often invited a dozen or fifteen persons to dinner and rose from the table before the soup was finished... The court was a regular galley where each rowed according to command."

[93] Madame de Rémusat, I., 114, 122, 206; II., 110, 112.

[94] Ibid., I., 277.

[95] "Hansard's Parliamentary History, " vol. XXXVI.,. 3I0. Lord Whitworth's dispatch to Lord Hawkesbury, March 14, 1803, and account of the scene with Napoleon. "All this took place loud enough for the two hundred persons present to hear it. "- Lord Whitworth (dispatch of March 17) complains of this to Talleyrand and informs him that he shall discontinue his visits to the Tuileries unless he is assured that similar scenes shall not occur again. - Lord Hawkesbury approves of this (dispatch of March 27), and declares that the proceeding is improper and offensive to the King of England. - Similar scenes, the same conceit and intemperate language, with M. de Metternich, at Paris, in 1809, also at Dresden, in 1813: again with Prince Korsakof, at Paris, in 1812; with M. de Balachof, at Wilna, in 1812, and with Prince Cardito, at Milan, in 1805.

[96] Before the rupture of the peace of Amiens ("Moniteur, " Aug. 8, 1802): The French government is now more firmly established than the English government. " - ("Moniteur" Sept. 10, 1802): "What a

difference between a people which conquers for love of glory and a people of traders who happen to become conquerors! " - ("Moniteur," Feb. 20, 1803): "The government declares with a just pride that England cannot now contend against France. " - Campaign of 1805, 9th bulletin, words of Napoleon in the presence of Mack's staff: "I recommend my brother the Emperor of Germany to make peace as quick as he can! Now is the time to remember that all empires come to an end; the idea that an end might come to the house of Lorraine ought to alarm him. " - Letter to the Queen of Naples, January 2, 1805: "Let your Majesty listen to what I predict. On the first war breaking out, of which she might be the cause, she and her children will have ceased to reign; her children would go wandering about among the different countries of Europe begging help from their relations. "

[97] 37th bulletin, announcing the march of an army on Naples "to punish the Queen's treachery and cast from the throne that criminal woman, who, with such shamelessness, has violated all that men hold sacred. " - Proclamation of May 13, 1809: "Vienna, which the princes of the house of Lorraine have abandoned, not as honorable soldiers yielding to circumstances and the chances of war, but as perjurers pursued by remorse. . ... In flying from Vienna their adieus to its inhabitants consisted of murder and fire. Like Medea, they have sacrificed their children with their own hands. " - 13th bulletin: "The rage of the house of Lorraine against the city of Vienna, "

[98] Letter to the King of Spain, Sept. 18, 1803, and a note to the Spanish minister of foreign affairs, on the Prince de la Paix: "This favorite, who has succeeded by the most criminal ways to a degree unheard of in the annals of history. . .. Let Your Majesty put away a man who, maintaining in his rank the low passions of his character, has lived wholly on his vices. " - After the battle of Jéna, 9th, 17th, 18th, and 19th bulletins, comparison of the Queen of Prussia with Lady Hamilton, open and repeated insinuations, imputing to her an intrigue with the Emperor Alexander. "Everybody admits that the Queen of Prussia is the author of the evils the Prussian nation suffers. This is heard everywhere. How changed she is since that fatal interview with the Emperor Alexander! . .. The portrait of the Emperor Alexander, presented to her by the Prince, was found in the apartment of the Queen at Potsdam. "

[99] "La Guerre patriotique" (1812-1815), according to the letters of contemporaries, by Doubravine (in Russian). The Report of the Russian envoy, M. de Balachof, is in French,

[100] An allusion to the murder of Paul I.

[101] Stanislas de Girardin, "Mémoires, " III., 249. (Reception of Niv'se 12, year X.) The First consul addresses the Senate: "Citizens, I warn you that I regard the nomination of Daunou to the senate as a personal insult, and you know that I have never put up with one. " - "Correspondance de Napoleon I. " (Letter of Sept. 23, 1809, to M. de Champagny): "The Emperor Francis insulted me in writing to me that I cede nothing to him, when, out of consideration for him, I have reduced my demands nearly one-half. " (Instead of 2,750,000 Austrian subjects he demanded only 1,600,000.) - Roederer, III., 377 (Jan. 24, 1801): "The French people must put up with my defects if they find I am of service to them; it is my fault that I cannot endure insults. "

[102] M. de Metternich, II., 378. (Letter to the Emperor of Austria, July 28, 1810.)

[103] Note presented by the French ambassador, Otto, Aug. 17, 1802.

[104] Stanislas Girardin, III., 296. (Words of the First consul, Floreal 24, year XI.): "I had proposed to the British minister, for several months, to make an arrangement by which a law should be passed in France and in England prohibiting newspapers and the members of the government from expressing either good or ill of foreign governments. He never would consent to it. " - St. Girardin: "He could not. " - Bonaparte: "Why? " - St. Girardin: "Because an agreement of that sort would have been opposed to the fundamental law of the country. " Bonaparte: "I have a poor opinion, " etc.

[105] Hansard, vol. XXXVI., p. 1298. (Dispatch of Lord Whitworth, Feb. 21, 1803, conversation with the First consul at the Tuileries.) - Seeley, 'A Short History of Napoleon the First. " "Trifles is a softened expression, Lord Whitworth adds in a parenthesis which has never been printed; "the expression he made use of is too insignificant and too low to have a place in a dispatch or anywhere else, save in the mouth of a hack-driver. "

[106] Lanfrey, "Histoire de Napoléon, " II., 482. (Words of the First consul to the Swiss delegates, conference of January 29, 1803.)

[107] Sir Neil Campbell, "Napoleon at Fontainebleau and Elba, " p. 201. (The words of Napoleon to Sir Neil Campbell and to the other commissioners.) - The Mémorial de Sainte Helene mentions the same plan in almost identical terms. - Pelet de la Lozère, "Opinions de Napoléon au conseil d'état, " p. 238 (session of March 4, 1806): "Within forty- eight hours after peace with England, I shall interdict foreign commodities and promulgate a navigation act forbidding any other than French vessels entering our ports, built of French timber, and with the crews two-thirds French. Even coal and English 'milords' shall land only under the French flag. " - Ibid., 32.

[108] Moniteur, January 30, 1803 (Sebastiani).

[109] Hansard, vol. XXXVI., p. 1298. (Lord Whitworth's dispatch, Feb. 21, 1803, the First Consul's words to Lord Whitworth.)

[110] "Memorial. " (Napoleon's own words, March 24, 1806.)

[111] Lanfrey, II., 476. (Note to Otto, October 23, 1802.) - Thiers, VI., 249.

[112] Letter to Clarke, Minister of War, Jan. 18, 1814. " If, at Leipsic, I had had 30,000 cannon balls to fire off on the evening of the 18th, I should to-day be master of the world. "

[113] "Memorial, " Nov. 30, 1815.

[114] Lanfrey, III., - 399. Letters of Talleyrand, October 11 and 27, 1805, and memorandum addressed to Napoleon.

[115] At the council held in relation to the future marriage of Napoleon, Cambacérès vainly supported an alliance with the Russians. The following week, he says to M. Pasquier: "When one has only one good reason to give and it cannot possibly be given, it is natural that one should be beaten. . ., You will see that it is so good that one phrase suffices to make its force fully understood. I am deeply convinced that in two years we shall have a war with that of two powers whose daughter the Emperor does not marry. Now a war with Austria does not cause me any uneasiness, and I tremble at a war with Russia. The consequences are incalculable. " "Souvenirs",

by PASQUIER (Etienne-Dennis, duc), Librarie Plon, Paris 1893. Vol I., p 293, p 378.).

[116] M. de Metternich, II., 305. (Letter to the Emperor of Austria, Aug. 10, 1809.) - Ibid. 403.. (Letter of Jan. 11, 1811.) "My appreciation of Napoleon's plans and projects, at bottom, has never varied. The monstrous purpose of the complete subjection of the continent under one head was, and is still, his object. "

[117] "Correspondance de Napoleon I. " (Letter to the King of Wurtemberg, April 2, 1814): "The war will take place in spite of him (the Emperor Alexander), in spite of me, in spite of the interests of France and those of Russia. Having already seen this so often, it is my past experience which enables me to unveil the future, "

[118] Mollien, III., 135, 190. - In 1810 "prices have increased 400% on sugar, and 100 % on cotton and dye stuffs. " - " More than 20,000 custom-house officers were employed on the frontier against more than 100,000 smugglers, in constant activity and favored by the population. " - "Souvenirs", by PASQUIER (Etienne-Dennis, duc), Librarie Plon, Paris 1893. -, I., 387. - There were licenses for importing colonial products, but on condition of exporting a proportionate quantity of French manufactures; now, England refused to receive them. Consequently, "not being allowed to bring these articles back to France, they were thrown overboard. " - "They began at first by devoting the refuse of manufactures to this trade, and then ended by manufacturing articles without other destination; for example, at Lyons, taffetas and satins. "

[119] Proclamation of Dec. 27, 1805: "The Naples dynasty has ceased to reign. Its existence is incompatible with the repose of Europe and the honor of my crown. " - Message to the Senate, Dec. 10, 1810: "Fresh guarantees having become necessary, the annexation to the Empire of the mouths of the Escaut, the Meuse, the Rhine, the Ems, the Weser, and the Elbe, seemed to me to be the first and most important. . .. The annexation of the Valais is an anticipated result of the vast works I have undertaken for the past ten years in that section of the Alps. "

[120] We are familiar with the Spanish affair. His treatment of Portugal is anterior and of same order. -" Correspondance. " (Letter to Junot, Oct. 31, 1807): - 'I have already informed you, that in authorizing you to enter as an auxiliary, it was to enable you to

possess yourself of the (Portuguese) fleet, but my mind was made up to take Portugal. " - (Letter to Junot, Dec. 23, 1807): "Disarm the country. Send all the Portuguese troops to France. . ... I want them out of the country. Have all princes, ministers, and other men who serve as rallying points, sent to France. " - (Decree of Dec. 23, 1807): " An extra contribution of 100 million francs shall be imposed on the kingdom of Portugal, to redeem all property, of whatever denomination, belonging to private parties. .. All property belonging to the Queen of Portugal, to the prince-regent, and to princes in appanage; . . .. all the possessions of the nobles who have followed the king, on his abandoning the country, and who had not returned to the kingdom before February 1, shall be put under sequestration. " - Cf. M. d'Haussonville, "L'Église Romaine et le premier Empire, " 5 vols. (especially the last volume). No other work enables one to see into Napoleon's object and proceedings better nor more closely.

[121] "Souvenirs du feu duc de Broglie, " p. 143. (As a specimen of steps taken in time of war, see the register of Marshal Bessières' orders, commandant at Valladolid from April 11 to July 15, 1811.) - "Correspondance du Roi Jérome, " letter of Jerome to Napoleon, Dec. 5, 1811. (Showing the situation of a vanquished people in times of peace): "If war should break out, all countries between the Rhine and the Oder will become the center of a vast and active insurrection. The mighty cause of this dangerous movement is not merely hatred of the French, and impatience of a foreign yoke, but rather in the misfortunes of the day, in the total ruin of all classes, in over-taxation, consisting of war levies, the maintenance of troops, soldiers traversing the country, and every sort of constantly renewed vexation. . .. At Hanover, Magdebourg, and in the principal towns of my kingdom, owners of property are abandoning their dwellings and vainly trying to dispose of them at the lowest prices. . .. Misery everywhere presses on families; capital is exhausted; the noble, the peasant, the bourgeois, are crushed with debt and want. . .. The despair of populations no longer having anything to lose, because all has been taken away, is to be feared. " - De Pradt, p. 73. (Specimen of military proceedings in allied countries.) At Wolburch, in the Bishop of Cujavie's chateau, "I found his secretary, canon of Cujavie, decorated with the ribbon and cross of his order, who showed me his jaw, broken by the vigorous blows administered to him the previous evening by General Count Vandamme, because he had refused to serve Tokay wine, imperiously demanded by the general; he was told that the King of Westphalia had lodged in the castle the day before, and had carted away all this wine. "

[122] Fievée, "Correspondance et relations avec Bonaparte, de 1802 à 1813, " III., 82. (Dec. 1811), (On the populations annexed or conquered): "There is no hesitation in depriving them of their patrimony, their language, their legislatures, in disturbing all their habits, and that without any warrant but throwing a bulletin des lois at their heads (inapplicable). . .. How could they be expected to recognize this, or even become resigned to it? . .. Is it possible not to feel that one no longer has a country, that one is under constraint, wounded in feeling and humiliated? . .. Prussia, and a large part of Germany, has been so impoverished that there is more to gain by taking a pitchfork to kill a man than to stir up a pile of manure. "

[123] "Correspondance, " letter to King Joseph, Feb. 18, 1814. "If I had signed the treaty reducing France to its ancient limits, I should have gone to war two years after - Marmont, V., 133 (1813): "Napoleon, in the last years of his reign, always preferred to lose all rather than to yield anything. "

[124] M. de Metternich, II., 205.

[125] Words of Richelieu on his death-bed: "Behold my judge, " said he, pointing to the Host, "the judge who will soon pronounce his verdict. I pray that he will condemn me, if, during my ministry, I have proposed to myself aught else than the good of religion and of the State. "

[126] Miot de Melito, "Mémoires, "II., 48, 152.

[127] "Souvenirs, " by Gaudin, duc de Gaëte (3rd vol. of the "Mémoires, " p. 67).

[128] M. de Metternich, II., 120. (Letter to Stadion, July 26, 1807.)

[129] Ibid., II., 291. (Letter of April 11, 1809.)

[130] Ibid., II., 400. (Letter of Jan. 17, 1811.) In lucid moments, Napoleon takes the same view. Cf. Pelet de la Lozère, "Opinions de Napoleon au conseil d'etat, " p. 15: "That will last as long as I do. After me, however, my son will deem himself fortunate if he has 40,000 francs a year. " - (De Ségur, "Histoire et Mémoires, " III., 155.): "How often at this time (1811) was he heard to foretell that the weight of his empire would crush his heir! " "Poor child, " said he, regarding the King of Rome, "what an entanglement I shall leave to

you! " From the beginning he frequently passed judgment on himself and foresaw the effect of his action in history. " On reaching the isle of Poplars, the First Consul stopped at Rousseau's grave, and said: 'It would have, been better for the repose of France, if that man had never existed. ' 'And why, citizen Consul? ' 'He is the man who made the French revolution. ' 'It seems to me that you need not complain of the French revolution! ' 'well, the future must decide whether it would not have been better for the repose of the whole world if neither myself nor Rousseau had ever lived. ' He then resumed his promenade in a revery. " - Stanislas Girardin; "Journal et Mémoires, " III., Visit of the French Consul to Ermenonville.

[131] Marmont, "Mémoires, " III., 337. (On returning from Wagram.)

[132] On this initial discord, cf. Armand Lefèvre, "Histoire des Cabinets de l'Europe, " vol.VI.

[133] "Correspondance de Napoléon I. " (Letter to the King of Wurtemberg, April 2, 1811.)

[134] Testament of April 25, 1821 "It is my desire that my remains rest on the banks of the Seine, amidst that French people I have so dearly loved. "

[135] "Correspondance de Napoleon I., XXII., 119. (Note by Napoleon, April, 1811.) "There will always be at Hamburg, Bremen, and Lubeck from 8000 to 10,000 Frenchmen, either as employees or as gendarmes, in the custom-houses and warehouses. "

[136] "Souvenirs", by PASQUIER (Etienne-Dennis, duc), Librarie Plon, Paris 1893. -, II., 88, and following pages: "During the year 1813, from Jan. 1 to Oct. 7, 840,000 men had already been drafted from imperial France and they had to be furnished. " - Other decrees in December, placing at the disposition of the government 300,000 conscripts for the years 1806 to 1814 inclusive. - Another decree in November organizing 140,000 men of the national guard in cohorts, intended for the defense of strongholds. - In all, 1,300,000 men summoned in one year. "Never has any nation been thus asked to let itself be voluntarily led in a mass to the slaughterhouse. - Ibid., II., 59. Senatus-consulte, and order of council for raising 10,000 young men, exempt or redeemed from conscription, as the prefects might choose, arbitrarily, from amongst the highest classes in society. The purpose was plainly " to secure hostages in every family of doubtful

loyalty. No measure created for Napoleon more irreconcilable enemies. " - Cf. De Ségur, II., 34. (He was charged with organizing and commanding a division of young men.) Many were sons of Vendéans or of Conventionalists, some torn from their wives the day after their marriage, or from the bedside of a wife in her confinement, of a dying father, or of a sick son; "some looked so feeble that they seemed dying. " One half perished in the campaign of 1814. - " Correspondance, " letter to Clarke, Minister of War, Oct. 23, 1813 (in relation to the new levies): "I rely on 100,000 refractory conscripts. "

[137] "Archives nationales, " A F., VI., 1297. (Documents 206 to 210.) (Report to the Emperor by Count Dumas, April 10, 1810.) Besides the 170 millions of penalties 1,675,457 francs of penalty were inflicted on 2335 individuals, " abettors or accomplices. " - Ibid., A F., VI., 1051. (Report of Gen. Lacoste on the department of Haute-Loire, Oct. 13, 1808.) "He always calculated in this department on the desertion of one-half of the conscripts. In most of the cantons the gendarmes traffic with the conscription shamefully; certain conscripts pension them to show them favors. " - Ibid., A F., VI., 1052. (Report by Pelet, Jan. 12, 1812.) "The operation of the conscription has improved (in the Herault); the contingents of 1811 have been furnished. There remained 1800 refractory, or deserters of the previous classes; 1600 have been arrested or made to surrender by the flying column; 200 have still to be pursued. " Faber, - "Notice (1807) sur l'intérieur de la France, " p. 141: "Desertion, especially on the frontiers, is occasionally frightful; 80 deserters out of 160 have sometimes been arrested. " - Ibid., p. 149: It has been stated in the public journals that in 1801 the court in session at Lille had condemned 135 refractory out of the annual conscription, and that which holds its sittings at Ghent had condemned 70. Now, 200 conscripts form the maximum of what an arrondissement in a department could furnish. " -Ibid, p. 145. "France resembles a vast house of detention where everybody is suspicious of his neighbor, where each avoids the other. .. One often sees a young man with a gendarme at his heels oftentimes, on looking closely, this young man's hands are found tied, or he is handcuffed. " - Mathieu Dumas, III., 507 (After the battle of Dresden, in the Dresden hospitals): "I observed, with sorrow, that many of these men were slightly wounded: most of them, young conscripts just arrived in the army, had not been wounded by the enemy's fire, but they had mutilated each other's feet and hands. Antecedents of this kind, of equally bad augury, had already been remarked in the campaign of 1809. "

[138] De Ségur, III., 474. - Thiers, XIV., 159. (One month after crossing the Niemen one hundred and fifty thousand men had dropped out of the ranks.)

[139] Bulletin 29 (December 3, 1812).

[140] De Pradt, Histoire de l'Ambassade de Varsovie, " p. 219.

[141] M. de Metternich, I., 147. - Fain, "Manuscript, " of 1813, II., 26. (Napoleon's address to his generals.) "What we want is a complete triumph. To abandon this or that province is not the question; our political superiority and our existence depend on it. " - II., 41, 42. (Words of Napoleon to Metternich.) "And it is my father-in-law who favors such a project! And he sends you! In what attitude does he wish to place me before the French people? He is strangely deluded if he thinks that a mutilated throne can offer an asylum to his daughter and grandson. . .. Ah, Metternich, how much has England given you to make you play this part against me? " (This last phrase, omitted in Metternich's narrative, is a characteristic trait; Napoleon at this decisive moment, remains insulting and aggressive, gratuitously and even to his own destruction.)

[142] "Souvenirs du feu duc de Broglie, " I., 235.

[143] Ibid., I., 230. Some days before Napoleon had said to M. de Narbonne, who told me that very evening: "After all, what has this (the Russian campaign) cost me? 300,000 men, among whom, again, were a good many Germans. " - "Souvenirs", by PASQUIER (Etienne-Dennis, duc, Librarie Plon, Paris 1893. II. 110. (Apropos of the Frankfurt basis, and accepted by Napoleon when too late.) "What characterizes this mistake is that it was committed much more against the interests of France than against his own. . .. He sacrificed her to the perplexities of his personal situation, to the mauvaise honte of his own ambition, to the difficulty he finds in standing alone to a certain extent before a nation which had done everything for him and which could justly reproach him with having sacrificed so much treasure and spilled so much blood on enterprises proved to have been foolish and impracticable. "

[144] Leonce de Lavergne, "Economie rurale de la France, " P. 40. (According to the former director of the conscription under the Empire.)

BOOK SECOND. FORMATION AND CHARACTER OF THE NEW
STATE.

CHAPTER I.

I. The Institution of Government.

Conditions on which the public power can act. - Two points
forgotten by the authors of the preceding constitutions. - Difficulty of
the undertaking and poor quality of the available materials.

Every human society requires government, that is to say an
authority. No other machinery is more useful. But a machinery is
useful only if it is adapted to its purpose; if not it will not work, or
may even work contrary to its purpose. Hence, during its
construction, one must first of all consider the magnitude of the
work it has to do as well as the quality of the materials one has at
one's disposal. It is very important to know beforehand whether it
will lift 100 or of 100,000 kilograms, whether the pieces fitted
together will be of iron or of steel, of sound or of unsound timber. -
But the legislators had not taken that into consideration during the
last ten years. They had set themselves up as theoreticians, and
likewise as optimists, without looking at the things, or else
imagining the them as they wished to have them. In the national
assemblies, as well as with the public, the task was deemed easy and
simple, whereas it was extraordinary and immense; for the matter in
hand consisted in effecting a social revolution and in carrying on an
European war. The materials were supposed to be excellent, as
manageable as they were substantial, while, in fact, they were very
poor, being both refractory and brittle, for these human materials
consisted of the Frenchmen of 1789 and of the following years; that is
to say, of exceedingly sensitive men doing each other all possible
harm, inexperienced in political business, Utopians, impatient,
intractable, and overexcited. Calculations had been made on these
prodigiously false data; consequently, although the calculations were
very exact, the results obtained were found absurd. Relying on these
data, the machine had been planned, and all its parts been adjusted,
assembled, and balanced. That is why the machine, irreproachable in
theory, remained unsuccessful in practice: the better it appeared on
paper the quicker it broke down when set up on the ground.

II. Default of previous government.

The consequences of the years 1789 to 1799. - Insubordination of the local powers, conflict of the central powers, suppression of liberal institutions, and the establishment of an unstable despotism. - Evildoing of the government thus formed.

A capital defect at once declared itself in the two principal compositions, in the working gear of the superposed powers and in the balance of the motor powers. - In the first place, the hold given to the central government on its local subordinates was evidently too feeble; with no right to appoint these, it could not select them as it pleased, according to the requirements of the service. Department, district, canton, and commune administrators, civil and criminal judges, assessors, appraisers, and collectors of taxes, officers of the national-guard and even of the gendarmerie, police-commissioners, and other agents who had to enforce laws on the spot, were nearly all recruited elsewhere: either in popular assemblies or provided ready- made by elected bodies. [1] They were for it merely borrowed instruments; thus originating, they escaped its control; it could not make them work as it wanted them to work. On most occasions they would shirk their duties; at other times, on receiving orders, they would stand inert; or, again, they would act outside of or beyond their special function, either going too far or acting in a contrary sense; never did they act with moderation and precision, with coherence and consequence. For this reason any desire of the government to do its job proved unsuccessful. Its legal subordinates - incapable, timid, lukewarm, unmanageable, or even hostile - obeyed badly, did not obey at all, or willfully disobeyed. The blade of the executive instrument, loose in the handle, glanced or broke off when the thrust had to be made.

In the second place, never could the two or three motor forces thrusting the handle act in harmony, owing to the clashing of so many of them; one always ended in breaking down the other. The Constituent Assembly had set aside the King, the Legislative Assembly had deposed him, the Convention had decapitated him. Afterward each fraction of the sovereign body in the Convention had proscribed the other; the Montagnards had guillotined the Girondists, and the Thermidorians had guillotined the Montagnards. Later, under the Constitution of the year III, the Fructidorians had banished the Constitutionalists, the Directory had purged the

Councils, and the Councils had purged the Directory. - Not only did the democratic and parliamentary institution fail in its work and break down on trial, but, again, through its own action, it became transformed into its opposite. In a year or two a coup d'état in Paris took place; a faction seized the central power and converted it into an absolute power in the hands of five or six ringleaders. The new government at once re-forged the executive instrument for its own advantage and refastened the blade firmly on the handle; in the provinces it dismissed those elected by the people and deprived the governed of the right to choose their own rulers; henceforth, through its proconsuls on mission, or through its resident commissioners, it alone appointed, superintended, and regulated on the spot all local authorities. [2]

Thus the liberal constitution, at its close, gave birth to a centralized despotism, and this was the worst of its species, at once formless and monstrous; for it was born out of a civil crime, while the government which used it had no support but a band of bigoted fanatics or political adventurers; without any legal authority over the nation, or any moral hold on the army, detested, threatened, discordant, exposed to the resistance of its own upholders, to the treachery of its own members, and living only from day to day, it could maintain itself only through a brutal absolutism and permanent terror, while the public power of which the first care is the protection of property, consciences, and lives, became in its hands the worst of persecutors, robbers, and murderers.

III.

In 1799, the undertaking is more difficult and the materials worse.

Twice in succession had the experiment been tried, the monarchical constitution of 1791, and the republican constitution of 1795; twice in succession had the same events followed the same course to attain the same end; twice in succession had the theoretical, cunningly-devised machine for universal protection changed into an efficient and brutal machine for universal oppression. It is evident that if the same machine were started the third time under analogous conditions, one might expect to see it work in the same manner; that is to say, contrary to its purpose.

Now, in 1799, the conditions were analogous, and even worse, for the work which the machine had to do was not less, while the human materials available for its construction were not so good. - Externally, the country was constantly at war with Europe; peace could not be secured except by great military effort, and peace was as difficult to preserve as to win. The European equilibrium had been too greatly disturbed; neighboring or rival States had suffered too much; the rancor and distrust provoked by the invading revolutionary republic were too active; these would have lasted a long time against pacified France even after she had concluded reasonable treaties. Even should she abandon a policy of propaganda and interference, return brilliant acquisitions, cease the domination of protectorates, and abandon the disguised annexation of Italy, Holland, and Switzerland, the nation was still bound to keep watch under arms. A government able to concentrate all its forces - that is to say, placed above and beyond all dispute and promptly obeyed-was indispensable, if only to remain intact and complete, to keep Belgium and the frontier of the Rhine. - Likewise internally, and for no other purpose than to restore civil order; for here, too, the outrages of the Revolution had been too great. There had been too much spoliation, too many imprisonments, exiles, and murders, too many violations of every kind, too many invasions of the rights of property and of persons, public and private. It was so much more difficult

* To insure respect for persons and all private and public possessions;
* to restrain at once both Royalists and Jacobins;

* to restore 140,000 émigrés to their country and yet satisfy 1,200,000 possessors of national property;
* to give back to 25,000,000 of orthodox Catholics the right, faculty, and means for worshipping, and yet not allow the schismatic clergy to be maltreated;
* to bring face to face in the same commune the dispossessed seigneur and the peasant holders of his domain;
* to compel the delegates of the Committee of Public Safety and their victims, the shooters and the shot of Vendémiaire, the Fructidorians and the Fructidorized, the Whites and the Blues of La Vendée and Brittany, to live in peace side by side,

because the future laborers in this immense work, from the village mayor to the state-senator and state-councilor, had borne a part in the Revolution, either in effecting it or under subjection to it - Monarchists, Feuillantists, Girondists, Montagnards, Thermidorians, moderate Jacobins or desperate Jacobins, all oppressed in turn and disappointed in their calculations. Their passions, under this régime, had become embittered; each brought personal bias and resentment into the performance of his duties; to prevent him from being unjust and mischievous demanded a tightened curb. [3] All sense of conviction, under this régime, had died out; no body would serve gratis as in 1789; [4] nobody would work without pay; disinterestedness had lost all charm; ostentatious zeal seemed hypocrisy; genuine zeal seemed self- dupery; each looked out for himself and not for the community; public spirit had yielded to indifference, to egotism, and to the need of security, of enjoyment, and of self-advancement. Human materials, deteriorated by the Revolution, were less than ever suited to providing citizens - they simply furnished functionaries. With such wheels combined together according to formula current between 1791 and 1795, the requisite work could not possibly be done. As a consequence, definitely and for a long time, any use of the two great liberal mechanisms were doomed. So long as the wheels remained of such poor quality and the task so hard, both the election of local powers and the division of the central power had to be abandoned.

IV.

Motives for suppressing the election of local powers. - The Electors. - Their egoism and partiality. - The Elected. - Their inertia, corruption, and disobedience.

All were agreed on the first point. If any still doubted, they had only to open their eyes, fix them on the local authorities, watch them as soon as born, and follow them throughout the exercise of their functions. - Naturally, in filling each office, the electors had chosen a man of their own species and caliber; their fixed and dominant disposition was accordingly well known; they were indifferent to public matters and therefore their candidate was as indifferent as themselves. Had they shown too great a concern for the nation this would have prevented their election; the State to them was a troublesome moralist and remote creditor. Their candidate must choose between them and this intruder, side with them against it, and not act as a pedagogue in its name or as bailiff on its behalf. When power is born on the spot and conferred to-day by constituents who are to submit to it to-morrow as subordinates, they do not put the whip in the hands of one who will flog them; they demand sentiments of him in conformity with their inclinations; in any event they will not tolerate in him the opposite ones. From the beginning, this resemblance between them and him is great, and it goes on increasing from day to day because the creature is always in the hands of his creators; subject to their daily pressure, he at last becomes as they are; after a certain period they have shaped him in their image. - Thus the candidate-elect, from the start or very soon after, became a confederate with his electors. At one time, and this occurred frequently, especially in the towns, he had been elected by a violent sectarian minority; he then subordinated general interests to the interests of a clique. At another, and especially in the rural districts, he had been elected by an ignorant and brutal majority, when he accordingly subordinated general interests to those of a village. - If he chanced to be conscientious and somewhat intelligent and was anxious to do his duty, he could not; he felt himself weak and was felt to be weak; [5] both authority and the means for exercising it were wanting in him. He had not the force which a power above communicates to its delegates below; nobody saw behind him the government and the army; his only resource was a national-guard, which either shirked or refused to do its duty, and which often did not exist at all. - On the contrary, he could prevaricate, pillage, and persecute for his own advantage and that of his clique with impunity; for there was no restraint on him from above; the Paris Jacobins would not be disposed to alienate the Jacobins of the province; they were partisans and allies, and the government had few others; it was bound to retain them, to let them intrigue and embezzle at will.

Suppose an extensive domain of which the steward is appointed, not by the absent owner, but by his tenants, debtors, farmers, and dependents: the reader may imagine whether rents will be paid and debts collected, whether road-taxes will be worked out, what care will be taken of the property, what its annual income will be to the owner, how abuses of commission and omission will be multiplied indefinitely, how great the disorder will be, the neglect, the waste, the fraud, the injustice, and the license. - The same in France, [6] and for the same reason:

* every public service disorganized, destroyed, or perverted;
* no justice, no police;
* authorities abstaining from prosecution, magistrates not daring to condemn, a gendarmerie which receives no orders or which stands still;
* rural marauding become a habit;
* roving bands of brigands in forty-five departments;
* mail wagons and coaches stopped and pillaged even up to the environs of Paris;
* highways broken up and rendered impassable;
* open smuggling, customs yielding nothing, national forests devastated, the public treasury empty, [7] its revenues intercepted and expended before being deposited, taxes decreed and not collected;
* everywhere arbitrary assessments of real and personal estate, no less wicked exemptions than overcharges;
* in many places no list prepared for tax assessments,
* communes which here and there, under pretext of defending the republic against neighboring consumers, exempt themselves from both tax and conscription;
* conscripts to whom their mayor gives false certificates of infirmity and marriage, who do not turn out when ordered out, who desert by hundreds on the way to headquarters, who form mobs and use guns in defending themselves against the troops, -

such were the fruits of the system.

The government could not constrain rural majorities with the officials chosen by the selfish and inept rural majorities. Neither could it repress the urban minorities with agents elected by the same partial and corrupt urban minorities. Hands are necessary, and hands as firm as tenacious, to seize conscripts by the collar, to rummage the pockets of taxpayers, and the State did not have such hands. They were required right away, if only to prepare and provide for urgent needs. If the western departments had to be subdued and tranquilized, relief furnished to Massena besieged in Genoa, Mélas prevented from invading Provence, Moreau's army transported over the Rhine, the first thing was to restore to the central government the appointment of local authorities.

V. Reasons for centralization.

Reasons for placing the executive central power in one hand. -
Sieyès' chimerical combinations. - Bonaparte's objections.

On this second point, the evidence was scarcely less. - And clearly,
the moment the local powers owed their appointment to the central
powers, it is plain that the central executive power, on which they
depend, should be unique. For, this great team of functionaries,
driven from aloft, could not have aloft several distinct drivers; being
several and distinct, the drivers would each pull his own way, while
the horses, pulling in opposite directions, would do nothing but
prance. In this respect the combinations of Sieyès do not bear
examination. A mere theorist and charged with preparing the plan of
a new constitution, he had reasoned as if the drivers on the box were
not men, but robots: perched above all, a grand-elector, a show
sovereign, with two places to dispose of and always passive, except
to appoint or revoke two active sovereigns, the two governing
consuls. One, a peace-consul, appointing all civil officers, and the
other a war-consul, making all military and diplomatic
appointments; each with his own ministers, his own council of state,
his own court of judicature. All these functionaries, ministers,
consuls, and the grand-elector himself, were revocable at the will of a
senate which from day to day could absorb them, that is to say, make
them senators with a salary of 30,000 francs and an embroidered
dress-coat. [8] Sieyès evidently had not taken into account either the
work to be done or the men who would have to do it, while
Bonaparte, who was doing the work at this very time, who
understood men and who understood himself, at once put his finger
on the weak spot of this complex mechanism, so badly adjusted and
so frail. Two consuls, [9] "one controlling the ministers of justice, of
the interior, of the police, of the treasury, and the other the ministers
of war, of the navy, and of foreign affairs. " The conflict between
them is certain; look at them facing each other, subject to contrary
influences and suggestions: around the former "only judges,
administrators, financiers, and men in long robes, " and round the
latter "only epaulets and men of the sword. " Certainly "one will
need money and recruits for his army which the other will not grant.
" - And it is not your grand-elector who will make them agree. "If he
conforms strictly to the functions which you assign to him he will be
the mere ghost, the fleshless phantom of a roi fainéant. Do you know
any man vile enough to take part in such contrivances? How can you

imagine any man of talent or at all honorable contentedly playing the part of a hog fattening himself on a few millions? " - And all the more because if he wants to abandon his part the door stands open. "Were I the grand-elector I would say to the war-consul and to the peace-consul on appointing them, If you put in a minister or sign a bill I don't like I'll put you out. " Thus does the grand-elector become an active, absolute monarch.

"But, " you may say, "the senate in its turn will absorb the grand-elector. " - " The remedy is worse than the disease; nobody, according to this plan, has any guarantees, " and each, therefore, will try to secure them to himself, the grand-elector against the senate, the consuls against the grand-elector, and the senate against the grand- elector and consuls combined, each uneasy, alarmed, threatened, threatening, and usurping to protect himself; these are the wheels which work the wrong way, in a machine constantly getting out of order, stopping, and finally breaking down entirely.

Thereupon, and as Bonaparte, moreover, was already master, all the executive powers were reduced to one, and this power was vested in him. [10] In reality, "to humor republican opinion"[11] they gave him two associates with the same title as his own; but they were appointed only for show, simply as consulting, inferior, and docile registrars, with no rights save that of signing their names after his and putting their signatures to the procès verbal declaring his orders; he alone commanded, "he alone had the say, he alone appointed to all offices, " so that they were already subjects as he alone was already the sovereign.

VI. Irreconcilable divisions.

Difficulty of organizing a legislative power. - Fraudulent and violent elections for ten years. - Spirit and diffusion of hatred against the men and dogmas of the Revolution. - Probable composition of a freely elected Assembly. - Its two irreconcilable divisions. - Sentiments of the army. - Proximity and probable meaning of a new coup d'État.

It remained to frame a legislative power as a counterpoise to this executive power, so concentrated and so strong. - In organized and tolerably sound communities this point is reached through an elective parliament which represents the public will; it represents this because it is a copy, a faithful reduction of that will on a small scale; it is so organized as to present a loyal and proportionate expression of diverse controlling opinions. In this case, the electoral selection has worked well; one superior right, that of election, has been respected, or, in other words, the passions excited have not proved too strong, which is owing to the most important interests not having proved too divergent. - Unfortunately, in France, rent asunder and discordant, all the most important interests were in sharp antagonism; the passions brought into play, consequently, were furious; no right was respected, and least of all that of election; hence the electoral test worked badly, and no elected parliament was or could be a veritable expression of the public will. Since 1791, the elections, violated and deserted, had brought intruders only to the legislative benches, under the name of mandatories. These were endured for lack of better; but nobody had any confidence in them, and nobody showed them any deference. People knew how they had been elected and how little their title was worth. Through inertness, fear, or disgust, the great majority of electors had not voted, while the voters at the polls fought among themselves, the strongest or least scrupulous expelling or constraining the rest. During the last three years of the Directory the electoral assembly was often divided; each faction elected its own deputy and protested against the election of the other. The government then chose between the two candidates elected, arbitrarily and always with barefaced partiality; and again, if but one candidate was elected, and that one an adversary, his election was invalidated. In sum, for nine years, the legislative body, imposed on the nation by a faction, was scarcely more legitimate than the executive power, another usurper, and which, later on, filled up or purged its ranks. Any remedy for this defect in the electoral machine was impossible; it was due to its internal structure, to the very quality of its materials. At this date, even under an impartial and strong government, the machine could not have answered its purpose, that of deriving from the nation a body of sober-minded and respected delegates, providing France with a parliament capable of playing its own part, or any part whatever, in the conduct of public business.

For, suppose

* that the new governors show uncommon loyalty, energy, and vigilance, remarkable political abnegation and administrative omnipresence,
* that the factions are contained without suppression of free speech,
* the central powers neutral yet active,
* no official candidature,
* no pressure from above,
* no constraint from below,
* the police-commissioners respectful and gendarmes protecting the entrance to every electoral assembly,
* all proceedings regular, no disturbance inside, voting perfectly free, the electors numerous, five or six millions of Frenchmen gathered at the polls,

and guess what choice they will make.

After Fructidor, there is a renewal of religious persecution and of excessive civil oppression; the brutality and unworthiness of the rulers have doubled and diffused hatred against the men and the ideas of the Revolution. - In Belgium, recently annexed, the regular and secular clergy had just been proscribed in a mass, [12] and a great rural insurrection had broken out. The uprising had spread from the Waes country and the ancient seignory of Malines, around Louvain as far as Tirlemont, and afterward to Brussels, to Campine, to South Brabant, to Flanders, to Luxembourg, in the Ardennes, and even to the frontiers of Liège; many villages had to be burned, and many of their inhabitants killed, and the survivors keep this in mind. In the twelve western departments, [13] at the beginning of the year 1800, the royalists were masters of nearly the whole country and had control of forty thousand armed men in regimental order; undoubtedly these were to be overcome and disarmed, but they were not to be deprived of their opinions, as of their guns. - In the month of August, 1799, [14] sixteen thousand insurgents in Haute

Garonne and the six neighboring departments, led by Count de Paulo, had unfurled the royal white flag; one of the cantons, Cadours, "had risen almost entirely; " a certain town, Muret, sent all its able-bodied men. They had penetrated even to the outskirts of Toulouse, and several engagements, including a pitched battle, were necessary to subdue them. On one occasion, at Montréjean, 2000 were slain or drowned. The peasants fought with fury, " a fury that bordered on frenzy; " "some were heard to exclaim with their last breath, 'Vive le Roi! ' and others were cut to pieces rather than shout, 'Vive la République! '" - From Marseilles to Lyons the revolt lasted five years on both banks of the Rh'ne, under the form of brigandage; the royalist bands, increased by refractory conscripts and favored by the inhabitants whom they spared, killed or pillaged the agents of the republic and the buyers of national possessions. [15] There were thus, in more than thirty departments, intermittent and scattered Vendées. In all the Catholic departments there was a latent Vendée. Had the elections been free during this state of exasperation it is probable that one-half of France would have voted for men of the ancient régime - Catholics, Royalists, or, at least, the Monarchists of 1790.

Let the reader imagine facing this party, in the same chamber, about an equal number of representatives elected by the other party; the only ones it could select, its notables, that is to say, the survivors of preceding assemblies, probably Constitutionalists of the year IV and the year V, Conventionalists of the Plain and of the Feuillants of 1792, from Lafayette and Dumolard to Daunou, Thibaudeau and Grégoire, among them Girondists and a few Montagnards, Barère, [16] with others, all of them wedded to the theory the same as their adversaries to traditions. To one who is familiar with the two groups, behold two inimical doctrines confronting each other; two irreconcilable systems of opinions and passions, two contradictory modes of conceiving sovereignty, law, society, the State, property, religion, the Church, the ancient régime, the Revolution, the present and the past; it is civil war transferred from the nation to the parliament. Certainly the Right would like to see the First Consul a Monck, which would lead to his becoming a Cromwell; for his power depends entirely on his credit with the army, then the sovereign force; at this date the army is still republican, at least in feeling if not intelligently, imbued with Jacobin prejudices, attached to revolutionary interests, and hence blindly hostile to aristocrats, kings, and priests. [17] At the first threat of a monarchical and Catholic restoration it will demand of him an eighteenth Fructidor];

otherwise, some Jacobin general, Jourdan, Bernadotte, or Augereau, will make one without him, against him, and they fall back into the rut from which they wished to escape, into the fatal circle of revolutions and coups d'état.

VII. Establishment of a new Dictatorship.

The electoral and legislative combinations of Sieyès. - Bonaparte's use of them. - Paralysis and submission of the three legislative bodies. - The Senate as the ruler's tool. -Senatus-consultes and Plebiscites. - Final establishment of the Dictatorship. - Its dangers and necessity. - Public power now able to do its work.

Sieyès comprehended this: he detects on the horizon the two specters which, for ten years, have haunted all the governments of France, legal anarchy and unstable despotism; he has found a magic formula with which to exorcise these two phantoms; henceforth "power is to come from above and confidence from below. "[19] - Consequently, the new constitutional act withdraws from the nation the right to elect its deputies; it will simply elect candidates to the deputation and through three degrees of election, one above the other; thus, it is to take part in the choice of its candidates only through "an illusory and metaphysical participation. "[20] The right of the electors of the first degree is wholly reduced to designating one-tenth among themselves; the right of those of the second degree is also reduced to designating one-tenth among themselves; the right of those of the third degree is finally reduced to designating one-tenth of their number, about six thousand candidates. On this list, the government itself, by right and by way of increasing the number, inscribes its own high functionaries; evidently, on such a long list, it will have no difficulty in finding men who, as simple tools, will be devoted to it. Through another excess of precaution, the government, on its sole authority, in the absence of any list, alone names the first legislature. Last of all, it is careful to attach handsome salaries to these legislative offices, 10,000 f., 15,000 f., and 30,000 f. a year; parties canvass with it for these places the very first day, the future depositaries of legislative power being, to begin with, solicitors of the antechamber. - To render their docility complete, there is a dismemberment of this legislative power in advance; it is divided among three bodies, born feeble and passive by institution. Neither of these has any initiative; their deliberations are confined to laws proposed by the government. Each possesses only a fragment of function; the "Tribunat" discusses without passing laws, the "Corps Législatif" decrees without discussion, the conservative" Sénat" is to maintain this general paralysis. "What do you want? " said Bonaparte to Lafayette. [21] "Sieyès everywhere put nothing but ghosts, the ghost of a legislative power, the ghost of a judiciary, the ghost of a government.

Something substantial had to be put in their place. Ma foi, I put it there, " in the executive power.

There it is, completely in his hands; other authorities to him are merely for show or as instruments. [22] The mutes of the Corps Législatif come annually to Paris to keep silent for four months; one day he will forget to convoke them, and nobody will remark their absence. - As to the Tribunat, which talks too much, he will at first reduce its words to a minimum "by putting it on the diet of laws; " afterward, through the interposition of the senate, which designates retiring members, he gets rid of troublesome babblers; finally, and always through the interposition of the senate, titular interpreter, guardian, and reformer of the constitution, he ventilates and then suppresses the Tribunat itself. - The senate is the grand instrument by which he reigns; he commands it to furnish the senatus-consultes of which he has need. Through this comedy played by him above, and through another complementary comedy which he plays below, the plebiscite, he transforms his ten-year consulate into a consulate for life, and then into an empire, that is to say, into a permanent, legal, full, and perfect dictatorship. In this way the nation is handed over to the absolutism of a man who, being a man, cannot fail to think of his own interest before all others. It remains to be seen how far and for how long a time this interest, as he comprehends it, or imagines it, will accord with the interest of the public. All the better for France should this accord prove complete and permanent; all the worse for France should it prove partial and temporary. It is a terrible risk, but inevitable. There is no escape from anarchy except through despotism, with the chance of encountering in one man, at first a savior and then a destroyer, with the certainty of henceforth belonging to an unknown will fashioned by genius and good sense, or by imagination and egoism, in a soul fiery and disturbed by the temptations of absolute power, by success and universal adulation, in a despot responsible to no one but himself, in a conqueror condemned by the impulses of conquest to regard himself and the world under a light growing falser and falser.

Such are the bitter fruits of social dissolution: the authority of the state will either perish or become perverted; each uses it for his own purposes, and nobody is disposed to entrust it to an external arbitrator, and the usurpers who seize it only remain trustee on condition that they abuse it; when it works in their hands it is only to work against its office. It must be accepted when, for want of better or fear of worse, through a final usurpation, it falls into the only hands able to restore it, organize it, and apply it at last to the service of the public.

Notes:

[1] "The Revolution, " and following pages, also and following pages. The provisions of the constitution of the year III, somewhat less anarchical, are analogous; those of the "Mountain" constitution (year II) are so anarchical that nobody thought of enforcing them.

[2] "The Revolution, " vol. III.

[3] Sauzay, "Histoire de la persecution révolutionnaire dans le département du Doubs, " X., 472 (Speech of Briot to the five-hundred, Aug. 29, 1799): "The country seeks in vain for its children; it finds the chouans, the Jacobins, the moderates, and the constitutionalists of '91 and '93, clubbists, the amnestied, fanatics, scissionists and antiscissionists; in vain does it call for republicans. "

[4] "The Revolution, " III., 427, 474. - Rocquain, "L'état de la France au 18 Brumaire, " 360, 362: "Inertia or absence of the national agents. .. It would be painful to think that a lack of salary was one of the causes of the difficulty in establishing municipal administrations. In 1790, 1791, and 1792, we found our fellow-citizens emulously striving after these gratuitous offices and even proud of the disinterestedness which the law prescribed. " (Report of the Directory, end of 1795.) After this date public spirit is extinguished, stifled by the Reign of Terror. - Ibid., 368, 369: "Deplorable indifference for public offices. . .. Out of seven town officials appointed in the commune of Laval, only one accepted, and that one the least capable. It is the same in the other communes. " - Ibid., 380 (Report of the year VII): "General decline of public spirit. " - Ibid., 287 (Report by Lacuée, on the 1st military division, Aisne, Eure-et-Loire, Loiret, Oise, Seine, Seine-et-Marne, (year IX): "Public spirit is dying out and is even gone. "

[5] Rocquain, Ibid., (Report of François de Nantes, on the 8th military division, Vaucluse, Bouches-du-Rh'ne, Var, Basses-Alpes, and Alpes-Maratimes, year IX): "Witnesses, in some communes, did not dare furnish testimony, and, in all, the justices of the peace were afraid of making enemies and of not being re-elected. It was the same with the town officials charged with prosecutions and whom their quality as elected and temporary officials always rendered timid. " - Ibid., 48:

"All the customs-directors complained of the partiality of the courts. I have myself examined several cases in which the courts of Marseilles and Toulon decided against the plain text the law and with criminal partiality. - Archives nationales, series F7, Reports "on the situation, on the spirit of the public, " in many hundreds of towns, cantons, and departments, from the year III to the year VIII and after.

[6] Cf. "The Revolution, " III., book IX., ch. I. - Rocquain, passim. - Schmidt, "Tableaux de la Révolution française, " III., parts 9 and 10. - Archives nationales, F7, 3250 (Letter of the commissioner of the executive directory, Fructidor 23, year VII): "Armed mobs on the road between Saint-Omer and Arras have dared fire on the diligences and rescue from the gendarmerie the drawn conscripts. " - Ibid., F7, 6565. Only on Seine-inferiure, of which the following are some of the reports of the gendarmerie for one year. - Messidor, year VII, seditious mobs of conscripts and others in the cantons of Motteville and Doudeville. "What shows the perverted spirit of the communes of Gremonville and of Héronville is that none of the inhabitants will make any declaration, while it is impossible that they should not have been in the rebels' secrets. " - Similar mobs in the communes of Guerville, Millebose, and in the forest of Eu: "It is stated that they have leaders, and that drilling goes on under their orders. - Vendémiaire 27, year VIII.) "Twenty-five armed brigands or drafted men in the cantons of Réauté and Bolbec have put farmers to ransom. " - (Niv'se 12~ year VIII.) In the canton of Cuny another band of brigands do the same thing. - (Germinal 14, year VIII.) Twelve brigands stop the diligence between Neufchatel and Rouen; a few days after, the diligence between Rouen and Paris is stopped and three of the escort are killed. - Analogous scenes and mobs in the other departments.

[7] "Souvenirs", by PASQUIER (Etienne-Dennis, duc), Librarie Plon, Paris 1893. I., 260. Under the Directory, " one day, in order to dispatch a special courier, the receipts of the Opera had to be taken because they were in coin. Another day, it was on the point of sending every gold piece in the musée of medals to be melted down (worth in the crucible from 5000 to 6000 francs). "

[8] "Théorie constitutionnelle de Sieyès. " (Extract from unpublished memoirs by Boulay de la Meurthe.) Paris, 1866, Renouard.

[9] "Correspondance de Napoleon 1er, " XXX.. 345. ("Mémoires. ") - "Mémorial de Sainte-Hélène

[10] "Extrait des Mémoires" de Boulay de la Meurthe, p. 50. (Words of Bonaparte to Roederer about Sieyès, who raised objections and wanted to retire.) "If Sieyès goes into the country, draw up for me at once the plan of a constitution. I will summon the primary assemblies in a week and make them accept it after discharging the (Constituant) committees. "

[11] "Correspondance de Napoléon 1er" XXX., 345, 346. ("Mémoires.") "Circumstances were such as to still make it necessary to disguise the unique magistracy of the president. "

[12] The Revolution, " III., 458, 417. - " Mercure britannique, " nos. for November 1798 and January 1799. (Letters from Belgium.) - " More than 300 millions have been seized by force in these desolated provinces; there is not a landowner whose fortune has not been ruined, or sequestrated, or fatally sapped by forced levies and the flood of taxes which followed these, by robberies of movable property and the bankruptcy due to France having discredited claims on the emperor and on the governments, in short through confiscation. " - The insurrection breaks out, as in Vendée, on account of the conscription; the war-cry of the insurgents is, "Better die here than elsewhere. "

[13] De Martel, "Les Historiens fantaisistes, " part 2 (on the Pacification of the West, according to reports of the royalist leaders and of the republican generals).

[14] Archives nationales, F7, 3218. (Summary of dispatches arranged according to dates. -Letters of Adjutant-General Vicose, Fructidor 3, year VII. - Letters of Lamagdelaine, commissioner of the executive Directory, Thermidor 26 and Fructidor 3, year VII.) - " The rascals who led the people astray had promised them, in the King's name, that they should not be called on for further taxes, that the conscripts and requisitionnaires should not leave, and, finally, that they should have the priests they wanted. " - Near Montréjean "the carnage was frightful, nearly 2000 men slain or drowned and 1000 prisoners. " - (Letter of M. Alquier to the first consul, Pluvi'se 18, year VIII.) "The insurrection of Thermidor caused the loss of 3000 cultivators. - (Letters of the department administrators and of the government commissioners, Niv'se 25 and 27, Pluvi'se 13, 15, 25, 27, and 30, year

VIII.) - The insurrection is prolonged through a vast number of isolated outrages, with sabers or guns, against republican functionaries and partisans, justices of the peace, mayors, etc. In the commune of Balbèze, fifty conscripts, armed deserters with their knapsacks, impose requisitions, give balls on Sunday, and make patriots give up their arms. Elsewhere, this or that known patriot is assaulted in his house by a band of ten or a dozen young folks who make him pay a ransom, shout "Vive le Roi! " etc. - Cf. "Histoire de l' insurrection royaliste de l'an VII, " by B. Lavigne, 1887.

[15] Archives nationales, F7, 3273 (Letter of the commissioner of the executive Directory, Vaucluse, Fructidor 6, year VII.): "Eighty armed royalists have carried off, near the forest of Suze, the cash-box of the collector, Bouchet, in the name of Louis XVIII. These rascals, it must be noted, did not take any of the money belonging to the collector himself. " - (Ibid., Thermidor 3, year VII.) "On looking around among our communes I find all of them under the control of royalist or town-councillors. That is the spirit of the peasants generally. . .. Public spirit it so perverted, so opposed to the constitutional regime, that a miracle only will bring them within the pale of freedom. " - Ibid., F7, 3199. (Similar documents on the department of Bouches-du-Rh'ne.) Outrages continue here far down into the consulate, in spite of the vigor and multitude of military executions. - (Letter of the sub-prefect of Tarascon, Germinal 15, year IX.) "In the commune of Eyragues, yesterday, at eight o'clock, a band of masked brigands surrounded the mayor's house, while some of them entered it and shot this public functionary without anybody daring to render him any assistance. ... Three-quarters of the inhabitants of Eyragues are royalists. "- In series F7, 7152 and those following may be found an enumeration of political crimes classified by department and by the month, especially for Messidor, year VII.

[16] Barère, representative of Hautes Pyrénées, had preserved a good deal of credit in this remote department, especially in the district of Argeles, with populations which knew nothing about the "Mountain. " In 1805, the electors presented him as a candidate for the legislative body and the senate; in 1815, they elected him deputy.

[17] "Souvenirs", by PASQUIER (Etienne-Dennis, duc), chancelier de France. in VI volumes, Librarie Plon, Paris 1893. I., 158. At the time the concordat was under consideration the aversion to " priest rule" was very great in the army; there were secret meetings held against it. Many of the superior officers took part in them, and even some of

the leading generals. Moreau was aware of them although he did not attend them. In one of these gatherings, things were carried far enough to resolve upon the assassination of the first consul. A certain Donnadieu, then of a low rank in the army, offered to strike the blow. General Oudinot, who was present, informed Davoust, and Donnadieu, imprisoned in the Temple, made revelations. Measures were at once taken to scatter the conspirators, who were all sent away more or less farther off; some were arrested and others exiled, among them General Mounier, who had commanded one of Desaix's brigades at Marengo. General Lecourbe was also one of the conspirators.

[19] "Extrait des Mémoires de Boulay de la Meurthe, ".

[20] Napoleon's words. ("Correspondance, " XXX., 343, memoirs dictated at Saint Helena.)

[21] Lafayette, " Mémoires, "II., 192.

[22] Pelet de la Lozère, " Opinions de Napoléon au conseil d'état, " "The senate is mistaken if it thinks it possesses a national and representative chamber. It is merely a constituted authority emanating from the government like the others. " - Ibid., P. 147: " It must not be in the power of a legislative body to impede government by refusing taxes; once the taxes are established they should be levied by simple decrees. The court of cassation regards my decrees as laws; otherwise, there would be no government. " (January 9, 1808.) - Ibid., p. 147: " If I ever had any fear of the senate I had only to put fifty young state-councillors into it. " (December 1, 1803.) - Ibid., p. 150: "If an opposition should spring up in the legislative corps I would fall back on the senate to prorogue, change it, or break it up. " (March 29, 1806.) - Ibid.: "Sixty legislators go out every year which one does not know what to do with; those who do not get places go and grumble in the departments. I should like to have old land-owners married, in a certain sense, to the state through their family or profession, attached by some tie to the commonwealth. Such men would come to Paris annually, converse with the emperor in his own circle, and be contented with this little bit of vanity relieving the monotony of their existence. " (Same date.) - Cf. Thibaudeau, "Mémoires sur le Consulat, " ch. XIII., and M. de Metternich, "Mémoires, " I., 120 (Words of Napoleon at Dresden, in the spring of 1812): "I shall give the senate and the council of state a new organization. The former will take the place of the upper

chamber, the latter that of the chamber of deputies. I shall continue to appoint the senators; I shall have the state councillors elected one-third at a time on triple lists; the rest I will appoint. Here will the budget be prepared and the laws elaborated. " - We see the corps législatif, docile as it is, still worrying him, and very justly; he foresaw the session of 1813.

CHAPTER II.

I.

Principal service rendered by the public power. - It is an instrumentality. - A common law for every instrumentality. - Mechanical instruments. - Physiological instruments. - Social instruments. - The perfection of an instrument increases with the convergence of its effects.

What is the service which the public power renders to the public? - The principal one is the protection of the community against the foreigner, and of private individuals against each other. - Evidently, to do this, it must in all cases be provided with indispensable means, namely: diplomats, an army, a fleet, arsenals, civil and criminal courts, prisons, a police, taxation and tax-collectors, a hierarchy of agents and local supervisors, who, each in his place and attending to his special duty, will co-operate in securing the desired effect. - Evidently, again, to apply all these instruments, the public power must have, according to the case, this or that form or constitution, this or that degree of impulse and energy: according to the nature and gravity of external or internal danger, it is proper that it should be concentrated or divided, emancipated from control or under control, authoritative or liberal. No indignation need be cherished beforehand against its mechanism. Strictly speaking, it is a vast piece appliance in the human community, such as a machine in a factory or such as organ in the human body. If this organ is the only on that can carry out the task, let us accept it and its structure: whoever wants the end wants the means. All we can ask is that the means shall be adapted to the end; in other terms, that the myriad of large or small local or central pieces shall be determined, adjusted, and coordinated in view of the final and total effect to which they co-operate nearly or remotely.

But, whether simple or compound, every engine which does any work is subject to one condition; the better it is suited to any distinct purpose the less it is suited to other purposes; as its perfection increases, so does its application become limited. - Accordingly, if there are two distinct instruments applied to two distinct objects, the more perfect they are, each of its kind, the more do their domains become circumscribed and opposed to each other; as one of them becomes more capable of doing its own work it becomes more incapable of doing the work of the other; finally, neither can take the place of the other, and this is true whatever the instrument may be, mechanical, physiological, or social.

At the very lowest grade of human industry the savage possesses but one tool; with his cutting or pointed bit of stone he kills, breaks, splits, bores, saws, and carves; the instrument suffices, in the main, for all sorts of services. After this come the lance, the hatchet, the hammer, the punch, the saw, the knife, each adapted to a distinct purpose and less efficacious outside of that purpose: one cannot saw well with a knife, and one cuts badly with a saw. Later, highly-perfected engines appear, and, wholly special, the sewing-machine and the typewriter: it is impossible to sew with the typewriter or write with the sewing-machine. - In like manner, when at the lowest round of the organic ladder the animal is simply a shapeless jelly, homogeneous and viscous, all parts of it are equally suited to all functions; the amoebae, indifferently and by all the cells of its body, can walk, seize, swallow, digest, breathe, and circulate all its fluids, expel its waste, and propagate its species. A little higher up, in fresh-water polyp, the internal sac which digests and the outer skin which serves to envelop it can, if absolutely necessary, change their functions; if you turn the animal inside out like a glove it continues to live; its skin, become internal, fulfills the office of a stomach; its stomach, become external, fulfills the office of an envelope. But, the higher we ascend, the more do the organs, complicated by the division and subdivision of labor, diverge, each to its own side, and refuse to take each other's place. The heart, with the mammal, is only good for impelling the blood, while the lungs only furnish the blood with oxygen; one cannot possibly do the work of the other; between the two domains the special structure of the former and the special structure of the latter interpose an impassable barrier. - In like manner, finally, at the very bottom of the social scale - lower down than the Andamans and the Fuegians - we find a primitive stage of humanity in which society consists wholly of a herd. In this herd there is no distinct association in view of a distinct purpose; there is not even a family - no permanent tie between male and female; there is simply a contact of the sexes. Gradually, in this herd of individuals, all equal and all alike, particular groups define themselves, take shape, and separate: we see appearing more and more precise relationships, more and more distinct habitations, more and more hereditary homesteads, fishing, hunting, and war groups, and small workshops; if the people is a conquering people, castes establish themselves. At length, we find in this expanded and solidly- organized social body provinces, communes, churches, hospitals, schools, corporate bodies and associations of every species and dimension, temporary or permanent, voluntary or involuntary, in brief, a multitude of social engines constructed out of human beings who, on account of personal interest, habit, and constraint, or through inclination, conscience, and generosity, co-operate according to a public or tacit statute in effecting in the material or spiritual order of things this or that determinate undertaking. In France, to- day, there are, besides the State, eighty-six departments, thirty-six thousand communes, four church bodies, forty thousand parishes, seven or eight millions of families, millions of agricultural, industrial, and commercial establishments, hundreds of institutions of science and art, thousands of educational and charitable institutions, benevolent and mutual-aid societies, and others for business or for pleasure by tens and hundreds and thousands, in short, innumerable associations of every kind, each with a purpose of its own, and, like a tool or a special organ, carrying out a distinct work.

Now, each of these associations so far as it is a tool or an organ is subject to the same law; the better it is in one direction, the more mediocre it is in other directions; its special competency constitutes its general incompetence. This is why, among developed nations, no specialized organization can replace another in a satisfactory manner. "An academy of painting which should also be a bank would, in all probability, exhibit very bad pictures and discount very bad bills. A gas company which should also be a kindergarten would, we expect, light the streets poorly and teach the children badly. " [1] And the reason is that an instrument, whatever it may be, a mechanical tool, or physiological organ, or human association, is always a system of pieces whose effects converge to a given end; it matters little whether the pieces are bits of wood and metal, as in the tool, cells and fibers, as in the organ, souls and understandings, as in the association; the essential thing is the convergence of their effects; for the more convergent these effects, the more efficient is the instrument in the realization of its end. But, through this convergence, it takes one direction exclusively and cannot take any other; it cannot operate at once in two different senses; it cannot possibly turn to the right and at the same time turn to the left. If any social instrument devised for a special service is made to act additionally for another, it will perform its own office badly as well the one it usurps. Of the two works executed by it, the first injures the second and the second injures the first one. The end, ordinarily, is the sacrifice of one to the other, and, most frequently, the failure of both.

II. Abusive Government Intervention.

Application of this law to the public power. - General effect of its intervention.

Let us follow out the effects of this law when it is the public power which, beyond its principal and peculiar task, undertakes a different task and puts itself in the place of corporate bodies to do their work; when the State, not content with protecting the community and individuals against external or internal oppression, takes upon itself additionally the government of churches, education, or charity, the direction of art, science, and of commercial, agricultural, municipal, or domestic affairs. - Undoubtedly, it can intervene in all corporate bodies other than itself; it has both the right and the duty to interfere; it is bound to do this through its very office as defender of persons and property, to repress in these bodies spoliation and oppression, to compel in them the observance of the primordial statute, charter, or contract, to maintain in the them rights of each member fixed by this statute, to decide according to this statute all conflicts which may arise between administrators and the administrated, between directors and stockholders, between pastors and parishioners, between deceased founders and their living successors. In doing this, it affords them its tribunals, its constables, and its gendarmes, and it affords these to them only with full consent after having looking into and accepted the statute. This, too, is one of the obligations of its office: its mandate hinders it from placing the public power at the service of despoiling and oppressive enterprises; it is interdicted from authorizing a contract for prostitution or slavery, and above all, for the best of reasons, a society for brigandage and insurrections, an armed league, or ready to arm itself, against the community, or a part of the community, or against itself. - But, between this legitimate intervention which enables it to maintain rights, and the abusive interference by which it usurps rights, the limit is visible and it oversteps this limit when, to its function of justiciary, it adds a second, that of governing or supporting another corporation. In this case two series of abuses unfold themselves; on the one side, the State acts contrary to its primary office, and, on the other, it discharges the duties of its superadded office badly. [2]

III. The State attacks persons and property.

It acts against its function. Its encroachments are attacks on persons and property.

For, in the first place, to govern another corporate body, for example the Church, the State at one time appoints its ecclesiastical heads, as under the old monarchy after the abolition of the Pragmatic Sanction by the Concordat of 1516; at another, as with the Constituent Assembly in 1791, without appointing its heads, it invents a new mode of appointment by imposing on the Church a discipline contrary to its spirit and even to its dogmas. Sometimes it goes further still and reduces a special body into a mere administrative branch, transforming its heads into revocable functionaries whose acts it orders and directs; such under the Empire as well as under the Restoration, were the mayor and common-councilors in a commune, and the professors and head-masters of the University. One step more and the invasion is complete: naturally, either through ambition or precaution, or through theory or prejudice, on undertaking a new service it is tempted to reserve to itself or delegate its monopoly. Before 1789 there existed one of these monopolies to the advantage of the Catholic Church, through the interdiction of other cults, also another to the advantage of each corporation of "Arts et Métiers, " through the interdiction of free labor; after 1800, there existed one for the benefit of the University through all sorts of shackles and constraints imposed on the establishment and maintenance of private schools. - Now, through each of these constraints the State encroaches on the domain of the individual; the more extended its encroachments the more does it prey upon and reduce the circle of spontaneous initiation and of independent action, which constitute the true life of the individual; if, in conformity with the Jacobin program, it pushes its interference to the end, it absorbs in itself all other lives; [3] henceforth, the community consists only of automata maneuvered from above, infinitely small residues of men, passive, mutilated, and, so to say, dead souls; the State, instituted to preserve persons, has reduced them to nonentities.

The effect is the same with property when the State supports other organizations than its own. For, to maintain these, it has no other funds than those of the taxpayers; consequently, using its collectors, it takes the money out of their pockets; all, indiscriminately, willingly or not, pay supplementary taxes for supplementary services, whether this service benefits them or is repugnant to them. If I am a Protestant in a Catholic State, or a Catholic in a Protestant State, I pay for religion which seems wrong to me and for a Church which seems to me mischievous. If I am a skeptic, a free-thinker, indifferent or hostile to positive religions in France, I pay to-day for the support of four cults which I regard as useless or pernicious. If I am a provincial or a peasant, I pay for maintaining an "Opéra" which I never attend and for a "Sèvres" and "Gobelins" of which I never see a vase or a piece of tapestry. - In times of tranquility the extortion is covered up, but in troubled times it is nakedly apparent. Under the revolutionary government, bands of collectors armed with pikes made raids on villages as in conquered countries; [4] the farmer, collared and kept down by blows from the butt end of a musket, sees his grain taken from his barn and his cattle from their stable; "all scampered off on the road to the town; " while around Paris, within a radius of forty leagues, the departments fasted in order that the capital might be fed. With gentler formalities, under a regular government, a similar extortion occurs when the State, employing a respectable collector in uniform, takes from our purse a crown too much for an office outside of its competency. If, as with the Jacobin State, it claims all offices, it empties the purse entirely; instituted for the conservation of property, it confiscates the whole of it. - Thus, with property, as with persons, when the state proposes to itself another purpose than the preservation of these, not only does it overstep its mandate but it acts contrary to its mandate.

IV. Abuse of State powers.

It badly fills the office of the bodies it supplant. - Cases in which it usurps their powers and refuses to be their substitute. - Cases in which it violates or profits by their mechanism. - In all cases it is bad or mediocre substitute. - Reasons derived from its structure compared with that of other bodies.

Let us consider the other series of abuses, and the way in which the State performs the service of the corporate bodies it supplants.

In the first place there is a chance that, sooner or later, it will shirk this work, for this new service is more or less costly, and, sooner or later, it seems too costly. - Undoubtedly the State has promised to defray expenses; sometimes even, like the Constituent and Legislative assemblies, the revenues for this having been confiscated, it has to furnish an equivalent; it is bound by contract to make good the local or special sources of revenue which it has appropriated or dried up, to furnish in exchange a supply of water from the grand central reservoir, the public treasury. - But if water becomes low in this reservoir, if the taxes in arrears stop the regular supply, if a war happens to open a large breach in it, if the prodigality and incapacity of the rulers, multiply its fissures and leaks, then there is no money on hand for accessory and secondary services. The State, which has adopted this service drops it: we have seen under the Convention and the Directory how, having taken the property of all corporations, provinces, and communes, of institutions of education, art, and science, of churches, hospitals, and asylums, it performed their functions; how, after having been a despoiler and a robber, it became insolvent and bankrupt; how its usurpation and bankruptcy ruined and then destroyed all other services; how, through the double effect of its intervention and desertion, it annihilated in France education, worship, and charity; why the streets in the towns were no longer lighted nor swept; why, in the provinces, roads went to decay, and dikes crumbled; why schools and churches stood empty or were closed; why, in the asylum and in the hospital, foundlings died for lack of milk, the infirm for lack of clothing and food, and the sick for lack of broth, medicines, and beds. [5]

In the second place, even when the State respects a service or provides the means for it, there is a chance that it will pervert this simply because it comes under its direction. - When rulers lay their hands on an institution it is almost always for the purpose of making something out of it for their own advantage and to its detriment: they render everything subordinate to their interests or theories, they put some essential piece or wheel out of shape or place; they derange its action and put the mechanism out of order; they make use of it as a fiscal, electoral, or doctrinal engine, as a reigning or sectarian instrument. - Such, in the eighteenth century, was the ecclesiastical staff with which we are familiar, [6] court bishops, drawing-room abbés imposed from above on their diocese or their abbey, non-residents, charged with functions which they do not fulfill, largely-paid idlers, parasites of the Church, and, besides all this, worldly, gallant, often unbelievers, strange leaders of a Christian clergy and which, one would say, were expressly selected to undermine Catholic faith in the minds of their flocks, or monastic discipline in their convents. - Such, in 1791, [7] is the new constitutional clergy, schismatic, excommunicated, interlopers, imposed on the orthodox majority to say masses which they deem sacrilegious and to administer sacraments which they refuse to accept.

In the last place, even when the rulers do not subordinate the interests of the institution to their passions, to their theories, or to their own interests, even when they avoid mutilating it and changing its nature, even when they loyally fulfill, as well as they know how, the supererogatory (distributive) mandate which they have adjudged to themselves, they infallibly fulfill it badly, at least worse than the special and spontaneous bodies for which they substitute themselves, for the structure of these bodies and the structure of the state are different. - Unique of its kind, alone wielding the sword, acting from above and afar by authority and constraints, the State acts over the entire territory through uniform laws, through imperative and minute regulations, by a hierarchy of obedient functionaries, which it maintains under strict instructions. Hence, it is not adapted to business which, to be well done, needs springs and processes of another species. Its springs, wholly exterior, are insufficient, too weak to support and push undertakings which require an internal motor like private interest, local patriotism, family affections, scientific curiosity, charitable instincts, and religious faith. Its wholly mechanical processes, too rigid and too limited, cannot urge on enterprises which demand of whoever undertakes them delicate and safe handling, supple manipulation, appreciation of circumstances, ready adaptation of means to ends, constant contrivance, the initiative, and perfect independence. On this account the State is a poor head of a family, a poor commercial or agricultural leader, a bad distributor of labor and of subsistence, a bad regulator of production, exchanges, and consumption, a mediocre administrator of the province and the commune, an undiscerning philanthropist, an incompetent director of the fine arts, of science, of instruction, and of worship. [8] In all these offices its action is either dilatory or bungling, according to routine or oppressive, always expensive, of little effect and feeble in returns, and always beyond or apart from the real wants it pretends to satisfy. The reason is that it starts from too high a point therefore extending over too vast a field. Transmitted by hierarchical procedures, it lags along in formalism, and loses itself in "red- tape. " On attaining its end and object it applies the same program to all territories alike a program devised beforehand in the Cabinet, all of a piece, without experimental groping and the necessary corrections;

* a program which, calculated approximately according to the average and the customary, is not exactly suited to any particular case;
* a program which imposes its fixed uniformity on things instead of adjusting itself to its diversity and change;
* a sort of model coat, obligatory in pattern and stuff, which the government dispatches by thousands from the center to the provinces, to be worn, willingly or not, by figures of all sizes and at all seasons.

V. Final Results of Abusive Government Intervention

Other consequences. - Suppressed or stunted bodies cease to grow. - Individuals become socially and politically incapable. - The hands into which public power then falls. - Impoverishment and degradation of the social body.

And much worse. Not only does the State do the work badly on a domain not its own, roughly, at greater cost, and with smaller yield than spontaneous organizations, but, again, through the legal monopoly which it deems its prerogative, or through its unfair competition, it kills and paralyzes these natural organizations or prevents their birth; and hence so many precious organs, which, absorbed, curbed or abandoned, are lost to the great social body. - And still worse, if this system lasts, and continues to crush them out, the human community loses the faculty of reproducing them; entirely extirpated, they do not grow again; even their germ has perished. Individuals no longer know how to form associations, how to co-operate under their own impulses, through their own initiative, free of outside and superior constraint, all together and for a long time in view of a definite purpose, according to regular forms under freely-chosen chiefs, frankly accepted and faithfully followed. Mutual confidence, respect for the law, loyalty, voluntary subordination, foresight, moderation, patience, perseverance, practical good sense, every disposition of head and heart, with which no association of any kind is efficacious or even viable, have died out for lack of exercise. Henceforth spontaneous, pacific, and fruitful co-operation, as practiced by a free people, is unattainable; men have arrived at social incapacity and, consequently, at political incapacity. - In fact they no longer choose their own constitution or their own rulers; they put with these, willingly or not, according as accident or usurpation furnishes them: now the public power belongs to the man, the faction, or the party sufficiently unscrupulous, sufficiently daring, sufficiently violent, to seize and hold on to it by force, to make the most of it as an egotist or charlatan, aided by parades and prestige, along with bravura songs and the usual din of ready-made phrases on the rights of Man and the public salvation. - This central power itself has in its hands no body who might give it an impetus and inspiration, it rules only over an impoverished, inert, or languid social body, solely capable of intermittent spasms or of artificial rigidity according to order, an organism deprived of its secondary organs, simplified to excess, of an inferior or degraded kind, a people no longer anything but an arithmetical sum of separate, unconnected units, in brief, human dust or mud. - This is what the interference of the State leads to.

There are laws in the social and moral world as in the physiological and physical world; we may misunderstand them, but we cannot elude them; they operate now against us, now for us, as we please, but always alike and without heeding us; it is for us to heed them; for the two conditions they couple together are inseparable; the moment the first appears the second inevitably follows.

Notes:

[1] Macaulay, "Essays: Gladstone on Church and State. " - This principle, of capital importance and of remarkable fecundity, may be called the principle of specialties. Adam Smith fist applied it to machines and to workmen. Macaulay extended it to human associations. Milne-Edwards applied it to the entire series of animal organs. Herbert Spencer largely develops it in connection with physiological organs and human societies in his "Principles of Biology" and "Principles of Sociology. " I have attempted here to show the three parallel branches of its consequences, and, again, their common root, a constitutive and primordial property inherent in every instrumentality.

[2] Cf. "The Revolution, " III., book VI., ch. 2 The encroachments of the State and their effect on individuals is there treated. Here, the question is their effects on corporations. Read, on the same subject, "Gladstone on Church and State, " by Macaulay, and "The Man versus the State, " by Herbert Spencer, two essays in which the close reasoning and abundance of illustrations are admirable.

[3] "The Revolution, " III, 346. (Laffont II.)

[4] Ibid., III. 284 Laff. 213.

[5] "The Revolution, " III., 353, 416. (Laffont II. notes pp 262 and 305 to 308.)

[6] "The Ancient Régime, " 64, 65, 76, 77, 120, 121, 292. (Laffont I.)

[7] "The Revolution, " I., 177 and following pages. (Laffont I,

[8] The essays of Herbert Spencer furnish examples for England under the title of "Over-legislation and Representative government." Examples for France may be found in "Liberté du Travail, " by Charles Dunoyer (1845). This work anticipates most of the ideas of Herbert Spencer, lacking only the physiological "illustrations. "

CHAPTER III. The New Government Organization.

I. Precedents of the new organization. - In practical operation. - Anterior usurpations of the public power. - Spontaneous bodies under the Ancient Regime and during the Revolution. - Ruin and discredit of their supports. - The central power their sole surviving dependence. -

Unfortunately, in France at the end of the eighteenth century the bent was taken and the wrong bent. For three centuries and more the public power had increasingly violated and discredited spontaneous bodies:

Sometimes it had mutilated them and decapitated them; for example, it had suppressed provincial governments (états) over three-quarters of the territory, in all the electoral districts; nothing remained of the old province but its name and an administrative circumscription.

Sometimes, without mutilating the corporate body it had upset and deformed it, or dislocated and disjointed it. - So that in the towns, through changes made in old democratic constitutions, through restrictions put upon electoral rights and repeated sales of municipal offices, [1] it had handed over municipal authority to a narrow oligarchy of bourgeois families, privileged at the expense of the taxpayer, half separated from the main body of the public, disliked by the lower classes, and no longer supported by the confidence or deference of the community. And in the parish and in the rural canton, it had taken away from the noble his office of resident protector and hereditary patron, reducing him to the odious position of a mere creditor, and, if he were a man of the court, to the yet worse position of an absentee creditor. [2] - So that in the parish and in the rural canton, it had taken away from the noble his office of resident protector and hereditary patron, reducing him to the odious position of a mere creditor, and, if he were a man of the court, to the yet worse position of an absentee creditor. [3] Thus, as to the clergy, it had almost separated the head from the trunk by superposing (through the concordat) a staff of gentleman prelates, rich, ostentatious, unemployed, and skeptical, upon an army of plain, poor, laborious, and believing curates. [4]

Finally, it had, through a protection as untimely as it was aggressive, sometimes conferred on the corporation oppressive privileges which rendered it offensive and mischievous, or else fossilized in an obsolete form which paralyzed its action or corrupted its service. Such was the case with the corporations of crafts and industries to which, in consideration of financial aid, it had conceded monopolies onerous to the consumer and a clog on industrial enterprises. Such was the case with the Catholic Church to which, every five years, it granted, in exchange for its voluntary gift (of money), cruel favors or obnoxious prerogatives, the prolonged persecution of Protestants, the censorship of intellectual speculation, and the right of controlling schools and education. [5] Such was the case with the universities benumbed by routine; with latest provincial "Ètats, " constituted in 1789, as in 1489. Such was the case with noble families subjected by law to the antique system of substitutions and of primogeniture, that is to say, to social constraint which, devised long ago for private as well as for public interest in order to secure the transmission of local patronage and political power. This system, however, became useless and corrupting, fecund in pernicious vanities, [6] in detestable calculations, domestic tyrannies, forced vocations, and private bickering, from the time when the nobles, become frequenters of the court, had lost political power and renounced local patronage.

Thus deprived of, or diverted from, their purpose, the corporate bodies had become unrecognizable under the crust of the abuses which disfigured them. Nobody, except a Montesquieu, could comprehend why they should exist; on the approach of the Revolution, they seemed, not organs, but outgrowths, deformities, and, so to say, superannuated monstrosities. Their historical and natural roots, their living germs far below the surface, their social necessity, their fundamental utility, their possible usefulness, were no longer visible. Only their present inconvenience was felt; people suffered by their friction and burden; their lack of harmony and incoherence created dissatisfaction; annoyance due to their degeneracy were attributed to radical defects; they were judged to be naturally unsound and were condemned, in principle, because of the deviations and laws which the public power had imposed on their development.

Suddenly, the public power, which had produced the evil by its intervention, pretended to remove it by a still greater intervention: in 1789 it again intruded itself on corporate bodies, not to reform them, not restore each to its proper channel, not to confine each with proper limits, but to destroy them outright. Through a radical, universal, and extraordinary amputation, the like of which is not mentioned in history, with the rashness of the theorist and the brutality of the butcher, the legislator extirpated them all, as far as he could, even including the family, while his fury extended beyond the present into the future. To legal abolition and total confiscation, he added the systematic hostility of his preventive laws, together with a fresh obstacle in the shape of his new constructions; during three successive legislatures[7] he provided against their future regeneration, against the permanent instincts and necessities which might one day resuscitate stable families, distinct provinces, and an orthodox church, against artistic, industrial, financial, charitable, and educational corporations, against every spontaneous and organized group, and against every collective, local, or special enterprise. In place of these he installed synthetic bodies or institutions:

* a Church without believers,
* schools without pupils,
* hospitals without incomes,
* a geometrical hierarchy of improvised powers in the commune, district, and department,

all badly organized, badly adjusted, out of gear at the start, overwhelmed with political functions, as incapable of performing their proper duties as their supplementary duties, and, from the very beginning, either powerless or mischievous. [8] Changes repeatedly marred by arbitrariness from above or from below, set aside or perverted now by the mob and again by the government, inert in the country, oppressive in the towns, we have seen the state into which they had fallen at the end of the Directory; how, instead of a refuge for liberty, they had become haunts of tyranny or sinks of egoism; why, in 1800, they were as much decried as their predecessors in 1788, why their two successive props, the old one and the most recent, historic custom and popular election, were now discredited and no longer resorted to. - After the disastrous experience of the monarchy and the still worse experience of the republic, another prop had to be sought for; but only one remained, that of the central power, the only one visible and which seemed substantial; in default of others they had recourse to this. [9] In any event, no protestation, even secret and moral, any longer prevented the State from attaching other corporate bodies to itself, in order to use them for its own purposes as instruments or appendages.

II. Doctrines of Government.

The theory. - Agreement of speculative ideas with practical necessities. - Public rights under the Ancient Regime. - The King's three original rights. - Labors of the jurists in extending royal prerogatives. - Historical impediments. - The primitive or ulterior limits of royal power. - The philosophic and revolutionary principle of popular sovereignty. - Unlimited extension of State power. - Application to spontaneous bodies. - Convergence of ancient and new doctrines. - Corporations considered as creations of the public power. - Centralization through the universal intervention of the State.

The theory here agreed with the need, and not alone the recent theory, but again the ancient theory. Long before 1789, public right had elevated the prerogative of centralized power into a dogma and exaggerated it beyond measure.

There are three titles under which this power was conferred. - Feudal seignior, and suzerain, that is to say, commander-in-chief of the great resident army whose willing forces had served to reconstruct society in the ninth century, the King, through the remotest of his origins - that is to say, through the immemorial confusion of sovereignty with property - was the owner of France, the same as an individual owns his private domain. [10] - Married, moreover, to the Church since the first Capets, consecrated and crowned at Rheims, anointed by God like a second David, [11] not only was he believed to be authorized from on high, like other monarchs, but, from Louis le Gros, and especially after the time of saint Louis, he appeared as the delegate from on high, invested with a laic sacerdotalism, clothed with moral power, minister of eternal justice, redresser of wrongs, protector of the weak, benefactor of the humble - in short, "His Most Christian Majesty. " - At length, after the thirteenth century, the recent discovery and diligent study of the ancient codes of Justinian had shown in his person the successor of the Caesars of Rome and of the Emperors of Constantinople. According to these codes the people in a body had transferred its rights to the prince; now, in antique cities, all rights were vested in the community, and the individual had none; [12] accordingly, through this transfer, all rights, public or private, passed into the hands of the prince; henceforth he could exercise them as he pleased, under no restriction and no control. He was above the law, since he made it; his powers were illimitable and his decision absolute. [13]

On this triple frame the jurists, like State spiders, had, from Philippe le Bel down, spun their web, and the instinctive concordance of their hereditary efforts had attached all its threads to the omnipotence of the King. - Being jurisconsults - that is to say, logicians - they were obliged to deduce, and their minds naturally recurred to the unique and rigid principle to which they might attach their arguments. - As advocates and councilors of the crown they espoused the case of their client and, through professional zeal, derived or forced precedents and texts to his advantage. - By virtue of being administrators and judges the grandeur of their master constituted their grandeur, and personal interest counseled them to expand a prerogative in which, through delegation, they took part. - Hence, during four centuries, they had spun the tissue of "regalian rights, " the great net in the meshes of which, since Louis XIV., all lives found themselves caught. [14]

Nevertheless, however tightly spun was the web, there were openings in it, or, at least, very weak spots. - And first, of the consequences flowing from these three principles in their hands, two of them had hindered the third from unwinding its skein to the end: owing to the fact that the King was formerly Count de Paris and Abbot of St. Denis, he could not become a veritable Augustus, an authentic Diocletian: his two French titles limited his Roman title. Without regard to the laws, so-called fundamental, which imposed his heir on him beforehand, also the entire line of his successive heirs, the tutor, male or female, of his minor heir, and which, if he derogated from immemorial usage, annulled his will like that of a private individual, his quality of suzerain and that of Most Christian, were for him a double impediment. As hereditary general of the feudal army he was bound to consider and respect the hereditary officers of the same army, his old peers and companions in arms - that is to say, the nobles. As outside bishop, he owed to the Church not alone his spiritual orthodoxy, but, again, his temporal esteem, his active zeal, and the aid furnished him by his secular arm. Hence, in applied right, the numerous privileges of the nobles and the Church, so many immunities and even liberties, so many remains of antique local independence, and even of antique local sovereignty, [15] so many prerogatives, honorific or serviceable, maintained by the law and by the tribunals. On this side, the meshes of the monarchical netting had not been well knit or remained loose; and the same elsewhere, with openings more or less wide, in the five provincial governments (états), in the Pyrenees districts, in Alsace, at Strasbourg, but especially in Languedoc and in Brittany, where the pact of incorporation, through a sort of bilateral contract, associated together on the same parchment and under the same seal the franchises of the province and the sovereignty of the King.

Add to these original lacunae the hole made by the Prince himself in his net already woven: he had with his own hand torn away its meshes, and by thousands. Extravagant to excess and always needy, he converted everything into money, even his own rights, and, in the military order, in the civil order, in commerce and in industry, in the administration, in the judicature, and in the finances. From one end of the territory to the other, he had sold innumerable offices, imposts, dignities, honors, monopolies, exemptions, survivorships, expectancies - in brief, privileges which, once conferred for a money consideration, became legal property, [16] often hereditary and transmissible by the individual or the corporation which had paid for them. In this way the King alienated a portion of his royalty for the benefit of the buyer. Now, in 1789, he had alienated a great many of these portions; accordingly, his present authority was everywhere restricted by the use he had previously made of it. - Sovereignty, thus, in his hands had suffered from the double effect of its historic origins and its historic exercise; the public power had not become, or had ceased to be, omnipotence. On the one hand it had not reached its plenitude, and on the other hand it had deprived itself of a portion of its own completeness.

The philosophers wished to find a solution for this double weakness, innate and acquired They had therefore transported sovereignty out of history into the ideal and abstract world, with an imaginary city of mankind reduced to the minimum of a human being Here men, infinitely simplified, all alike, equal, separate from their surroundings and from their past, veritable puppets, were all lifting their hands in common rectangular motion to vote unanimously for the contrat social. In this contract "all classes are reduced to one, [17] the complete surrender of each associate, with all his rights, to the community, each giving himself up entirely, just as he actually is, himself and all his forces, of which whatever he possesses forms a part, " each becoming with respect to himself and every act of his private life a delegate of the State, a responsible clerk, in short, a functionary, a functionary of the people, henceforth the unique, the absolute, and the universal sovereign. A terrible principle, proclaimed and applied for ten years, below by the mob and above by the government! Popular opinion had adopted it; accordingly the passage from the sovereignty of the King to the sovereignty of the people was easy, smooth, [18] and to the novice in reasoning, the old-fashioned taxable and workable subject, to whom the principle conferred a portion of the sovereignty, the temptation was too great.

At once, according to their custom, the jurists put themselves at the service of the new reign. And no dogma was better suited their to authoritative instinct; no axiom furnished them so convenient a fulcrum on which to set up and turn their logical wheel. This wheel, which they had latterly managed with care and caution under the ancient Régime, had suddenly in their hands turned with frightful speed and effect in order to convert the rigid, universal, and applied laws, the intermittent processes, the theoretical pretensions, and the worst precedents of the monarchy into practice. This meant

* the use of extraordinary commissions,
* accusations of lésé majesté,
* the suppression of legal formalities,
* the persecution of religious beliefs and of personal opinions,
* the right of condemning publications and of coercing thought,
* the right of instruction and education,
* the rights of pre-emption, of requisition, of confiscation, and of proscription,

in short, pure and perfect arbitrariness. The result is visible in the deeds of Treilhard, of Berlier, of Merlin de Douai, of Cambacérès, in those of the Constituant and Legislative Assemblies, in the Convention, under the Directory, in their Jacobin zeal or hypocrisy, in their talent for combining despotic tradition with tyrannical innovation, in their professional skill in fabricating on all occasions a snare of plausible arguments with which to properly strangle the individual, their adversary, to the profit of the State, their eternal master.

In effect, not only had they almost strangled their adversary, but likewise, through an aftereffect, their master: France which, after fourteen months of suffocation, was approaching physical suicide. [19] Such success, too great, had obliged them to stop; they had abandoned one-half of their destructive creed, retaining only the other half, the effect of which, less imminent, was less apparent. If they no longer dared paralyze individual acts in the man, they persisted in paralyzing in the individual all collective acts. - There must be no special associations in general society; no corporations within the State, especially no spontaneous bodies endowed with the initiative, proprietary and permanent: such is Article II. of the Revolutionary Creed, and the direct consequence of the previous one which posits axiomatically the sovereignty of the people and the omnipotence of the State. Rousseau, [20] inventor of the first, had like-wise enunciated the second; the constituent assembly had solemnly decreed it and applied it on a grand scale, [21] and successive assemblies had applied it on a still grander scale; [22] it was a faith with the Jacobins, and, besides, in conformity with the spirit of Roman imperial right and with the leading maxim of French monarchical right. On this point the three known jurisprudential systems were in accord, while their convergence brought together around the same table the jurists of the three doctrines in a common task, ex-parliamentarians and ex-members of the Committee of Public Safety, former pro-scribers and the proscribed, the purveyors of Sinamari with Treilhard and Merlin de Douai, returned from Guiana, alongside of Simeon, Portalis, and Barbé- Marbois. There was nobody in this conclave to maintain the rights of spontaneous bodies; the theory, on all three sides, no matter from whom it proceeded, refused to recognize them for what they are originally and essentially, that is to say, distinct organisms equally natural with the State, equally indispensable in their way, and, therefore, as legitimate as itself; it allowed them only a life on trust, derived from above and from the center. But, since the State created them, it might and ought to treat them as its creatures, keep them indefinitely under its thumb, use them for its purposes, act through them as through other agencies, and transform their chiefs into functionaries of the central power.

III. Brilliant Statesman and Administrator.

The Organizer. - Influence of Napoleon's character and mind on his internal and French system. - Exigencies of his external and European r'le. - Suppression of all centers of combination and concord. - Extension of the public domain and what it embraces. - Reasons for maintaining the private domain. - The part of the individual. - His reserved enclosure. - Outlets for him beyond that. - His talents are enlisted in the service of public power. - Special aptitude and temporary vigor, lack of balance, and doubtful future of the social body thus formed.

A new France, not the chimerical, communistic, equalized, and Spartan France of Robespierre and Saint-Just, but a possible real, durable, and yet leveled and uniform France, logically struck out at one blow, all of a piece, according to one general principle, a France, centralized, administrative, and, save the petty egoistic play of individuals, managed in one entire body from top to bottom, - in short, the France which Richelieu and Louis XIV. had longed for, which Mirabeau after 1790 had foreseen, [23] is now the work which the theories of the monarchy and of the Revolution had prepared, and toward which the final concurrence of events, that is to say, "the alliance of philosophy and the saber, " led the sovereign hands of the First Consul.

Accordingly, considering his well-known character, the promptitude, the activity, the reach, the universality, and the cast of his intellect, he could not have proposed to himself a different work nor reduced himself to a lower standard. His need of governing and of administrating was too great; his capacity for governing and administrating was too great: his was an exacting genius. - Moreover, for the outward task that he undertook he required internally, not only undisputed possession of all executive and legislative powers, not only perfect obedience from all legal authorities, but, again, the annihilation of all moral authority but his own, that is to say, the silence of public opinion and the isolation of each individual, and therefore the abolition, preventive and systematic, of any religious, ecclesiastic, pedagogic, charitable, literary, departmental, or communal initiative that might, now or in the future gather men against him or alongside of him. Like a good general he secures his rear. At strife with all Europe, he so arranges it as not to allow in the France he drags along after him refractory souls or bodies which might form platoons in his rear. Consequently, and through precaution, he suppresses in advance all eventual rallying points or centers of combination Henceforth, every wire which can stir up and bring a company of men together for the same object terminates in his hands; he holds in his firm grasp all these combined wires, guards them with jealous care, in order to strain them to the utmost. Let no one attempt to loosen them, and, above all, let no one entertain a thought of getting hold of them; they belong to him and to him alone, and compose the public domain, which is his domain proper.

But, alongside of his proper domain, he recognizes another in which he himself assigns a limit to the complete absorption of all wills by his own; he does not admit, of course in his own interest, that the public power, at least in the civil order of things and in common practice, should be illimitable nor, especially, arbitrary. [24] - This is due to his not being an utopian or a theorist, like his predecessors of the Convention, but a perspicacious statesman, who is in the habit of using his own eyes. He sees things directly, in themselves; he does not imagine them through book formulae or party phrases, by a process of verbal reasoning, employing the gratuitous suppositions of humanitarian optimism or the dogmatic prejudices of Jacobin nonsense. He sees Man just as he is, not Man in himself, an abstract citizen, the philosophic puppet of the Contrat Social, but the real individual, the entire living man, with his profound instincts, his tenacious necessities, which, whether tolerated or not by legislation, still subsist and operate infallibly, and which the legislator must take into consideration if he wants to turn them to account. - This individual, a civilized European and a modern Frenchman, constituted as he is by several centuries of tolerable police discipline, of respected rights and hereditary property, must have a private domain, an enclosed area, large or small, which belongs and is reserved to him personally, to which the public power interdicts access and before which it mounts guard to prevent other individuals from intruding on it. Otherwise his condition seems intolerable to him; he is no longer disposed to exert himself, to set his wits to work, or to enter upon any enterprise. Let us be careful not to snap or loosen this powerful and precious spring of action; let him continue to work, to produce, to economize, if only that he may be in a condition to pay taxes; let him continue to marry, to bring forth and raise up sons, if only to serve the conscription. Let us ease his mind with regard to his enclosure; [25] let him exercise full proprietorship over it and enjoy it exclusively; let him feel himself at home in his own house in perpetuity, safe from any intrusion, protected by the code and by the courts, not alone against his enemies, but against the administration itself. Let him in this well-defined, circumscribed abode be free to turn round and range as he pleases, free to browse at will, and, if he chooses, to consume all his hay himself. It is not essential that his meadows should be very extensive: most men live with their nose to the ground; very few look beyond a very narrow circle; men are not much troubled by being penned up; the egoism and urgent needs of daily life are already for them ready-made limits: within these natural barriers they ask for nothing but to be allowed to graze in security. Let us give them this assurance and leave them free to consult their own welfare. - As to the rest, in very small number, more or less imaginative, energetic, and ardent, there is, outside the enclosure, an issue expressly provided for them: the new administrative and military professions offer an outlet to their ambition and to their vanity which, from the start, keeps on expanding until, suddenly, the first Consul points to an infinite perspective on the horizon. [26] According to an expression attributed to him, henceforth,

"the field is open to all talents, "

and hence all talents, gathered into the central current and precipitated headlong through competition, swell with their inflow the immensity of the public power.

This done, the principal features of modern France are traced; a tool of a new and strange type arises, defines itself, and issues forth, its structure determining its destiny. It consists of a social body organized by a despot and for a despot, calculated for the use of one man, excellent for action under the impulsion of a unique will, with a superior intelligence, admirable so long as this intelligence remains lucid and this will remains healthy. It is adapted to a military life and not to civil life, and therefore badly balanced, hampered (géné) in its development, exposed to periodical crises, condemned to precocious debility, but viable for a long time, and, for the present robust, alone able to bear the weight of the new reign and to furnish for fifteen successive years the crushing labor, the conquering obedience, the superhuman, murderous, insensate effort which its master exacts.

IV. Napoleon's barracks.

General aspect and characteristics of the new State. - Contrast between its structure and that of other contemporary or pre-existing States. - The plurality, complexity, and irregularity of ancient France. - The unity, simplicity, and regularity of modern France. - To what class of works it belongs. - It is the modern masterpiece of the classic spirit in the political and social order of things.

Let us take a nearer view of the master's idea and of the way in which, at this moment, he figures to himself the society which is assuming new shape in his hands. All the leading features of the plan are fixed beforehand in his mind: they are already deeply graven on it through his education and through his instinct. By virtue of this instinct, which is despotic, by virtue of this education, which is classic and Latin, he conceives human associations not in the modern fashion, Germanic and Christian, as a concert of initiations starting from below, but in the antique fashion, pagan and Roman, as a hierarchy of authorities imposed from above. He puts his own spirit into his civil institutions, the military spirit; consequently, he constructs a huge barracks wherein, to begin with, he lodges thirty million, men, women, and children, and, later on, forty-two million, all the way from Hamburg to Rome.

The edifice is, of course, superb and of a new style. On comparing it with other societies in surrounding Europe, and particularly France as she was previous to 1789, the contrast is striking. - Everywhere else the social edifice is a composition of many distinct structures - provinces, cities, seignories, churches, universities, and corporations. Each has begun by being a more or less isolated block of buildings where, on an enclosed area, a population has lived apart. Little by little the barriers have given way; either they have been broken in or have tumbled down of their own accord; passages have been made between one and the other and new additions have been put up; at last, these scattered buildings have all become connected and soldered on as annexes to the central pile. But they combine with it only through a visible and clumsy juxtaposition, through incomplete and bizarre communications: the vestiges of their former independence are still apparent athwart their actual dependence. Each still rests on its own primitive and appropriate foundations; its grand lines subsist; its main work is often almost intact. In France, on the eve of 1789, it is easily recognized what she formerly was; for example, it is clear that Languedoc and Brittany were once sovereign States, Strasbourg a sovereign town, the Bishop of Mende and the Abbess of Remiremont, sovereign princes; [27] every seignior, laic, or ecclesiastic, was so in his own domain, and he still possessed some remnants of public power. In brief, we see thousands of states within the State, absorbed, but not assimilated, each with its own statutes, its own legal customs, its own civil law, its own weights and measures; several with special privileges and immunities; some with their own jurisdiction and their own peculiar administration, with their own imposts and tariffs like so many more or less dismantled fortresses, but whose old feudal, municipal, or provincial walls still rose lofty and thick on the soil comprehended within the national enclosure.

Nothing could be more irregular than this total aggregate thus formed; it is not really an entire whole, but an agglomeration. No plan, good or bad, has been followed out; the architecture is of ten different styles and of ten different epochs. That of the dioceses is Roman and of the fourth century; that of the seignories is Gothic and of the ninth century; one structure dates from the Capetians, another from the Valois, and each bears the character of its date. Because each has been built for itself and with no regard to the others, adapted to an urgent service according to the exigencies or requirements of time, place, and circumstance; afterward, when circumstances changed, it had to adapt itself to other services, and this constantly from century to century, under Philippe le Bel, under Louis XI., under Francis I., under Richelieu, under Louis XIV., through constant revision which never consists of entire destruction, through a series of partial demolitions and of partial reconstructions, in such a way as to maintain itself, during the transformation, in conciliating, well or ill, new demands and rooted habits, in reconciling the work of the passing generation with the works of generations gone before. - The central seignory itself is merely a donjon of the tenth century, a military tower of which the enclosure has extended so as to embrace the entire territory, and of which the other buildings, more or less incorporated with it, have become prolongations. - A similar medley of constructions - disfigured by such mutilations, adjuncts, and patches, a pell-mell so complicated with such incongruous bits and fragments - can be comprehended only by antiquaries and historians; ordinary spectators- - the public - pronounce it absurd; it finds no favor with that class of reasoners who, in social architecture as in physical architecture, repudiate disorder, posit theories, deduce consequences, and require that every work shall proceed from the application of a simple idea.

And worse still, not only is good taste offended but, again, good sense often murmurs. Practically, the edifice fails in its object, for, erected for men to dwell in, it is in many places scarcely habitable. Because it endures it is found superannuated, ill-adapted to prevailing customs; it formerly suited, and still suits, the feudal, scattered, and militant way of living; hence it no longer suits the unity and repose of modern life. New-born rights obtain no place in it alongside of established rights; it is either not sufficiently transformed or it has been transformed in an opposite sense, in such a way as to be inconvenient or unhealthy, badly accommodating people who are useful and giving good accommodations to useless people, costing too much to keep up and causing discomfort and discontent to nearly all its occupants. - In France, in particular, the best apartments, especially that of the King, are for a century past too high and too large, too sumptuous and too expensive. Since Louis XIV. these have imperceptibly ceased to be government and business bureaus; they have become in their disposition, decoration, and furnishing, saloons for pomp and conversation, the occupants of which, for lack of other employment, delight in discussing architecture and in tracing plans on paper for an imaginary edifice in which everybody will find himself comfortable. Now, underneath these, everybody finds himself uncomfortable, the bourgeoisie in its small scanty lodgings on the ground-floor and the people in their holes in the cellar, which are low and damp, wherein light and air never penetrate. Innumerable vagabonds and vagrants are still worse off, for, with no shelter or fireside, they sleep under the stars, and as they are without anything to care for, they are disposed to pull everything down. - Under the double pressure of insurrection and theory the demolition begins, while the fury of destruction goes on increasing until nothing is left of the razed edifice but the soil it stood on.

The new one rises on this cleared ground and, historically as well as structurally, it differs from all the others. - In less than ten years it springs up and is finished according to a plan which, from the first day, is definite and complete. It forms one unique, vast, monumental block, in which all branches of the service are lodged under one roof; in addition to the national and general services belonging to the public power, we find here others also, local and special, which do not belong to it, such as worship, education, charity, fine arts, literature, departmental and communal interests, each installed in a distinct compartment. All the compartments are ordered and arranged alike, forming a circle around the magnificent central apartment, with which each is in communication by a bell; as soon as the bell rings and the sound spreads from division to sub- division, the entire service, from the chief clerk down to the lowest employee, is instantly in motion; in this respect the arrangement, as regards despatch, co-ordination, exactitude, and working facilities, is admirable. [28]

On the other hand, its advantages and attractions for employees and aspirants of every kind and degree are not mediocre. There is no separation between the stories, no insurmountable barrier or enclosure between large and small apartments; all, from the least to the finest, from the outside as well as from the inside, have free access. Spacious entrances around the exterior terminate in broad, well- lighted staircases open to the public; everybody can clamber up that pleases, and to mount these one must clamber; from top to bottom there is no other communication than that which they present. There is no concealed and privileged passage, no private stairway or false door; glancing along the whole rectilinear, uniform flight, we behold the innumerable body of clerks, functionaries, supernumeraries, and postulants, an entire multitude, ranged tier beyond tier and attentive; nobody advances except at the word and in his turn. - Nowhere in Europe are human lives so well regulated, within lines of demarcation so universal, so simple, and so satisfactory to the eye and to logic: the edifice in which Frenchmen are henceforth to move and act is regular from top to bottom, in its entirety as well as in its details, outside as well as inside; its stories, one above the other, are adjusted with exact symmetry; its juxtaposed masses form pendants and counterpoise; all its lines and forms, every dimension and proportion, all its props and buttresses combine, through their mutual dependencies, to compose a harmony and to maintain an equilibrium. In this respect the structure is classic, belonging to the same family of productions which the same spirit, guided by the same method, had produced in Europe for the previous one hundred and fifty years. [29] Its analogues, in the physical order of things, are the architectural productions of Mansard, Le Notre, and their successors, from the structures and gardens of Versailles down to and embracing the Madeleine and the Rue de Rivoli. In the intellectual order, its analogues consist of the literary forms of the seventeenth and eighteenth centuries, the superb oratorical prose and correct, eloquent poetry, especially epics and tragedies, including those still manufactured according to rule about the year 1810. It corresponds to these and forms their pendant in the political and social order of things, because it emanates from the same deliberate purpose. Four constitutions, in the same style, preceded it; but these were good only on paper, while this one stands firm on the ground. For the first time in modern history we see a society due to ratiocination and, at the same time, substantial; the new France, under these two heads, is the masterpiece of the classic spirit.

V. Modeled after Rome.

Its analogue in the antique world. - The Roman State from Diocletian to Constantine. - Causes and bearing of this analogy. - Survival of the Roman idea in Napoleon's mind. - The new Empire of the West.

Nevertheless, if we go back in time, beyond modern times, beyond the Middle Ages, as far as the antique world, we encounter during the Roman emperors Diocletian's and Constantine's era another monument whose architecture, equally regular, is developed on a still grander scale: back then we are in the natal atmosphere and stand on the natal soil of the classic spirit. - At this time, the human material, more reduced and better prepared than in France, existed similarly in the requisite condition. At this date, we likewise see at work the prearranging reasoning-faculty

* which simplifies in order to deduce,
* which leaves out historic customs and local diversities,
* which considers the basic human being,
* which treats individuals as units and the people as totals,
* which forcibly applies its general outlines to all special lives, and
* which glories in constituting, legislating, and administering by rule
according to the measurements of square and compass.

At this date, in effect, the turn of mind, the talent, the ways of the Roman architect, his object, his resources and his means of execution, are already those of his French successor; the conditions around him in the Roman world are equivalent; behind him in Roman history the precedents, ancient and recent, are almost the same.

In the first place, [30] there is, since emperor Augustus, the absolute monarchy, and, since the Antonines, administrative centralization the result of which is that

* all the old national and municipal communities are broken up or crushed out,
* all collective existences chilled or extinguished,
* local patriotism slowly worn away,
* an increasing diminution of individual initiative,

and, under the invasive interference, direction, and providence of the State, one hundred millions of men become more and more passive and separated from each other. [31]

And as a result, in full enjoyment of peace and internal prosperity under the appearances of union, force, and health, latent feebleness, and, as in France on the approach of 1789, a coming dissolution.

There is next, as after 1789 in France, the total collapse, not from below and among the people, but from above and through the army, a worse collapse than in France, prolonged for fifty years of anarchy, civil wars, local usurpations, ephemeral tyrannies, urban seditions, rural jacqueries, brigandage, famines, and invasions along the whole frontier, with such a ruin of agriculture and other useful activities, with such a diminution of public and private capital, with such a destruction of human lives that, in twenty years, the number of the population seems to have diminished one half. [32] There is, finally, as after 1799, in France, the re-establishment of order brought about more slowly, but by the same means, the army and a dictatorship, in the rude hands of three or four great military parvenus, Pannonians or Dalmatians, Bonapartes of Sirmium or of Scutari, they too, of a new race or of intact energy, adventurers and children of their own deeds, the last Diocletian, like Napoleon, a restorer and an innovator. Around them, as around Napoleon, to aid them in their civil undertakings, is a crowd of expert administrators and eminent jurisconsults, all practitioners, statesmen, and businessmen, and yet men of culture, logicians, and philosophers. They were imbued with the double governmental and humanitarian view, which for three centuries Greek speculation and Roman practice had introduced into minds and imaginations. This view, at once leveling and authoritative, tending to exaggerate the attributes of the State and the supreme power of the prince, [33] was nevertheless inclined

* to put natural right in the place of positive law, [34]
* to preferring equity and logic to antiquity and to custom,
* to reinstate the dignity of man among the qualities of mankind,
* to enhance the condition of the slave, of the provincial, of the debtor, of the bastard, of woman, of the child, and
* to recover for the human community all its inferior members, foreign or degraded, which the ancient constitution of the family and of the city had excluded from it.

Therefore Napoleon could find the outlines of his construction in the political, legislative, and judicial organizations extending from Diocletian to Constantine, and beyond these down to Theodosius. At the base, popular sovereignty; [35] the powers of the people delegated unconditionally to one man. This omnipotence conferred, theoretically or apparently, through the free choice of citizens, but really through the will of the army. No protection against the Prince's arbitrary edict, except a no less arbitrary rescript from the same hand. His successor designated, adopted, and qualified by himself. A senate for show, a council of state for administration; all local powers conferred from above; cities under tutelage. All subjects endowed with the showy title of citizen, and all citizens reduced to the humble condition of taxpayers and of people under control. An administration of a hundred thousand officials taking all services into its hands, comprising public instruction, public succor, and public supplies of food, together with systems of worship. This was at first pagan cults, and after Constantine, the Christian cult. All these services were classified, ranked, co-coordinated, carefully defined in such a way as not to encroach on each other, and carefully combined in such a way as to complete each other. An immense hierarchy of transferable functionaries was kept at work from above on one hundred and eighty square leagues of territory; thirty populations of different race and language-Syrians, Egyptians, Numidians, Spaniards, Gauls, Britons, Germans, Greeks, Italians - subject to the same uniform Régime. The territory was divided like a checker-board, on arithmetical and geometrical principles, into one hundred or one hundred and twenty small provinces; old nations or States dismembered and purposely cut up so as to put an end forever to natural, spontaneous, and viable groups. A minute and verified census taking place every fifteen years to correctly assign land taxes. An official and universal language; a State system of worship, and, very soon, a Church and State orthodoxy. A systematic code of laws, full and precise, admirable for the rule of private life, a sort of moral geometry in which the theorems, rigorously linked together, are attached to the definitions and axioms of abstract justice. A scale of grades, one above the other, which everybody may ascend from the first to the last; titles of nobility more and more advanced, suited to more and more advanced functions; spectabiles, illustres, clarissimi, perfectissimi, analogous to Napoleon's Barons, Counts, Dukes, and Princes. A programme of promotion once exhibiting, and on which are still seen, common soldiers, peasants, a shepherd, a barbarian, the son of a cultivator (colon), the grandson of a slave, mounting gradually upward to the highest dignities, becoming patrician, Count, Duke, commander of the cavalry, Cœsar, Augustus, and donning the imperial purple, enthroned amid the most sumptuous magnificence and the most elaborate ceremonial prostrations, a being called God during his lifetime, and after death adored as a divinity, and dead or alive, a complete divinity on earth. [36]

So colossal an edifice, so admirably adjusted, so mathematical, could not wholly perish; its hewn stones were too massive, too nicely squared; too exactly fitted, and the demolisher's hammer could not reach down to its deepest foundations. - This one, through its shaping and its structure, through its history and its duration, resembles the stone edifices which the same people at the same epoch elevated on the same soil, the aqueducts, amphitheatres, and triumphal arches, the Coliseum, the baths of Diocletian and of Caracalla.

The medieval man, using their intact foundations and their shattered fragments, built here and there, haphazard, according to the necessities of the moment, planting his Gothic towers between Corinthian columns against the panels of walls still standing. [37] But, under his incoherent masonry, he observed the beautiful forms, the precious marbles, the architectural combinations, the symmetrical taste of an anterior and superior art; he felt that his own work was rude. The new world, to all thinking minds, was miserable compared with the old one; its languages seemed a patois (crude dialect), its literature mere stammering or driveling, its law a mass of abuses or a mere routine, its feudality anarchy, and its social arrangements, disorder. - In vain had the medieval man striven to escape through all issues, by the temporal road and by the spiritual road, by the universal and absolute monarchy of the German Cesars, and by the universal and absolute monarchy of the Roman pontiffs. At the end of the fifteenth century the Emperor still possessed the golden globe, the golden crown, the scepter of Charlemagne and of Otho the Great, but, after the death of Frederick II., he was nothing more than a majesty for show; the Pope still wore the tiara, still held the pastoral staff and the keys of Gregory VII. and of Innocent III., but, after the death of Boniface VIII., he was nothing more than a majesty of the Church. Both abortive restorations had merely added ruins to ruins, while the phantom of the ancient empire alone remained erect amid so many fragments. Grand in its outlines and decorations, it stood there, august, dazzling, in a halo, the unique masterpiece of art and of reason, as the ideal form of human society.

For ten centuries this specter haunted the medieval epoch, and nowhere to such an extent as in Italy. [38]

It reappears the last time in 1800, starting up in and taking firm hold of the magnificent, benighted imagination of the great Italian, [39] to whom the opportunity afforded the means for executing the grand Italian dream of the Middle Ages; it is according to this retrospective vision that the Diocletian of Ajaccio, the Constantine of the Concordat, the Justinian of the Civil Code, the Theodosius of the Tuileries and of St. Cloud reconstructed France.

This does not mean that he copies - he restores; his conception is not plagiarism, but a case of atavism; it comes to him through the nature of his intellect and through racial traditions. In the way of social and political conceptions, as in literature and in art, his spontaneous taste is ultra-classic. We detect this in his mode of comprehending the history of France; State historians, "encouraged by the police, " must make it to order; they must trace it "from the end of Louis XIV. to the year VIII, " and their object must be to show how superior the new architecture is to the old one. [40] "The constant disturbance of the finances must be noted, the chaos of the provincial assemblies, . .. the pretensions of the parliaments, the lack of energy and order in the administration, that parti-colored France with no unity of laws or of administration, being rather a union of twenty kingdoms than one single State, so that one breathes on reaching the epoch in which people enjoy the benefits of the unity of the laws, of the administration, and of the territory. " In effect, he breathes; in thus passing from the former to the latter spectacle, he finds real intellectual pleasure; his eyes, offended with Gothic disorder, turn with relief and satisfaction to majestic simplicity and classic regularity; his eyes are those of a Latin architect brought up in the "École de Rome. "

This is so true that, outside of this style, he admits of no other. Societies of a different type seem to him absurd. He misconceives their local propriety and the historical reasons for their existence. He takes no account of their solidity. He is going to dash himself against Spain and against Russia, and he has no comprehension whatever of England. [41] -This is so true that, wherever he places his hand he applies his own social system; he imposes on annexed territories and on vassal[42] countries the same uniform arrangements, his own administrative hierarchy, his own territorial divisions and sub-divisions, his own conscription, his civil code, his constitutional and ecclesiastical system, his university, his system of equality and promotion, the entire French system, and, as far as possible, the language, literature, drama, and even the spirit of his France, - in brief, civilization as he conceives it, so that conquest becomes propaganda, and, as with his predecessors, the Cesars of Rome, he sometimes really fancies that the establishment of his universal monarchy is a great benefit to Europe.

Notes:

[1] De Tocqueville, "L'Ancien régime et la Revolution. "and following pages, also and following pages. - "The Ancient Régime, "

[2] "The Revolution, " I., book I.,. (Laffont I.)

[3] "The Ancient Regime, " Laff. I)

[4] Ibid. (Laff. I.)

[5] Ibid., (Laff. I)

[6] Cf. Frédéric Masson, "Le Marquis de Grignan, " vol. I.

[7] The Revolution, " I, and following pages; II., book VI., ch. I., especially and following pages. (Laffont I and II)

[8] Ibid., I., and following pages, and p. 226 and following pages. (Ed. Laffont. I. 449 to 452, 473 to 481.)

[9] "Souvenirs", by PASQUIER (Etienne-Dennis, duc), chancelier de France. in VI volumes, Librarie Plon, Paris 1893. I., 148 (in relation to the institution prefects and sub-prefects): "The perceptible good resulting from this change was the satisfaction arising from being delivered in one day from a herd of insignificant men, mostly without any merit or shadow of capacity and to who the administration of department and arrondissement had been surrendered for the past ten years. As nearly all of them sprung from the lowest ranks in society, they were only the more disposed to make the weight of their authority felt. "

[10] Guyot, "Répertoire de jurisprudence" (1785), article King: "It is a maxim of feudal law that the veritable ownership of lands, the domain, directum dominium, is vested in the dominant seignior or

suzerain. The domain in use, belonging to the vassal or tenant, affords him really no right except to its produce. "

[11] Luchaire, " Histoire des institutions monarchiques de la France sous les premiers Capétiens, " I., 28, 46. (Texts of Henry I., Philip I., Louis VI., and Louis VII.) "A divine minister. " - (Kings are) "servants of the kingdom of God. " - "Gird on the ecclesiastical sword for the punishment of the wicked. " - " Kings and priests alone, by ecclesiastical ordination, are made sacred by the anointing of holy oils. "

[12] "The Revolution, " III., p. 94. (Laffont II,)

[13] Janssen, "L'Allemagne à la fin du moyen âge " (French translation), I., 457. (On the introduction of Roman law into Germany.) - Declaration of the jurists at the Diet of Roncaglia: "Quod principi placuit, legis habet vigorem. " - Edict of Frederick I., 1165: "Vestigia praedecessorum suorum, divorum imperatorum, magni Constantini scilicet et Justiniani et Valentini, . .. sacras eorum leges, . .. divina oracula. . .. Quodcumque imperator constituerit, vel cognoscens decreverit, vel edicto praeceperit, legem esse constat. " - Frederick II. : "Princeps legibus solutus est. " - Louis of Bavaria: "Nos qui sumus supra jus. "

[14] Guyot, ibid., article Régales. "The great 'régales, ' majora regalia, are those which belong to the King, jure singulari et proprio, and which are incommunicable to another, considering that they cannot be divorced from the scepter, being the attributes of sovereignty, such as . .. the making of laws, the interpretation or change of these, the last appeal from the decisions of magistrates, the creation of offices, the declaration of war or of peace, . .. the coining of money, the augmentation of titles or of values, the imposition of taxes on the subjects, . .. the exemption of certain persons from these, the award of pardon for crimes, . .. the creation of nobles, the foundation of universities, . .. the assembling of the états-généraux or provinciaux, etc. " - Bossuet, "Politique tirée de l'Écriture sainte": The entire state exists in the person of the prince. " - Louis XIV., "Œuvres, " I., 50 (to his son): "You should be aware that kings can naturally dispose fully and freely of all possessions belonging as well to persons of the church as to laymen, to make use of at all times with wise economy, that is to say, according to the general requirements of their government. " - Sorel, "L'Europe et la Révolution française, " I., 231 (Letter of the "intendant" Foucault): "It is an illusion, which cannot

proceed from anything but blind preoccupation, that of making any distinction between obligations of conscience and the obedience which is due to the King. "

[15] "The Ancient Régime, " and following pages. - "Correspondance de Mirabeau et du Comte de le Marck, " II., 74 (Note by Mirabeau, July 3, 1790): "Previous to the present revolution, royal authority was incomplete: the king was compelled to humor his nobles, to treat with the parliaments,, to be prodigal of favors to the court. "

[16] "The Revolution, " III., p. 318. (Laff. II.). - " The Ancient Régime, " p. 10 (Laff. I. 25n.) Speech by the Chancellor Séguier, 1775: "Our kings have themselves declared that they are fortunately powerless to attack property. "

[17] Rousseau's text in the "Contrat Social. " - On the meaning and effect of this principle cf "The Revolution, " I., 217 and following pages, and III., book VI., ch. I. Laff. 182-186 et II. 47 to 74).

[18] The opinion, or rather the resignation which confers omnipotence on the central power, goes back to the second half of the fifteenth century, after the Hundred Years' war, and is due to that war; the omnipotence of the king was then the only refuge against the English invaders, and the ravages of the Écorcheurs. - Cf. Fortescue, "In leges Angliœ, " and" "The Difference between an Absolute and a Limited Monarchy" (end of the fifteenth century), on the difference at this date between the English and the French government. - The same decision is found in the dispatches of the Venetian ambassadors of this date: "In France everything is based on the will of the king. Nobody, whatever might be his conscientious scruples, would dare express an opinion opposed to his. The French respect their king to such an extent that they would not only sacrifice their property for him, but again their souls. " (Janssen, "L'Allemagne à la fin du moyen âge. I. 484.) - As to the passage of the monarchical to the democratic idea, we see it plainly in the following quotations from Restif de la Bretonne: "I entertained no doubt that the king could legally oblige any man to give me his wife or his daughter, and everybody in my village (Sacy in Burgundy) thought so too. " ("Monsieur Nicolas, " I., 443.) - In relation to the September massacres: "No, I do not pity them, those fanatical priests. .. When a community or its majority wants anything, it is right. The minority is always culpable, even when right morally. Common sense is that is needed to appreciate that truth. It is

indisputable that the nation has the power to sacrifice even an innocent person. " ("Nuits de Paris, " XVth, p. 377.)

[19] "The Revolution, " III., 393. (Laff. II.)

[20] "Contrat Social, " book 1st, ch. III. : "It is accordingly essential that, for the enunciation of the general will, no special organization should exist in the State, and that the opinion of each citizen should accord with that. Such was the unique and sublime law of the great Lycurgus. "

[21] "The Revolution, " I., 170. (Laff. I.)

[22] Ibid., II., 93; III., 78-82. (Laff. I and II.)

[23] "Correspondance de Mirabeau et du Comte de la Marck, "II., 74 (Letter of Mirabeau to the King, July 3, 1790): "Compare the new state of things with the ancient régime. . .. One portion of the acts of the national assembly (and that the largest) is evidently favorable to monarchical government. Is it to have nothing, then, to have no parliaments, no provincial governments, no privileged classes, no clerical bodies, no nobility? The idea of forming one body of citizens would have pleased Richelieu: this equalized surface facilitates the exercise of power. Many years of absolute rule could not have done so much for royal authority as this one year of revolution. " - Sainte-Beuve, "Port-Royal, " V., 25 (M. Harlay conversing with the supérieure of Port-Royal): "People are constantly talking about Port-Royal, about these Port-Royal gentlemen: the King dislikes whatever excites talk. Only lately he caused M. Arnaud to be informed that he did not approve of the meetings at his house; that there is no objection to his seeing all sorts of people indifferently like everybody else, but why should certain persons always be found in his rooms and such an intimate association among these gentlemen? . .. The King does not want any rallying point; a headless assemblage in a State is always dangerous. "- Ibid.,: "The reputation of this establishment was too great. People were anxious to put their children in it. Persons of rank sent theirs there. Everybody expressed satisfaction with it. This provided it with friends who joined those of the establishment and who together formed a platoon against the State. The King would not consent to this: he regarded such unions as dangerous in a State. "

[24] "Napoleon Ire et ses lois civiles, " by Honoré Pérouse, 280: Words of Napoleon: "I have for a long time given a great deal of thought and calculation to the re-establishment of the social edifice. I am to-day obliged to watch over the maintenance of public liberty. I have no idea of the French people becoming serfs. " -"The prefects are wrong in straining their authority. " - "The repose and freedom of citizens should not depend on the exaggeration or arbitrariness of a mere administrator. " - "Let authority be felt by the people as little as possible and not bear down on them needlessly. " - (Letters of January 15, 1806, March 6, 1807, January 12, 1809, to Fouché, and of March 6, 1807, to Regnault.) -Thibaudeau, "Mémoires sur le Consulat, "(Words of the first consul before the council of state): "True civil liberty depends on the security of property. In no country can the rate of the tax-payer be changed every year. A man with 3000 francs income does not know how much he will have left to live on the following year; his entire income may be absorbed by the assessment on it. .. A mere clerk, with a dash of his pen, may overcharge you thousands of francs... Nothing has ever been done in France in behalf of real estate. Whoever has a good law passed on the cadastre (official valuation of all the land in France) will deserve a statue. "

[25] Honoré Pérouse, Ibid, 274 (Speech of Napoleon to the council of state on the law on mines): " "Myself, with many armies at my disposition, I could not take possession of any one's field, for the violation of the right of property in one case would be violating it in all. The secret is to have mines become actual property, and hence sacred in fact and by law. " - Ibid., 279: " "What is the right of property? It is not only the right of using but, again, of abusing it. . .. One must always keep in mind the advantage of owning property. The best protection to the owner of property is the interest of the individual; one may always rely on his activity. . .. A government makes a great mistake in trying to be too paternal; liberty and property are both ruined by over-solicitude. " -"If the government prescribes the way in which property shall be used it no longer exists. ". - Ibid., 284 (Letters of Aug. 21 and Sept. 7, 1809, on expropriations by public authority): "It is indispensable that the courts should supervise, stop expropriation, receive complaints of and guarantee property-owners against the enterprises of our prefects, our prefecture councils and all other agents. . .. Expropriation is a judicial proceeding.. .. I cannot conceive how France can have proprietors if anybody can be deprived of his field simply by an administrative decision. " - In relation to the ownership

of mines, to the cadastre, to expropriation, and to the portion of property which a man might bequeath, Napoleon was more liberal than his jurists. Madame de Staël, "Dix années d'exil, " ch. XVIII. (Napoleon conversing with the tribune Gallois): "Liberty consists of a good civil code, while modern nations care for nothing but property. " - "Correspondance, " letter to Fouché, Jan. 15, 1805. (This letter gives a good summary of his ideas on government.) "In France, whatever is not forbidden is allowed, and nothing can be forbidden except by the laws, by the courts, or police measures in all matters relating to public order and morality. "

[26] Roederer, "Œuvres complètes, " III., 339 (Speech by the First Consul, October 21, 1800): "Rank, now, is a recompense for every faithful service - the great advantage of equality, which has converted 20,000 lieutenancies, formerly useless in relation to emulation, into the legitimate ambition and honorable reward of 400,000 soldiers. " - Lafayette, "Mémoires, " V., 350: "Under Napoleon, the soldiers said, he has been promoted King of Naples, of Holland, of Sweden, or of Spain, as formerly it was said that a than had been promoted sergeant in this or that company. "

[27] "The Ancient Régime, " book I., ch. 2, the Structure of Society, especially pp. 19-21. (Laff. I. p. 21-22)

[28] Mémorial de Sainte-Hélène" - Napoleon, speaking of his imperial organization, said that he had made the most compact government, one with the quickest circulation and the most nervous energy, that ever existed. And, he remarked, nothing but this would have answered in overcoming the immense difficulties around us, and for effecting the wonderful things we accomplished. The organization of prefectures, their action, their results, were admirable and prodigious. The same impulsion affected at the same time more than forty millions of men, and, aided by centers of local activity, the action was as rapid at every extremity as at the heart. "

[29] "The Ancient Régime, " book III., chs. 2 and 3. (Laff. I,)

[30] Gibbon, "Decline and Fall of the Roman Empire, " chs. I, 2, 3, and 13. - Duruy, Histoire des Romains" (illustrated edition), tenth period, chs. 82, 83, 84, and 85; twelfth period, chs. 95 and 99; fourteenth period, ch. 104. - (The reader will find in these two excellent works the texts and monuments indicated to which it is necessary to resort for a direct and satisfactory impression.)

[31] See in Plutarch (Principles of Political Government) the situation of a Greek city under the Antonines.

[32] Gibbon, ch. 10. - Duruy, ch. 95. (Decrease of the population of Alexandria under Gallien, according to the registers of the alimentary institution, letter of the bishop Dionysius.)

[33] "Digest, " I., 4, I. : "Quod principi placuit legis habet vigorem, utpote, cum lege regia, quœ de imperio ejus lata est, populus ei et in eum omne suum imperium et potestatem conferat. Quodcumque igitur imperator per epistolam et subscriptionem statuit, vel cognoscens decrevit, vel de plano interlocutus est, vel edicto prœcepit, legis habet vigorem. " (Extracts from Ulpian.) - Gaius, Institutes, I., 5: "Quod imperator constituit, non dubium est quin id vicem legis obtineat, quum ipse imperator per legem imperium obtineat. "

[34] "Digest, " I, 2. (Extracts from Ulpian): "Jus est a justitia appellatum; nam, ut eleganter Celsus definit, jus est ars boni et œqui. Cujus merito quis nos sacerdotes appellat: justitiam namque colimus, et boni et œqui notitiam profitemur, œquum ab iniquo separantes, licitum ab illicito discernentes, . .. veram, nisi fallor, philosophiam, non simulatam affectantes. . .. Juris prœcepta sunt hœc: honeste vivere, alterum non lœdere, suum cuique tribuere. " - cf. Duruy, 12th period, ch. 87.

[35] Cf., on this immemorial principle of the entire body of Roman public law, cf. Fustel de Coulanges, "Histoire des institutions politiques et privées de l'ancienne France, " vol. I., book II., ch. I, and following pages.

[36] Read the "Notitia dignitatum tam civilium quam militarium in partibus orientis et occidentis. " It is the imperial almanac for the beginning of the fifth century. There are eleven ministers at the centre, each with his bureaux, divisions, subdivisions and squads of superposed functionaries,

[37] Cf. Piranesi's engravings.

38 Cf., among other clues see Dante's: "De Monarchia".

[39] We can trace in Napoleon's brain and date the formation of this leading idea. At first, it is simply a classic reminiscence, as with his

contemporaries; but suddenly it takes a turn and has an environment in his mind which is lacking in theirs, and which prevents the idea from remaining a purely literary phrase. From the beginning he speaks of Rome in the fashion of a Rienzi. (Proclamation of May 20, 1796.) "We are the friends of every people, and especially of the Brutuses, the Scipios, and of the great men whom we have chosen as models. To re-establish the Capitol, to place there with honor the statues of heroes who render it famous, to arouse the Roman people benumbed by centuries of slavery, such will be the fruit of our victories. " - Fifteen months afterwards, on becoming master of Italy, his historic meditations turn into positive ambition henceforth, the possession of Italy and of the Mediterranean is to be with him a central and preponderant idea. (Letter to the Directory, Aug. 16, 1797, and correspondence on the subject of Corsica, Sardinia, Naples, and Genoa; letters to the pasha of Scutari, to the Maniotes, etc.) "The islands of Corfu, Zante, and Cephalonia are of more interest to us than all Italy put together. . .. The Turkish empire is daily tottering; the possession of these islands will enable us to support it as long as possible, or to take our portion of it. The time is not remote when we shall feel that, for the real destruction of England, we must get possession of Egypt. " Formerly, the Mediterranean was a Roman lake; it must become a French lake. (Cf. "Souvenirs d'un Sexagénaire, " by Arnault, vol. IV., on his dream, in 1798, of making Paris a colossal Rome.) - At this same date, his conception of the State is fixed and wholly Roman. (Conversations with Miot, June 1797, and letter to Talleyrand, Sep. 19, 1797.) "I do not see but one thing in fifty years well defined, and that is the sovereignty of the people. . .. The organization of the French nation is still only sketched out. . .. The power of the government, with the full latitude I give to it, should be considered as really representing the nation. " In this government, "the legislative power, without rank in the republic, deaf and blind to all around it, would not be ambitious and would no longer inundate us with a thousand chance laws, worthless on account of their absurdity. " It is evident that he describes in anticipation his future senate and legislative corps. - Repeatedly, the following year, and during the expedition into Egypt, he presents the Romans as an example to his soldiers, and views himself as a successor to Scipio and Cœsar. - (Proclamation of June 22, 1798.): "Be as tolerant to the ceremonies enjoined by the Koran as you are for the religion of Moses and Jesus. The Roman legions protected all religions. " - (Proclamation of May 10, 1798.) " The Roman legions that you have often imitated but not yet equaled fought Carthage in turn on this wall and in the vicinity of Zama. " - Carthage at this time is England: his hatred of this community of merchants which destroys his fleet at Aboukir, which forces him to raise the siege of Saint-Jean d'Acre, which holds on to Malta, which robs him of his substance, his patrimony, his Mediterranean, is that of a Roman consul against Carthage; it leads him to conquer all western Europe against her and to "resuscitate the empire of the Occident. " (Note to Otto, his ambassador at London, Oct.. 23, 1802.) - Emperor of the French, king of Italy, master of Rome, suzerain of the Pope, protector of the confederation of the Rhine, he succeeds the German emperors, the titularies of the Holy Roman Empire which has just ended in 1806; he is accordingly the heir of Charlemagne and, through Charlemagne, the heir of the ancient Cœsars. - In fact, he reproduces the work of the ancient Cœsars by analogies of imagination, situation and character, but in a different Europe, and where this posthumous reproduction can be only an anachronism.

[40] "Correspondance, " note for M. Cretet, minister of the interior, April 12, 1808.

[41] Metternich, "Mémoires, " I., 107 (Conversations with Napoleon,, 1810): "I was surprised to find that this man, so wonderfully endowed, had such completely false ideas concerning England, its vital forces and intellectual progress. He would not admit any ideas contrary to his own, and sought to explain these by prejudices which he condemned. " - Cf. Forsyth, "History of the Captivity of Napoleon at Saint-Helena, " III., 306, (False calculations of Napoleon at Saint-Helena based on his ignorance of the English parliamentary system,) and Stanislas Girardin, III., 296, (Words of the First Consul, Floreal 24, year XI, quoted above.)

[42] Cf., amongst other documents, his letter to Jerome, King of Westphalia, October 15, 1807, and the constitution he gives to that kingdom on that date, and especially titles 4 to 12: "The welfare of your people concerns me, not only through the influence it may exercise on your fame and my own, but likewise from the point of view of the general European system. . .. Individuals who have talent and are not noble must enjoy equal consideration and employment from you. . .. Let every species of serfage and of intermediary lien between the sovereign and the lowest class of people be abolished. The benefits of the code Napoleon, the publicity of proceedings, the establishment of juries, will form so many distinctive characteristics of your monarchy. " - His leading object is the suppression of feudalism, that is to say, of the great families and old historic

authorities. He relies for this especially on his civil code: "That is the great advantage of the code; . .. it is what has induced me to preach a civil code and made me decide on establishing it. " (Letter to Joseph, King of Naples, June 5, 1806.) - "The code Napoleon is adopted throughout Italy. Florence has it, and Rome will soon have it. " (Letter to Joachim, King of the Two Sicilies, Nov. 27, 1808.) - " My intention is to have the Hanseatic towns adopt the code Napoleon and be governed by it from and after the 1st of January. " - The same with Dantzic: "Insinuate gently and not by writing to the King of Bavaria, the Prince-primate, the grand-dukes of Hesse-Darmstadt and of Baden, that the civil code should be established in their states by suppressing all customary law and confining themselves wholly to the code Napoleon. " (Letter to M. de Champagny, Oct. 31, 1807.) - " The Romans gave their laws to their allies. Why should not France have its laws adopted in Holland? . .. It is equally essential that you should adopt the French monetary system. " (Letter to Louis, King of Holland, Nov. 13, 1807.) - To the Spaniards: "Your nephews will honor me as their regenerator. " (Allocution addressed to Madrid Dec. 9, 1808.) - "Spain must be French. The country must be French and the government must be French. " (Roederer, III., 529, 536, words of Napoleon, Feb. 11, 1809.) - In short, following the example of Rome, which had Latinized the entire Mediterranean coast, he wanted to render all western Europe French. The object was, as he declared, "to establish and consecrate at last the empire of reason and the full exercise, the complete enjoyment of every human faculty. " (Mémorial.)

BOOK THIRD. Object and Merits of the System.

CHAPTER I. Recovery of Social Order.

I. Rule as the mass want to be ruled.

How Napoleon comprehends the sovereignty of the people. - His maxim on the will of the majority and on the office of government. - Two groups of prominent and obvious desires in 1799.

HOWEVER clear and energetic his artistic convictions may be, his mind is absorbed by the preoccupations of the ruler: It is not enough for him that his edifice should be monumental, symmetrical, and beautiful. As he lives in it and derives the greatest benefit from it, he wants first of all that it should be fit to live in, habitable for Frenchmen of the year 1800. Consequently, he takes into account the habits and dispositions of his tenants, the pressing and permanent wants. But these needs must not be theoretic and vague, but verified and defined; for he is as accurate as he is shrewd, and deals only with positive facts.

"My political system, " says he to the Council of State, [1] "is to rule men as the mass want to be ruled. .. By constituting myself a Catholic I put an end to the war in La Vendée; by turning into a Moslem I established myself in Egypt: by turning ultramontane I gained over the priests in Italy. Were I to govern a population of Jews, I would restore the temple of Solomon. I shall speak just in this fashion about liberty in the free part of St. Domingo; I shall confirm slavery in the Ile-de-France and even in the slave section of St. Domingo, with the reservation of diminishing and limiting slavery where I maintain it, and of restoring order and keeping up discipline where I maintain freedom. I think that is the way to recognize the sovereignty of the people. "

" Now, in France, at this epoch, there are two groups of preponderant desires which evidently outweigh all others, one dating back the past ten years, and the other for a century or more: the question is how to satisfy these, and the sagacious constructor, who estimates them for what they are worth, combines to this end the proportions, plan, arrangement, and entire interior economy of his edifice.

II. The Revolution Ends.

Necessities dating from the Revolution. - Lack of security for Persons, Property, and Consciences. - Requisite conditions for the establishment of order. - End of Civil war, Brigandage, and Anarchy. - Universal relief and final security.

The first of these two needs is urgent, almost physical. For the last ten years, the government has not done its duty, or has ruled in a contrary sense. By turns or at the same time its impotence and injustice have been deplorable. It has committed or allowed too many outrages on persons, property, and consciences. All in all the Revolution did nothing else, and it is time that this should stop. Safety and security for consciences, property, and persons is the loud and unanimous outcry vibrating in all hears. [3] - To calm things down, many novelties are required: To start with, the political and administrative concentration just described, a centralization of all powers in one hand, local powers conferred by the central power, and, to exercise this supreme power a resolute chief, equal in intelligence to his high position. Next, a regularly paid army, [4] carefully equipped, properly clothed and fed, strictly disciplined and therefore obedient and able to do its duty without wavering or faltering, like any other instrument of precision. An active police force and gendarmerie kept on a tight rein. Administrators independent of those under their jurisdiction, and judges independent of those due to be tried. All appointed, maintained, watched, and restrained from above, as impartial as possible, sufficiently competent, and, in their official spheres, capable functionaries. Finally, freedom of worship, and, accordingly, a treaty with Rome and the restoration of the Catholic Church, that is to say, a legal recognition of the orthodox hierarchy and of the only clergy which the faithful may accept as legitimate, in other words, the institution of bishops by the Pope, and of priests by the bishops.

This done, the rest is easily accomplished. A well-led army corps marches along and tramples out the embers of the conflagration now kindling in the West, while religious toleration extinguishes the smoldering fires of popular insurrection. Henceforth, there is an end to civil war. [5] Regiments ready to act in harmony with the military commissions[6] purge the South and the valley of the Rh'ne; thenceforth, there are no more roving bands in the rural districts, while brigandage on a grand scale, constantly repressed, ceases, and after this, that on a small scale. No more chouans, chauffeurs, or barbets; [7] The mail-coach travels without a guard, and the highways are safe. [8] There is longer any class or category of citizens oppressed or excluded from the common law, the latest Jacobin decrees and the forced loan have been at once revoked: noble or plebeian, ecclesiastic or layman, rich or poor, former émigré or former terrorist, every man, whatever his past, his condition, or his opinions, now enjoys his private property and his legal rights; he has no longer to fear the violence of the opposite party; he may relay on the protection of the authorities, [9] and on the equity of the magistrates. [10] So long as he respects the law he can go to bed at night and sleep tranquilly with the certainty of awaking in freedom on the morrow, and with the certainty of doing as he pleases the entire day; with the privilege of working, buying, selling, thinking, amusing himself, [11] going and coming at his pleasure, and especially of going to mass or of staying away if he chooses. No more jacqueries either rural or urban, no more proscriptions or persecutions and legal or illegal spoliations, no more intestine and social wars waged with pikes or by decrees, no more conquests and confiscations made by Frenchmen against each other. With universal and unutterable relief people emerge from the barbarous and anarchical régime which reduced them to living from one day to another, and return to the pacific and regular régime which permits them to count on the morrow and make provision for it. After ten years of harassing subjection to the incoherent absolutism of unstable despotism, here, for the first time, they find a rational and stable government, or, at least, a reasonable, tolerable, and fixed degree of it. The First Consul is carrying out his declarations and he has declared that "The Revolution has ended. "[12]

III. Return of the Emigrés.

Lasting effect of revolutionary laws. - Condition of the Émigrés. -
Progressive and final amnesty. -They return. - They recover a portion
of their possessions. - Many of them enter the new hierarchy. -
Indemnities for them incomplete.

The main thing now is to dress the severe wounds it has made and
which are still bleeding, with as little torture as possible, for it has
cut down to the quick, and its amputations, whether foolish or
outrageous, have left sharp pains or mute suffering in the social
organism.

One hundred and ninety-two thousand names have been inscribed
on the list of émigrés[13] the terms of the law, every émigré is civilly
dead, and his possessions have become the property of the
Republic;" if he dared return to France, the same law condemned
him to death; there could be no appeal, petition, or respite; it sufficed
to prove identity and the squad of executioners was at once ordered
out. Now, at the beginning of the Consulate, this murderous law is
still in force; summary proceedings are always applicable, [14] and
one hundred and forty-six thousand names still appear on the
mortuary list. This constitutes a loss to France of 146,000 Frenchmen,
and not those of the least importance - gentlemen, army and navy
officers, members of parliaments, priests, prominent men of all
classes, conscientious Catholics, liberals of 1789, Feuillantists of the
Legislative assembly, and Constitutionalists of the years III and V.
Worse still, through their poverty or hostility abroad, they are a
discredit or even a danger for France, as formerly with the
Protestants driven out of the country by Louis XIV. [15] - To these
146,000 exiled Frenchmen add 200,000 or 300,000 others, residents,
but semi-proscribed: [16] First, those nearly related and allied to each
émigré, excluded by the law from "every legislative, administrative,
municipal and judicial function, " and even deprived of the elective
vote. Next, all former nobles or ennobled, deprived by the law of
their status as Frenchmen and obliged to re-naturalize themselves
according to the formalities.

It is, accordingly, almost the entire elite of old France which is
wanting in the new France, like a limb violently wrenched and half-
detached by the unskillful and brutal scalpel of the revolutionary
"sawbones"; for both the organ and the body are not only living, but

they are still feverish and extremely sensitive; it is important to avoid too great irritation; inflammation of any kind would be dangerous. A skilful surgeon, therefore, must mark the places for the stitches, not force the junctures, but anticipate and prepare for the final healing process, and await the gradual and slow results of vital effort and spontaneous renewal. Above all he must not alarm the patient. The First Consul is far from doing this; on the contrary his expressions are all encouraging. Let the patient keep quiet, there shall be no re-stitching, the wound shall not be touched. The constitution solemnly declares that the French people shall never allow the return of the émigrés, [17] and, on this point, the hands of future legislators are already tied fast; it prohibits any exception being added to the old ones. - But, first, by virtue of the same constitution, every Frenchman not an émigré or banished has the right to vote, to be elected, to exercise every species of public function; consequently, twelve days later, [18] a mere order of the Council of State restores civil and political rights to former nobles and the ennobled, to the kinsmen and relations of émigrés, to all who have been dubbed émigrés of the interior and whom Jacobin intolerance had excluded, if not from the territory, at least from the civic body: here are 200,000 or 300,000 Frenchmen already brought back into political communion if not to the soil. - They had succumbed to the coup-d'état of Fructidor; naturally, the leading fugitives or those transported, suffering under the same coup-d'état, were restored to political rights along with them and thus to the territory - Carnot, Barthélémy, Lafont-Ladébat, Siméon, Poissy d'Anglas, Mathieu Dumas, in all thirty-nine, designated by name; [19] very soon after. Through a simple extension of the same resolution, others of the Fructidor victims, a crowd of priests huddled together and pining away on the Ile-de-Ré, the most unfortunate and most inoffensive of all. [20] - Two months later, a law declares that the list of émigrés is definitely closed; [21] a resolution orders immediate investigation into the claims of those who are to be struck off the list; a second resolution strikes off the first founders of the new order of things, the members of the National Assembly "who voted for the establishment of equality and the abolition of nobility; " and, day after day, new erasures succeed each other, all specific and by name, under cover of toleration, pardon, and exception: [22] on the 19th of October 1800, there are already 1200 of them. Bonaparte, at this date, had gained the battle of Marengo; the surgical restorer feels that his hands are more free; he can operate on a larger scale and take in whole bodies collectively. On the 20th of October 1800, a resolution strikes off entire categories from the list, all whose condemnation is too grossly unjust or malicious, [23] at first, minors under sixteen and the wives of émigrés; next, farmers, artisans, workmen, journeymen and servants with their wives and children and at last 18,000 ecclesiastics who, banished by law, left the country only in obedience to the law. Besides these, "all individuals inscribed collectively and without individual denomination, " those already struck off, but provisionally, by local administrations; also still other classes. Moreover, a good many emigrants, yet standing on the lists, steal back one by one into France, and the government tolerates them. [24] Finally, eighteen months later, after the peace of Amiens and the Concord at, [25] a sénatus-consulte ends the great operation; an amnesty relieves all who are not yet struck off, except the declared leaders of the militant emigration, its notables, and who are not to exceed one thousand; the rest may come back and enjoy their civic rights; only, they must promise "loyalty to the government established under the constitution and not maintain directly or indirectly any connection or correspondence with the enemies of the State. " On this condition the doors of France are thrown open to them and they return in crowds.

But their bodily presence is not of itself sufficient; it is moreover essential that they should not be absent in feeling, as strangers and merely domiciliated in the new society. Were these mutilated fragments of old France, these human shreds put back in their old places, simply attached or placed in juxtaposition to modern France, they would prove useless, troublesome and even mischievous. Let us strive, then, to have them grafted on afresh through adherence or complete fusion; and first, to effect this, they must not be allowed to die of inanition; they must take root physically and be able to live. In private life, how can former proprietors, the noblesse, the parliamentarians, the upper bourgeoisie, support themselves, especially those without a profession or pursuit, and who, before 1789, maintained themselves, not by their labor, but by their income? Once at home, they can no longer earn their living as they did abroad; they can no longer give lessons in French, in dancing, or in fencing. - There is no doubt but that the sénatus-consulte which amnesties them restores to them a part of their unsold possessions; [26] but most of these are sold and, on the other hand, the First Consul, who is not disposed to re-establish large fortunes for royalists, [27] retains and maintains the largest portion of what they have been despoiled of in the national domain: all woods and forests of 300 arpents[28] and over, their stock and property rights in the great canals, and their personal property already devoted to the public service. The effective restitution is therefore only moderate; the émigrés who return recover but little more than one-twentieth of their patrimony, one hundred millions[29] out of more than two milliards. Observe, besides, that by virtue even of the law and as admitted by the First Consul, [30] this alms is badly distributed; the most needy and the greatest number remain empty- handed, consisting of the lesser and medium class of rural proprietors, especially of country gentlemen whose domain, worth less than 50,000 francs, brings in only 2000 or 3000 francs income; [31] a domain of this size came within reach of a great many purses, and hence found purchasers more readily and with greater facility than a large holding; the State was almost always the seller, and thenceforth the old proprietor could make no further claim or pretension. - Thus, for many of the émigrés, "the sénatus-consulte of the year X is simply a permit to starve to death in France "and, [32] four years later, [33] Napoleon himself estimates that "40,000 are without the means of subsistence. " They manage to keep life and soul together and nothing more; [34] many, taken in and cared for by their friends or relations, are supported as guests or parasites, somewhat through compassion and again on humanitarian grounds. One recovers his silver plate, buried in a cellar; another finds notes payable to bearer, forgotten in an old chest. Sometimes, the purchaser of a piece of property, an honest man, gives it back at the price he paid for it, or even gratis, if, during the time he had held it, he had derived sufficient profit from it. Occasionally, when the adjudication happens to have been fraudulent, or the sale too irregular, and subject to legal proceedings, the dishonest purchaser does not refuse a compromise. But these cases are rare, and the evicted owner, if he desires to dine regularly, will wisely seek a small remunerative position and serve as clerk, book-keeper or accountant. M. des Echerolles, formerly a brigadier-general, keeps the office of the new line of diligences at Lyons, and earns 1200 francs a year. M. de Puymaigre, who, in 1789, was worth two millions, becomes a contr'leur des droits réunis at Briey with a salary of 2400 francs. - In every branch of the new administration a royalist is welcome to apply for a post; [35] however slightly recommended, he obtains the place. Sometimes he even receives one without having asked for it; M. de Vitrolles[36] thus becomes, in spite of himself, inspector of the imperial sheepfolds; this fixes his position and makes it appear as if he had given in his adhesion to the government. - Naturally, the great political recruiter singles out the tallest and most imposing subjects, that is to say, belonging to the first families of the ancient monarchy, and, like one who knows his business, he brings to bear every means, constraint and seduction, threats and cajoleries, supplies in ready money, promises of promotion with the influence of a uniform and gold-lace embroidery. [37] It matters little whether the enlistment is voluntary or extorted; the moment a man becomes a functionary and is enrolled in the hierarchy, he loses the best portion of his independence; once a dignitary and placed at the top of the hierarchy, he gives his entire individuality up, for henceforth he lives under the eye of the master, feels the daily and direct pressure of the terrible hand which grasps him, and he forcibly becomes a mere tool. [38] These historic names, moreover, contribute to the embellishment of the reign. Napoleon hauls in a good many of them, and the most illustrious among the old noblesse, of the court of the robe and of the sword. He can enumerate among his magistrates, M. Pasquier, M. Séguier, M. Molé; among his prelates, M. de Boisgelin, M. du Barral, M. du Belley, M. de Roquelaure, M. de Broglie; among his military officers, M. de Fézensac, M. de Ségur, M. de Mortemart, M. de Narbonne; [39] among the dignitaries of his palace, chaplains, chamberlains and ladies of honor - the Rohan, Croy, Chevreuse, Montmorency, Chabot, Montesquiou, Noailles, Brancas, Gontaut, Grammont, Beauvau, Saint-Aignan, Montalembert, Haussonville, Choiseul-Praslin, Mercy d'Argenteau, Aubusson de la Feuillade, and many others, recorded in the imperial almanac as formerly in the royal almanac.

But they are only with him nominally and in the almanac. Except certain individuals, M. de las Cases and M. Philippe de Ségur, who gave themselves up body and soul, even to following him to Saint Helena, to glorifying, admiring and loving him beyond the grave, the others are submissive conscripts and who remain more or less refractory spirits. He does nothing to win them over. His court is not, like the old court, a conversational ball-room, but a hall of inspection, the most sumptuous apartment in his vast barracks; the civil parade is a continuation of the military parade; one finds one's self constrained, stiff, mute and uncomfortable. [40]

He does not know how to entertain as the head of his household, how to welcome guests and be gracious or even polite to his pretended courtiers; he himself declares that[41] "they go two years without speaking to him, and six months without seeing him; he does not like them, their conversation displeases him. " When he addresses them it is to browbeat them; his familiarities with their wives are those of the gendarme or the pedagogue, while the little attentions he inflicts upon them are indecorous criticisms or compliments in bad taste. They know that they are spied upon in their own homes and responsible for whatever is said there; "the upper police is constantly hovering over all drawing-rooms. ". For every word uttered in privacy, for any lack of compliance, every individual, man or woman, runs the risk of exile or of being relegated to the interior at a distance of forty leagues. [43] And the same with the resident gentry in the provinces; they are obliged to pay court to the prefect, to be on good terms with him, or at least attend his receptions; it is important that their cards should be seen on his mantel piece. [44] Otherwise, let them take heed, for it is he who reports on their conduct to the minister Fouché or to Savary who replaced him. In vain do they live circumspectly and confine themselves to a private life; a refusal to accept an office is unpardonable; there is a grudge against them if they do not employ their local influence in behalf of the reign. [45] Accordingly, they are, under the empire as under the republic, in law as in fact, in the provinces as well as at Paris, privileged persons the wrong way, a suspicious class under a special surveillance" and subject to exceptional rigor. [46] In 1808, [47] Napoleon orders Fouché "to draw up . .. among the old and wealthy families who are not in the system . ... a list of ten in each department, and of fifty for Paris, " of which the sons from sixteen to eighteen years of age shall be forced to enter Saint-Cyr and from thence go into the army as second lieutenants. In 1813, still "in the highest classes of society, " and arbitrarily selected by the prefects, he takes ten thousand other persons, exempt or redeemed from the conscription, even the married, even fathers of families, who, under the title of guards of honor, become soldiers, at first to be slaughtered in his service, and next, and in the mean time, to answer for the fidelity of their relatives. It is the old law of hostages, a resumption of the worst proceedings of the Directory for his account and aggravated for his profit. - Decidedly, the imperial Régime, for the old royalists, resembles too much the Jacobin régime; they are about as repugnant to one as to the other, and their aversion naturally extends to the whole of the new society. - As they comprehend it, they are more or less robbed and oppressed for a quarter of a century. In order that their hostility may cease, the indemnity of 1825 is essential, fifty years of gradual adaptation, the slow elimination of two or three generations of fathers and the slow elimination of two or three generations of sons.

Nothing is so difficult as the reparation of great social wrongs. In this case the incomplete reparation did not prove sufficient; the treatment which began with gentleness ended with violence, and, as a whole, the operation only half succeeded.

IV. Education and Medical Care.

Confiscation of collective fortunes. - Ruin of the Hospitals and Schools.

Other wounds are not less deep, and their cure is not less urgent; for they cause suffering, not only to one class, but to the whole people - that vast majority which the government strives to satisfy. Along with the property of the émigrés, the Revolution has confiscated that of all local or special societies, ecclesiastic or laic, of churches and congregations, universities and academies, schools and colleges, asylums and hospitals, and even the property of the communes. All these fortunes have been swallowed up by the public treasury, which is a bottomless pit, and are gone forever. - Consequently, all services thus maintained, especially charitable institutions, public worship and education, die or languish for lack of sustenance; the State, which has no money for itself, has none for them. And what is worse, it hinders private parties from taking them in charge; being Jacobin, that is to say intolerant and partisan, it has proscribed worship, driven nuns out of the hospitals, closed Christian schools, and, with its vast power, it prevents others from carrying out at their own expense the social enterprises which it no longer cares for.

And yet the needs for which this work provides have never been so great nor so imperative. In ten years, [48] the number of foundlings increased from 23,000 to 62,000; it is, as the reports state, a deluge: there are 1097 instead of 400 in Aisne, 1500 in Lot-et- Garonne, 2035 in la Manche, 2043 in Bouches-du-Rh'ne, 2673 in Calvados. From 3000 to 4000 beggars are enumerated in each department and about 300,000 in all France. [49] As to the sick, the infirm, the mutilated, unable to earn their living, it suffices, for an idea of their multitude, to consider the régime to which the political doctors have just subjected France, the Régime of fasting and bloodletting. Two millions of Frenchmen have marched under the national flag, and eight hundred thousand have died under it; [50] among the survivors, how many cripples, how many with one arm and with wooden legs! All Frenchmen have eaten dog-bread for three years and often have not had enough of that to live on; over a million have died of starvation and poverty; all the wealthy and well-to-do Frenchmen have been ruined and have lived in constant fear of the guillotine; four hundred thousand have wasted away in prisons; of the survivors, how many shattered constitutions, how many bodies and brains disordered by an excess of suffering and anxiety, by physical and moral wear and tear!

Now, in 1800, assistance is lacking for this crowd of civil and military invalids, the charitable establishments being no longer in a condition to furnish it. Under the Constituent Assembly, through the suppression of ecclesiastical property and the abolition of octrois, a large portion of their revenue had been cut off, that assigned to them out of octrois and the tithes. Under the Legislative Assembly and the Convention, through the dispersion and persecution of nuns and monks, they were deprived of a body of able male and female volunteer servants who, instituted for centuries, gave their labor without stint. Under the Convention, all their possessions, the real-estate and the debts due them, had been confiscated; [52] and, in the restitution to them of the remainder at the end of three years, a portion of their real-estate is found to have been sold, while their claims, settled by assignats or converted into state securities, had died out or dwindled to such an extent that, in 1800, after the final bankruptcy of the assignats and of the state debt, the ancient patrimony of the poor is two-thirds or one-half reduced. [53] It is for this reason that the eight hundred charitable institutions which, in 1789, had one hundred thousand or one hundred and ten thousand occupants, could not support more than one-third or one-half of them; on the other hand, it may be estimated that the number of applicants tripled; from which it follows that, in 1800, there is less than one bed in the hospitals and asylums for six children, either sick or infirm.

V. Old and New.

Complaints of the Poor, of Parents, and of Believers. - Contrast between old and new educational facilities. - Clandestine instruction. - Jacobin teachers.

Under this wail of the wretched who vainly appeal for help, for nursing and for beds, another moan is heard, not so loud, but more extensive, that of parents unable to educate their children, boys or girls, and give them any species of instruction either primary or secondary.

Previous to the Revolution "small schools" were innumerable: in Normandy, Picardy, Artois, French Flanders, Lorraine and Alsace, in the Ile-de-France, in Burgundy and Franche-Comté, in the Dombes, Dauphiny and Lyonnais, in the Comtat, in the Cévennes and in Béarn, [54] almost as many schools could be counted as there were parishes, in all probably twenty or twenty-five thousand for the thirty-seven thousand parishes in France, and all frequented and serviceable; for, in 1789, forty-seven men out of a hundred, and twenty-six girls or women out of a hundred, could read and write or, at least, sign their names. [55] - And these schools cost the treasury nothing, next to nothing to the tax-payer, and very little to parents. In many places, the congregations, supported by their own property, furnished male or female teachers, - Frères de la Doctrine Chrétienne, Frères de Saint-Antoine, Ursulines, Visitandines, Filles de la Charité, Sœurs de Saint-Charles, Sœurs de la Providence, Sœurs de la Sagesse, Sœurs de Notre-Dame de la Croix, Vatelottes, Miramiones, Manettes du Tiers Ordre, and many others. Elsewhere, the curate of the parish was obliged through a parish regulation to teach himself, or to see that his vicar taught. A very large number of factories or of communes had received legacies for maintaining a school; the instructor often enjoyed, through an endowment, a métayer farm or a piece of ground; he was generally provided with a lodging; if he was a layman he was exempt, besides, from the most onerous taxes; as sexton, beadle, chorister or bell-ringer, he had small perquisites; finally, he was paid for each child four or five sous a month; sometimes, especially in poor districts, he taught only from All Saints' day down to the spring, and followed another occupation during the summer. In short, his salary and his comfort were about those of a rural vicar or of a suitably paid curate.

Higher education (éducation secondaire) was provided for in the same manner, and still better by local and private enterprise. More than one hundred and eight establishments furnished it completely, and more than four hundred and fifty-four partially. [57] Like the others, and not less liberally than the smaller schools, these were supported by endowments, some of which were very ample and even magnificent; a certain upper school in the provinces, Rodez, [58] possessed twenty- seven thousand livres income, and one in Paris, Louis-le-Grand, an income of four hundred and fifty thousand livres, each of these, large or small, having its own distinct endowment, in real property, lands and houses, and in revenues on privileges derived from the hotel-de- ville, the octroi and from transportation lines. - And, in each of them, the scholarships, or half-scholarships, were numerous-six hundred alone in Louis-le-Grand. In total, out of the seventy-two thousand scholars in the kingdom, there were forty thousand for whom a high-school education was gratuitous or half-gratuitous; nowadays, it is less than five thousand out of seventy-nine thousand. [59] The reason why is that, before 1789, the revenues were not only large, but the expenses were small. The salary of a head-master, teacher, or assistant-teacher was not large, say four hundred and fifty, six hundred, nine hundred, or twelve hundred livres per annum at most, just enough for a single man to live on; in effect, most of the teachers were priests or monks, Benedictines, regular canons, Oratorians, the latter alone officiating in thirty colleges. Not subject to the expenses and necessities which a family imposes, they were abstemious through piety, or at least through discipline, habit, and respect for persons; frequently, the statutes of the school obliged them to live in common, [60] which was much cheaper than living apart. - The same economical accord is found with all the wheels, in the arrangement and working of the entire system. A family, even a rural one, never lived far away from a high-school, for there were high-schools in nearly all the small towns, seven or eight in each department, fifteen in Ain, seventeen in Aisne. [61] The child or youth, from eight to eighteen, had not to endure the solitude and promiscuity of a civil barracks; he remained within reach of his parents. If they were too poor to pay the three hundred francs board required by the school, they placed their son in a respectable family, in that of some artisan or acquaintance in the town; there, with three or four others, he was lodged, had his washing done, was cared for and watched, had a seat at the family table and by the fireside, and was provided with light; every week, he received from the country his supply of bread and other provisions; the mistress of the house cooked for him and mended his clothes, the whole for two or three livres a month. [62] - Thus do institutions flourish that arise spontaneously on the spot; they adapt themselves to circumstances, conform to necessities, utilize resources and afford the maximum of returns for the minimum of expense.

This great organization disappears entirely, bodily and with all its possessions, like a ship that sinks beneath the waves. The teachers are dismissed, exiled, transported, and proscribed; its property is confiscated, sold and destroyed, and the remainder in the hands of the State is not restored and again applied to its former service. Public education, worse treated than public charity, does not recover a shred of its former endowment. Consequently, in the last years of the Directory, and even early in the Consulate, [63] there is scarcely any instruction given in France; in fact, for the past eight or nine years it has ceased, [64] or become private and clandestine. Here and there, a few returned priests, in spite of the intolerant law and with the connivance of the local authorities, also a few scattered nuns, teach in a contraband fashion a few small groups of Catholic children; five or six little girls around a disguised Ursuline nun spell out the alphabet in a back room; [65] a priest without tonsure or cassock secretly receives in the evening two or three youths whom he makes translate the De Viris. - During the intervals, indeed, of the Reign of Terror, before the 13th of Vendémiaire and the 18th of Fructidor, sundry schools spring up again like tufts of grass in a mowed pasture- ground, but only in certain spots and meagerly; moreover, as soon as the Jacobin returns to power he stubbornly stamps them out; [66] he wants to have teaching all to himself. - Now the institution by which the State pretends to replace the old and free establishments makes a figure only on paper. One école centrale in each department is installed or decreed, making eighty eight on the territory of ancient France; this hardly supplies the place of the eight or nine hundred high-schools (collèges), especially as these new schools are hardly viable, being in ruin at the very start, [67] poorly maintained, badly furnished, with no preparatory schools nor adjacent boarding- houses, [68] the programme of studies being badly arranged and parents suspicious of the spirit of the studies. [69] Thus, there is little or no attendance at most of the courses of lectures; only those on mathematics are followed, particularly on drawing, and especially mechanical and geometrical drawing, probably by the future surveyors and engineers of roads and bridges, by building contractors and a few aspirants to the École Polytechnique. As to the other courses, on literature, history, and the moral sciences, as comprehended by the Republic and imposed by it, these obtain not over a thousand auditors in all France; instead of 72,000 pupils, only 7000 or 8000 seek superior education, while six out of seven, instead of seeking self- culture, simply prepare themselves for some practical pursuit. [70]

It is much worse with primary instruction. This task is given to the local authorities. But, as they have no money, they generally shirk this duty, and, if they do set up a school, are unable to maintain it. [71] On the other hand, as instruction must be laic and Jacobin, "almost everywhere, "[72] the teacher is an outcast layman, a fallen Jacobin, some old, starving party member, unemployed, foul-mouthed and of ill-repute. Families, naturally, refuse to trust their children with him; even when honorable, they avoid him; and the reason is that, in 1800, Jacobin and scoundrel have become synonymous terms. Henceforth, parents desire that their children should learn to read in the catechism and not in the declaration of rights: [73] as they view it, the old manual formed polite and civilized youths and respectful sons; the new one forms only insolent rascals and precocious, slovenly blackguards. [74] Consequently, the few primary schools in which the Republic has placed its people and imposed its educational system remain three-quarters empty; in vain does she close the doors of those in which other masters teach with other books; fathers persist in their repugnance and distaste; they prefer for their sons utter ignorance to unsound instruction. [75] - A secular establishment, created and provided for by twenty generations of benefactors, gave gratis, or at a much lower rate, the first crumbs of intellectual food to more than 1,200,000 children. [76] It was demolished; in its place, a few improvised and wretched barracks distributed here and there a small ration of moldy and indigestible bread. Thereupon, one long, low murmur, a long time suppressed, breaks out and keeps on increasing, that of parents whose children are condemned to go hungry; in any event, they demand that their sons and daughters be no longer forced, under penalty of fasting, to consume the patent flour of the State, that is to say a nauseous, unsatisfactory, badly-kneaded, badly-baked paste which, on trial, proves offensive to the palate and ruinous to the stomach.

VI. Religion

The Spirit and Ministrations of Catholicism. - How the Revolution develops a sense of this.

Another plaint is heard, deeper and more universal, that of all souls in which regret for their established church and forms of worship still subsists or is revived.

In every religious system discipline and rites depend upon faith, for it is faith alone which suggests or prescribes these; they are the outcome and expansion of this; it attains its ends through these, and manifests itself by them; they are the exterior of which it is the interior; thus, let these be attacked and it is in distress; the living, palpitating flesh suffers through the sensitive skin. - In Catholicism, this skin is more sensitive than elsewhere, for it clings to the flesh, not alone through ordinary adhesiveness, the effect of adaptation and custom, but again through a special organic attachment, consisting of dogmatic doctrine; theology, in its articles of belief, has here set up the absolute necessity of the sacraments and of the priesthood; consequently, between the superficial and central divisions of religion the union is complete. The Catholic sacraments, therefore, are not merely symbols; they possess in themselves "an efficacious power, a sanctifying virtue. " "That which they represent, they really work out. "[77] If I am denied access to them, I am cut off from the fountains to which my soul resorts to drink in grace, pardon, purity, health and salvation. If my children cannot be regularly baptized, they are not Christians; if extreme unction cannot be administered to my dying mother, she sets out on the long journey without the viaticum; if I am married by the mayor only, my wife and I live in concubinage; if I cannot confess my sins, I am not absolved from them, and my burdened conscience seeks in vain for the helping hand which will ease the too heavy load; if I cannot perform my Easter duties, my spiritual life is a failure; the supreme and sublime act by which it perfects itself through the mystic union of my body and soul with the body, soul, and divinity of Jesus Christ, is wanting. - Now, none of these sacraments are valid if they have not been conferred by a priest, one who bears the stamp of a superior, unique, ineffaceable character, through a final sacrament consisting of ordination and which is conferred only on certain conditions; among other conditions, it is essential that this priest should have been ordained by a bishop; among other conditions, it is essential that this bishop[78] should have been installed by the Pope. Consequently, without the Pope there are no bishops; without bishops no priests; without priests no sacraments; without the sacraments no salvation. The ecclesiastical institution is therefore indispensable to the believer. The canonical priesthood, the canonical hierarchy is necessary to him for the exercise of his faith. - He must have yet more, if fervent and animated with true old Christian sentiment, ascetic and mystic, which separates the soul from this world and ever maintains it in the presence of God. Several things are requisite to this end:

* First, vows of chastity, poverty and obedience, that is to say, the steady and voluntary repression of the most powerful animal instinct and of the strongest worldly appetites;
* Next, unceasing prayer, especially prayer in common, where the emotion of the prostrate soul increases through the emotion of the souls that surround it; in the same degree, active piety, meaning by this the doing of good works, education and charity, especially the accomplishment of repulsive tasks, such as attending the sick, the infirm, the incurable, idiots, maniacs and repentant prostitutes;
* Finally, the strict daily rule which, a sort of rigorous and minute countersign, enjoining and compelling the repetition of the same acts at the same hours, renders habit the auxiliary of will, adds mechanical enthusiasm to a serious determination, and ends in making the task easy.

Hence, communities of men and of women, congregations and convents, these likewise, the same as the sacraments, the priesthood and the hierarchy, form a body along with belief and thus constitute the inseparable organs of faith.

Before 1789, the ignorant or indifferent Catholic, the peasant at his plow, the artisan at his work-bench, the good wife attending to her household, were unconscious of this innermost suture. Thanks to the Revolution, they have acquired the sentiment of it and even the physical sensation. They had never asked themselves in what respect orthodoxy differed from schism, nor how positive religion was opposed to natural religion; it is the civil organization of the clergy which has led them to distinguish the difference between the unsworn curé and the interloper, between the right mass and the wrong mass; it is the prohibition of the mass which has led them to comprehend its importance; it is the revolutionary government which has transformed them into theologians and canonists. [79]

Compelled, under the Reign of Terror, to sing and dance before the goddess Reason, and next, in the temple of the "Étre Supreme, " subjected, under the Directory, to the new-fangled republican calendar, and to the insipidity of the decade festivals, they have measured, with their own eyes, the distance which separates a present, personal, incarnate deity, redeemer and savior, from a deity without form or substance, or, in any event, absent; a living, revealed, and time-honored religion, and an abstract, manufactured, improvised religion; their spontaneous worship, which is an act of faith, and a worship imposed on them which is only frigid parade; their priest, in a surplice, sworn to continence, delegated from on high to open out to them the infinite perspectives of heaven or hell beyond the grave, and the republican substitute, officiating in a municipal scarf, Peter or Paul, a lay-man like themselves, more or less married and convivialist, sent from Paris to preach a course of Jacobin morality. [80] - Their attachment to their clergy, to the entire body regular and secular, is due to this contrast. Previously, they were not always well-disposed to it; the peasantry, nowhere, were content to pay tithes, and the artisan, as well as the peasant, regarded the idle, well-endowed, meditative monks as but little more than so many fat drones. The man of the people in France, by virtue of being a Gaul, has a dry, limited imagination; he is not inclined to veneration, but is rather mocking, critical and insubordinate at the powers above him, with a hereditary undertone of distrust and envy at every man who wears a cloth suit and who eats and drinks without doing manual labor. - At this time, his clergy do not excite his envy, but his pity; monks and nuns, cure's and prelates, roofless, without bread, imprisoned, transported, guillotined, or, at best, fugitives, hunted down and more unfortunate than wild beasts - it is he who, during the persecutions of the years II, IV and VI, harbors them, conceals them, lodges them and feeds them. He sees them suffering for their faith, which is his faith, and, before their constancy, equal to that of the legendary martyrs, his indifference changes into respect and next into zeal. From the year IV, [81] the orthodox priests have again recovered their place and ascendancy in his soul which the creed assigns to them; they have again become his serviceable guides, his accepted directors, the only warranted interpreters of Christian truth, the only authorized dispensers and ministers of divine grace. He attends their mass immediately on their return and will put up with no other. Brutalized as he may be, or indifferent and dull, and his mind filled with nothing but animal concerns, he needs them; [82] he misses their solemnities, the great festivals, the Sunday; and this privation is a periodical want both for eyes and ears; he misses the ceremonial, the lights, the chants, the ringing of the bells, the morning and evening Angelus. - Thus, whether he knows it or not, his heart and senses are Catholic[83] and he demands the old church back again. Before the Revolution, this church lived on its own revenues; 70,000 priests, 37,000 nuns, 23,000 monks, supported by endowments, cost the State nothing, and scarcely anything to the tax-payer; at any rate, they cost nothing to the actual, existing tax-payer not even the tithes, for, established many centuries ago, the tithes were a tax on the soil, not on the owner in possession, nor on the farmer who tilled the ground, who has purchased or hired it with this tax deducted. In any case, the real property of the Church belonged to it, without prejudice to anybody, through the strongest legal and most legitimate of property titles, the last will and testament of thousands of the dead, its founders and benefactors. All is taken from it, even the houses of prayer which, in their use, disposition and architecture, were, in the most manifest manner, Christian works and ecclesiastical objects, 38,000 parsonages, 4000 convents, over 40,000 parochial churches, cathedrals and chapels. Every morning, the man or woman of the people, in whom the need of worship has revived, passes in front of one of these buildings robbed of its cult; these declare aloud to them through their form and name what they have been and what they should be to-day. This voice is heard by incredulous philosophers and former Conventionalists; [84] all Catholics hear it, and out of thirty- five millions of Frenchmen, [85] thirty-two millions are Catholics.

VII. The Confiscated Property.

Reasons for the concordat. - Napoleon's economical organization of the Church institution. - A good bargainer. - Compromise with the old state of things.

How withstand such a just complaint, the universal complaint of the destitute, of relatives, and of believers? - The fundamental difficulty reappears, the nearly insurmountable dilemma into which the Revolution has plunged every steady government, that is to say the lasting effect of revolutionary confiscations and the conflict which sets two rights to the same property against each other, the right of the despoiled owner and the right of the owner in possession. This time, again the fault is on the side of the State, which has converted itself from a policeman into a brigand and violently appropriated to itself the fortune of the hospitals, schools, and churches; the State must return this in money or in kind. In kind, it is no longer able; everything has passed out of its hands; it has alienated what it could, and now holds on only to the leavings. In money, nothing more can be done; it is itself ruined, has just become bankrupt, lives on expedients from day to day and has neither funds nor credit. Nobody dreams of taking back property that is sold; nothing is more opposed to the spirit of the new Régime: not only would this be a robbery as before, since its buyers have paid for it and got their receipts, but again, in disputing their title the government would invalidate its own. For its authority is derived from the same source as their property: it is established on the same principle as their rights of possession and by virtue of the same accomplished facts

* because things are as they are and could not be different,
* because ten years of revolution and eight years of war bear down on the present with too heavy a weight,
* because too many and too deep interests are involved and enlisted on the same side,
* because the interests of twelve hundred thousand purchasers are incorporated with those of the thirty thousand officers to whom the Revolution has provided a rank, along with that of all the new functionaries and dignitaries, including the First Consul himself, who, in this universal transposition of fortunes and ranks, is the greatest of parvenus and who must maintain the others if he wants to be maintained by them.

Naturally, he protects everybody, through calculation as well as sympathy, in the civil as in the military order of things, particularly the new property-owners, especially the smaller and the average ones, his best clients, attached to his reign and to his person through love of property, the strongest passion of the ordinary man, and through love of the soil, the strongest passion of the peasant. [86] Their loyalty depends on their security, and consequently he is lavish of guarantees. In his constitution of the year VIII, [87] he declares in the name of the French nation that after a legally consummated sale of national property, whatever its origin, the legitimate purchaser cannot be divested of it. " Through the institution of the Legion of Honor he obliges each member "to swear, on his honor, to devote himself to the conservation of property sanctioned by the laws of the republic. "[88] According to the terms of the imperial constitution[89] "he swears" himself "to respect and to enforce respect for the irrevocability of the sale of national possessions. "

Unfortunately, a cannon-ball on the battle-field, an infernal machine in the street, an illness at home, may carry off the guarantor and the guarantees. [90] On the other hand, confiscated goods preserve their original taint. Rarely is the purchaser regarded favorably in his commune; the bargain he has made excites envy; he is not alone in his enjoyment of it, but the rest suffer from it. Formerly, this or that field of which he reaps the produce, this or that domain of which he enjoys the rental, once provided for the parsonage, the asylum and the school; now the school, the asylum and the parsonage die through inanition for his advantage; he fattens on their fasting. In his own house, his wife and mother often look melancholy, especially during Easter week; if he is old, or becomes ill, his conscience disturbs him; this conscience, through habit and heredity, is Catholic: he craves absolution at the last moment at the priest's hands, and says to himself that, at the last moment, he may not probably be absolved. [91] In other respects, he would find it difficult to satisfy himself that his legal property is legitimate property; for, not only is it not so rightfully before the tribunal of conscience, but again it is not so in fact on the market; the figures, in this particular, are convincing, daily and notorious. A patrimonial domain which brings in 3000 francs finds a purchaser at 100,000 francs; alongside of this a national domain which brings in just as much, finds a purchaser only at 60,000 francs; after several sales and resale, the depreciation continues and 40 % of the value of the confiscated property is lost. [92] A low, indistinct murmur is heard, and reverberates from sale to sale, the muttering of private probity protesting against public probity, declaring to the new proprietor that his title is defective; it lacks one clause and a capital one, that of the surrender and cession, the formal renunciation, the authentic withdrawal of the former owner. The State, the first seller, owes this voucher to the purchasers; let it procure this and negotiate accordingly; let it apply for this to the rightful party, to the owners whom it has dispossessed, to the immemorial and legitimate authorities, I mean to the ancient corporations. These have been dissolved by revolutionary law and have no longer a representative who can sign for them. Nevertheless, in spite of revolutionary law, one of these corporations, with more vitality than the rest, still subsists with its proper, if not legal, representative, its regular and undisputed chief. This chief is qualified and authorized to bind the body; for, institutionally, he is supreme, and the conscience of all its members is in his hand. His signature is of the highest value; it is very important to obtain this, and the First Consul concludes the Concordat with the Pope.

By this Concordat, the Pope "declares that neither himself nor his successors shall in any manner disturb the purchasers of alienated ecclesiastical property, and that the ownership of the said property, the rights and revenues derived there from, shall consequently remain in commutable in their hands or in those of their assigns. "[93] Henceforth the possession of this property is no longer a sin; at least, it is not condemned by the spiritual authority, by that external conscience which, in Catholic countries, governs the inward conscience and often supplies its place; the Church, the moral head, removes with its own hands the moral scruple, the last small stone, troublesome and dangerous, which, lying underneath the cornerstone of lay society, breaks the level of the entire structure and compromises the equilibrium of the new government. - In exchange, the State endows the Church. By the same Concordat, and by the decrees which follow it, "the government[94] ensures a suitable salary to bishops and cure's, " 15,000 francs to each archbishop, 10,000 francs to each bishop, 1500 francs to each curé of the first class and 1000 francs to each curé of the second class, [95] also, later on, [96] a maximum of 500 francs and a minimum of 300 francs to each assistant-priest or vicar. "If circumstances require it, [97] the conseils-généraux of the large communes may grant to prelates or to curés an increase of salary out of their rural possessions or octrois. " In all cases, archbishops, bishops, curés and priests shall be lodged, or receive a lodging indemnity. So much for the support of persons. -

As to real property, [98] "all the metropolitan churches, cathedrals, parochial buildings and others, not alienated, and needed for the purposes of worship, shall be subject to the disposition of the bishops. " - The parsonages and gardens attached to these, not alienated, shall be given up to the curés and assistant-priests. " - " The possessions of the fabriques, [99] not alienated, as well as the rentals they enjoyed, and which have not been transferred, shall be restored to their original purpose. - As to the outlay and expenditure for worship, [100] for the parochial center or cathedral, if its revenue is not sufficient, this shall receive aid from its commune or from its department; besides, "an assessment of 10 %. [101] shall be laid on the revenues of all the real estate of the communes, such as houses, woods, and rural possessions, for the formation of a common fund of subsidy, " a general sum with which to provide for "acquisitions, reconstructions or repairs of churches, . .. seminaries and parsonages. " Moreover, [102] the government allows "the French Catholics to make endowments, if so disposed, in favor of churches . .. for the support of ministers and the exercise of worship, " that is to say to bequeath or make gifts to the fabriques or seminaries; in fine, it exempts seminarists, the future cure's, from the conscription.

It also exempts the "Ignorantins, " or brethren of the Christian schools, who are the instructors of the common people. With respect to these and in relation to every other Catholic institution, it follows the same utilitarian principle, the fundamental maxim of laic and practical good sense: when religious vocations make their appearance and serve the public, it welcomes and makes use of them; it grants them facilities, dispensations and favors, its protection, its donations, or at least its tolerance. Not only does it turn their zeal to account, but it authorizes their association. [103] Numerous societies of men or of women again spring up with the assent of the public authorities - the "Ignorantins, " the "Filles de la Charité, " the "Seurs Hospitalières, " the "Sœurs de Saint-Thomas, " the "Sœurs de Saint-Charles, " the "Sœurs Vatelottes. " The Council of State accepts and approves of their statutes, vows, hierarchy, and internal regulations. They again become proprietors; they may accept donations and legacies. The State frequently makes presents to them. In 1808, [104] thirty-one communities of Sisters of Charity, and mostly educational, thus obtain the buildings and furniture they ask for, in full possession and gratuitously. The State, also, frequently supports them; [105] it repeatedly decides that in this asylum, or in that school, the "sisters" designated by the ancient foundation shall resume their work and be paid out of the income of the asylum or school. Better still, and notwithstanding threatening decrees, [106] Napoleon, between 1804 and 1814, allows fifty-four communities to arise and exist, outside of the congregations authorized by him, which do not submit their statutes to him and which dispense with his permission to exist; he lets them live and does not disturb them; he judges[107] "that there is every sort of character and imagination, that eccentricities even should not be repressed when they do no harm, " that, for certain people, an ascetic life in common is the only refuge; if that is all they desire they should not be disturbed, and it is easy to feign ignorance of them; but let them remain quiet and be sufficient unto themselves! - Such is the new growth of the regular clergy alongside of the secular clergy, the two main branches of the Catholic trunk. Owing to the help, or to the authorization, or to the connivance of the State, inside or outside of its limitations, both clerical bodies, legally or in reality, recover a civil existence, and thus obtain, or at least nearly so, their physical maintenance. [108]

And nothing more. Nobody, better than Napoleon, knows how to make a good bargain, that is to say, to give a little in order to gain a great deal. In this treaty with the Church he tightens his purse-strings and especially avoids parting with his ready money. Six hundred and fifty thousand francs for fifty bishops and ten archbishops, a little more than four million francs for the three or four thousand cantonal curés, in all five million francs per annum, is all that the State promises to the new clergy. Later on, [109] he takes it on himself to pay those who officiate in the branch chapels; nevertheless, in 1807, the entire appropriation for public worship costs the State only twelve million francs a year; [110] the rest, as a rule, and especially the salaries of the forty thousand assistant-priests and vicars, must be provided by the fabriques and the communes. [111] Let the clergy benefit by occasional contributions; [112] let it appeal to the piety of believers for its monstrances, chalices, albs and chasubles, for decorations and the other expenses of worship; they are not prohibited from being liberal to it, not only during the services, on making collections, but in their houses, within closed doors, from hand to hand. Moreover, they have the right of making gifts or bequests before a notary, of establishing foundations in favor of seminaries and churches; the foundation, after verification and approval by the Council of State, becomes operative; only, [113] it must consist of state securities, because, in this shape, it helps maintain their value and the credit of the government; in no case must it be composed of real estate; [114]

should the clergy become land-owners it would enjoy too much local influence. No bishop, no curé must feel himself independent; he must be and always remain a mere functionary, a hired workman for whom the State provides work in a shop with a roof overhead, a suitable and indispensable atelier, in other words, the house of prayer well known in each parish as "one of the edifices formerly assigned to worship. " This edifice is not restored to the Christian community, nor to its representatives; it is simply "placed at the disposition of the bishop. "[115] The State retains the ownership of it, or transfers this to the communes; it concedes to the clergy merely the right of using it, and, in that, loses but little. Parish and cathedral churches in its hands are, for the most part, dead capital, nearly useless and almost valueless; through their structure, they are not fitted for civil offices; it does not know what to do with them except to make barns of them; if it sells them it is to demolishers for their value as building material, and then at great scandal. Among the parsonages and gardens that have been surrendered, several have become communal property, [116] and, in this case, it is not the State which loses its title but the commune which is deprived of its investment. In short, in the matter of available real estate, land or buildings, from which the State might derive a rent, that which it sets off from its domain and hands over to the clergy is of very little account. As to military service, it makes no greater concessions. Neither the Concordat nor the organic articles stipulate any exemption for the clergy; the dispensation granted is simply a favor; this is provisional for the seminarians and only becomes permanent under ordination; now, the government fixes the number of the ordained, and it keeps this down as much as possible; [117] for the diocese of Grenoble, it allows only eight in seven years. [118] In this way, it not only saves conscripts, but again, for lack of young priests, it forces the bishops to appoint old priests, even constitutionalists, nearly all pensioners on the treasury, and which either relieves the treasury of a pension or the commune of a subsidy. [119] - Thus, in the reconstruction of the ecclesiastical fortune the State spares itself and the portion it contributes remains very small: it furnishes scarcely more than the plan, a few corner and foundation stones and the permission or injunction to build; the rest concerns the communes and private individuals. They must exert themselves, continue and complete it, by order or spontaneously and under its permanent direction.

VIII. Public Education.

State appropriations very small. - Toleration of educational institutions. - The interest of the public in them invited. - The University. - Its monopoly. - Practically, his restrictions and conditions are effective. - Satisfaction given to the first group of requirements.

Invariably the government proceeds in the same manner with the reorganization of the other two collective fortunes. - As regards the charitable institutions, under the Directory, the asylums and hospitals had their unsold property restored to them, and in the place of what had been sold they were promised national property of equal value. [120] But this was a complicated operation; things had dragged along in the universal disorder and, to carry it out, the First Consul reduced and simplified it. He at once sets aside a portion of the national domain, several distinct morsels in each district or department, amounting in all to four millions of annual income derived from productive real-estate, [121] which he distributes among the asylums, pro rata, according to their losses. He assigns to them, moreover, all the rents, in money or in kind, due for foundations to parishes, curés, fabriques and corporations; finally, "he applies to their wants" various outstanding claims, all national domains which have been usurped by individuals or communes and which may be subsequently recovered, "all rentals be-longing to the Republic, the recognition and payment of which have been interrupted. "[122] In short, he rummages every corner and picks out the scraps which may help them along; then, resuming and extending another undertaking of the Directory, he assigns to them, not merely in Paris, but in many other towns, a portion of the product derived from theatres and octrois. [123] - Having thus increased their income, he applies himself to diminishing their expenses. On the one hand, he gives them back their special servants, those who cost the least and work the best, I mean the Sisters of Charity. On the other hand, he binds them down rigidly to exact accounts; he subjects them to strict supervision; he selects for them competent and suitable administrators; he stops, here as everywhere else, waste and peculation. Henceforth, the public reservoir to which the poor come to quench their thirst is repaired and cleaned; the water remains pure and no longer oozes out; private charity may therefore pour into it its fresh streams with full security; on this side, they flow in naturally, and, at this moment, with more force than usual, for, in the reservoir, half-emptied by revolutionary confiscations, the level is always low.

There remain the institutions for instruction. With respect to these, the restoration seems more difficult, for their ancient endowment is almost entirely wasted; the government has nothing to give back but dilapidated buildings, a few scattered investments formerly intended for the maintenance of a college scholarship, [124] or for a village schoolhouse. And to whom should these be returned since the college and the schoolhouse no longer exist? - Fortunately, instruction is an article of such necessity that a father almost always tries to procure it for his children; even if poor, he is willing to pay for it, if not too dear; only, he wants that which pleases him in kind and in quality and, therefore, from a particular source, bearing this or that factory stamp or label. If you want him to buy it do not drive the purveyors of it from the market who enjoy his confidence and who sell it cheaply; on the contrary, welcome them and allow them to display their wares. This is the first step, an act of toleration; the conseils- généraux demand it and the government yields. [125] It permits the return of the Ignorantin brethren, allows them to teach and authorizes the towns to employ them; later on, it graduates them at its University: in 1810, they already possess 41 schoolhouses and 8400 pupils. [126] Still more liberally, it authorizes and favors female educational congregations; down to the end of the empire and afterwards, nuns are about the only instructors of young girls, especially in primary education. - Owing to the same toleration, the upper schools are likewise reorganized, and not less spontaneously, through the initiative of private individuals, communes, bishops, colleges or pensionnats, at Reims, Fontainebleau, Metz, Évreux, Sorrèze, Juilly, La Fléche and elsewhere small seminaries in all the dioceses. Offer and demand have come together; instructors meet the children half-way, and education begins on all sides. [127]

Thought can now be given to its endowment, and the State invites everybody, the communes as well as private persons, to the undertaking. It is on their liberality that it relies for replacing the ancient foundations; it solicits gifts and legacies in favor of new establishments, and it promises "to surround these donations with the most invariable respect. "[128] Meanwhile, and as a precautionary measure, it assigns to each its eventual duty; [129] if the commune establishes a primary school for itself, it must provide the tutor with a lodging and the parents must compensate him; if the commune founds a college or accepts a lycée, it must pay for the annual support of the building, [130] while the pupils, either day-scholars or boarders, pay accordingly. In this way, the heavy expenses are already met, and the State, the general-manager of the service, furnishes simply a very small quota; and this quota, mediocre as a rule, is found almost null in fact, for its main largess consists in 6400 scholarships which it establishes and engages to support; but it confers only about 3000 of them, [131] and it distributes nearly all of these among the children of its military or civilian employees This way a son's scholarship becomes additional pay or an increased salary for the father; thus, the 2 millions which the State seems, under this head, to assign to the lycées are actually gratifications which it distributes among its functionaries and officials: it takes back with one hand what it be-stows with the other. - Having put this in place, it establishes the University. It is not at its own expense, however, but at the expense of others, at the expense of private persons and parents, of the communes, and above all at the expense of rival schools and private boarding-schools, of the free institutions, and all this in favor of the University monopoly which subjects these to special taxation as ingenious as it is multifarious. [132] A private individual obtaining diploma to open on a boarding school must pay from 200 to 300 francs to the University; likewise, every person obtaining a diploma to open an institution shall pay from 400 to 600 francs to the University; likewise every person obtaining permission to lecture on law or medicine. [133] Every student, boarder, half- boarder or day-scholar in any school, institution, seminary, college or lycée, must pay to the University one-twentieth of the sum which the establishment to which he belongs demands of each of its pupils. In the higher schools, in the faculties of law, medicine, science and literature, the students pay entrance and examination fees and for diplomas, so that the day comes when superior instruction provides for its expenditures out of its receipts and even shows on its budget a net surplus of profit. The new University, with its expenses thus defrayed, will support itself alone; accordingly, all that the State really grants to it, as a veritable gift, in ready cash, is 400,000 francs annual income on the public ledger, a little less than the donation of one single college, Louis-le-Grand, in 1789. [134] It may even be said that it is exactly the fortune of the old college which, after being made use of in many ways, turned aside and with other mischance, becomes the patrimony of the new University. [135] From high-school to University, the State has effected the transfer. Such is its generosity. This is especially apparent in connection with primary instruction; in 1812, for the first time, it allows 25,000 francs for this purpose, of which only 4,500 are received. [136]

Such is the final liquidation of the great collective fortunes. A settlement of accounts, an express or tacit bargain, intervenes between the State and all institutions for instruction, worship and charity. It has taken from the poor, from the young and from believers, 5 milliards of capital and 270 millions of revenue; [137] it gives back to them, in public income and treasury interest, about 17 millions per annum. As it has the might and makes the law it has no difficulty in obtaining or in giving itself its own discharge; it is a bankrupt who, having spent his creditors money, bestows on these 6%. of their claim by way of alms.

Naturally, it takes the opportunity to bring them under its strict and permanent dependence, in adding other claims to those with which the old monarchy had already burdened the corporations that administered collective fortunes. Napoleon increases the weight of these chains and screws them tighter. Not only does he take it upon himself to impose order, probity, and economy on the administrators, but, again, he appoints them, dismisses them, and prescribes or authorizes each of their acts. He puts words in their mouths; he wants to be the great bishop, the universal genius, the sole tutor and professor, in short, the dictator of opinion, the creator and director of every political, social and moral idea throughout his empire. - With what rigidity and pertinacious intent, with what variety and convergence of means, with what plenitude and certainty of execution, with what detriment and with what danger, present and to come, for corporations, for the public, for the State, for himself, we shall see presently; he himself, living and reigning, is to realize this. For his interference, pushed to extremes, is to end in encountering resistance in a body which he considers as his own creature, the Church: here, forgetting that she has roots of her own, deep down and out of his reach, he carries off the Pope, holds him captive, sends cardinals into the interior, (Page 198/504)imprisons bishops, banishes priests, and incorporates seminarians in his regiments. [138] He decrees the closing of all small seminaries, [139] alienates forever the Catholic clergy like the royalist nobility, precisely at the same moment and through the same absolutism, through the same abuse of power, through the same recurrence to revolutionary tradition, to Jacobin infatuation and brutality, even to the frustration of his Concordat of 1802 as with his amnesty of 1802, even to compromising his capital work of the attempted reconciliation and reunion of old France with the new France. His work, nevertheless, although incomplete, even interrupted and marred by himself, remains substantial and salutary. The three grand machines which the Revolution had demolished with so little foresight, and which he had reconstructed at so little cost, are in working order, and, with deviations or shortcomings in result, they render to the public the required services, each its own, worship, charity and instruction. Full toleration and legal protection to the three leading Christian cults, and even to Judaism, would of itself already satisfy the most sensitive of religious demands; owing to the donation furnished by the State and communes and by private individuals, the necessary complement is not wanting.

The Catholic community, in particular, the most numerous of all, exercises and celebrates its system of worship in conformity with its faith, according to ecclesiastical canons under its own orthodox hierarchy; in each parish, or within reach of each parish, dwells one authorized priest who administers valid sacraments; in his stole he says mass publicly in a consecrated edifice, plainly decorated at first but gradually beautified; not less publicly, various congregations of monks and nuns, the former in black robes and the "sisters in wimples and white caps, serve in the schools and asylums.

On the other hand, in these well-equipped and well-governed asylums and hospitals, in the bureaux of charity, their resources are no longer inferior to their needs, while Christian charity and philanthropic generosity are constantly operating in all directions to fill the empty drawers; legacies and private donations, after 1802, authorized by the Council of State, multiply; we see them swelling the pages of the "Bulletin des Lois. "[140] From 1800 to 1845, the hospitals and asylums are thus to receive more than 72 millions, and the charity bureaux over 49 millions; from 1800 to 1878, all together will thus receive more than 415 millions. [141] The old patrimony of the poor is again reconstituted piece by piece; and on January 1st, 1833, asylums and hospitals, with their 51 millions of revenue, are able to support 154,000 elderly and the sickly. [142]

Like public charity, public education again becomes effective; Fourcroy, after 1806, [143] lists 29 organized and full lycées; besides these, 370 communal secondary schools and 377 private secondary schools are open and receive 50,200; there are 25,000 children in the 4500 schools. Finally, in 1815, [144] we find in France, restored to its ancient boundaries, 12 faculties of Law or Medicine with 6,329 students, 36 lycées with 9000 pupils, 368 colleges with 28,000 pupils, 41 small seminaries with 5233 pupils, 1255 boarding-schools and private institutions with 39,623 pupils, and 22,348 primary schools with 737,369 scholars; as far as can be gathered, the proportion of men and women able to read and to sign their name is raised under the empire up to and beyond the figures[145] it had reached previous to 1789.

In this manner are the worst damages repaired. The three new administrative services, with a different set-up, do the job of the old ones and, at the expiration of twenty-five years, give an almost equal return. - In sum, the new proprietor of the great structure sacked by the Revolution has again set up the indispensable apparatus for warming, lighting and ventilation; as he knows his own interests perfectly, and is poorly off in ready money, he contributes only a minimum of the expense; in other respects, he has grouped together his tenants into syndicates, into barracks, in apartments, and, voluntarily or involuntarily, he has put upon them the burden of cost. In the meantime, he has kept the three keys of the three engines in his own cabinet, in his own hands, for himself alone; henceforth, it is he who distributes throughout the building, on each story and in every room, light, air and heat. If he does not distribute the same quantity as before he at least distributes whatever is necessary; the tenants can, at last, breathe comfortably, see clearly and not shiver; after ten years of suffocation, darkness and cold they are too well satisfied to wrangle with the proprietor, discuss his ways, and dispute over the monopoly by which he has constituted himself the arbitrator of their wants. - The same thing is done in the material order of things, in relation to the highways, dikes, canals, and structures useful to the people: here also he repairs or creates through the same despotic initiative,

* with the same economy, [146]
* the same apportionment of expense, [147]
* the same spontaneous or forced aid to those interested,
* the same practical efficiency. [148]

Summing it up and if we take things as a whole, and if we offset the worse with the better, it may be said that the French people have recovered the possessions they had been missing since 1789:

* internal peace,
* public tranquility,

* administrative regularity,
* impartial justice,
* a strict police,
* security of persons, property and consciences,
* liberty in private life,
* enjoyment of one's native land, and, on leaving it, the privilege of coming back;
* the satisfactory endowment, gratuitous celebration and full exercise of worship;
* schools and instruction for the young;
* beds, nursing and assistance for the sick, the indigent and for foundlings;
* the maintenance of roads and public buildings.

So that of the two groups of cravings which troubled men in 1800, the first one, that which dated from the Revolution, has, towards 1808 or 1810, obtained reasonable satisfaction.

Notes:

[1] Roederer, III., 334 (August 6, 1800).

[3] Stanislas Girardin, "Mémoires, " I., 273 (22 Thermidor, year X): "The only craving, the only sentiment in France, disturbed for so many years, is repose. Whatever secures this will gain its assent. Its inhabitants, accustomed to take an active part in all political questions, now seem to take no interest in them. " - Roederer, III., 484 (Report on the Sénatorerie of Caen, Dec. 1, 1803): "The people of the rural districts, busy with its new affairs, . .. are perfectly submissive, because they now find security for persons and property. . .. They show no enthusiasm for the monarch, but are full of respect for and trust in a gendarme; they stop and salute him on passing him on the roads. "

[4] Rocquam, "l'État de la France au 18 Brumaire. " (Report by Barbé- Marbois, p. 72, 81.) Cash-boxes broken open and exclamations by the officers "Money and fortune belong to the brave. Let us help ourselves. Our accounts will be settled at the cannon's mouth. " - " The subordinates, " adds Barbé-Marbois, "fully aware of their superior's drafts on the public treasury, stipulate for their share of the booty; accustomed to exacting contributions from outside enemies they are not averse to treating as conquered enemies the departments they were called upon to defend. "

[5] Ibid. (Reports of Barbe-Marbois and Fourcroy while on their missions in the 12th and 13th military divisions, year IX., p. 158, on the tranquility of La Vendée.) "I could have gone anywhere without an escort. During my stay in some of the villages I was not disturbed by any fear or suspicion whatever. . .. The tranquility they now enjoy and the cessation of persecutions keep them from insurrection. "

[6] Archives nationales, F7,3273 (Reports by Gen. Ferino, Pluvi'se, year IX, with a table of verdicts by the military commission since Floreal, year VIII.) The commission mentions 53 assassinations, 3 rapes, 44 pillagings of houses, by brigands in Vaucluse, Dr'me, and the Lower Alps; 66 brigands taken in the act are shot, 87 after condemnation, and 6, who are wounded, die in the hospital. - Rocquain, ibid., p. 17, (Reports of Français, from Nantes, on his mission in the 8th military division.) "The South may be considered as purged by the destruction of about 200 brigands who have been shot. There remains only three or four bands of 7 or S men each. "

[7] Three classes of insurrectionary peasants or marauders. - Tr.

[8] Archives Nationales, F7, 7152 (on the prolongation of brigandage). Letter from Lhoste, agent, to the minister of justice, Lyons, Pluvi'se 8, year VIII. "The diligences are robbed every week." - Ibid., F7,3267, (Seine-et-Oise, bulletins of the military police and correspondence of the gendarmerie). Brumaire 25, year VIII, attack on the Paris mail near Arpajon by 5 brigands armed with guns. Fructidor, year VIII, at three o'clock P. M., a cart loaded with 10,860 francs sent by the collector at Mantes to the collector at Versailles is stopped near the Marly water-works, by 8 or 10 armed brigands on horseback. - Similar facts abound. It is evident that more than a year is required to put an end to brigandage. - It is always done by employing an impartial military force. (Rocquam, Ibid, p. 10.) "There are at Marseilles three companies of paid national guards, 60 men each, at a franc per man. The fund for this guard is supplied by a contribution of 5 francs a month paid by every man subject to this duty who wishes to be exempt. The officers . .. are all strangers in the country. Robberies, murders, and conflicts have ceased in Marseilles since the establishment of this guard. "

[9] Archives Nationales, 3144 and 3145, No. 1004. (Reports of the councillors of State on mission during the year IX, published by Rocquam, with omissions, among which is the following, in the report of François de Nantes.) "The steps taken by the mayors of

Marseilles are sufficiently effective to enable an émigré under surveillance and just landed, to walk about Marseilles without being knocked down or knocking anybody else down, an alternative to which they have been thus far subject. And yet there are in this town nearly 500 men who have slaughtered with their own hands, or been the accomplices of slaughterers, at different times during the Revolution. . .. The inhabitants of this town are so accustomed to being annoyed and despoiled, and to being treated like those of a rebellious town or colony, that arbitrary power no longer frightens them, and they simply ask that their lives and property be protected against murderers and pillagers, and that things be entrusted to sure and impartial hands. "

[10] Roederer, III., 481. (Report on the Sénatorerie of Caen, Germinal 2, year XIII.)- Faber, "Notice sur l'intérieur de la France"(1807), p. 110, 112. "Justice is one of the bright sides of France of to-day. It is costly, but it cannot be called venal. "

[11] Rocquain, ibid., 19. (Report of François de Nantes on the 8th military division.) "For the past eighteen months a calm has prevailed here equal to that which existed before the Revolution. Balls and parties have been resumed in the towns, while the old dances of Provence, suspended for ten years, now gladden the people of the country. "

[12] Proclamation to the French people, Dec. 15, 1799.

[13] See "The Revolution, " vol. III., p. 292. (Notes.) (Laff. II, the notes on pp. 218-219.)

[14] Decision of the Council of State, Pluvi'se 5, year VIII (Jan. 25, 1800).

[15] Forneron, "Histoire générale des émigrés, " II., 374. In 1800, the army of Condé still comprised 1007 officers and 5840 volunteers.

[16] Decrees of Brumaire 3, year IV, and of Frimaire 9, year VI. (Cf. "The Revolution, " pp. 433, 460.)

[17] Constitution of Frimaire 22, year VIII. (December 13, 1799), article 93. "The French nation declares that in no case will it suffer the return of the Frenchmen who, having abandoned their country since the 14th of July 1789, are not comprised in the exceptions made

to the laws rendered against émigrés. It interdicts every new exception in this respect. "

[18] Opinion of the Council of State, Dec. 25, 1799.

[19] Resolution of Dec. 26, 1799. - Two ultra-Jacobins, exiled after Thermidor, are added to the list, Barère and Vadier, undoubtedly by way of compensation and not to let it appear that the scales inclined too much on one side.

[20] Resolution of Dec. 30, 1799.

[21] Resolutions of February 26, March 2, and March 3, 1800.

[22] Thibaudeau, "Mémoires sur le Consulat, " 199. (Stated by the First Consul at Regnault at a meeting of the council of state, Aug. 12, 1801.) "I am glad to hear the denunciation of striking off names. How many have you yourselves not asked for? It could not be otherwise. Everybody has some relation or friend on the lists. "

[23] Thibaudeau. ibid. (Speech by the First Consul.) "Never have there been lists of émigrés; " there are only lists of absentees. The proof of this is that names have always been struck off. I have seen members of the Convention and even generals on the lists. Citizen Monge was inscribed. "

[24] Thibaudeau, ibid., 97. - "The minister of police made a great hue and cry over the arrest and sending back of a few émigrés who returned without permission, or who annoyed the buyers of their property, while, at the same time, it granted surveillance to all who asked for it, paying no attention to the distinction made by the resolution of Vendémiaire 28. "

[25] Sénatus-consulte of April 26, 1802.

[26] Sénatus-consulte of April 26, 1802, title II., articles 16 and 17. - Gaudin, Duc de Gaëte, "Mémoires, " I., 183. (Report on the administration of the Finances in 1803.) "The old proprietors have been reinstated in more than 20,000 hectares of forests. "

[27] Thibaudeau, ibid., p. 98. (Speech of the First Consul, Thermidor 24, year IX.) Some of the émigrés who have been pardoned are cutting down their forests, either from necessity or to send money

abroad. I will not allow the worst enemies of the republic, the defenders of ancient prejudices, to recover their fortunes and despoil France. I am glad to welcome them back; but it is important that the nation should preserve its forests; the navy needs them. "

[28] An arpent measures about an acre and a half. (TR.)

[29] Stourm, "Les Finances de l'ancien régime et de la révolution, "II., 459 to 461. - (According to the figures appended to the projected law of 1825.) - This relates only to their patrimony in real estate; their personal estate was wholly swept away, at first through the abolition, without indemnity, of their available feudal rights under the Constituent and Legislative assemblies, and afterwards through the legal and forced transformation of their personal capital into national bonds (titres sur le grand-livre, rentes) which the final bankruptcy of the Directory reduced to almost nothing.

[30] Pelet de la Lozère, "Opinions de Napoléon au conseil d'état" (March 15th and July 1st, 1806): "One of the most unjust effects of the revolution was to let an émigré; whose property was found to be sold, starve to death, and give back 100,000 crowns of rente to another whose property happened to be still in the hands of the government. How odd, again, to have returned unsold fields and to have kept the woods! It would have been better, starting from the legal forfeiture of all property, to return only 6000 francs of rente to one alone and distribute what remained among the rest. "

[31] Léonce de Lavergne, "Economie rurale de la France, " p. 26. (According to the table of names with indemnities awarded by the law of 1825.) - Duc de Rovigo, Mémoires, " IV., 400.

[32] De Puymaigre, "Souvenirs de l'émigration de l'empire et de la restauration, " p. 94.

[33] Pelet de la Lozère, ibid., p. 272.

[34] De Puymaigre, ibid., passim. - Alexandrine des Écherolles, "Une famille noble pendant la Terreur, " pp. 328, 402, 408. - I add to published documents personal souvenirs and family narrations.

[35] Duc de Rovigo, "Mémoires, " IV., 399. (On the provincial noblesse which had emigrated and returned.) "The First Consul quietly gave orders that none of the applications made by the large

number of those who asked for minor situations in various branches of the administration should be rejected on account of emigration. "

[36] M. de Vitrolles, "Mémoires. " - M. d'Haussonville, "Ma jeunesse," p. 6o: "One morning, my father learns that he has been appointed chamberlain, with a certain number of other persons belonging to the greatest families of the faubourg Saint-Germain. "

[37] Madame de Rémusat, "Mémoires, " II., 312, 315 and following pages, 373. - Madame de Staël, "Considérations sur la révolution française, " 4th part, ch IV.

[38] Roederer, III., 459. (Speech by Napoleon, December 30, 1802.)" Very well, I do protect the nobles of France; but they must see that they need protection. . .. I give places to many of them; I restore them to public distinction and even to the honors of the drawing-room; but they feel that it is alone through my good will. - Ibid., III., 558 (January 1809): "I repent daily of a mistake I have made in my government; the most serious one I ever made, and I perceive its bad effects every day. It was the giving back to the émigrés the totality of their possessions. I ought to have massed them in common and given each one simply the chance of an income of 6000 francs. As soon as I saw my mistake I withdrew from thirty to forty millions of forests; but far too many are still in the hands of a great number of them. " - We here see the attitude he would impose on them, that of clients and grateful pensioners. They do not stand in this attitude. (Roederer, III., 472. Report on the Sénatorerie of Caen, 1803.) - "The returned émigrés are not friendly nor even satisfied; their enjoyment of what they have recovered is less than their indignation at what they have lost. They speak of the amnesty without gratitude, and as only partial justice. . .. In other respects they appear submissive. "

[39] Duc de Rovigo1 "Memoires. " V., 297. Towards the end, large numbers of the young nobles went into the army. "In 1812, there, was not a marshal, or even a general, who had not some of these on his staff, or as aids-de-camp. Nearly all the cavalry regiments in the army were commanded by officers belonging to these families. They had already attracted notice in the infantry. All these young nobles had openly joined the emperor because they were easily influenced by love of glory. "

[40] Madame de Rémusat II., 299 (1806): "He began to surround himself about this time with so much ceremony that none of us had

scarcely any intimate relations with him. . ... The court became more and more crowded and monotonous, each doing on the minute what he had to do. Nobody thought of venturing outside the brief series of ideas which are generated within the restricted circle of the same duties. . ... Increasing despotism, . .. fear of a reproof if one failed in the slightest particular, silence kept by us all. . ... There was no opportunity to indulge emotion or interchange any observation of the slightest importance. "

[41] Roederer, III., 558 (January 1809). - "The Modern Régime, " ante, book I., ch. II.

[43] Madame de Staël, "Considérations sur la révolution française" and "Dix ans d'exil. " Exile of Madame de Balbi, of Madame de Chevreuse, of Madame de Duras, of Madame d'Aveaux, of Madame de Staël, of Madame de Récamier, etc. - Duc de Rovigo, Ibid., IV., 389: "The first exiles dated from 1805; I think there were fourteen. "

[44] Roederer, III., 472. (Report on the Sénatorerie of Caen, 1803.) The nobles "have no social relations either with citizens or with the public functionaries, except with the prefect of Caen and the general in command. . ... Their association with the prefect intimates their belief that they might need him. All pay their respects to the general of division; his mantelpiece is strewed with visiting-cards. "

[45] Madame de la Rochejaquelein, "Mémoires, " 423: "We lived exposed to a tyranny which left us neither calm nor contentment. At one time a spy was placed amongst our servants, at another some of our relations would be exiled far from their homes, accused of exercising a charity which secured them too much affection from their neighbors. Sometimes, my husband would be obliged to go to Paris to explain his conduct. Again, a hunting-party would be represented as a meeting of Vendéans. Occasionally, we were blamed for going into Poitou because our influence was regarded as too dangerous; again, we were reproached for not living there and not exercising our influence in behalf of the conscription. " - Her brother-in-law, Auguste de la Rochejaquelein, invited to take service in the army comes to Paris to present his objections. He is arrested, and at the end of two months "the minister signifies to him that he must remain a prisoner so long as he refuses to be a second-lieutenant. "

[46] Sénatus-consulte of April 26, 1802: "Considering that this measure is merely one of pardon to the large number who are always more led astray than criminal . .. the amnestied will remain for ten years under a special government surveillance. " It may oblige each one "to leave his usual residence and go to a distance of twenty leagues, and even farther if circumstances demand it. "

[47] Thiers, X., 41. (Letter to Fouché, Dec. 31, 1808, not inserted in the correspondence.) - "The Modern Régime, " book I., ch. II.

[48] Rocquain, "État de la France au 18 brumaire, " pp. 33, 189, 190. (Reports of Français de Nantes and of Fourcroy.) - "Statistique elementaire de la France, " by Peuchet (according to a statement published by the minister of the interior, year IX), p. 260. - "Statistiques des préfets, " Aube, by Aubray, p. 23; Aisne, by Dauchet, p. 87; Lot-et-Garonne, by Pieyre, p. 45: "It is during the Revolution that the number of foundlings increased to this extraordinary extent by the too easy admission in the asylums of girls who had become mothers, along with their infants; through the passing sojourn of soldiers in their houses; through the subversion of every principle of religion and morality. " - Gers, by Balguerie: "Many defenders of the country became fathers before their departure. . .. The soldiers, on their return, maintained the habits of their conquests. . .. Many of the girls, besides, for lack of a husband took a lover. "- Moselle, by Coichen, p. 91: "Morals are more lax. In 1789, at Metz, there are 524 illegitimate births; in the year IX, 646; in 1789, 70 prostitutes; in the year IX, 260. There is the same increase of kept women. " - Peuchet, " Essai d'une statistique générale de la France, " year IX, p. 28. "The number of illegitimate births, from one forty-seventh in 1780, increased to nearly one eleventh of the total births, according to the comparative estimates of M. Necker and M. Mourgue. "

[49] Rocquam, ibid., p. 93. (Report of Barbé-Marbois.)

[50] "The Revolution, " III., p. 416 (note), P. 471 (note). (Laff. II. pp. 307-308, p 348.)

[52] Decrees of March 19, 1793, and Messidor 23, year II. - Decrees of Brumaire 2, year IV, and Vendémiaire 16 year V.

[53] "Statistiques des préfets, " Rh'ne, by Verminac, year X. Income of the Lyons Asylums in 1789,1.510,827 francs; to-day, 459,371 francs.

- Indre, by Dalphonse, year XII. The principal asylum of Issoudun, founded in the twelfth century, had 27,939 francs revenue, on which it loses 16,232. Another asylum, that of the Incurables, loses, on an income of 12,062 francs, 7457 francs. - Eure, by Masson Saint-Amand, year XIII: "14 asylums and 3 small charity establishments in the department, with about 100,000 francs income in 1789, have lost at least 60,000 francs of it. - Vosges, by Desgouttes, year X: "10 asylums in the department. Most of these have been stripped of nearly the whole of their property and capital on account of the law of Messidor 23, year II; on the suspension of the execution of this law, the property had been sold and the capital returned. - Cher, by Luçay: "15 asylums before the revolution; they remain almost wholly without resources through the loss of their possessions. - Lozère, by Jerphaniou, year X: "The property belonging to the asylums, either in real estate or state securities, has passed into other hands. " - Doubs, analysis by Ferrieres: "Situation of the asylums much inferior to that of 1789, because they could not have property restored to them in proportion to the value of that which had been alienated. The asylum of Pontarlier lost one-half of its revenue through reimbursements in paper-money. All the property of the Ornans asylum has been sold, " etc. - Rocquain, p. 187. (Report by Fourcroy.) Asylums of Orne: their revenue, instead of 123,189 francs, is no more than 68,239. - Asylums of Calvados: they have lost 173,648 francs of income, there remains of this only 85,955 francs. - Passim, heart-rending details on the destitution of the asylums and their inmates, children, the sick and the infirm. - The figures by which I have tried to show the disproportion between requirements and resources are a minimum.

[54] Abbé Allain, "l'Instruction primaire en France avant la Révolution, " and Albert Duruy, "l'Instruction publique et la Révolution, " passim.

[55] "Statistique de l'enseignement primaire" (1880), II., CCIV. The proportion of instructed and uninstructed people has been ascertained in 79 departments, and at various periods, from 1680 down to the year 1876, according to the signatures on 1,699,985 marriage-records. - In the "Dictionnaire de pédagogie et d'instruction primaire, " published by M. Buisson, M. Maggiolo, director of these vast statistics, has given the proportion of literate and illiterate people for the different departments; now, from department to department, the figures furnished by the signatures on marriage records correspond with sufficient exactness to the

number of schools, verified moreover by pastoral visits and by other documents. The most illiterate departments are Cantal, Puy-de-Dome, Nièvre, Allier, Vienne, Haute- Vienne, Deux-Sèvres, Vendée and the departments of Brittany.

[57] Albert Duruy, ibid., p. 25. (According to the report of M. Villemain on common-school education in 1843.) - Abbé Allain, "la Question d'enseignement en 1789, " p. 88 - A. Silvy, "les Collèges en France avant la Révolution, " p. 5. The researches of M. Silvy show that the number of high-schools (collèges) given by M. Villemain is much too low: "The number of these schools under the ancient Régime cannot be estimated at less than about 900. . .. I have ascertained 800. . .. I must add that my search is not yet finished and that I find new institutions every day. "

[58] Lunet, "Histoire du collège de Rodez, " p. 110. - Edmond, "Histoire du collège de Louis-le-Grand, " p. 238. - "Statistiques des préfets, " Moselle. (Analysis by Ferrière, year XII.) Before 1789, 4 high-schools at Metz, very complete, conducted by regular canons, Benedictines, with 33 professors, 38 assistant teachers, 63 servants, 259 day-scholars and 217 boarders. All this was broken up. In the year IX there is only one central school, very inadequate, with 9 professors, 5 assistants, 3 servants and 233 day-scholars.

[59] Albert Duruy, ibid., p. 25.

[60] Lunet, ibid, p. 110,

[61] "Statistiques des préfets, " Ain, by Bossi, p. 368. At Bourg, before the revolution, 220 pupils, of which 70 were boarders, 8000 livres income in real property confiscated during the revolution. - At Belley, the teachers consist of the congregationist of Saint-Joseph; 250 pupils, 9950 francs revenue from capital invested in the pays d'état, swept away by the revolution. - At Thoissy, 8000 francs rental of real property sold, etc. - Deux-Sèvres, by Dupin, year IX, and "analyse" by Ferrière, P. 48: "Previous to the revolution, each department town had its high-school. - At Thouars, 60 boarders at 300 livres per annum, and 40 day-scholars. At Niort, 80 boarders at 450 livres per annum, and 100 day-scholars". -Aisne, by Dauchy, p. 88. Before 1789, nearly all the small high-schools were gratuitous, and, in the large ones, there were scholarships open to competition. All their possessions, except large buildings, were alienated and sold, as well as those of the 60 communities in which girls were taught

gratuitously. - Eure, by Masson Saint-Amand. There were previous to 1789, 8 high-schools which were all suppressed and destroyed. - Dr'me, by Collin, p. 66. Before the revolution, each town had its high- school, " etc.

[62] Cf. Marmontel, "Mémoires, " I., 16, for details of these customs; M. Jules Simon found the same customs afterwards and describes them in the souvenirs of his youth. - La Chalotais, at the end of the reign of Louis XV., had already described the efficiency of the institution. "Even the people want to study. Farmers and craftsmen send their children to the schools in these small towns where living is cheap. " — This rapid spread of secondary education contributed a good deal towards bringing on the revolution.

[63] "Statistiques des préfets, " Indre, by Dalphonse, year XII, p. 104: "The universities, the colleges, the seminaries, the religious establishments, the free schools are all destroyed; vast plans only remain for a new system of education raised on their ruins. Nearly all of these rest unexecuted. . .. Primary schools have nowhere, one may say, been organized, and those which have been are so poor they had better not have been organized at all. With a pompous and costly system of public instruction, ten years have been lost for instruction. "

[64] Moniteur, XXI., 644. (Session of Fructidor 19, year II.) One of the members says: "It is very certain, and my colleagues see it with pain, that public instruction is null. " - Fourcroy: "Reading and writing are no longer taught. " - Albert Duruy, p. 208. (Report to the Directory executive, Germinal 13, year IV.) "For nearly six years no public instruction exists. " - De La Sicotiere, "Histoire du collège de Alençon, " p. 33: "In 1794, there were only two pupils in the college. " - Lunet, "Histoire du collège de Rodez, " p. 157: "The recitation-rooms remained empty of pupils and teachers from March 1793 to May 16, 1796. " - " Statistiques des préfets, " Eure, by Masson Saint-Amand year XIII: "In the larger section of the department, school-houses existed with special endowments for teachers of both sexes. The school-houses have been alienated like other national domains; the endowments due to religious corporations or establishments have been extinguished - As to girls, that portion of society has suffered an immense loss, relatively to its education, in the suppression of religious communities which provided them with an almost gratuitous and sufficiently steady instruction. "

[65] My maternal grandmother learned how to read from a nun concealed in the cellar of the house.

[66] Albert Duruy, ibid., 349. (Decree of the Directory, Pluvi'se 17, year V, and circular of the minister Letourneur against free schools which are "dens of royalism and superstition. " - Hence the decrees of the authorities in the departments of Eure, Pas de Calais, Dr'me, Mayenne and La Manche, closing these dens.) "From Thermidor 27, year VI, to Messidor 2, year VII, say the authorities of La Manche, we have revoked fifty-eight teachers on their denunciation by the municipalities and by popular clubs. "

[67] Archives nationales, cartons 3144 to 3145, No. l04. (Reports of the Councillors of State on mission in the year IX.) Report by Lacuée on the first military division. Three central schools at Paris, one called the Quatre-Nations. "This school must be visited in order to form any idea of the state of destruction and dilapidation which all the national buildings are in. No repairs have been made since the reopening of the schools; everything is going to ruin. . .. Walls are down and the floors fallen in. To preserve the pupils from the risks which the occupation of these buildings hourly presents, it is necessary to give lessons in rooms which are very unhealthy on account of their small dimensions and dampness. In the drawing-class the papers and models in the portfolios become moldy. "

[68] Albert Duruy, ibid., 484. ("Procès-verbaux des conseils-généraux, " year IX, passim.)

[69] Ibid., 476. ("Statistiques des préfets, " Sarthe, year X.) "Prejudices which it is difficult to overcome, as well on the stability of this school as on the morality of some of the teachers, prevented its being frequented for a time. " - 483. (Procès-verbaux des conseils-généraux, " Bas-Rhin.) "The overthrow of religion has excited prejudices against the central schools. " - 482. (Ibid., Lot.) "Most of the teachers in the central school took part in the revolution in a not very honorable way. Their reputation affects the success of their teaching. Their schools are deserted. "

[70] Albert Duruy, ibid., '94. (According to the reports of 15 central schools, from the year VI. to the year VIII.) The average for each central school is for drawing, 89 pupils; for mathematics, 28; for the classics, 24; for physics, chemistry and natural history, 19; for general grammar, 5; for history, 10; for legislation, 8: for belles- lettres, 6. -

Rocquam, ibid., P. 29. (Reports of Français de Nantes, on the departments of the South-east.) "There, as elsewhere, the courses on general grammar, on belles-lettres, history and legislation, are unfrequented. Those on mathematics, chemistry, Latin and drawing are better attended, because these sciences open up lucrative careers. - Ibid., p. 108. (Report by Barbé-Marboi on the Brittany departments.)

[71] Statistiques des préfets, " Meurthe, by Marquis, year XIII, p. 120. "In the communal schools of the rural districts, the fee was so small that the poorest families could contribute to the (teacher's) salary. Assessments on the communal property, besides, helped almost everywhere in providing the teacher with a satisfactory salary, so that these functions were sought after and commonly well fulfilled. . .. Most of the villages had Sisters of Saint-Vincent de Paul for instructors, or others well known under the name of Vatelottes. " - "The partition of communal property, and the sale of that assigned to old endowments, had deprived the communes of resources which afforded a fair compensation to schoolmasters and schoolmistresses. The product of the additional centimes scarcely sufficed for administrative expenses. - Thus, there is but little else now than people without means, who take poorly compensated places; again, they neglect their, schools just as soon as they see an opportunity to earn something elsewhere. " - Archives nationales, No. 1004, cartons 3044 and 3145. (Report of the councillors of state on mission in the year IX. - First military division, Report of Lacuée.) Aisne: "There is now no primary school according to legal institution. " - The situation is the same in Oise, also in Seine for the districts of Sceaux and SaintDenis.

[72] Albert Duruy, 178. (Report drawn up in the bureaux of the ministry of the interior, year VIII.) "A detestable selection of those called instructors; almost everywhere, they are men without morals or education, who owe their nomination solely to a pretended civism, consisting of nothing but an insensibility to morality and propriety. . .. They affect an insolent contempt for the (old) religious opinions. " - Ibid., p. 497. (Procès-verbaux des conseils-généraux.) On primary school-teachers, Hérault: "Most are blockheads and vagabonds. " - Pas-de-Calais: " Most are blockheads or ignoramuses."

[73] Rocquam, '94. (Report by Fourcroy on the 14th military division, Manche, Orne, Calvados.) "Besides bad conduct, drunkenness, and the immorality of many of these teachers, it seems certain that the

lack of instruction in religion is the principal motive which prevents parents from sending their children to these schools. " - Archives nationales, ibid. (Report by Lacuée on the 1st military division.) "The teachers, male and female, who desired to conform to the law of Brumaire 3 and to the different rules prescribed by the central administration, on placing the constitution and the rights of man in the hands of their pupils, found their schools abandoned one after the other. The schools the best attended are those where the Testament, the catechism, and the life of Christ are used. . .. The instructors, obliged to pursue the line marked out by the government, could not do otherwise than carry out the principles which opposed the prejudices and habits of the parents; hence their loss of credit, and the almost total desertion of the pupils. "

[74] "The Revolution, " vol. III., p. 81, note 2. (Laff. II. pp. 68-69, note 4.)

[75] "Statistiques des préfets, " Moselle. (Analysis by Ferrière.) At Metz, in 1789, there were five free schools for young children, of which one was for boys and four for girls, kept by monks or nuns; in the year XII there were none: "An entire generation was given up to ignorance. " Ibid., Ain, by Bossi, 1808: "In 1800, there were scarcely any primary schools in the department, as in the rest of France. " In 1808, there are scarcely thirty. - Albert Duruy, p. 480, 496. (Procès-verbaux des conseils-généraux, year IX.) Vosges: "Scarcely any primary instruction. " - Sarthe: "Primary instruction, none. " - Meuse- Inférieure: "It is feared that in fifteen years or so there will not be one man in a hundred able to write, " etc.

[76] These are the minimum figures, and they are arrived at through the following calculation. Before 1789, 47 men out of 100, and 26 women out of 100, that is to say 36 or 37 persons in 100, received primary instruction. Now, according to the census from 1876 to 1881 (official statistics of primary instruction, III., XVI.), children from six to thirteen number about twelve % of the entire population. Accordingly, in 1789, out of a population of 26 millions, the children from 6 to 13 numbered 3,120,000, of whom 1,138,000 learned to read and write. It must be noted that, in 1800, the adult population had greatly diminished, and that the infantine population had largely increased. France, moreover, is enlarged by 12 departments (Belgium, Savoy, Comtat, Nice), where the old schools had equally perished. - If all the old schools had been kept up, it is probable that

the children who would have had primary instruction would have numbered nearly 1,400,000.

[77] Saint Thomas, "Summa theologica, " pars III., questio 60 usque ad 85: "Sacramenta efficiunt quod figurant. . .. Sant necessaria ad salutem hominum. . .. Ab ipso verbo incarnata efficaciam habent. Ex sua institutione habent quod conferant gratiam. . .. Sacramentum est causa gratiœ, causa agens, principalis et instrumentalis. "

[78] Except priests ordained by a bishop of the Greek church.

[79] "The Revolution, " I. 161. - Archives nationales. (Reports of the Directory commissioners from the cantons and departments. - There are hundreds of these reports, of which the following are specimens.) - F7, 7108. (Canton of Passavent, Doubs, Vent'se 7, year IV.) "The sway of religious opinions is much more extensive here than before the revolution, because the mass of the people did not concern themselves about them, while nowadays they form among the generality the subject of conversation and complaint. " - F7, 7127. (Canton of Goux, Doubs, Pluvi'se 13, year IV.) "The hunting down of unsworn priests, coupled with the dilapidation and destruction of the temples, displeased the people, who want a religion and a cult; the government became hateful to them. " - Ibid. (Dordogne, canton of Livrac, Vent'se 13, year IV.) "The demolition of altars, the closing of the churches, had rendered the people furious under the Tyranny." - F7, 7129. (Seine-Infèrieure, canton of Canteleu, Pluvi'se 12, year IV.) "I knew enlightened men who, in the ancient regime, never went near a church, and yet who harbored refractory priests. " - Archives nationales, cartons 3144- 3145, No. 1004. (Missions of the councillors of state in the year IX.) At this date, worship was everywhere established and spontaneously. (Report by Lacuée.) In Eure-et-Loire, "nearly every village has its church and minister; the temples are open in the towns and are well attended. " - In Seine-et-Oise, "the Roman Catholic cult prevails in all the communes of the department. " - In Oise, "worship is carried on in all the communes of the department. "-In Loiret, "the churches are attended by the multitude almost as regularly as before 1788. One- sixth of the communes (only) have neither worship nor minister and, in these communes, both are strongly desired. "

[80] Archives nationales, F7, 7129. (Tarn, canton of Vielmur, Germinal 10, year IV.) "The ignorant now regard patriot and brigand as synonymous. "

[81] Archives nationales, F7, 7108. (Doubs, canton of Vercel, Pluvi'se 20, year IV.) "Under the law of Prairial II, the unsworn priests were all recalled by their former parishioners. Their hold on the people is so strong that there is no sacrifice that they will not make, no ruse nor measures that they will not employ to keep them and elude the rigor of the laws bearing on them" - (Ibid., canton of Pontarlier, Pluvi'se 3, year IV.) "In the primary assemblies, the aristocracy, together with spite, have induced the ignorant people not to accept the constitution except on condition of the recall of their transported or emigrant priests for the exercise of their worship. " - (Ibid., canton of Labergement, Pluvi'se 14, year IV.) "The cultivators adore them. . .. I am the only citizen of my canton who, along with my, family, offers up prayers to the Eternal without any intermediary. " - F7, 7127. (C'te-d'Or, canton of Beaune, Vent'se 5, year IV.) "Fanaticism is a power of great influence. " - (Ibid., canton of Frolois, Pluvi'se 9, year IV.) "Two unsworn priests returned eighteen months ago; they are hidden away and hold nocturnal meetings. .. They have seduced and corrupted at least three-quarters of the people of both sexes. " - (Ibid., canton of Ivry, Pluvi'se 1, year IV.) "Fanaticism and popery have perverted the public mind. " - F7, 7119. (Puy-de-D'me, canton of Ambert, Vent'se 15, year IV.) "Five returned priests have celebrated the mass here, and each time were followed by 3000 or 4000 persons. " - F7, 7127. (Dordogne, canton of Carlux, Pluvi'se 18, year IV.) "The people are so attached to the Catholic faith, they walk fully two leagues to attend mass. " - F7, 7119. (Ardèche, canton of Saint-Barthélemy, Pluvi'se 15, year IV.) "The unsubmissive priests have become absolute masters of popular opinion. " - (Orne, canton of Alençon, Vent'se 22, year IV.) "Presidents, members of the municipal councils, instead of arresting the refractory priests and bringing them into court, admit them to their table, lodge them and impart to them the secrets of the government. " - F7, 7129. (Seine-et-Oise, canton of Jouy, Pluvi'se 8, year IV.) "Forty-nine out of fifty citizens seem to have the greatest desire to profess the Catholic faith. " - Ibid., canton of Dammartin, Pluvi'se 7, year IV.) "The Catholic religion has full sway; those who do not accept it are frowned upon. " - At the same date (Pluvi'se 9, year IV), the commissioner at Chamarande writes: "I see persons giving what they call blessed bread and yet having nothing to eat. "

[82] Ibid., cartons 3144 and 3145, No. 1004, missions of the councillors of state, year IX. - (Report of Barbé-Marbois on Brittany.) "At Vannes, I entered the cathedral on the jour des Rois, where the constitutional mass was being celebrated; there were only one priest

and two or three poor people there. A little farther on I found a large crowd barring the way in the street; these people could not enter a chapel which was already full and where the mass called for by the Catholics was being celebrated. - Elsewhere, the churches in the town were likewise deserted, and the people went to hear mass by a priest just arrived from England. " - (Report by Français de Nantes on Vaucluse and Provence.) One tenth of the population follows the constitutional priests; the rest follow the returned emigré priests; the latter have on their side the rich and influential portion of society. " - (Report of Lacuée on Paris and the seven surrounding departments.) "The situation of the unsubmissive priests is more advantageous than that of the submissive priests. . .. The latter are neglected and abandoned; it is not fashionable to join them. .. (The former) are venerated by their adherents as martyrs; they excite tender interest, especially from the women. "

[83] Archives nationales, cartons 3144 and 3145, No. 1004, missions of the councillors of state, year IX. - (Report by Lacuée.) "The wants of the people in this way seem at this moment to be confined. .. to a vain spectacle, to ceremonies: going to mass, the sermon and vespers, which is all very well; but confession, the communion, fasting, doing without meat, is not common anywhere. . .. In the country, where there are no priests, the village schoolmaster officiates, and people are content; they would prefer bells without priests rather than priests without bells. " - This regret for bells is very frequent and survives even in the cantons which are lukewarm. - (Creuse, Pluvi'se 10, year IV.) "They persist in replanting the crosses which the priests have dug up; they put back the ropes to the bells which the magistrate has taken away. "

[84] Archives nationales, cartons 3144 and 3145, No. 1004, missions of the councilors of state, year IX. - (Report by Fourcroy.) "The keeping of Sunday and the attendance on the churches, which is seen everywhere, shows that the mass of Frenchmen desire a return to ancient usages, and that the time has gone by for resisting this national tendency. .. The mass of mankind require a religion, a system of worship and a priesthood. It is an error of certain modern philosophers, into which I have myself been led, to believe in the possibility of any instruction sufficiently widespread to destroy religious prejudices; they are a source of consolation for the vast number of the unfortunate. . .. Priests, altars and worship must accordingly be left to the mass of the people. "

[85] Peuchet, "Statistique élémentaire de la France" (published in 1805), p. 228. According to statements furnished by prefects in the years IX and X, the population is 33,111,962 persons; the annexation of the island of Elbe and of Piedmont adds 1,864,350 Total, 34,976,313. - Pelet de la Lozère, P. 203. (Speech by Napoleon to the council of state, February 4, 1804, on the Protestant seminaries of Geneva and Strasbourg, and on the number of Protestants in his states.) "Their population numbers only 3 millions. "

[86] Roederer, III., 330 (July 1800): "The First Consul spoke to me about the steps necessary to be taken to prevent the (emigrés) who had been struck off from getting back their possessions, in view of maintaining the interest in the revolution of about 1,200,000 purchasers of national domains. " - Rocquain, "État de la France au 18 Brumaire. " (Report by Barbé-Marbois on Morbihan, Finisterre, Ile-et- Vilaine, and C'tes-du-Nord, year IX.) "In every place I have just passed through the proprietors recognize that their existence is attached to that of the First Consul. "

[87] Constitution of Frimaire 22, year VIII, art. 94. - Article 93, moreover, declares that "the possessions of the émigrés are irrevocably acquired by the republic. "

[88] Law of Floréal 29, year X, title I, article 8. The member also swears "to combat with all the means which justice, reason and the law authorize, every enterprise tending to restore the feudal régime," and, consequently, feudal rights and tithes

[89] Organic Sénatus-consulte, Floreal 28, year XII (18th May 1804). Title VII., art. 53.

[90] Roederer, III., 430-432 (April 4, 1802, May I, 1802): "Defermon remarked to me yesterday, 'This will all go on well as long as the First Consul lives; the day after his death we shall all emigrate. ' " - " Every one, from the sailor to the worker, says to himself, 'All this is very well, but will it last? . .. - This work we undertake, this capital we risk, this house we build, these trees we plant, what will become of them if he dies? "

[91] Ibid., 340. (Words of the First Consul, November 4, 1800.) "Who is the rich man to-day? The buyer of national domains, the contractor. the robber. " -These details, above, are provided for me by family narrations and souvenirs.

[92] Napoleon, "Correspondance, " letter of September 5, 1795. "National and émigré property is not dear; patrimonies are priceless." - Archives nationales, cartons 3144 to 3145, No. 1004, missions of the councillors of state, year IX. (Report by Lacuée on the seven departments of the division of the Seine.) "The proportion of value, in Seine, between national and patrimonial properties is from 8 to 15. " - In Eure, national property of every kind is sold about 10 %. off, and patrimonial at about 4 %. off. There are two sorts of national property, one of first origin (that of the clergy), and the other of second origin (that of the émigrés). The latter is much more depreciated than the former. Compared with patrimonial property, in Aisne, the former loses a fifth or a quarter of its value and the latter a third; in Loiret, the former loses a quarter and the latter one-half; in Seine-et-Oise the former loses one-third and the latter three-fifths; in Oise the former is at about par, the latter loses a quarter. - Roederer, III., 472 (December 1803). Depreciation of national property in Normandy: "But little is bought above 7 %. off; this, however, is the fate of this sort of property throughout France. " - Ibid., III., 534 (January 1809): "In Normandy, investments on patrimonial property bring only 3 %., while State property brings 5 %. " - Moniteur (January 4, 1825). Report of M. de Martignac: "The confiscated property of the emigrés finds its purchasers with difficulty, and its commercial value is not in proportion to its real value. " - Duclosonge, former inspector of domains, "Moyens de porter les domaines nationaux à la valeur des biens patrimoniaux, " p. 7. "Since 1815, national property has generally been bought at a rate of income of 3 %. or, at the most, 4 %. The difference for this epoch is accordingly one-fifth, and even two-fifths. "

[93] Treaty between the Pope and the French government, July '5, 1801. Ratifications exchanged September 1, 1801, and published with its articles April 8, 1802. - Article 13.

[94] Ibid., article 14.

[95] Articles organiques, 64, 65, 66.

[96] Law of November 30, 1809, and opinion of the Council of State, May 19, 1811.

[97] Articles organiques, 68.

[98] Articles organiques, 71, 72. - Concordat, article 12. - Law passed July 26, 1803.

[99] Councils of laymen entrusted with the administration of parish incomes.

[100] Law of December 30, 1809, articles 39, 92 and following articles, 105 and following articles.

[101] Law of September 15, 1807, title IX.

[102] Concordat, article 15. - Articles organiques, 73.

[103] Alexis Chevalier, "les Frères des écoles chrétiennes et l'Enseignement primaire après la révolution, " passim. (Act of Vendémiaire 24 and Prairial 28, year XI, and Frimaire II, year XII; laws of May 14, 1806, March 7, 1808, February 17, 1809, Dec. 26, 1810.)

[104] Alexis Chevalier, ibid., 189.

[105] Ibid., p. 185 sequitur. (Decision of Aug. 8, 1803, of March 25, of May 30, 1806.)

[106] Decree of June 22, 1804 (articles I and 4). - "Consultation sur les decrets du 29 Mars 1880, " by Edmond Rousse, p. 32. (Out of 54 communities, there were two of men, the "Pères du tiers-ordre de Saint-François" and the priests of "la Miséricorde, " one founded in 1806 and the other in 1808.)

[107] "Mémorial de Sainte-Héléne. " Napoleon adds" that an empire like France may and must have some refuge for maniacs called Trappists. " - Pelet de la Lozère, p. 208. (Session of the council of state, May 22, 1804.) "My intention is to have the house of foreign missions restored; these monks will be of great use to me in Asia, Africa, and America. . .. I will give them a capital of 15,000 francs a year to begin with. . ... I shall also re-establish the 'Sisters of Charity; ' I have already had them put in possession of their old buildings. I think it necessary also, whatever may be said of it, to re-establish the 'Ignorantins. ' "

[108] Roederer, III., 481. (Sénatorerie of Caen, Germinal 17, year XIII.) Constant lamentations of bishops and most of the priests he has met.

"A poor curé, an unfortunate curé, . .. The bishop invites you to dinner, to partake of the poor cheer of an unfortunate bishop on 12,000 francs salary. " - The episcopal palaces are superb, but their furniture is that of a village curé; one can scarcely find a chair in the finest room. - "The officiating priests have not yet found a fixed salary in any commune. . .. The peasants ardently longed for their usual mass and Sunday service as in the past, but to pay for this is another thing. "

[109] Decrees of May 31 and Dec. 26, 1804, assigning to the Treasury the salaries of 24,000 and then 30,000 assistant-priests.

[110] Charles Nicolas, "le Budget de la France depuis le commencement du XIXe siecle; " appropriation in 1807, 12,341,537 francs.

[111] Decrees of Prairial 2, year XII, Niv'se 5. year XIII, and Sep. 30, 1807. - Decree of Dec. 30, 1809 (articles 37, 39, 40, 49 and ch. IV.)- - Opinion of the council of state, May 19, 1811.

[112] These are limited (articles organiques, 5): "All ecclesiastical functions are gratuitous except the authorized oblations fixed by the regulations. "

[113] Articles organiques, 73.

[114] Ibid., 74: " Real property other than dwellings with their adjoining gardens, shall not be held under ecclesiastical titles or possessed by ministers of worship by reason of their functions. "

[115] Opinion of the Council of State, January 22, 1805, on the question whether the communes have become owners of the churches and parsonages abandoned to them by the law of Germinal 18, year X (articles organiques). - The Council of State is of the opinion that "the said churches and parsonages must be considered as communal property. " If the State renounces ownership in these buildings it is not in favor of the fabrique, curé or bishop, but in favor of the commune.

[116] In 1790 and 1791 a number of communes had made offers for national property with a view to re-sell it afterwards, and much of this, remaining unsold, was on their hands.

[117] Articles organiques, 26. "The bishops will make no ordination before submitting the number of persons to the government for its acceptance. "

[118] "Archives de Grenoble. " (Documents communicated by Mdlle. de Franclieu.) Letter of the bishop, Monseigneur Claude Simon, to the Minister of Worship, April 18, 1809. "For seven years that I have been bishop of Grenoble, I have ordained thus far only eight priests; during this period I have lost at least one hundred and fifty. The survivors threaten me with a more rapid gap; either they are infirm, bent with the weight of years, or wearied or overworked. It is therefore urgent that I be authorized to confer sacred orders on those who are old enough and have the necessary instruction. Meanwhile, you are limited to asking authorization for the first eight on the aforesaid list, of whom the youngest is twenty-four. . .. I beg Your Excellency to present the others on this list for the authorization of His Imperial Majesty. " - Ibid., October 6, 1811. "I have only one deacon and one subdeacon, whilst I am losing three or four priests monthly. "

[119] Articles organiques, 68, 69. "The pensions enjoyed by the curés by virtue of the laws of the constituent assembly shall be deducted from their salary. The vicars and assistants shall be taken from the pensioned ecclesiastics according to the laws of the constituent assembly. The amount of these pensions and the product of oblations shall constitute their salary. "

[120] Laws of Vendémiaire 16, year V, and Vent'se 20, year V..

[121] Decree of Nov. 6, 1800.

[122] Decisions of February 23, 1801, and June 26, 1801. (We find, through subsequent decisions, that these recoveries were frequently effected.)

[123] Law of Frimaire 7, year V (imposing one decime per franc above the cost of a ticket in every theatre for the benefit of the poor not in the asylums). - Also the decree of Dec. 9, 1809. - Decisions of Vendémiaire 27, year VII, and the restoration of the Paris octroi, "considering that the distress of the civil asylums and the interruption of succor at domiciles admit of no further delay. " - Also the law of Frimaire 19, year VIII, with the addition of 2 decimes per franc to the octroi duties, established for the support of the asylums

of the commune of Paris. - Paul Leroy-Beaulieu, "Traité de la science des finances, " I., 685. Many towns follow this example: "Two years had scarcely passed when there were 293 Octrois in France. "

[124] Law of Messidor 25, year V. - Alexis Chevalier, ibid., p. 185. (Decisions of Thermidor 20, year XI, and Germinal 4, year XIII.) - Law of Dec.. 11, 1808 (article 1.)

[125] Albert Duruy, "l'Instruction publique et la Révolution, " p. 480 et seq. ("Procès-verbaux des conseils-généraux de l'an IX; " among others, the petitions from Gironde, Ile-et-Vilaine, Maine-et-Loire, Puy.de-D'me, Haute-Sa'ne, Haute Vienne, la Manche, Lot-et-Garonne, Sarthe, Aisne, Aude, C'te-d'Or, Pas-de-Calais, BassePyrénées, Pyrénées-Orientales, and Lot.)

[126] Alexis Chevalier, ibid., p. 182. (According to statistical returns of the parent establishment, rue Oudinot. - These figures are probably too low.)

[127] "Recueil des lois et réglemens sur l'enseignement supérieur, " by A. de Beauchamp, I., 65. (Report by Fourcroy, April 20, 1802.) "Old schools, since the suppression of upper schools and universities, have taken a new extension, and a pretty large number of private institutions have been formed for the literary education of the young. "

[128] Ibid., 65 and 71. (Report by Fourcroy.) "As to the primary schools, the zeal of the municipalities must be aroused, the emulation of the functionaries excited, and charitable tendencies revived, so natural to the French heart and which will so promptly spring up when the religious respect of the government for local endowments becomes known. "

[129] Ibid., p. 81. (Decree of May 1st, 1802, titles 2 and 9. - Decree of Sept. 17, 1808, article 23.)

130] "Histoire du collège des Bons-Enfans de l'université de Reims, " by abbé Cauly, p. 649. - The lycée of Reims, decreed May 6, 1802, was not opened until the 24th of September, 1803. The town was to furnish accommodations for 150 pupils. It spent nearly 200,000 francs to put buildings in order. . .. This sum was provided, on the one hand, by a voluntary subscription which realized 45,000 francs and, on the other hand, by an additional tax.

[131] Law of May 1, 1802, articles 32, 33, and 34. - Guizot, "Essai sur l'instruction publique, I., 59. Bonaparte maintained and brought up in the lycées, at his own expense and for his own advantage, about 3000 children . .. commonly selected from the sons of soldiers or from poor families. " - Fabry, "Mémoires pour servir à l'histoire de l'instruction publique, " III., 802. "Children of soldiers whose wives lived in Paris, the sons of office-holders who were prevented by luxury from bringing up their families - such were the scholarships of Paris. " - "In the provinces, the employees in the tax- and post-offices, with other nomadic functionaries - such were the communal scholarships. " - Lunet, "Histoire du collège de Rodez, " 219, 224. Out of 150 scholarships, 87 are filled, on the average.

[132] "Recueil, " etc., by A. de Beauchamp, I, 171, 187, 192. (Law of September 17, 1808, article 27, and decision of April 7, 1809.)

[133] Ibid. Masters of private schools and heads of institutions must pay additionally every year one-quarter of the sums above fixed. (Law of Sept. 17, 1808, article 25. Law of March 17, 1808, title 17. - Law of February 17, 1809.)

[134] Ibid., I., 189. (Decree of March 24, 1808, on the endowment of the University.)

[135] Emond, "Histoire du collège Louis-le-Grand, " p. 238. (This college, previous to 1789, enjoyed an income of 450,000 livres.) - Guizot, ibid., I., 62. - This college was maintained during the revolution under the name of the "Prytanée Français" and received in 1800 the property of the University of Louvain. Many of its pupils enlisted in 1792, and were promised that their scholarships should be retained for them on their return; hence the military spirit of the "Prytanée. " - By virtue of a decree, March 5, 1806, a perpetual income of 400,000 francs was transferred to the Prytanée de Saint-Cyr. It is this income which, by the decree of March 24, 1808, becomes the endowment of the imperial University. Henceforth, the expenses of the Prytanée de Saint-Cyr are assigned to the war department.

[136] Alexis Chevalier, Ibid., p. 265. Allocution to the "Ignorantin" brethren.

[137] "The Ancient Régime, " pp. 13-15. (Laff. I. pp. 17 and 18.)- "The Revolution, " III., p. 54. (Laff. II. pp. 48-49) - Alexis Chevalier,

"Les Frères des écoles chrétiennes, " p. 341. "Before the revolution, the revenues of public instruction exceeded 30 millions. " - Peuchet, "Statistique elementaire de la France (published in 1805), p. 256. Revenue of the asylums and hospitals in the time of Necker, 40 millions, of which 23 are the annual income from real-estate and 17 provided by personal property, contracts, the public funds, and a portion from octrois, etc.

[138] D'Haussonville, "l'Église romaine et le premier Empire, " vol. IV. et V., passim - Ibid., III., 370, 375. (13 Italian cardinals and 19 bishops of the Roman states are transported and assigned places in France, as well as many of their grand-vicars and chanoines; about the same date over 200 Italian priests are banished to Corsica). - V., 181. (July 12, 1811, the bishops of Troyes, Tournay and Ghent are sent to (the fortress-prison of) Vincennes.) - V., 286. (236 pupils in the Ghent seminary are enrol1ed in an artillery brigade and sent off to Wesel, where about fifty of them die in the hospital.) - "Souvenirs", by PASQUIER (Etienne-Dennis, duc) Librarie Plon, Paris 1893. (Numbers of Belgian priests confined in the castles of Ham, Bouillon and Pierre-Châtel were set free after the Restoration.)

[139] Decree of November 15, 1811, art. 28, 29, and 30. (Owing to M. de Fontanes, the small seminaries were not all closed, many of them, 41, still existing in 1815.)

[140] Collection of laws and decrees, passim, after 1802.

[141] Documents furnished by M. Alexis Chevalier, former director of public charities. The total amount of legacies and bequests is as follows: 1st Asylums and hospitals, from January 1, 1800, to December 31, 1845, 72,593,360 francs; from January 1st, 1846, to December 31, 1855, 37,107,812; from January 1st, 1856, to December 31, 1877, 121,197,774. in all, 230,898,346 francs. - 2d. Charity bureaux. From January 1st, 1800, to December 31, 1845, 49,911,090; from January 1st, 1846, to December 31, 1873, 115,629,925; from January 1st 1874, to December 31, 1877, 19,261,065. In all, 184,802,080 francs. - Sum total, 415,701,026 francs.

[142] According to the statements of M. de Watteville and M. de Gasparin.

[143] Report by Fourcroy, annexed to the exposition of the empire and presented to the Corps Législatif, March 5, 1806.

[144] Coup d'œil général sur l'éducation et l'instruction publique en France, " by Basset, censor of studies at Charlemagne college (1816), - p. 21.

[145] "Statistique de l'enseignement primaire, " II., CCIV. (From 1786 to 1789, 47 out of 100 married men and 26 married women out of a hundred signed their marriage contract. From 1816 to 1820, the figures show 54 husbands and 34 wives.) - Morris Birbeck, "Notes of a Journey through France in July, August and September 1814. " p. 3 (London, 1815). "I am told that all the children of the laboring classes learn to read, and are generally instructed by their parents. "

[146] Madame de Rémusat, I., 243. (Journey in the north of France and in Belgium with the First Consul, 1803.) "On journeys of this kind he was in the habit, after obtaining information about the public buildings a town needed, to order them as he passed along, and, for this munificence, he bore away the blessings of the people. " - Some time after this a letter came from the minister of the interior: "In conformity with the favor extended to you by the First Consul (later, emperor) you are required, citizen mayor, to order the construction of this or that building, taking care to charge the expenses on the funds of your commune, " and which the prefect of the department obliges him to do, even when available funds are exhausted or otherwise applied.

[147] Thiers, VIII., 117 (August 1807) and 124. 13,400 leagues of highways were constructed or repaired; 10 canals were dug or continued, at the expense of the public treasury; 32 departments contribute to the expense of these through the extra centimes tax, which is imposed on them. The State and the department, on the average, contribute each one-half. - Among the material evils caused by the Revolution, the most striking and the most seriously felt was the abandonment and running down of roads which had become impracticable, also the still more formidable degeneracy of the dikes and barriers against rivers and the sea. (Cf. in Rocquain, "État de la France au 18 Brumaire, " the reports of Français de Nantes, Fourcroy, Barbeé-Marbois, etc.) - The Directory had imagined barrriers with toll-gates on each road to provide expenses, which brought in scarcely 16 millions to offset 30 and 35 millions of expenditure. Napoleon substitutes for these tolls the product of the salt-tax. (Decree of April 24, 1806, art. 59.)

[148] "Souvenirs", by PASQUIER (Etienne-Dennis, duc) Librarie Plon, Paris 1893. "Scarcely two or three highways remained in decent order. . .. Navigation on the rivers and canals became impossible Public buildings and monuments were everywhere falling to ruin. . .. If the rapidity of destruction was prodigious, that of restoration was no less so.

CHAPTER II. TAXATION AND CONSCRIPTION.

I. Distributive Justice in Allotment of Burdens and Benefits.

Requirements previous to the Revolution. - Lack of distributive justice. - Wrongs committed in the allotment of social sacrifices and benefits. - Under the ancient Regime. - During the Revolution. - Napoleon's personal and public motives in the application of distributive justice. - The circumstances favorable to him. - His principle of apportionment. - He exacts proportion in what he grants.

The other group of needs, dating from long before 1789, involve wants which have survived the Revolution, because the Revolution has not satisfied these. The first, the most tenacious, the most profound, the most inveterate, the most frustrated of all is the desire for distributive justice. - In political society, as in every other society, there are burdens and benefits to be allotted. When the apportionment of these is unbiased, it takes place according to a very simple, self-evident principle:

For each individual the costs must be in proportion to the benefits and the benefits to the costs, so that, for each one, the final expense and the final receipt may exactly compensate each other, the larger or smaller share of expense being always equal to the larger or smaller share of profits.

Now, in France, this proportion had been wanting for many centuries; it had even given way to the inverse proportion. If, towards the middle of the eighteenth century, two sum-totals of the budget, material and moral, had been calculated, assets on one side and liabilities on the other:

On the one hand the sum of the apportionments exacted by the State, taxes in ready money, enforced labor, military service, civil subordination, every species of obedience and subjection, in short, every sacrifice of leisure, comfort and self-esteem.

On the other hand the sum of dividends distributed by the State of whatever kind or shape, security for persons and property, use and convenience of roads, delegations of public authority land liens on the public treasury, dignities, ranks, grades, honors, lucrative salaries, sinecures, pensions, and the like, that is to say, every gratification belonging to leisure, comfort, or pride - one might have concluded that the more a man contributed to the receipts the less would his dividend be, and the greater his dividend the less would he furnish to the general contribution.

Consequently, every social or local group consisted of two other groups: a majority which suffered for the benefit of the minority, and a minority which benefited at the expense of the majority, to such an extent that the privations of the greatest number defrayed the luxury of the small number. This was the case in all compartments as on every story, owing to the multitude, enormity and diversity of honorific or useful privileges, owing to the legal prerogatives and effective preferences by which the court nobles benefited at the expense of the provincial nobility,

* the noblesse at the expense of plebeians,
* the prelates and beneficiaries at the expense of poorly-paid curés and vicars,
* the two highest orders of the clergy at the expense of the third,
* the bourgeoisie at the expense of the people,
* the towns at the expense of the rural districts,
* this or that town or province at the expense of the rest,
* the artisan member of a corporation at the expense of the free workman,

and, in general, the strong, more or less well-to-do, in league and protected, at the expense of the weak, more or less needy, isolated and unprotected (indéfendus). [1]

One hundred years before the Revolution a few clairvoyant, open-hearted and generous spirits had already been aroused by this scandalous disproportion. [2] Finally, everybody is shocked by it, for, in each local or social group, nearly everybody is a sufferer, not alone the rural, the peasant, the artisan, and the plebeian, not alone the citizen, the curé and the bourgeois notable, " but again the gentleman, the grand seignior, the prelate and the King himself. [3] Each is denouncing the privileges of all others that affect his interests, each striving to diminish another's share in the public cake and to keep his own, all concurring in citing natural right and in claiming or accepting as a principle liberty and equality, but all concurring in misconception and solely unanimous in destroying and in allowing destruction, [4] to such an extent that, at last, the attack being universal and no defense anywhere, social order itself perishes, entirely owing to the abuses of it.

On the reappearance of the same abuses, the lack of distributive justice in revolutionary France became still more apparent than in monarchical France. Through a sudden transposition, the preferred of the former Régime had become the disgraced, while the disgraced of the former Régime had become the preferred; unjust favor and unjust disfavor still subsisted, but with a change of object. Before 1789, the nation was subject to an oligarchy of nobles and notables; after 1789, it became subject to an oligarchy of Jacobins big or little. Before the Revolution, there were in France three or four hundred thousand privileged individuals, recognizable by their red heels or silver shoe-buckles. After the Revolution, there were three or four hundred thousand of the privileged, recognizable by their red caps or their carmagnoles. The most privileged of all, the three or four thousand verified nobles, presented at court and of racial antiquity, who, by virtue of their parchments, rode in the royal carriages, were succeeded by three or four thousand Jacobins of a fresh sprout, no less verified and accepted, who, by virtue of their civic patent, sat in the club of the rue Saint-Honoré and the latter coterie was still more dominant, more exclusive, more partial than the former one. Consequently, before the Revolution, the burden of taxation was light for the rich or the well-to-do, crushing for the peasants or the common people; after the Revolution, on the contrary, the peasants, the common people, paid no more taxes, [6] while from the rich and the well-to-do the government took all, not alone their income but their capital. - On the other hand, after having fed the court of Versailles, the public treasury had to feed the rabble of Paris, still more voracious; and, from 1793 to 1796, the maintenance of this rabble cost it twenty-five times as much as, from 1783 to 1786, the maintenance of the court. [7] Finally, at Paris as at Versailles, the subordinates who lived on the favored spot, close to the central manger, seized on all they could get and ate much more than their allowance. Under the ancient Régime, "the ladies of honor, every time they travel from one royal country-house to another, gain 80 %. on the cost of the journey, " while the queen's first chambermaid gains, over and above her wages, 38,000 francs a year out of the sales of half- burnt candles. [8] Under the new Régime, in the distribution of food, "the matadors of the quarter, " the patriots of the revolutionary committees, deduct their portions in advance, and a very ample portion, to the prejudice of the hungry who await their turn, one taking seven rations and another twenty. [9] Thus did the injustice remain; in knocking it over, they had simply made matters worse; and had they wished to build permanently, now was the time to put an end to it; for, in every social edifice it introduced an imbalance. Whether the plumb-line deflects right or left is of little consequence; sooner or later the building falls in, and thus had the French edifice already fallen twice, the first time in 1789, through imminent bankruptcy and hatred of the ancient Régime, and the second time in 1799, through an actual bankruptcy and hatred of the Revolution.

An architect like the French Consul is on his guard against a financial, social and moral danger of this sort. He is aware that, in a well-organized society, there must be neither surcharge nor discharge, no favors, no exemptions and no exclusions. Moreover, "l'Etat c'est lui; "[10] thus is the public interest confounded with his personal interest, and, in the management of this double interest, his hands are free. Proprietor; and first inhabitant of France in the fashion of its former kings, he is not obliged and embarrassed as they were by immemorial precedents, by the concessions they have sanctioned or the rights they have acquired. At the public table over which he presides and which is his table, he does not, like Louis XV. or Louis XVI., encounter messmates already installed there, the heirs or purchasers of the seats they occupy, [11] extending in long rows from one end of the room to the other, each in his place according to rank, in an arm-chair, or common chair, or on a footstool, all being the legitimate and recognized owners of their seats, all of them the King's messmates and all authorized by law, tradition and custom to eat a free dinner or pay for it at less than cost, to find fault with the dishes passed around, to reach out for those not near by, to help themselves to what they want and to carry off the dessert in their pockets. At the new table there are no places secured beforehand. It is Napoleon himself who arranges the table, and on sitting down, he is the master who has invited whomsoever he pleases, who assigns to each his portion, who regulates meals as he thinks best for his own and the common interest, and who introduces into the entire service order, watchfulness and economy. Instead of a prodigal and negligent grand- seignior, here at last is a modern administrator who orders supplies, distributes portions and limits consumption, a contractor who feels his responsibility, a man of business able to calculate. Henceforth, each is to pay for his portion, estimated according to his ration, and each is to enjoy his ration according to his quota. - Judge of this by one example: In his own house, customarily a center of abuses and sinecures, there must be no more parasites. From the grooms and scullions of his palace up to its grand officials, even to the chamberlains and ladies of honor, all his domestics, with or without titles, work and perform their daily tasks in person, administrative or decorative, day or night, at the appointed time, for exact compensation, without pickings or stealing and without waste. His train and his parades, as pompous as under the old monarchy, admit of the same ordinary and extraordinary expenses - stables, chapel, food, hunts, journeys, private theatricals, renewals of plate and furniture, and the maintenance of twelve palaces or châteaux. While, under Louis XV., it was estimated that "coffee with one roll for each lady of honor cost the King 2,000 livres a year, " and under Louis XVI., " the grand broth night and day" which Madame Royale, aged two years, sometimes drank and which figured in the annual accounts at 5201 livres, [12] under Napoleon "in the pantries, in the kitchens, the smallest dish, a mere plate of soup, a glass of sugared water, would not have been served without the authorization or check of grand- marshal Duroc. Every abuse is watched; the gains of each are calculated and regulated beforehand. "[13] Consequently, this or that journey to Fontainebleau which had cost Louis XVI. nearly 2 million livres, cost Napoleon, with the same series of fêtes, only 150,000 francs, while the total expense of his civil household, instead of amounting to 25 million livres, remains under 3 million francs. [14] The pomp is thus equal, but the expense is ten times less; the new master is able to derive a tenfold return from persons and money, because he squeezes the full value out of every man he employs and every crown he spends. Nobody has surpassed him in the art of turning money and men to account, and he is as shrewd, as careful, as sharp in procuring them as he is in profiting by them.

II. Equitable Taxation.

The apportionment of charges. - New fiscal principle and new fiscal machinery.

In the assignment of public burdens and of public offices Napoleon therefore applies the maxims of the new system of rights, and his practice is in conformity with the theory. For the social order, which, according to the philosophers, is the only just one in itself, is at the same time the most profitable for him: he adds equity because equity is profitable to him. - And first, in the matter of public burdens, there shall be no more exemptions. To relieve any category of taxpayers or of conscripts from taxation or from military service would annually impoverish the treasury by so many millions of crowns, and diminish the army by so many thousands of soldiers. Napoleon is not the man to deprive himself without reason of either a soldier or a franc; above all things, he wants his army complete and his treasury full; to supply their deficits he seizes whatever he can lay his hands on, both taxable material as well as recruitable material. But all material is limited; if he took too little on the one hand he would be obliged to take too much on the other; it is impossible to relieve these without oppressing those, and oppression, especially in the matter of taxation, is what, in 1789, excited the universal jacquerie, perverted the Revolution, and broke France to pieces. - At present, in the matter of taxation, distributive justice lays down a universal and fixed law; whatever the property may be, large or small, and of whatever kind or form, whether lands, buildings, indebtedness, ready money, profits, incomes or salaries, it is the State which, through its laws, tribunals, police, gendarmes and army, preserves it from ever ready aggression within and without; the State guarantees, procures and ensures the enjoyment of it. Consequently, property of every species owes the State its premium of assurance, so many centimes on the franc. The quality, the fortune, the age or the sex of the owner is of little importance; each franc assured, no matter in whose hands, must pay the same number of centimes, not one too much, not one too little. - Such is the new principle. To announce it is easy enough; all that is necessary is to combine speculative ideas, and any Academy can do that. The National Assembly of 1789 had proclaimed it with the rattling of drums, but merely as a right and with no practical effect. Napoleon turns it into a reality, and henceforth the ideal rule is applied as strictly as is possible with human material, thanks to two pieces of fiscal machinery of a new type, superior of their kind, and which, compared with those of the ancient Régime, or with those of the Revolution, are masterpieces.

III. Formation of Honest, Efficient Tax Collectors

Direct real and personal taxation. - In what respect the new machinery is superior to the old. - Full and quick returns. - Relief to taxpayers. - Greater relief to the poor workman and small farmer.

The collection of a direct tax is a surgical operation performed on the taxpayer, one which removes a piece of his substance: he suffers on account of this and submits to it only because he is obliged to. If the operation is performed on him by other hands he submits to it willingly or not. But that he should do it himself, spontaneously and with his own hands, it is not to be thought of. On the other hand, the collection of a direct tax according to the prescriptions of distributive justice, is a subjection of each taxpayer to an amputation proportionate to his bulk or, at least, to his surface; this requires delicate calculation and is not to be entrusted to the patients themselves, for, not only are they surgical novices and poor calculators, but, again, they are interested in calculating falsely. They have been ordered to assess their group with a certain total weight of human substance, and to apportion to each individual in their group the lighter or heavier portion he must provide. Everyone will soon understand that, the more that is cut from the others, the less will be required of him. And as each is more sensitive to his own suffering, although moderate, than to another's suffering, even excessive, each, therefore, be his neighbor little or big, is inclined, in order to unjustly diminish his own sacrifice by an ounce, to add a pound unjustly to that of his neighbor.

Up to this time, in the construction of the fiscal machine, nobody knew or had been disposed to take into account such natural and powerful sentiments; through negligence or through optimism, the taxpayer had been introduced into the mechanism in the quality of first agent; before 1789, in the quality of a responsible and constrained agent; after 1789, in the quality of a voluntary and philanthropic agent. Hence, before 1789, the machine had proved mischievous, and after 1789, impotent; before 1789, its working had been almost fatal, [15] and after 1789 its returns scarcely amounted to anything. [16] Finally, Napoleon establishes independent, special and competent operators, enlightened by local informers, but withdrawn from local influences. These are appointed, paid and supported by the central government, forced to act impartially by the appeal of the taxpayer to the council of the prefecture, and forced to keep correct accounts by the final auditing of a special court (cour des comptes). The are kept interested, through the security they have given as well as by commissions, in the integral recovery of unpaid arrears and in the prompt returns of collected taxes. All, assessors, auditors, directors, inspectors and collectors, being good accountants, are watched by good accountants, kept to their duties by fear, and made aware that embezzlements, lucrative under the Directory, [17] are punished under the Consulate. [18] They are soon led to consider necessity a virtue, to pride themselves inwardly on compulsory rectitude, to imagine that they have a conscience and hence to acquiring one, in short, to voluntarily imposing on themselves probity and exactitude through amour-propre and honorable scruples. - For the first time in ten years lists of taxes are prepared and their collection begun at the beginning of the year. [19] Previous to 1789, the taxpayer was always in arrears, while the treasury received only three-fifths of that which was due in the current year. [20] After 1800, direct taxes are nearly always fully returned before the end of the current year, and half a century later, the taxpayers, instead of being in arrears, are often in advance. [21] To do this work required, before 1789, about 200,000 collectors, besides the administrative corps, [22] occupied one half of their time for two successive years in running from door to door, miserable and detested, ruined by their ruinous office, fleecers and the fleeced, and always escorted by bailiffs and constables. Since 1800, from five thousand to six thousand collectors, and other fiscal agents, honorable and respected, have only to do their office-work at home and make regular rounds on given days, in order to collect more than double the amount without any vexation and using very little constraint. Before 1780, direct taxation brought in about 170 millions; [23] after the year XI, it brought in 360 millions. [24] By the same measure, an extraordinary counter-measure, the taxable party, especially the peasant-proprietor, the small farmer with nobody to protect him, diametrically opposite to the privileged class, the drudge of the monarchy, is relieved of three-fourths of his immemorial burden. [25] At first, through the abolition of tithes and of feudal privileges, he gets back one-quarter of his net income, that quarter which he paid to the seignior and to the clergy; next, through the application of direct taxation to all lands and to all persons, his quota is reduced one-half. Before 1789, he paid, on 100 francs net income, 14 to the seignior, 14 to the clergy, 53 to the State, and kept only 18 or 19 for himself. After 1800, he pays nothing out of 100 francs of income to the seignior or to the clergy; he pays but little to the State, only 21 francs to the commune and department, and keeps 79 francs in his pocket. [26]

If each franc insured pays so many centimes insurance premium, each franc of manual gain and of salary should pay as many centimes as each franc of industrial or commercial gain, also as each franc of personal or land revenue; that is to say, more than one-fifth of a franc, or 21 centimes. - At this rate, the workman who lives on his own labor, the day-laborer, the journeyman who earns 1 franc 15 centimes per day and who works 300 days of the year, ought to pay out of his 345 francs wages 69 francs to the public treasury. At this rate; the ordinary peasant or cultivator of his own field, owner of a cottage and a small tract of ground which he might rent at 100 francs a year, should pay into the public treasury, out of his land income and from manual labor, 89 francs. [27] The deduction, accordingly, on such small earnings would be enormous; for this gain, earned from day to day, is just enough to live on, and very poorly, for a man and his family: were it cut down one-fifth he and his family would be obliged to fast; he would be nothing but a serf or half-serf, exploited by the exchequer, his seignior and his proprietor. Because the exchequer, as formerly the proprietary seigniors, would appropriate to itself 60 days of labor out of the 300. Such was the condition of many millions of men, the great majority of Frenchmen, under the ancient Régime. Indeed, the five direct taxes, the taille, its accessories, the road- tax, the capitatim and the vingtièmes, were a tax on the taxpayer, not only according to the net revenue of his property, if he had any, but again and especially "of his faculties" and presumed resources whatever these might be, comprising his manual earnings or daily wages. - Consequently, "a poor laborer owning nothing, "[28] who earned 19 sous a day, or 270 livres a year, [29] was taxed 18 or 20 livres. Out of 300 days' work there were 20 or 22 which belonged beforehand to the public treasury. - Three-fifths[30] of the French people were in this situation, and the inevitable consequences of such a fiscal system have been seen - the excess of extortions and of suffering, the spoliation, privations and deep-seated resentment of the humble and the poor. Every government is bound to care for these, if not from compassion, at least through prudential considerations, and this one more than any other, since it is founded on the will of the greatest number, on the repeated votes of majorities counted by heads.

To this end, it establishes two divisions of direct taxation: one, the real-estate tax, which has no bearing on the taxpayer without any property; and the other, the personal tax, which does affect him, but lightly: calculated on the rate of rent, it is insignificant on an attic, furnished lodging, hut or any other hovel belonging to a laborer or peasant; again, when very poor or indigent, if the octroi is burdensome, the exchequer sooner or later relieves them; add to this the poll-tax which takes from them1 franc and a half up to 4.50 francs per annum, also a very small tax on doors and windows, say 60 centimes per annum in the villages on a tenement with only one door and one window, and, in the towns, from 60 to 75 centimes per annum for one room above the second story with but one window. [31] In this way, the old tax which was crushing becomes light: instead of paying 18 or 20 livres for his taille, capitatim and the rest, the journeyman or the artisan with no property pays no more than 6 or 7 francs; [32] instead of paying 53 livres for his vingtièmes for his poll, real and industrial tax, his capitatim and the rest, the small cultivator and owner pays no more than 21 francs. Through this reduction of their fiscal charges (corvée) and through the augmentation of their day wages, poor people, or those badly off, who depended on the hard and steady labor of their hands, the plowmen, masons, carpenters, weavers, blacksmiths, wheelwrights and porters, every hired man and artisan, in short, all the laborious and tough hands, again became almost free; these formerly owed, out of their 300 working days, from 20 to 59 to the exchequer; they now owe only from 6 to 19, and thus gain from 14 to 40 free days during which, instead of working for the exchequer, they work for themselves. - The reader may estimate the value to a small household of such an alleviation of the burden of discomfort and care.

IV. Various Taxes.

Other direct taxes. - Tax on business licenses. - Tax on real-estate transactions. - The earnings of manual labor almost exempt from direct taxation. - Compensation on another side. - Indirect taxation. - In what respect the new machinery is superior to the old. - Summary effect of the new fiscal régime. - Increased receipts of the public treasury. - Lighter burdens of the taxpayer. - Change in the condition of the small taxpayer.

This infraction of the principle of distributive justice is in favor of the poor. Through the almost complete exemption of those who have no property the burden of direct taxation falls almost entirely on those who own property. If they are manufacturers, or in commerce, they support still another burden, that of the license tax, which is a supplementary impost proportioned to their probable gains. [34] Finally, to all these annual and extra taxes, levied on the probable or certain income derived from invested or floating capital, the exchequer adds an eventual tax on capital itself, consisting of the mutation tax, assessed on property every time it changes hands through gift, inheritance or by contract, obtaining its title under free donation or by sale, and which tax, aggravated by the timbre, [35] is enormous[36] since, in most cases, it takes 5, 7, 9, and up to 10 1/2 % on the capital transmitted, that is to say, in the case of real- estate, 2, 3 and even 4 years' income from it. Thus, in the first shearing of the sheep the exchequer cuts deep, as deep as possible; but it has sheared only the sheep whose fleece is more or less ample; its scissors have scarcely touched the others, much more numerous, whose wool, short, thin and scant, is maintained only by day-wages, the petty gains of manual labor. - Compensation is to come when the exchequer, resuming its scissors, shears the second time: it is the indirect tax which, although properly levied and properly collected, is, in its nature, more burdensome for the poor than for the rich and well-off.

Through this tax, and through to the previous action of customs-duties, tolls, octrois or monopolies, the State collects a certain percentage on the price of various kinds of merchandise sold. In this way it participates in trade and commerce and itself becomes a merchant. It knows, therefore, like all able merchants, that, to obtain large profits, it must sell large quantities, that it must have a very large body of customers, that the largest body is that which ensures to it and embraces all its subjects, in short, that its customers must consist not only of the rich, who number merely tens of thousands, not only the well-to-do, who number merely hundreds of thousands, but likewise the poor and the half-poor, who number millions and tens of millions. Hence, in the merchandise by the sale of which it is to profit, it takes care to include staple articles which everybody needs, for example, salt, sugar, tobacco and beverages in universal and popular use. This accomplished, let us follow out the consequences, and look in at the shops over the whole surface of the territory, in the towns or in the villages, where these articles are disposed of. Daily and all day long, consumers abound; their large coppers and small change constantly rattle on the counter; and out of every large copper and every small piece of silver the national treasury gets so many centimes: that is its share, and it is very sure of it, for it is already in hand, having received it in advance. At the end of the year, these countless centimes fill its cash-box with millions, as many and more millions than it gathers through direct taxation.

And this second crop causes less trouble than the first one for the taxpayer who is subject to it has less trouble and like-wise the State which collects it. - In the first place, the tax-payer suffers less. In relation to the exchequer, he is no longer a mere debtor, obliged to pay over a particular sum at a particular date; his payments are optional; neither the date nor the sum are fixed; he pays on buying and in proportion to what he buys, that is to say, when he pleases and as little as he wants. He is free to choose his time, to wait until his purse is not so empty; there is nothing to hinder him from thinking before he enters the shop, from counting his coppers and small change, from giving the preference to more urgent expenditure, from reducing his consumption. If he is not a frequenter of the cabaret, his quota, in the hundreds of millions of francs obtained from beverages, is almost nothing; if he does not smoke or snuff, his quota, in the hundreds of millions derived from the tax on tobacco, is nothing at all; because he is economical, prudent, a good provider for his family and capable of self-sacrifice for those belonging to him, he escapes the shearing of the exchequer. Moreover, when he does come under the scissors, these hardly graze his skin; so long as tariff regulations and monopolies levy nothing on articles which are physically indispensable to him, as on bread in France, indirect taxation does not touch his flesh. In general, fiscal or protective duties, especially those which increase the price of tobacco, coffee, sugar, and beverages, do not affect his daily life, but merely deprive him of some of its pleasures and comforts. - And, on the other hand, in the collection of these duties, the exchequer may not show its hand; if it does its business properly, the anterior and partial operation is lost sight of in the total operation which completes and covers this up; it screens itself behind the merchant. The shears are invisible to the buyer who presents himself to be sheared; in any event, he has no distinct sensation of them. Now, with the man of the people, the common run of sheep, it is the positive, actual, animal sensation which is the cause of his cries, his convulsive shudders, and contagious alarms and panics. As long as he is not being excited he can be manipulated; at the utmost, he grumbles at the hard times; the high prices from which he suffers are not imputed to the government; he does not know how to reckon, check off and consider for himself the surplus price which the fiscal impost extorts from him. Even at the present day, one might tell a peasant in vain that the State takes fifteen out of the forty sous which he pays for a pound of coffee, and five centimes out of every two sous he pays for a pound of salt; for him, this is simply a barren notion, a vague calculation at random; the impression on his mind would be very different if, standing before the grocer who weighs out his coffee and salt, he saw with his own eyes, right before him, the clerk of the customs and of the salt-tax actually taking the fifteen sous and the five centimes off the counter.

Such are the good indirect taxes: in order that they may be correct, that is to say, tolerable and tolerated, three conditions, as we see, are requisite. In the first place, the taxpayer, in his own interest, must be free to buy or not to buy the merchandise taxed. Next, in the interest of the taxpayer and of the exchequer, the merchandise must not be so taxed as to be rendered too dear. After that, in the interest of the exchequer, its interference must not be perceptible. Owing to these precautions, indirect taxes can be levied, even on the smaller taxpayers, without either fleecing or irritating them. It is for lack of these precautions before 1789, when people were fleeced in such a clumsy way, [37] that, in 1789, they first rebelled against indirect taxation, [38] against the meal-tax, the salt-tax, the tax on liquors, the internal tariffs, and the town octrois, against fiscal officers, bureaux and registries, by murdering, pillaging, and burning, beginning in the month of March in Provence and after the 13th of July in Paris, and then throughout France, with such a universal, determined and persistent hostility that the National Assembly, after having vainly attempted to restore the suspended tax- levies and enforce the law on the populace, ended in subjecting the law to the populace and in decreeing the suppression of indirect taxation entirely. [39]

Such, in the matter of taxation, is the work of the Revolution. Of the two sources which, through their regular afflux, fill the public Treasury, and of which the ancient Régime took possession and managed badly, violently, through loose and bungling measures, it has nearly dried up the first one, direct taxation, and completely exhausted the second one, indirect taxation. At present, as the empty Treasury must be filled, the latter must be taken in hand the same as the former, its waters newly gathered in and gently conducted without loss. The new government sets about this, not like the old one, in a rude, conventional manner, but as an engineer and calculator who knows the ground, its inclination and other obstacles, in short, who comprehends human sensibility and the popular imagination. [40] - And, first of all, there is to be no more farming-out (of the collection of the revenues): the State no longer sells its duties on salt or on beverages to a company of speculators, mere contractors, who care for nothing but their temporary lease and annual incomes, solely concerned with coming dividends, bleeding the tax-payer like so many leeches and invited to suck him freely, interested in multiplying affidavits by the fines they get, and creating infractions, authorized by a needy government which, supporting itself on their advances, places the public force at their disposal and surrenders the people to their exactions. Henceforth, the exchequer collects for itself and for its own account. It is the same as a proprietor who, instead of leasing or renting out, improves his property and becomes his own farmer. The State, therefore, considers the future in its own interest; it limits the receipts of the current year so as not to compromise the receipts of coming years; it avoids ruining the present tax-payer who is also the future taxpayer; it does not indulge in gratuitous chicanery, in expensive lawsuits, in warrants of execution and imprisonment; it is averse to converting a profitable laborer into a beggar who brings in nothing, or into a prisoner for debt who costs it something. Through this course, the relief is immense; ten years previous to the Revolution, [41] it was estimated that, in principal and in accessories, especially in costs of collection and in fines, indirect taxation cost the nation twice as much the king derived from it, that it paid 371 millions to enable him to receive 184 millions, that the salt-tax alone took out of the pockets of the taxpayer 100 millions for 45 millions deposited in his coffers. Under the new government, fines became rarer; seizures, executions and sales of personal property still rarer, while the costs of collection, reduced by increasing consumption, are not to exceed one-twentieth in-stead of one-fifth of the receipts. [42] - In the second place, the consumer becomes free again, in law as in fact, not to purchase taxed goods. He is no longer constrained, as formerly, in the provinces subject to high salt-tax, to accept, consume, and pay for duty-salt, 7 pounds per head at 13 sous the pound. Provincial, town or seignorial taxes on Bread, a commodity which he cannot do without, no longer exist; there is no piquet, or duty on flour, as in Provence, [43] no duties on the sale or of grinding wheat, no impediments to the circulation or commerce of grain. And, on the other hand, through the lowering of fiscal charges, in the suppression of internal duties, and the abolition of multitudinous tolls, other commodities, apart from bread reached by a different tax, now becomes affordable for those of small means. Salt, instead of costing thirteen sous and over, no longer costs more than two sous the pound. A cask of Bordeaux wine no longer pays two hundred livres before it is retailed by the tavern-keeper at Rennes. [44] Except in Paris, and even at Paris, so long as the extravagance of municipal expenditure does not increase the octroi the total tax on wine, cider and beer does not add, even at retail, more than 18 % to their selling price, [45] while, throughout France, the vine-grower, or the wine-maker, who gathers in and manufactures his own wine, drinks this and even his brandy, without paying one cent of tax under this heading. [46] - Consequently, consumption increases, and, as there are no longer any exempt or half-exempt provinces, no more free salt (franc salé), [47] no more privileges arising from birth, condition, profession or residence, the Treasury, with fewer duties, collected or gained as much as before the Revolution: In 1809 and 1810, 20 millions on tobacco, 54 millions on salt, 100 millions on liquors, and then, as the taxpayer became richer and spent more, still larger and larger sums: in 1884, 305 millions on tobacco: in 1885, 429 millions on liquors, [48] without counting another 100 millions again raised on liquors through town octrois. - And lastly, the exchequer, with extreme prudence, keeps out of sight and succeeds in almost saving the taxpayer from contact with, or the presence of, its agents. There is an end to a domestic inquisition. The excise man no longer pounces in on the housewife to taste the pickle, to find out whether the ham has been cured with bogus salt, to certify that all the dutiable salt has been used in "the pot and the salt-cellar. " The wine-inspector no longer comes suddenly on the wine-grower, or even on the consumer, to gauge his casks, to demand an account of what he drinks, to make an affidavit in case of deficit or over-consumption, to impose a fine should a bottle have been given to a sick person or to a poor one. The 50,000 customs officers or clerks of the ferme, the 23,000 soldiers without a uniform who, posted in the interior along a line of 1200 leagues, guarded the heavily taxed salt districts against the provinces which were less taxed, redeemed or free, the innumerable employees at the barriers, forming a confused and complicated band around each province, town, district or canton, levying on twenty or thirty different sorts of merchandise forty-five principal duties, general, provincial, or municipal, and nearly sixteen hundred tolls, in short, the entire body of officials of the old system of indirect taxation has almost wholly disappeared. Save at the entrance of towns, and for the octroi the eye no longer encounters an official clerk. The carters who, from Roussillon or Languedoc, transport a cask of wine to Paris, are no longer subject to his levies, humiliations and moods in twenty different places, nor to ascribe to him the dozen or fifteen days' useless extension of their trip due to his predecessor, and during which they had to wait in his office until he wrote a receipt or a permit. There is scarcely any one now but the inn-keeper who sees his green uniform on his premises. After the abolition of the house- inventory, nearly two millions of proprietors and wine métayers are forever free of his visits; [49] from now on, for consumers, especially for the people, he seems absent and non existent. In effect, he has been transferred one or two hundred leagues off, to the salt- establishments in the interior and on the coasts, and on the frontier. There only is the system at fault, nakedly exposing its vice, - a war against exchanges, the proscription of international commerce, prohibition pushed to extreme, the continental blockade, an inquisition of 20,000 customs officials, the hostility of 100,000 defrauders, the brutal destruction of seized goods, an augmentation in price of 100 % on cottons and 400% on sugar, a dearth of colonial articles, privation to the consumer, the ruin of the manufacturer and trader, and accumulated bankruptcies one after the other in 1811 in all the large towns from Hamburg to Rome. [50] This vice, however, belongs to the militant policy and personal character of the master; the error that taints the external side of his fiscal system does not reach the internal side. After him, under pacific reigns, it is gradually modified; prohibition gives way to protection and then changes from excessive protection to limited protection. France remains, along with secondary improvements and partial amendments, on the course marked out by the Consulate and the Empire; this course, in all its main lines, is clearly traced, straight, and yet adapted to all things, by the plurality, establishment, distribution, rate of taxation and returns of the various direct and indirect taxes, nearly in conformity with the new principles of political economy, as well as in conformity with the ancient maxims of distributive justice, carefully directed between the two important interests that have to be cared for, that of the people who pays and of the State which collects.

Consider, in effect, what both have gained. - In 1789, the State had a revenue of only 475 millions; afterwards, during the Revolution, it scarcely collected any of its revenues; it lived on the capital it stole, like a genuine brigand, or on the debts it contracted, like a dishonest and insolvent bankrupt. Under the Consulate and during the first years of the Empire, its revenue amounts to 750 to 800 millions, its subjects being no longer robbed of their capital, while it no longer runs in debt. - In 1789, the ordinary taxpayer paid a direct tax to his three former or late sovereigns, namely, to the King, the clergy and the seigniors, more than three-quarters of his net income. After 1800, he pays to the State less than one-quarter, the one sovereign alone who replaces the other three. We have seen how relief came to the old taxable subject, to the rural, to the small proprietor, to the man without any property, who lived on the labor of his own hands; the lightening of the direct tax restored to him from 14 to 43 free days, during which, instead of working for the exchequer, he worked for himself. If married, and the father of two children over 7 years of age, the alleviation of one direct tax alone, that of the salt-tax, again restores to him 12 days more, in all from one to two complete months each year during which he is no longer, as formerly, a man doing statute-work, but the free proprietor, the absolute master of his time and of his own hands. - At the same time, through the re-casting of other taxes and owing to the increasing price of labor, his physical privations decrease. He is no longer reduced to consuming only the refuse of his crop, the wheat of poor quality, the damaged rye, the badly-bolted flour mixed with bran, nor to drink water poured over the lees of his grapes, nor to sell his pigs before Christmas because the salt he needs is too dear. [51] He salts his pork and eats it, and likewise butcher's meat; he enjoys his boiled beef and broth on Sunday; he drinks wine; his bread is more nutritious, not so black and healthier; he no longer lacks it and has no fear of lacking it. Formerly, he entertained a lugubrious phantom, the fatal image of famine which haunted him day and night for centuries, an almost periodical famine under the monarchy, a chronic famine and then severe and excruciating during the Revolution, a famine which, under the republic, had in three years destroyed over a million of lives. [52] The immemorial specter recedes and vanishes; after two accidental and local recurrences, in 1812 and 1817, it never again appears in France. [53]

V. Conscription or Professional soldiers.

Military service. - Under the Ancient Regime. - The militia and regular troops. - Number of soldiers. - Quality of the recruits. - Advantages of the institution. - Results of the new system. - The obligation universal. - Comparison between the burdens of citizens and subjects. - The Conscription under Napoleon. - He lightens and then increases its weight. - What it became after him. - The law of 1818.

One tax remains, and the last, that by which the State takes, no longer money, but the person himself, the entire man, soul and body, and for the best years of his life, namely military service. It is the Revolution which has rendered this so burdensome; formerly, it was light, for, in principle, it was voluntary. The militia, alone, was raised by force, and, in general, among the country people; the peasants furnished men for it by casting lots. [54] But it was simply a supplement to the active army, a territorial and provincial reserve, a distinct, sedentary body of reinforcements and of inferior rank which, except in case of war, never marched; it turned out but nine days of the year, and, after 1778, never turned out again. In 1789, it comprised in all 72,260 men, and for eleven years their names, inscribed on the registers, alone constituted their presence in the ranks. [55] There were no other conscripts under the monarchy; in this matter, its exactions were not great, ten times less than those of the Republic and of the Empire, since both the Republic and the Empire, using the same constraint, were to levy more than ten times the number of drafted men or conscripts. [56]

Alongside of this militia body, the entire army properly so called, the "regular" troops were, under, the ancient Régime, all recruited by free enlistment, not only the twenty-five foreign regiments, Swiss, Irish, Germans, and Liégeois, but again the hundred and forty-five French regiments, 177 000 men. [57] The enlistment, indeed, was not free enough; frequently, through the maneuvers of the recruiting-agent, it was tainted with inveigling and surprises, and sometimes with fraud or violence; but, owing to the remonstrances due to the prevailing philanthropic spirit, these abuses had diminished; the law of 1788 had suppressed the most serious of them and, even with its abuses, the institution had two great advantages. - The army, in the first place, served as an issue: through it the social body purged itself of its bad humors, of its overheated or vitiated blood. At this date, although the profession of soldier was one of the lowest and least esteemed, a barren career, without promotion and almost without escape, a recruit was obtainable for about one hundred francs bounty and a "tip"; add to this two or three days and nights of revel in the grog-shop, which indicates the kind and quality of the recruits; in fact, very few could be obtained except among men more or less disqualified for civil and domestic life, incapable of spontaneous discipline and of steady labor, adventurers and outcasts, half-savage or half-blackguard, some of them sons of respectable parents thrown into the army in an angry fit, and others again, regular vagabonds picked up in beggars' haunts, mostly stray workmen and loafers, in short, "the most debauched, the most hot-brained, the most turbulent people in an ardent, turbulent and somewhat debauched community. "[58] In this way, the anti-social class was utilized for the public good. Let the reader imagine an ill-kept domain overrun by a lot of stray curs that might prove dangerous: they are enticed and caught; a collar, with a chain attached to it, is put on their necks and they become good watch-dogs. - In the second place, this institution preserved to the subject the first and most precious of all liberties, the full possession and the unrestricted management of one's own person, the complete mastery of body and being. This was assured to him, guaranteed to him against the encroachments of the State. It was better guaranteed than by the wisest constitution, for the institution was a recognized custom accepted by everybody. In other words, it was a tacit, immemorial convention, [59] between the subject and the State, proclaiming that, if the State had a right to draw on purses it had no right to draft persons: in reality and in fact, the King, in his principal function, was merely a contractor like any other; he undertook natural defense and public security the same as others undertook cleaning the streets or the maintenance of a dike. It was his business to hire military workmen as they hired their civil workmen, by mutual agreement, at an understood price and at current market rates. Accordingly, the sub-contractors with whom he treated, the colonel and captains of each regiment, were subject as he was to the law of supply and demand; he allowed them so much for each recruit, [60] to replace those dropped out, and they agreed to keep their companies full. They were obliged to procure men at their own risk and at their own expense, while the recruiting-agent whom they dispatched with a bag of money among the taverns, enlisted artillerymen, horsemen or foot-soldiers, after bargaining with them, the same as one would hire men to sweep or pave the street and to clean the sewers.

Against this practice and this principle comes the theory of the Contrat-Social. It declares that the people are sovereign. Now, in this divided Europe, where a conflict between rival States is always imminent, sovereigns are military men; they are such by birth, education, and profession, and by necessity; the title carries along with it and involves the function. Consequently, the subject, in assuming their rights, imposes upon himself their duties; in his quota (of responsibility) he, in his turn, is sovereign; but, in his turn and in his person, he is a soldier. [61] Henceforth, if he is born an elector, he is born a conscript; he has contracted an obligation of a new species and of infinite reach; the State, which formerly had a claim only on his possessions, now has one on his entire body; never does a creditor let his claims rest and the State always finds reasons or pretexts to enforce its claims. Under the threats or trials of invasion the people, at first, had consented to pay this one; they regarded it as accidental and temporary. After victory and when peace came, its government continues to enforce the claim; it becomes settled and permanent. After the treaties of Luneville and Amiens, Napoleon maintains it in France; after the treaties of Paris and Vienna, the Prussian government is to maintain it in Prussia. One war after another and the institution becomes worse and worse; like a contagion, it has spread from State to State. At the present time, it has overspread the whole of continental Europe and here it reigns along with its natural companion which always precedes or follows it, its twin-brother, universal suffrage. Each more or less conspicuously "trotted out" and dragging the other along, more or less incomplete and disguised, both being the blind and formidable leaders or regulators of future history, one thrusting a ballot into the hands of every adult, and the other putting a soldier's knapsack on every adult's back:

* with what promises of massacre and bankruptcy for the twentieth century,
* with what exasperation of international rancor and distrust,
* with what waste of human labor,
* through what perversion of productive discoveries,
* through what perfection of destructive appliances,
* through what a recoil to the lower and most unwholesome forms of old militant societies,
* through what retrograde steps towards brutal and selfish instincts,
* towards the sentiments, habits and morality of the antique city and of the barbarous tribe

is only too well known. It is sufficient for us to place the two military systems face to face, that of former times and that of to- day: formerly, in Europe, a few soldiers, some hundreds of thousands; to-day, in Europe, 18 millions of actual or eventual soldiers, all the adults, even the married, even fathers of families summoned or subject to call for twenty-five years of their life, that is to say, as long as they continue able-bodied men; formerly, for the heaviest part of the service in France, no lives are confiscated by decree, only those bought by contract, and lives suited to this business and elsewhere idle or mischievous; about one hundred and fifty thousand lives of inferior quality, of mediocre value, which the State could expend with less regret than others, and the sacrifice of which is not a serious injury to society or to civilization. To-day, for the same service in France, 4 millions of lives are taken by authority, and, if they attempt to escape, taken by force; all of them, from the twentieth year onward, employed in the same manual and murderous pursuit, including the least suited to the purpose and the best adapted to other purposes, including the most inventive and the most fecund, the most delicate and the most cultivated, those remarkable for superior talent (Page 232/526)who are of almost infinite social value, and whose forced collapse, or precocious end, is a calamity for the human species.

Such is the terminal fruit of the new Régime; military duty is here the counterpart, and as it were, the ransom of political right; the modern citizen may balance one with the other like two weights in the scale. On the one side, he may place his prerogative as sovereign, that is to say, in point of fact, the faculty every four years of giving one vote among ten thousand for the election or non-election of one deputy among six hundred and fifty; on the other side, he may place his positive, active service, three, four or five years of barrack life and of passive obedience, and then twenty-eight days more, then a thirteen-days' summons in honor of the flag, and, for twenty years, at each rumor of war, anxiously waiting for the word of command which obliges him to shoulder his gun and slay with his own hand, or be slain. He will probably end by discovering that the two sides of the scales do not balance and that a right so hollow is poor compensation for so heavy a burden.

Of course, in 1789, he foresaw nothing like that; he was optimistic, pacific, liberal, humanitarian; he knew nothing of Europe nor of history, nothing of the past nor of the present. When the Constituent Assembly constituted him a sovereign, he let things go on; he did not know what he engaged to do, he had no idea of having allowed such a heavy claim against him. But, in signing the social contract, he made himself responsible; in 1793, the note came due and the Convention collected it. [63] Then comes Napoleon who put things in order. Henceforth, every male, able-bodied adult must pay the debt of blood; no more exemptions in the way of military service: [64] all young men who had reached the required age drew lots in the conscription and set out in turn according to the order fixed by their drafted number. [65] But Napoleon is an intelligent creditor; he knows that this debt is "most frightful and most detestable for families, " that his debtors are real, living men and therefore different in kind, that the head of the State should keep these differences in mind, that is to say their condition, their education, their sensibility and their vocation; that, not only in their private interest, but again in the interest of the public, not merely through prudence but also through equity, all should not be indistinguishably restricted to the same mechanical pursuit, to the same manual labor, to the same prolonged and indefinite servitude of soul and body. Already, under the Directory, the law had exempted young married men and widowers or divorced persons who were fathers. [66] Napoleon also exempts the conscript who has a brother in the active army, the only son of a widow, the eldest of three orphans, the son of a father seventy-one years old dependent on his labor, all of whom are family supports. He joins with these all young men who enlist in one of his civil militias, in his ecclesiastical militia or in his university militia, pupils of the École Normale, ignorantin brothers, seminarians for the priesthood, on condition that they shall engage to do service in their vocation and do it effectively, some for ten years, others for life, subject to a discipline more rigid, or nearly as rigid, as military discipline. [67] Finally, he sanctions or institutes volunteer substitutes, through private agreement between a conscript and the able-bodied, certified volunteer substitute for whom the conscript is responsible. [68] If such a bargain is made between them it is done freely, knowing what they are about, and because each man finds the exchange to his advantage; the State has no right to deprive either of them uselessly of this advantage, and oppose an exchange by which it does not suffer. So far from suffering it often gains by it. For, what it needs is not this or that man, Peter or Paul, but a man as capable as Peter or Paul of firing a gun, of marching long distances, of resisting inclemencies, and such are the substitutes it accepts. They must all be[69] "of sound health and robust constitution, " and sufficiently tall; as a matter of fact, being poorer than those replaced, they are more accustomed to privation and fatigue; most of them, having reached maturity, are worth more for the service than youths who have been recruited by anticipation and too young; some are old soldiers: and in this case the substitute is worth twice as much as the new conscript who has never donned the knapsack or bivouacked in the open air. Consequently, those who are allowed to obtain substitutes are "the drafted and conscripts of all classes, . .. unable to endure the fatigues of war, and those who shall be recognized of greater use to the State by continuing their labors and studies than in forming a part of the army. . .. "[70]

Napoleon had too much sense to be led by the blind existences of democratic formulae; his eyes, which penetrated beyond mere words, at once perceived that the life of a simple soldier, for a young man well brought up and a peasant or for day-laborer, is unequal. A tolerable bed, sufficient clothing, good shoes, certainty of daily bread, a piece of meat regularly, are novelties for the latter but not for the former, and, consequently, enjoyments; that the promiscuity and odor of the barrack chamber, the corporal's cursing and swearing and rude orders, the mess-dish and camp-bread, physical hardships all day and every other day, are for the former, but not for the latter, novelties and, consequently, sufferings. From which it follows that, if literal equality is applied, positive inequality is established, and that by virtue even of the new creed, it is necessary, in the name of true equality as in the name of true liberty, to allow the former, who would suffer most, to treat fairly and squarely with the latter, who will suffer less. And all the more because, by this arrangement, the civil staff preserves for itself its future recruits; it is from nineteen to twenty-six that the future chiefs and under-chiefs of the great work of peaceful and fruitful labor, the savants, artists or scholars, the jurisconsults, engineers or physicians, the enterprising men of commerce or of industry, receive and undertake for themselves a special and superior education, discover or acquire their leading ideas, and elaborate their originality or their competency. If talent is to be deprived of these productive years their growth is arrested in full vegetation, and civil capacities, not less precious for the State than military capacities, are rendered abortive. [71] - Towards 1804, [72] owing to substitution, one conscript out of five in the rural districts, one conscript out of seven in the towns, and, on the average, one conscript out of ten in France, escapes this forced abortive condition; in 1806, the price of a substitute varies from eighteen hundred to four thousand francs, [73] and as capital is scarce, and ready money still more so, a sum like this is sufficiently large. Accordingly, it is the rich or well-to-do class, in other words the more or less cultivated class, which buys off its sons: reliance may be placed on their giving them more or less complete culture. In this way, it prevents the State from mowing down all its sprouting wheat and preserves a nursery of subjects among which society is to find its future élite. - Thus attenuated, the military law is still rigid enough: nevertheless it remains endurable. It is only towards 1807[74] that it becomes monstrous and grows worse and worse from year to year until it becomes the sepulcher of all French youth, even to taking as canon fodder the adolescent under age and men already exempt or free by purchase. But, as before these excesses, it may still be maintained with certain modifications; it suffices almost to retouch it, to establish exemptions and the privilege of substitution as rights, which were once simply favors, [75] reduce the annual contingent, limit the term of service, guarantee their lasting freedom to those liberated, and thus secure in 1818 a recruiting law satisfactory and efficacious which, for more than half a century, will attain its ends without being too detrimental or too odious, and which, among so many laws of the same sort, all mischievous, is perhaps the least pernicious.

Notes:

[1] "The Ancient Régime, " book II., ch. 2, 3, 4, and book V. (Laff. I. pp. 95 to 125 and pp. 245 to 308.)

[2] La Bruyère is, I believe, the first of these precursors. Cf. his chapters on "The Great, " on "Personal Merit, " on "The Sovereign and the Republic, " and his chapter on "Man, " his passages on "The Peasants, " on "Provincial Notes, " etc. These appeals, later on, excite the applause given to the "Marriage of Figaro. " But, in the anticipatory indictment, they strike deeper; there is no gayety in them, the dominant sentiment being one of sadness, resignation, and bitterness.

[3] "Discours prononcé par l'ordre du roi et en sa presence, le 22 février 1787, " by M. de Calonne, contr'1eur-général, p. 22. "What remains then to fill this fearful void (in the finances)? Abuses. The abuses now demanding suppression for the public weal are the most considerable and the best protected, those that are the deepest rooted and which send out the most branches. They are the abuses which weigh most heavily on the working and producing classes, the abuses of financial privileges, the exceptions to the common law and

to so many unjust exemptions which relieve only a portion of the taxpayers by aggravating the lot of the others; general inequality in the distribution of subsidies and the enormous disproportion which exists in the taxation of different provinces and among the offices filled by subjects of the same sovereign; severity and arbitrariness in the collection of the taille; bureaux of internal transportation, and obstacles that render different parts of the same kingdom strangers to each other; rights that discourage industry; those of which the collection requires excessive expenditure and innumerable collectors."

[4] De Ségur, " Mémoires, " III., 591. In 1791, on his return from Russia, his brother says to him, speaking of the Revolution: "Everybody, at first, wanted it .. From the king down to the most insignificant man in the kingdom, everybody did something to help it along; one let it come on up to his shoe-buckle, another up to his garter, another to his waist, another to his breast, and some will not be content until their head is attacked! "

[6] "The Revolution, " pp. 271-279. (Laff. I. 505 to 509.) -Stourm " Les Finances de l'ancien régime et de la Révolution, " I., 171 to 177. - (Report by Ramel, January 31, 1796.) "One would scarcely believe it - the holders of real-estate now owe the public treasury over 13 milliards. "- (Report by Gaudin, Germinal, year X. on the assessment and collection of direct taxes.) "This state of things constituted a permanent, annual deficit of 200 millions. "

[7] "The Ancient Régime, " p. 99, and "The Revolution, " p. 407. (Laff. I. pp 77-78 and II. 300) (About 1,200 millions per annum in bread for Paris, instead of 45 millions for the civil and military household of the King at Versailles.)

[8] "The Ancient Régime, " p. 68. (Laff. I. p. 55) - Madame Campan, "Mémoires, " I., 291, 292.

[9] "The Revolution, " II., 151, and III., 500. (Laff. II. 282-283)

[10] "Mémorial. " (Napoleon's own words.) "The day when, adopting the unity and concentration of power, which could alone save us, . .. the destinies of France depended solely on the character, measures and conscience of him who had been clothed with this accidental dictatorship - beginning with that day, public affairs, that is to stay the State, was myself . .. I was the keystone of an entirely

new building and how slight the foundation! Its destiny depended on each of my battles. Had I been defeated at Marengo you would have then had a complete 1814 and 1815. "

[11] Beugnot, "Mémoires, "II., 317. "To be dressed, taxed, and ordered to take up arms, like most folks, seemed a punishment as soon as one had found a privilege within reach, " such, for example, as the title of "déchireur de bateaux" (one who condemns unseaworthy craft and profits by it), or inspector of fresh butter (using his fingers in tasting it), or tide-waiter and inspector of salt fish. These titles raised a man above the common level, and there were over twenty thousand of them.

[12] See "The Ancient Régime, " p. 129. (Laff. I. p. 99)

[13] Madame de Rémusat, "Mémoires, " III., 316, 317.

[14] De Beausset, "Intérieur du palais de Napoléon " I., p. 9 et seq.. For the year 1805 the total expense is 2,338,167 francs; for the year 1806 it reaches 2,770,861 francs, because funds were assigned "for the annual augmentation of plate, 1,000 silver plates and other objects. " - "Napoleon knew, every New Year's day, what he expended (for his household) and nobody ever dared overpass the credits he allowed."

[15] "The Ancient Régime, " pp. 35o-357. (Laff. I. 259-266)

[16] "The Revolution, " I. pp. 276-281. (Laff. pp. 508-510) - Stourm, ibid., 168-171. (Speech by Bénard-Lagrave to the Five Hundred, Pluvi'se II, year IV.) "It cannot be concealed that, for many years, people were willingly accustoming themselves to the non-payment of taxes. "

[17] Stourm, ibid., II., 365. (Speech of Ozanam to the Five Hundred, Pluvi'se 14, year VII.) "Scandalous traffic. . .. Most of the (tax) collectors in the republic are heads and managers of banks. " - (Circular of the minister of the finances, Floréal 25 year VII.) "Stock-jobbing of the worst kind to which many collectors give themselves up, using bonds and other public securities received in payment of taxes. " - (Report by Gros-Cassaud Florimond, Sep. 19, 1799.) "Among the corruptible and corrupting agents there are only too many public functionaries. " - Mollien, "Mémoires, " I., 222. (In 1800, he had just been appointed director of the sinking-fund.) "The commonplace compliment which was everywhere paid to me (and

even by statesmen who affected the sternest morality) was as follows - you are very fortunate to have an office in which one may legitimately accumulate the largest fortune in France. " - Cf. Rocquain, "État de la France au 18 Brumaire. " (Reports by Lacuée, Fourcroy and Barbé- Marbois.)

[18] Charlotte de Sohr, "Napoléon en Belgique et en Hollande, " 1811, vol. I., 243. (On a high functionary condemned for forgery and whom Napoleon kept in prison in spite of every solicitation.) "Never will I pardon those who squander the public funds. . .. Ah! parbleu! We should have the good old times of the contractors worse than ever if I did not show myself inexorable for these odious crimes."

[19] Stourm, ibid., I., 177. (Report by Gaudin, Sep. 15, 1799.) "A few (tax) rolls for the year V, and one-third of those for the year VII, are behindhand. " - (Report by the same, Germinal I, year X.) "Everything remained to do, on the advent of the consulate, for the assessment and collection of direct taxes; 35,000 rolls for the year VII still remained to be drawn up. With the help of the new office, the rolls for the year VII have been completed; those of the year VIII were made out as promptly as could be expected, and those of the year IX have been prepared with a dispatch which, for the first time since the revolution, enables the collections to be begun in the very year to which they belong. "

[20] "Archives parlementaires, " VIII., p. 11. (Report by Necker to the States-General, May 5, 1789.) "These two-fifths, although legitimately due to the king, are always in arrears. . .. (To-day) these arrears amount in full to about 80 millions. "

[21] De Foville, "la France économique, " p. 354.

[22] "The Ancient Régime, " p. 354. (Laff. I. p. 263.)

[23] Necker, "De l'administration des finances, " I., 164, and "Rapport aux états-généraux, " May 5th, 1789. (We arrive at these figures, 179 millions, by combining these documents, on both sides, with the observation that the 3rd vingtième is suppressed in 1789.)

[24] Charles Nicolas, "les Budgets de la France depuis le commencement du XIXème siècle" (in tabular form). - De Foville, ibid., 356. —In the year IX, the sum-total of direct taxes is 308

millions; in the year XI. 360, and in the year XII, 376. The total income from real- estate in France towards 1800 is 1,500 millions.

[25] It is only after 1816 that the total of each of the four direct taxes can be got at (land, individual, personal, doors and windows). In 1821, the land-tax amounts to 265 millions, and the three others together to 67 millions. Taking the sum of 1,580 millions, estimated by the government as the net revenue at this date in France, we find that, out of this revenue, 16.77 % is deducted for land, and that, with the other three, it then abstracts from the same revenue 21 % - On the contrary, before 1789, the five corresponding direct taxes, added to tithes and feudal privileges, abstracted 81.71 % from the net income of the taxable party. (Cf. "The Ancient Régime, " pp. 346, 347, 351 et seq. Laff. I. pp. 258, 259, 261 and following pages.)

[26] These figures are capital, and measure the distance which separates the old from the new condition of the laboring and poor class, especially in the rural districts; hence the tenacious sentiments and judgments of the people with respect to the Ancient Régime, the Revolution and the Empire. - All local information converges in this sense. I have verified the above figures as well as I could: 1st, by the "Statistiques des préfets, " of the year IX and year XIII and afterwards (printed); 2nd, by the reports of the councillors of state on mission during the year IX (published by Rocquam, and in manuscript in the Archives nationales); 3rd, by the reports of the senators on their sénatories and by the prefects on their departments, in 1806, 1809, 1812, 1814 and 1815, and from 1818 to 1823 (in manuscript in the Archives nationales); 4th, by the observations of foreigners travelling in France from 1802 to 1815. - For example ("A Tour through several of the Middle and Western Departments of France, " 1802, p. 23): "There are no tithes, no church taxes, no taxation of the poor. . .. All the taxes together do not go beyond one-sixth of a man's rent-roll, that is to say, three shillings and sixpence on the pound sterling. " - ("Travels in the South of France, 1807 and 1808, " by Lieutenant-Colonel Pinkney, citizen of the United States, p. 162.) At Tours a two-story house, with six or eight windows on the front, a stable, carriagehouse, garden and orchard, rents at £20 sterling per annum, with the taxes which are from £1,10, to £2, for the state and about ten shillings for the commune. - ("Notes on a Journey through July, August and September, 1814, " by Morris Birkbeck, p. 23.) Near Cosne (Orléanais), an estate of 1,000 acres of tillable land and 500 acres of woods is rented for nine years, for about 9,000 francs a year, together with the taxes, about 1,600 francs

more. - (Ibid., p. 91.) "Visited the Brie. Well cultivated on the old system of wheat, oats and fallow. Average rent 16 francs the acre with taxes, which are about one-fifth of the rent. " - Roederer, III., 474 (on the sénatorerie of Caen, Dec.. 1, 1803): "The direct tax is here in very moderate proportion to the income, it being paid without much inconvenience. - The travellers above quoted and many others are unanimous in stating the new prosperity of the peasant, the cultivation of the entire soil and the abundance and cheapness of provisions. (Morris Birkbeck, p. 11.) "Everybody assures me that the riches and comfort of the cultivators of the soil have been doubled since twenty-five years. " (Ibid., p. 43, at Tournon-sur- le-Rh'ne.) "I had no conception of a country so entirely cultivated as we have found from Dieppe to this place. " - (Ibid., P. 51,, at Montpellier.) "From Dieppe to this place we have not seen among the laboring people one such famished, worn-out, wretched figure as may be met in every parish of England, I had almost said on almost every farm. . .. A really rich country, and yet there are few rich individuals. " - Robert, " De l'Influence de la révolution sur la population, 1802, " p. 41. "Since the Revolution I have noticed in the little village of Sainte-Tulle that the consumption of meat has doubled; the peasants who formerly lived on salt pork and ate beef only at Easter and at Christmas, frequently enjoy a pot-à-feu during the week, and have given up rye-bread for wheat-bread. "

[27] The sum of 1 fr. 15 for a day's manual labor is an average, derived from the statistics furnished by the prefects of the year IX to the year XIII, especially for Charente, Deux-Sèvres, Meurthe, Moselle and Doubs.

[28] "The Ancient Régime. " p. 353. (Laff. I. p. 262).

[29] Arthur Young, II., 259. (Average rate for a day's work throughout France in 1789.)

[30] About 15 millions out of 26 millions, in the opinion of Mallet-Dupan and other observers. - Towards the middle of the 18th century, in a population estimated at 20 millions, Voltaire reckons that "many inhabitants possess only the value of 10 crowns rental, that others have only 4 or 5, and that more than 6 millions of inhabitants have nothing. " ("L'homme aux quarante écus. ")- A little later, Chamfort (I., 178) adds: "It is an incontestable truth that, in France, 7 millions of men beg, and 12 millions of men are incapable of giving anything. "

[31] Law of Floréal 3, year X, title II, articles 13, 14, § 3 and 4.

[32] Charles Nicolas, ibid. - In 1821, the personal and poll tax yields 46 millions; the tax on doors and windows, 21 millions: total, 67 millions. According to these sums we see that, if the recipient of 100 francs income from real-estate pays 16 fr. 77 real-estate tax, he pays only 4 fr. 01 for his three other direct taxes. - These figures, 6 to 7 francs, can nowadays be arrived at through direct observation. - To omit nothing, the assessment in kind, renewed in principle after 1802 on all parish and departmental roads, should be added; this tax, demanded by rural interests, laid by local authorities, adapted to the accommodation of the taxpayer, and at once accepted by the inhabitants, has nothing in common with the former covée, save in appearance; in fact, it is as easy as the corvée was burdensome. (Stourm, I., 122.)

[34] Charles Nicolas, "Les Budgets de la France depuis le commencement du XIXe Siècle, " and de Foville, "La France économique, " p. 365, 373. - Returns of licenses in 1816, 40 millions; in 1820, 22 millions; in 1860, 80 millions; in 1887, 171 millions.

[35] The mutation tax is that levied in France on all property transmitted by inheritance. or which changes hands through formal sale (other than in ordinary business transactions), as in the case of transfers of real-estate, effected through purchase or sale. Timbre designates stamp duties imposed on the various kinds of legal documents. -Tr.

[36] Ibid. Returns of the mutation tax (registration and timbre). Registration in 1820, 127 millions; in 1860, 306 millions; in 1886, 518 millions. - Timbre, in 1820, 26 millions; in 1860, 56 millions; in 1886, 156 millions. Sum-total in 1886, 674 millions. - The rate of corresponding taxes under the ancient régime (contr'le, insinuation centième denier, formule) was very much lower; the principal one, or tax of centieme denier, took only 1 per 100, and on the mutations of real-estate. This mutation tax is the only one rendered worse; it was immediately aggravated by the Constituent Assembly, and it is rendered all the more exorbitant on successions in which liabilities are not deducted from assets. (That is to say, the inheritor of an indebted estate in France must pay a mutation tax on its full value. He has the privilege, however, of renouncing the estate if he does not choose to accept it along with its indebtedness.) - The taxpayer's resignation to this tax is explained by the exchequer collecting it at a

unique moment, when proprietorship just comes into being or is just at the point of birth. In effect, if property changes hands under inheritance or through free donation it is probable that the new owner, suddenly enriched, will be only too glad to enter into possession of it, and not object to an impost which, although taking about a tenth, still leaves him only a little less wealthy. When property is transferred by contract or sale, neither of the contracting parties, probably, sees clearly which pays the fiscal tax; the seller may think that it is the buyer, and the buyer that it is the seller. Owing to this illusion both are less sensible of the shearing, each offering his own back in the belief that it is the back of the other.

[37] See "The Ancient Régime, " pp. 358-362. (Ed. Laff. I. 266-268.)

[38] See "The Revolution, " vol. I., pp. 16, 38. (ED. Laff. I. pp. 326, 342.)

[39] Decree of Oct. 31 - Nov. 5, 1789, abolishing the boundary taxes between the provinces and suppressing all the collection offices in the kingdom. - Decree of 21-30 March 1790, abolishing the salt-tax. Decree of 1-17 March 1791, abolishing all taxes on liquors, and decree of 19-25 Feb. 1791, abolishing all octroi taxes. - Decree of 20-27 March 1791, in relation to freedom of growing, manufacturing and selling tobacco; customs-duties on the importation of leaf-tobacco alone are maintained, and give but an insignificant revenue, from 1,500,000 to 1,800,000 francs in the year V.

[40] Gaudin, Duc de Gaëte, "Mémoires, " I., 215-217. - The advantages of indirect taxation are well explained by Gaudin. "The taxpayer pays only when he is willing and has the means. On the other hand, when the duties imposed by the exchequer are confounded with the price of the article, the taxpayer, in paying his due, thinks only of satisfying a want or of procuring an enjoyment. " - Decrees of March 16 and 27, and May 4, 1806 (on salt), of February 25, 1804, April 24, 1806, Nov. 25, 1808 (on liquors), May 19, 1802, March 6, 1804, April 24, 1806, Dec.. 29, 1810 (on tobacco).

[41] Letrosne, "De l'administration des finances et de la réforme de l'imp't" (1779) pp. 148, 162. - Laboulaye, "De l'administration française sous Louis XVI. " (Revue des cours littéraires, 1864-1865, p. 677). "I believe that, under Louis XIII., they took at least five and, under Louis XIV, four to get two. "

[42] Paul Leroy-Bealieu, "Traité de la science des finances, " I., 261. (In 1875, these costs amount to 5.20 %.) - De Foville, ibid. (Cost of customs and salt-tax, in 1828, 16.2 %; in 1876, 10.2 %. - Cost of indirect taxation, in 1828, 14.90 %; in 1876, 3.7 %.) - De Calonné, "Collection des mémoires présentés à l'assemblée des notables, " 1787, p. 63.

[43] See "The Ancient Régime, " P. 23, 370. - " The Revolution, " I., 10, 16, 17. (Ed. Laff. I. pp. 23-24, 274, 322, 326-327.)

[44] See "The Ancient Régime, " p. 361. (Ed. Laff. I. p. 268.)

[45] Leroy-Beaulieu, ibid., I., 643.

[46] Decrees of November 25, 1808, and December 8, 1824.

[47] Certain persons under the ancient régime enjoyed an exemption from the tax on salt.

[48] Stourm, I., 360, 389. - De Foville, 382, 385, 398.

[49] These figures are given by Gaudin.

[50] Thiers, XIII., pp. 20 to 25.

[51] Lafayette, "Mémoires. " (Letter of October 17, 1779, and notes made in Auvergne, August 1800.) "You know how many beggars there were, people dying of hunger in our country. We see no more of them. The peasants are richer, the land better tilled and the women better clad. " - "The Ancient Régime, " 340, 34, 342. - " The Revolution, " III., p. 366, 402.

[52] "The Ancient Régime, " P. 340. (ED. Laff. I. pp. 254, 256.)-" The Revolution, " III., 212. (Ed. Laff. II. p. 271, 297.)

[53] These two famines were due to inclement seasons and were aggravated, the last one by the consequences of invasion and the necessity of supporting 150,000 foreign troops, and the former by the course taken by Napoleon who applies the maximum afresh, with the same intermeddling, the same despotism and the same failure as under the Convention. ("Souvenirs", by PASQUIER (Etienne-Dennis, duc), chancelier de France. in VI volumes, Librarie Plon, Paris 1893.) "I do not exaggerate in stating that our operations in the

purchase and transport (of grain) required a full quarter of the time, and often one-third, more than would have been required in commerce. " - Prolongation of the famine in Normandy. "Bands of famished beggars overran the country. . .. Riots and pillaging around Caen; several mills burnt. . .. Suppression of these by the imperial guard. In the executions which resulted from these even women were not spared. " - The two principal guarantees at the present day against this public danger are, first, easier circumstances, and next the multiplication of good roads and of railroads, the dispatch and cheapness of transportation, and the superabundant crops of Russia and the United States.

[54] J. Gebelin, "Histoire des milices provinciales" (1882), p. 87, 143, 157, 288. - Most of the texts and details may be found in this excellent work. - Many towns, Paris, Lyons, Reims, Rouen, Bordeaux, Tours, Agen, Sedan and the two generalities of Flanders and Hainault are examples of drawing by lot; they furnished their contingent by volunteers enlisted at their own expense; the merchants and artisans, or the community itself, paying the bounty for enlistment. Besides this there were many exemptions in the lower class. - Cf. "The Ancient Régime, " p. 390. (Ed. Laff. p. 289.)

[55] J. Gebelin, ibid., 239, 279, 288. (Except the eight regiments of royal grenadiers in the militia who turned out for one month in the year.)

[56] Example afforded by one department. ("Statistics of Ain, " by Rossi, prefect, 1808.) Number of soldiers on duty in the department, in 1789, 323; in 1801, 6,729; in 1806, 6,764. - " The department of Ain furnished nearly 30,000 men to the armies, conscripts and those under requisition. " - It is noticeable, consequently, that in the population of 1801, there is a sensible diminution of persons between twenty and thirty and, in the population of 1806, of those between twenty-five and thirty-five years of age. The number between twenty and thirty is as follows: in 1789, 39,828; in 1801, 35,648; in 1806, 34,083.

[57] De Dampmartin. "Evénemens qui se sont passés sous mes yeux pendant la révolution française, " V. II. (State of the French army, Jan. 1, 1789.) Total on a peace footing, 177,890 men. - This is the nominal force; the real force under arms was 154,000; in March 1791, it had fallen to 115,000, through the multitude of desertions and the

scarcity of enlistments, (Yung, "Dubois-Crancé et la Révolution, " I., 158. Speech by Dubois-Crancé.)

[58] "The Ancient Régime, " P 390, 391. - "The Revolution, " p. 328-330. (Ed. Laff. I. 289 and 290, pp. 542-543) - Albert Babeau, "le Recrutement militaire sous l'ancien Régime. " (In "la Réforme sociale" of Sept. I, 1888, p. 229, 238.)- An officer says, "only the rabble are enlisted because it is cheaper. " - Yung, ibid., I., 32. (Speech by M. de Liancourt in the tribune.) "The soldier is classed apart and is too little esteemed. " - Ibid., p. 39. ("Vices et abus de la constitution actuelle française, " memorial signed by officers in most of the regiments, Sept. 6, 1789.) "The majority of soldiers are derived from the offscourings of the large towns and are men without occupation. "

[59] Gebelin, p. 270. Almost all the cahiers of the third-estate in 1789 demand the abolition of drafting by lot, and nearly all of those of the three orders are for volunteer service, as opposed to obligatory service; most of these demand, for the army, a volunteer militia enlisted through a bounty; this bounty or security in money to be furnished by communities of inhabitants which, in fact, was already the case in several towns.

[60] Albert Babeau, ibid., 238. "Colonels were allowed only 100 francs per man; this sum, however, being insufficient, the balance was assessed on the pay of the officers. "

[61] This principle was at once adopted by the Jacobins. (Yung, ibid., 19, 22, 145. Speech by Dubois-Crancé at the session held Dec. 12, 1789.) "Every citizen will become a soldier of the Constitution. " No more casting lots nor substitution. "Each citizen must be a soldier and each soldier a citizen. " - The first application of the principle is a call for 300,000 men (Feb. 26, 1793), then through a levy on the masses which brings 500,000 men under the flag, nominally volunteers, but conscripts in reality. (Baron Poisson, "l'Armée et la Garde Nationale, "III, 475.)

[63] Baron Poisson, "l'Armée et la Garde nationale, " III., 475. (Summing up.) "Popular tradition has converted the volunteer of the Republic into a conventional personage which history cannot accept. . .. 1st. The first contingent of volunteers demanded of the country consisted of 97,000 men (i1791). 60,000 enthusiasts responded to the call, enlisted for a year and fulfilled their

engagement; but for no consideration would they remain longer. 2nd. Second call for volunteers in April 1792. Only mixed levies, partial, raised by money, most of them even without occupation, outcasts and unable to withstand the enemy. 3rd. 300,000 men recruited, which measure partly fails; the recruit can always get off by furnishing a substitute. 4th. Levy in mass of 500,000 men, called volunteers, but really conscripts. "

[64] "Mémorial" (Speech by Napoleon before the Council of State). "I am inflexible on exemptions; they would be crimes; how relieve one's conscience of having caused one man to die in the place of another? " - "The conscription was an unprivileged militia: it was an eminently national institution and already far advanced in our customs; only mothers were still afflicted by it, while the time was coming when a girl would not have a man who had not paid his debt to his country. "

[65] Law of Fructidor 8, year XIII, article 10. - Pelet de La Lozère, 229. (Speech by Napoleon, Council of State, May 29, 1804.) - Pelet adds: "The duration of the service was not fixed. . .. As a fact in itself, the man was exiled from his home for the rest of his life, regarding it as a desolating, permanent exile. . .. Entire sacrifice of existence. . .. An annual crop of young men torn from their families and sent to death." - Archives nationales, F7, 3014. (Reports of prefects, 1806.) After this date, and even from the beginning, there is extreme repugnance which is only overcome by severe means. . .. (Ardeche.) "If the state of the country were to be judged of by the results of the conscription one would have a poor idea of it. " - (Ariège.) "At Brussac, district of Foix, four or five individuals arm themselves with stones and knives to help a conscript escape, arrested by the gendarmes. . .. A garrison was ordered to this commune. " - At Massat, district of Saint-Girons, on a few brigades of gendarmes entering this commune to establish a garrison, in order to hasten the departure of refractory conscripts, they were stoned; a shot even was fired at this troop. . .. A garrison was placed in these hamlets as in the rest of the commune. - During the night of Frimaire 16-17 last, six strange men presented themselves before the prison of Saint-Girons and loudly demanded Gouazé, a deserter and condemned. On the jailor coming down they seized him and struck him down. " - (Haute-Loire.) "'The flying column is under constant orders simultaneously against the refractory and disobedient among the classes of the years IX, X, XI, XII, and XIII, and against the laggards of that of year IV, of which 134 men yet remain to be supplied. " -

(Bouches-du-Rh'ne.) "50 deserter sailors and 84 deserters or conscripts of different classes have been arrested. " - (Dordogne.) "Out of 1353 conscripts, 134 have failed to reach their destination; 124 refractory or deserters from the country and 41 others have been arrested; 81 conscripts have surrendered as a result of placing a garrison amongst them; 186 have not surrendered. Out of 892 conscripts of the year XIV on the march, 101 deserted on the road. " - (Gard.) "76 refractory or deserters arrested. " - (Landes.) "Out of 406 men who left, 51 deserted on the way, " etc. - This repugnance becomes more and more aggravated. (Cf. analogous reports of 1812 and 1813, F7, 3018 and 3019, in "Journal d'un bourgeois d'Evreux, " p. 150 to 214, and "Histoire de 1814, " by Henry Houssaye, p. 8 to 24.)

[66] Law of Fructidor, year VI.

[67] Decree of July 29, 1811 (on the exemption of pupils in the École Normale). - Decree of March 30, 1810, title II., articles 2, 4, 5, 6 (on the police and system of the École Normale). - Decree on the organization of the University, titles 6 and 13, March 7, 1808.

[68] Law of Vent'se 17, year VIII, title III., articles I and 13. - Law of Fructidor 8, year XIII, articles 50, 54, and 55.

[69] Law of Fructidor 8, year XIII, article 51

[70] Law of Vent'se 17, year VIII, title 3, article I.

[71] Thibaudeau, p. 108. (Speech of the First Consul before the Council of State.) "Art, science and the professions must be thought of. We are not Spartans. . .. As to substitution, it must be allowed. In a nation where fortunes are equal each individual should serve personally; but, with a people whose existence depends on the inequality of fortunes, the rich must be allowed the right of substitution; only we must take care that the substitutes be good, and that conscripts pay some of the money serving to defray the expense of a part of the equipment of the army of reserve. "

[72] Pelet de La Lozère, 228.

[73] Archives nationales, F7, 3014. (Reports of prefects, 1806.) Average price of a substitute: Basses Alpes, from 2,000 to 2,500 francs; Bouches-du-Rh'ne, from 1,800 to 3,000; Dordogne, 2,400;

Gard, 3,000; Gers, 4,000; Haute-Garonne, from 2,000 to 3,000; Hérault, 4,000; Vaucluse, 2,500; Landes, 4,000. Average rate of interest (Ardèche): "Money, which was from 11/4 to 11/2 %, has declined; it is now at 3 1/4 % a month or 10 % per annum. " - (Basses Alpes): "The rate of money has varied in commerce from 1 to 3/4 % per month. " - (Gard): "Interest is at 1 % a month in commerce; proprietors can readily borrow at 9 or 10 % per annum. " - (Hérault): "The interest on money is 1 1/4 % per month. " - (Vaucluse): "Money is from 3/4 to 11/4 % per month. "

[74] Thiers, VII., p. 23 and 467. In November 1806, Napoleon orders the conscription of 1807; in March 1807, he orders the conscription of 1808, and so on, always from worse to worse. - Decrees of 1808 and 1813 against young men of family already bought off or exempted. - "Journal d'un Bourgeois d'Evreux, " 214. Desolate state of things in 1813, "general depression and discouragement. " - Miot de Mélito, III., 304. (Report of Miot to the Emperor after a tour in the departments in 1815.) "Everywhere, almost, the women are your declared enemies. "

[75] Law of Vent'se 17, year VIII, title 3, articles 6, 7, 8, 9. - Exemption is granted as a favor only to the ignorantin brothers and to seminarians assigned to the priesthood. - Cf. the law of March 10, 1818, articles 15 and 18.

CHAPTER III. Ambition and Self-esteem.

I. Rights and benefits.

The assignment of right. - Those out of favor and the preferred under former governments. - Under the Ancient Regime. - During the Revolution. - French conception of Equality and Rights. - Its ingredients and its excesses. - The satisfaction it obtains under the new regime. - Abolition of legal incapacity and equality in the possession of rights. - Confiscation of collective action and equality in the deprivation of rights. - Careers in the modern State. - Equal right of all to offices and to promotion. - Napoleon's distribution of employments. - His staff of officials recruited from all classes and parties.

Now that the State has just made a new allotment of the burdens and duties which it imposes it must make a new assignment of the rights and benefits it confers. Distributive justice, on both sides, and long before 1789, was defective, and, under the monarchy, exclusions had become as obnoxious as exemptions; all the more because, through a double iniquity, the ancient Régime in each group distinguished two other groups, one to which it granted every exemption, and the other which it made subject to every exclusion. The reason is that, from the first, the king, in the formation and government of the kingdom, in order to secure the services, money, collaboration or connivance which he needed, was obliged to negotiate always with corporations, orders, provinces, seignories, the clergy, churches, monasteries, universities, parliaments, professional bodies or industrial guilds and families, that is to say with constituted powers, more or less difficult to bring under subjection and which, to be kept in subjection, stipulated conditions. Hence, in France, so many different conditions: each distinct body had yielded through one or several distinct capitulations and possessed its own separate statute. Hence, again, such diversely unequal conditions: the bodies, the best able to protect themselves, had, of course, defended themselves the best. Their statutes, written or unwritten, guaranteed to them precious privileges which the other bodies, much weaker, could neither acquire nor preserve. These were not merely immunities but likewise prerogatives, not alone alleviations of taxation and militia dispensations, but likewise political and administrative liberties, remnants of their primitive sovereignty, with many other positive advantages. The very least being precedence, preferences, social priority, with an incontestable right to rank, honors, offices, and favors. Such, notably, were the regions-states possessing their own government (pays d'états), compared with those which elected the magistrates who apportioned taxation (pays d'élection), [1] the two highest orders, the clergy and the nobles, compared with the third-estate, and the bourgeoisie, and the town corporations compared with the rest of the inhabitants. On the other hand, opposed to these historical favorites were the historical disinherited, the latter much more numerous and counting by millions - the taxable commons, all subjects without rank or quality, in short, the ordinary run of men, especially the common herd of the towns and particularly of the country, all the more ground down on account of their lower status, along with the Jews lower yet, a sort of foreign class scarcely tolerated, with the Calvinists, not only deprived of the humblest rights but, again, persecuted by the State for the past one hundred years.

All these people, who have been transported far outside of civic relationships by historic right, are brought back, in 1789, by philosophic right. After the declarations of the Constituent Assembly, there are no longer in France either Bretons, Provençals, Burgundians or Alsatians, Catholics, Protestants or Israelites, nobles or plebeians, bourgeois or rurals, but simply Frenchmen,

* all with the one title of citizens,
* all endowed with the same civil, religious and political rights,
* all equal before the State,
* all introduced by law into every career, collectively, on an equal footing and without fear or favor from anybody;
* all free to follow this out to the end without distinction of rank, birth, faith or fortune;
* all, if they are good runners, to receive the highest prizes at the end of the race, any office or rank, especially the leading honors and positions which, thus far reserved to a class or coterie, had not been allowed previously to the great multitude.

Henceforth, all Frenchmen, in theory, enjoy rights in common; unfortunately, this is only the theory. In reality, in all state relationships (dans la cité), the new-comers appropriate to themselves the offices, the pretensions, and more than the privileges of their predecessors; the latter, consisting of large and small land-owners, gentlemen, parliamentarians, officials, ecclesiastics, notables of every kind and degree, are immediately deprived of the rights of man. Surrendered to rural jacqueries and to town mobs, they undergo, first, the neglect and, next, the hostility of the State: the public gendarme has ceased to protect them and refuses his services; afterwards, on becoming a Jacobin, he declares himself their enemy, treats them as enemies, plunders them, imprisons them, murders them, expels or transports them, inflicts on them civil death, and shoots them if they dare return; he deprives their friends or kindred who remain in France of their civil rights; he deprives the nobles or the ennobled of their quality as Frenchmen, and compels them to naturalize themselves afresh according to prescribed formalities; he renews against the Catholics the interdictions, persecutions and brutalities which the old government had practiced against the Calvinist minority. - Thus, in 1799 as in 1789, there are two classes of Frenchmen, two different varieties of men, the first one superior, installed in the civic fold, and the second, inferior and excluded from it; only, in 1799, the greatest inequality consigned the inferior and excluded class to a still lower, more remote, and much worse condition.

The principle (of equalite), nevertheless, subsists. Since 1789 it is inscribed at the top of every constitution; it is still proclaimed in the new constitution. It has remained popular, although perverted and disfigured by the Jacobins; their false and gross interpretation of it could not bring it into discredit; athwart the hideous grotesque caricature, all minds and sentiments ever recur to the ideal form of the cité to the veritable social contract, to the impartial, active, and permanent reign of distributive justice. Their entire education, all the literature, philosophy and culture of the eighteenth century, leads them onward to this conception of society and of rights; more profoundly still, they are predisposed to it by the inner structure of their intelligence, by the original cast of their sensibility7 by the hereditary defects and qualities of their nature and of their race. - The Frenchman easily and quickly grasps some general trait of objects and persons, some characteristic in common; here, this characteristic is the inherent quality of man which he dexterously makes prominent, clearly isolates, and then, stepping along briskly and confidently, rushes ahead on the high-road to consequences. [2] He has forgotten that his summary notion merely corresponds to an extract, and a very brief one, of man in his completeness; his decisive, precipitate process hinders him from seeing the largest portion of the real individual; he has overlooked numerous traits, the most important and most efficacious, those which geography, history, habit, condition, manual labor, or a liberal education, stamp on intellect, soul and body and which, through their differences, constitute different local or social groups. Not only does he overlook all these characteristics, but he sets them aside; they are too numerous and too complex; they would interfere with and disturb his thoughts; however fitted for clear and comprehensive logic he is so much the less fitted for complex and comprehensive ideas; consequently, he avoids them and, through an innate operation of which he is unconscious, he involuntarily condenses, simplifies and curtails henceforth, his idea, partial and superficial as it is, seems to him adequate and complete; in his eyes the abstract quality of man takes precedence of and absorbs all others; not only has this a value, but the sole value. One man, therefore, is as good as another and the law should treat all alike. - Here, amour-propre (self-esteem, pride or arrogance), so keen in France, and so readily excited, comes in to interpret and apply the formula: [3]

"Since all men equal each other, I am as good as any man; if the law confers a right on people of this or that condition, fortune or birth, it must confer the same right on me. Every door that is open to them must be open to me; every door that is closed to me must be closed to them. Otherwise, I am treated as an inferior and wounded in my deepest feelings. When the legislator places a ballot in their hands he is bound to place another just like it in my hands, even if they know how to use it and I do not, even if a limited suffrage is of use to the community and universal suffrage is not. So much the worse if I am sovereign only in name, and through the imagination; I consent to my sovereignty being illusory, but with the understanding that the sovereignty of others is regarded likewise; so I prefer servitude and privation for all, rather than liberties and advantages for a few, and, provided the same level is passed over all heads, I submit to the yoke for all heads, including my own. "

Such is the internal composition of the instinct of' equality, and such is the natural instinct of Frenchmen. It is beneficial or mischievous according as one or the other of its ingredients predominates, at one time the noble sentiment of equity and at another time the low envy of foolish vanity; [4] healthy or unhealthy, however, its power in France is enormous, and the new Régime gratifies it in every possible way, good or bad. No more legal disqualifications! On the one hand, the republican laws of proscription or of exception were all repealed: we have seen an amnesty and the return of the émigrés, the Concordat, the restoration of Catholic worship, the compulsory reconciliation of the constitutionalists with the orthodox; the First

Consul admits no difference between them; his new clergy are recruited from both groups and, in this respect, he forces the Pope to yield. [5] He gives twelve of the sixty episcopal thrones to former schismatics; he wants them to take their places boldly; he relieves them from ecclesiastical penitence and from any humiliating recantation; he takes care that, in the other forty-eight dioceses, the priests who formerly took the civic oath shall be employed and well treated by their superiors who, at the same epoch, refused to take the civic oath. On the other hand, all the exclusions, inequalities and distinctions of the monarchy remain abolished. Not only are the Calvinist and even Israelite cults legally authorized, the same as the Catholic cult, but, again, the Protestant consistories and Jewish synagogues[6] are constituted and organized on the same footing as the Catholic churches. Pastors and rabbis likewise become functionaries under the same title as bishops and cure's; all are recognized or sanctioned by the government and all equally benefit by its patronage: it is an unique thing in Europe to find the small churches of the minority obtaining the same measure of indifference and good will from the State as the great church of the majority, and, henceforth, in fact as in law, the ministers of the three cults, formerly ignored, tolerated or proscribed, enjoy their rank, titles and honors in the social as well as in the legal hierarchy, equally with the ministers of that cult which was once the only one dominant or allowed

Similarly, in the civilian status, no inferiority or discredit must legally attach to any condition whatever, either to plebeian, villager, peasant or poor man as such, as formerly under the monarchy; nor to noble, bourgeois, citizen, notable or rich man, as recently under the Republic. Each of these two classes is relieved of its degradation; no class is burdened by taxation or by the conscription beyond its due; all persons and all property find in the government, in the administration, in the tribunals, in the gendarme, the same reliable protection. - So much for equity and the true spirit of equality. - Let us now turn around and consider envy and the bad spirit of equality. The plebiscite, undoubtedly, as well as the election of deputies to the Corps Legislatif are simply comedies; but, in these comedies, one r'le is as good as another and the duke of the old or new pattern, a mere figurant among hundreds and thousands of others, votes only once like the corner-grocer. Undoubtedly, the private individual of the commune or department, in institutions of charity, worship or education, is deprived of any independence, of any initiation, of any control, as the State has confiscated for itself all collective action; but the classes deprived of this are especially the upper classes, alone sufficiently enlightened and wealthy to take the lead, form projects and provide for expenditure: in this usurpation, the State has encroached upon and eaten deeper into the large body of superior existences scattered about than into the limited circle where humbler lives clamber and crawl along; nearly the entire loss, all perceptible privation, is for the large landed proprietor and not for his hired hands, for the large manufacturer or city merchant and not for their workmen or clerks, [7] while the clerk, the workman, the journeyman, the handicraftsman, who grumble at being the groundlings, find themselves less badly off since their masters or patrons, fallen from a higher point, are where they are and they can elbow them.

Now that men are born on the ground, all on the same level, and are confined within universal and uniform limits, social life no longer appears to them other than a competition, a rivalry instituted and proclaimed by the State, and of which it is the umpire; for, through its interference, all are comprised within its enclosure and shut up and kept there; no other field is open to run on; on the contrary, every career within these bounds, indicated and staked out beforehand, offers an opportunity for all runners: the government has laid out and leveled the ground, established compartments, divided off and prepared rectilinear lists which converge to the goal; there, it presides, the unique arbiter of the race, exposing to all competitors the innumerable prizes which it proposes for them. - These prizes consist of offices, the various employments of the State, political, military, ecclesiastical, judiciary, administrative and university, all the honors and dignities which it dispenses, all the grades of its hierarchy from the lowest to the highest, from that of corporal, college-regent, alderman, office - supernumerary, assistant priest up to that of senator, marshal of France, grand master of the university, cardinal, and minister of State. It confers on its possessor, according to the greater or lesser importance of the place, a greater or lesser portion of the advantages which all men crave and seek for money, power, patronage, influence, consideration, importance and social pre-eminence; thus, according to the rank one attains in the hierarchy, one is something, or of some account; outside of the hierarchy, one is nothing.

Consequently, the faculty for getting in and advancing one's self in these lists is the most precious of all: in the new Régime it is guaranteed by the law as a common right and is open to all

Frenchmen. As no other outlet for them is allowed by the State it owes them this one; since it invites them and reduces everybody to competing under its direction it is bound to be an impartial arbiter; since the quality of citizen, in itself and through it alone, confers the right to make one's way, all citizens indifferently must enjoy the right of succeeding in any employment, the very highest, and without any distinction as to birth, fortune, cult or party. There must be no more preliminary exclusions; no more gratuitous preferences, undeserved favors, anticipated promotions; no more special favors. - Such is the rule of the modern State: constituted as it is, that is to say, monopolizer and omnipresent, it cannot violate this rule for any length of time with impunity. In France, at least, the good and bad spirits of equality agree in exacting adherence to it: on this point, the French are unanimous; no article of their social code is more cherished by them; this one flatters their amour-propre and tickles their imagination; it exalts hope, nourishes illusion, intensifies the energy and enjoyment of life. - Thus far, the principle has remained inert, powerless, held in suspension in the air, in the great void of speculative declarations and of constitutional promises. Napoleon brings it down to the ground and renders it practical; that which the assemblies had decreed in vain for ten years he brings about for the first time and in his own interest. To exclude a class or category of men from offices and promotion would be equivalent to depriving one's self gratuitously of all the talents it contains, and, moreover, to incurring, besides the inevitable rancor of these frustrated talents, the sullen and lasting discontent of the entire class or category. The First Consul would do himself a wrong were he to curb his right to choose: he needs every available capacity, and he takes them where he finds them, to the right, to the left, above or below, in order to keep his regiments full and enroll in his service every legitimate ambition and every justifiable pretension.

Under the monarchy, an obscure birth debarred even the best endowed men from the principal offices. Under the Consulate and the Empire the two leading personages of the State are Lebrun, Maupeou's old secretary, a productive translator, [8] a lawyer, formerly councilor in a provincial court of justice, then third-consul, then Duc de Plaisance and arch-chancellor of the Empire and Cambacérès, second- consul, then Duc de Parme and arch-chancellor of the Empire, both of them being princes. Similarly, the marshals are new men and soldiers of fortune, a few of them born in the class of inferior nobles or in the ordinary bourgeois class, mostly among the people or even amongst the populace, and, in its lowest ranks,

Masséna, the son of a wine- dealer, once a cabin-boy and then common soldier and non-commissioned officer for fourteen years; Ney, son of a cooper, Lefebvre, son of a miller, Murat, son of a tavern-keeper, Lannes, son of an hostler, and Augereau, son of a mason and a female dealer in fruit and vegetables. - Under the Republic, noble birth consigned, or confined, the ablest and best qualified men for their posts to a voluntary obscurity, only too glad when their names did not condemn them to exile, imprisonment or to the guillotine. Under the Empire, M. de Talleyrand is prince of Benevento, minister of foreign affairs and vice-grand-elector with a salary of five hundred thousand francs. We see personages of old nobility figuring in the first ranks: among the clergy M. de Roquelaure, M. de Boisgelin, M. de Broglie, M. Ferdinand de Rohan; in the magistracy, M. Séguier, M. Pasquier, M. Molé; on the domestic and decorative staff of the palace, Comte de Ségur, grand-master of ceremonies, Comte de Montesquiou-Fézensac, grand-chamberlain, also as chamberlains, Comtes d'Aubusson de la Feuillade, de Brigode, de Croy, de Coutades, de Louvois, de Brancas, de Gontaut, de Grammont, de Beauvau, de Lur-Saluces, d'Haussonville, de Noailles, de Chabot, de Turenne, [9] and other bearers of historic names. - During the Revolution, at each new parliamentarian, popular or military coup d'état the notabilities of the vanquished party were always excluded from office and generally outlawed. After the coup d'état of Brumaire, not only are the vanquished of the old parties all brought back under the protection of the law, but, again, their notables are promoted to the highest offices. Among the monarchists of the Constituent Assembly Mabuet is made councilor of State, and Maury archbishop of Paris; forty-seven other ecclesiastics who, like himself, refused to take the oath to the civil constitution of the clergy, are appointed, like him, to episcopal thrones. Among the Feuillants of the Legislative Assembly, Vaublanc is made prefect, Beugnot a councilor of State and minister of the finances in the grand-duchy of Berg, Matthieu Dumas a brigadier-general and director of reviews, Narbonne becomes the aid- de-camp and the intimate interlocutor of Napoleon, and then ambassador to Vienna; if Lafayette had been willing, not to ask for but to accept the post, he would have been made a marshal of France. - Among the few Girondists or Federalists who did not perish after the 2nd June, Riouffe is prefect and baron, Lanjuinais is senator and count; among others proscribed, or half proscribed, the new Régime restores to and places at the head of affairs the superior and special employees whom the Reign of Terror had driven away, or singled out for slaughter, particularly the heads of the financial and diplomatic services who, denounced by Robespierre on the 8th Thermidor, or arrested on the morning of the 9th already felt their necks under the blade of the guillotine; Reinhart and Otto are ambassadors, Mollien is count and treasury minister, Miot becomes councilor of state, Comte de Melito minister of finances at Naples, while Gaudin is made minister of finances in France and Duc de Gaëte. Among the transported or fugitives of Fructidor, Barthélemy becomes senator, Barbé-Marbois director of the Treasury and first president of the Cour des Comptes; Siméon, councilor of State and then minister of justice in Westphalia; Portalis is made minister of worship, and Fontanes grand-master of the University. The First Consul passes the sponge over all political antecedents: not only does he summon to his side the moderates and half-moderates of the Constituent and Legislative Assemblies, of the Convention and of the Directory, but again he seeks recruits among pure royalists and pure Jacobins, among the men the most devoted to the ancient Régime and amongst those most compromised by the Revolution, at both extremities of the most extreme opinions. We have just seen, on the one side, what hereditary favorites of a venerable royalty, what born supporters of the deposed dynasty, are elevated by him to the first of his magisterial, clerical and court dignities. On the other hand, apart from Chasset, Roederer and Grégoire, apart from Fourcroy, Bérlier and Réal, apart from Treilhard and Boulay de La Meurthe, he employs others branded or noted for terrible acts, Barère himself, at least for a certain period, and in the sole office he was fitted for, that of a denunciator, gazetteer and stimulator of public opinion; everybody has a place according to his faculties, and each has rank according to his usefulness and merit. Barère, consequently, becomes a paid spy and pamphleteer; Drouet, the postmaster, who arrested the royal family at Varennes, becomes sub-prefect at Sainte-Menehould; Jean-Bon Saint-André, one of the Committee of Public Safety, is made prefect at Mayence; Merlin de Douai, reporter of the law against suspects, is prosecuting attorney in the court of cassation; Fouché, whose name tells all, becomes minister of state and Duke of Otranto; nearly all of the survivors of the Convention are made judges of première instancc or of appeal, revenue-collectors, deputies, prefects, foreign consuls, police commissioners, inspectors of reviews, head-clerks in the post-offices, custom-houses and tax- offices, while, in 1808, among these functionaries, one hundred and thirty were regicides. [10]

II. Ambitions during the Ancient Regime.

The need of success. - Initiation and conditions of promotion under the old monarchy. - Effect on minds. - Ambitions are limited. - The external outlets open to them. -

To make one's way, get ahead, and succeed in the world is now the dominant thought in the minds of men. Before 1789, this thought had not acquired sovereign control in their minds; it found that there were rival ideas to contend with, and it had only half-developed itself; its roots had not sunk down deep enough to monopolize the activity of the imagination, to absorb the will and possess the mind entirely; and the reason is that it lacked both air and victuals. Promotion, under the old monarchy, was slow, and in the first place, because the monarchy was old and because in every order which is not new each new generation finds that every office is filled, and next, because, in this old order founded on tradition and heredity, future vacancies were supplied long beforehand. The great social staircase led to several stories; each man could ascend every step of his own flight, but he could not mount above it; the landing reached, he found closed doors and nearly insurmountable barriers. The story above was reserved to its own inhabitants; they occupied it now and were still to occupy it in time to come; the inevitable successors of the titular possessor were seen around him on each step, his equals, peers and neighbors, one or the other often designated by name as his legal heir, the purchaser of his survivorship. In those days, not only was the individual himself considered, his merits and his services, but likewise his family and ancestry, his state and condition, the society he entered into, the "salon" he maintained, his fortune and his followers; these antecedents and surroundings composed the quality of the personage; without this requisite quality, he could not go beyond the landing-place. Strictly speaking, a personage born on the upper steps of one story might sometimes succeed in mounting the lowest steps of the next story, but there he stopped. In short, it was always considered by those on the lower story that the upper story was inaccessible and, moreover, uninhabitable.

Accordingly, most of the public offices, in the finances, in the administration, in the judiciary, in the parliaments, in the army, at court, were private property as is now the case with the places of advocates, notaries and brokers; they had to be bought to enable one to follow these pursuits, and were very dear; one had to possess a large capital and be content beforehand to derive only a mediocre revenue from it, 10, 5 and sometimes 3 % on the purchase-money. [11] The place once acquired, especially if an important one, involved official parade, receptions, an open table, a large annual outlay; [12] it often ran the purchaser in debt; he knew that his acquisition would bring him more consideration than crowns. On the other hand, to obtain possession of it, he had to secure the good-will of the body of which he became a member, or of the patron who bestowed the office. That is to say, he must be regarded by his future colleagues as acceptable, or by the patron as a guest, invited, and feasible friend, in other words, provide sponsors for himself, furnish guarantees, prove that he was well-off and well-educated, that his ways and manners qualified him for the post, and that, in the society he was about to enter, he would not turn out unsuitable. To maintain one's self in office at court one was obliged to possess the tone of Versailles, quite different from that of Paris and the provinces. [13] To maintain one's self in a high parliamentary position, one was expected to possess local alliances, moral authority, the traditions and deportment handed down from father to son in the old magistrate families, and which a mere advocate, an ordinary pleader, could not arrive at. [14] In short, on this staircase, each distinct story imposed on its inmates a sort of distinct costume, more or less costly, embroidered and gilded, I mean a sum of outward and inward habits and connections, all obligatory and indispensable, comprising title, particle and name: the announcement of any bourgeois name by a lackey in the ante-chamber would be considered a discord; consequently, one had one's self ennobled in the current coin, or assumed a noble name gratis. Caron, son of a watchmaker, became Beaumarchais; Nicolas, a foundling, called himself M. de Champfort; Danton, in public documents, signed himself d'Anton; in the same way, a man without a dress-coat hires or borrows one, no matter how, on going out to dine; all this was tolerated and accepted as a sign of good behavior and of final conformity with custom, as in testimony of respect for the usages of good society.

Through this visible separation of stories, people had acquired the habit of remaining in the condition in which they were placed; they were not irritated by being obliged to stay in it; the soldier who enlisted did not aspire to become an officer; the young officer of the lower noblesse and of small means did not aspire to the post of colonel or lieutenant-general; a limited perspective kept hopes and the imagination from fruitlessly launching forth into a boundless future: ambition, humbled to the ground at the start, walked instead of flying; it recognized at the outset that the summits were beyond its reach; to be able to mount upward one or two steps was enough. - In general, a man obtained promotion on the spot, in his town, corporation or parliament. The assistant-counselor who pleaded his first case in the court of Grenoble or of Rennes calculated that, in twenty years, he would become first judge at Grenoble or at Rennes, rest twenty years or more in office, and he aimed at nothing better. Alongside of the counselor of a (court) presidency, or of an "election" magistrate, of a clerk in the salt-tax bureau, or in the frontier custom-house, or in the bureau of "rivers and forests, " alongside of a clerk in the treasury or ministry of foreign affairs, or of a lawyer or prosecuting attorney, there was always some son, son-in-law or nephew, fitted by domestic training, by a technical apprenticeship, by moral adaptation, not only to perform the duties of the office, but to be contented in it, pretend to nothing beyond it, not to look above himself with regret or envy, satisfied with the society around him, and feel, moreover, that elsewhere he would be out of his element and uncomfortable.

Life, thus restricted and circumscribed, was more cheerful then than at the present day; souls, less disturbed and less strained, less exhausted and less burdened with cares, were healthier. The Frenchman, exempt from modern preoccupations, followed amiable and social instincts, inclined to take things easily, and of a playful disposition owing to his natural talent for amusing himself by amusing others, in mutual enjoyment of each other's company and without calculation, through easy and considerate intercourse, smiling or laughing, in short, in a constant flow of inspiration, good-humor and gayety. [15] It is probable that, if the Revolution had not intervened, the great parvenus of the time and of the Empire would, like their forerunners, have submitted to prevailing necessities and readily accommodated themselves to the discipline of the established Régime. Cambacérès, who had succeeded to his father as counselor at the bar of Montpellier, would have become president (of the tribunal) in his turn; meanwhile, he would have composed able jurisprudential treatises and invented some new pâté de becfigues; Lebrun, former collaborator with Maupeou, might have become counselor in the court of excise at Paris, or chief-clerk in the Treasury department; he would have kept up a philosophical salon, with fashionable ladies and polished men of letters to praise his elegant and faulty translations. Amongst the future marshals, some of them, pure plebeians, Masséna, Augereau, Lannes, Ney, Lefebvre, might have succeeded through brilliant actions and have become "officers of fortune, " while others, taking in hand specially difficult services, like commandant Fischer who undertook the destruction of Mandrin's band, and again, like the hero Chevert, and the veteran Lückner, might have become lieutenant-generals. Rough as these men were, they would have found, even in the lower ranks, if not full employment for their superior faculties, at least sufficient food for their strong and coarse appetites; they would have uttered just the same oaths, at just as extravagant suppers, with mistresses of just the same caliber. [16] Had their temperament, character and genius been indomitable, had they reared and pranced to escape bridle and harness and been driven like ordinary men, they need not have broken out of the traces for all that; there were plenty of openings and issues for them on either side of the highway on which others were trotting along. Many families often contained, among numerous children, some hot-headed, imaginative youth, some independent nature rebellious in advance, in short, a refractory spirit, unwilling or incapable of being disciplined; a regular life, mediocrity, even the certainty of getting ahead, were distasteful to him; he would abandon the hereditary homestead or purchased office to the docile elder brother, son-in-law or nephew, by which the domain or the post remained in the family; as for himself, tempted by illimitable prospects, he would leave France and go abroad; Voltaire says[17] that "Frenchmen were found everywhere, " in Canada, in Louisiana, as surgeons, fencing-masters, riding-masters, officers, engineers, adventurers especially, and even filibusters, trappers and backwoodsmen, the supplest, most sympathetic and boldest of colonizers and civilizers, alone capable of bringing the natives under assimilation by assimilating with them, by adopting their customs and by marrying their women, mixing bloods, and forming new and intermediary races, like Dumas de La Pailleterie, whose descendants have furnished original and superior men for the past three generations, and like the Canada half-breeds by which the aboriginal race succeeds in transforming itself and in surviving. They were the first explorers of the great lakes, the first to trace the Mississippi to its mouth, and found colonial empires with Champlain and Lasalle in North America and with Dupleix and La Bourdonnais in Hindustan. Such was the outlet for daring, uncontrollable spirits, restive temperaments under constraint and subject to the routine of an old civilization, souls astray and unclassed from their birth, in which the primitive instincts of the nomad and barbarian sprouted afresh, in which insubordination was innate, and in which energy and capacity to take the initiative remained intact. - Mirabeau, having compromised his family by scandals, was on the point of being dispatched by his father to the Dutch Indies, where deaths were common; it might happen that he would be hanged or become governor of some large district in Java or Sumatra, the venerated and adored sovereign of five hundred thousand Malays, both ends being within the compass of his merits. Had Danton been well advised, instead of borrowing the money with which to buy an advocate's place in the Council at about seventy thousand livres, which brought him only three cases in four years and obliged him to hang on to the skirts of his father-in-law, he would have gone to Pondicherry or to the palace of some indigenous rajah or king as agent, councilor or companion of his pleasures; he might have become prime-minister to Tippoo Sahib, or other potentate, lived in a palace, kept a harem and had lacs of rupees; undoubtedly, he would have filled his prisons and occasionally emptied them by a massacre, as at Paris in September, but it would have been according to local custom, and operating only on the lives of Sheikhs and Mahrattas. Bonaparte, after the fall of his protectors, the two Robespierres, finding his career arrested, wanted to enter the Sultan's service; accompanied by Junot, Muiron, Marmont and other comrades, he could have carried to Constantinople rarer commodities, much better compensated in the Orient than in the Occident, namely military honor and administrative talent; he would have dealt in these two products, as he did in Egypt, at the right time and in the right place, at the highest price, without our conscientious scruples and without our European refinements of probity and humanity. No imagination can picture what he would have become there: certainly some pasha, like Djezzar in Syria, or a khedive like Mahomet-Ali, afterwards at Cairo; he already saw himself in the light of a conqueror, like Ghengis-Khan, [18] a founder like Alexander or Baber, a prophet like Mahomet; as he himself declares, "one could work only on a grand scale in the Orient, " and there he would have worked on a grand scale; Europe, perhaps, would have gained by it, and especially France.

III. Ambition and Selection.

The Revolution provides an internal outlet and an unlimited career. - Effect of this. - Exigencies and pretensions of the modern man. - Theoretical rule of selection among rivals. - Popular suffrage raised to be lord and judge. - Consequence of its verdict. - Unworthiness of its choice.

But the Revolution arrived and the ambitions which, under the ancient Régime, found a field abroad or cooled down at home, arose on the natal soil and suddenly expanded beyond all calculation. After 1789, France resembles a hive in a state of excitement; in a few hours, in the brief interval of an August morning, each insect puts forth two huge wings, soars aloft and "all whirl together pell-mell; " many fall to the ground half cut to pieces and begin to crawl upward as before; others, with more strength or with better luck, ascend and glitter on the highways of the atmosphere. - Every great highway and every other road is open to everybody through the decrees of the Constituent- Assembly, not only for the future, but even immediately. The sudden dismissal of the entire ruling staff, executive, or consultative, political, administrative, provincial, municipal, ecclesiastical, educational, military, judicial and financial, summon to take office all who covet it and who have a good opinion of themselves. All previously existing conditions, birth, fortune, education, old family and all apprenticeships, customs and ways which retard and limit advancement, are abolished: There are no longer any guarantees or sponsors; all Frenchmen are eligible to all employments; all grades of the legal and social hierarchy are conferred by a more or less direct election, a suffrage becoming more and more popular, by a mere numerical majority. Consequently, in all branches of the government under central or local authority and patronage, there is the installation of a new staff of officials. The transposition which everywhere substitutes the old inferior to the old superior, is universal, [19] "lawyers for judges, bourgeois for statesmen, former plebeians for former nobles, soldiers for officers, officers for generals, curés for bishops, vicars for curés, monks for vicars, stock-jobbers for financiers, self-taught persons for administrators, journalists for publicists, rhetoricians for legislators, and the poor for the rich. " A sudden jump from the bottom to the top of the social ladder by a few, from the lowest to the highest rung, from the rank of sergeant to that of major-general, from the condition of a pettifogger or starving newspaper-hack to the possession of supreme authority, even to the effective exercise of omnipotence and dictatorship - such is the capital, positive, striking work of the Revolution.

At the same time, and as an after-effect, a revolution is going on in minds and the moral effect of the show is greater and more lasting than the events themselves. The minds have been stirred to their very depths; stagnant passions and slumbering pretensions are aroused. The multitude of offices presented and expected vacancies "has excited the thirst for power, stimulated self-esteem, and fired the hopes of men the most inept. An fierce, gross presumption has freed the ignorant and the foolish of any feeling of modesty or incompetence; they have deemed themselves capable of everything because the law awards public office simply to the able. Everybody had a perspective glimpse of gratified ambition; the soldier dreamt only of displacing the officer, the officer of becoming general, the clerk of supplanting the head administrator, the lawyer of yesterday of the supreme court, the curé of becoming bishop, the most frivolous littérateur of seating himself on the legislative bench. Places and positions, vacant due to the promotion of so many parvenus, provided in their turn a vast career to the lower classes. Seeing a public functionary issue out of nothingness, where is the shoeblack whose soul would not stir with ambition? " - This new sentiment must be taken into account: for, whether reasonable or not, it is going to last, maintain its energy, stimulate men with extraordinary force[20] and become one of the great incentives of will and action. Henceforth, government and administration are to become difficult matters; the forms and plans of the old social architecture are no longer applicable; like construction is not possible with materials of a different kind, whether with stable or unstable materials, with men who do not dream of quitting their condition or with men who think of nothing but that.

In effect, whatever vacancy may occur, each aspirant thinks himself fit for it, and only one of the aspirants can obtain it. Accordingly some rule of preference must be adopted outside of the opinion that each candidate entertains of himself. Accordingly, at a very early date, one was established, and there could be no better one, namely, that, among the competitors for the place, the most competent to fill it should be chosen. Unfortunately, the judge, ordinary, extraordinary and supreme, instituted to decide in this case, was the plurality of male, adult Frenchmen, counted by heads, that is to say a collective being in which the small intelligent, élite body is drowned in the great rude mass; of all juries, the most incompetent, the easiest duped and misled, the least able to comprehend the questions laid before it and the consequences of its answer; the worst informed, the most inattentive, the most blinded by preconceived sympathies or antipathies, the most willingly absent, a mere flock of enlisted sheep always robbed or cheated out of their vote, and whose verdict, forced or simulated, depended on politicians beforehand, above and below, through the clubs as well as through the revolutionary government, the latter, consequently, maneuvering in such a way as to impose itself along with their favorites on the choice of the French people. Between 1792 and 1799, the republican official staff just described is thus obtained. - It is only in the army where the daily and keen sense of a common physical and mortal danger ends in dictating the choice of the best, and raises tried merit to the highest rank; and yet it must be noted that Jacobin infatuation bore down as rigorously on the army as elsewhere and on two occasions: at the outset through the election of a superior officer conferred on subordinates, which handed rank over to the noisy disputants and intemperate intriguers of the mess-room; and again during the Reign of Terror, and even later, [21] in the persecution or dismissal of so many patriotic and deserving officers, which led Gouvion-Saint-Cyr and his comrades, through disgust, to avoid or decline accepting high rank, in the scandalous promotion of club brawlers and docile nullities, in the military dictatorship of the civil proconsuls, in the supremacy conferred on Léchelle and Rossignol, in the subordination forced on Kléber and Marceau, in the absurd plans of a demagogue with huge epaulettes like Cartaux, [22] in the grotesque orders of the day issued by a swaggering inebriate like Henriot, [23] in the disgrace of Bonaparte, and in the detention of Hoche. - In the civil order of things, it was worse. Not only was the rule of regulating promotion by merit not recognized but it was applied in an inverse sense. In the central government as in the local government, and from top to bottom of the hierarchy, from the post of minister of foreign affairs down to that of president of a petty revolutionary committee, all offices were for the unworthy. Their unfitness kept on increasing inasmuch as incessant weeding out worked against them, the functionary, degraded by his work, growing worse along with his function. - Thus the constitutional rights of merit and capacity ended in the practical privilege of incapacity and demerit. And in the allotment of grades and social advantages, distributive justice had given way to distributive injustice, while practice, contrary to theory, instituted permanently, on the one hand, the exclusion or retirement of competent, instructed, expert, well-bred, honorable and respected men and, on the other hand, brought forward illiterate, inept and rude novices, coarse and vulgar brutes, common blackguards, men used up or of tarnished reputations, rogues ready for anything, fugitives from justice, in short the adventurers and outcasts of every kind and degree. [24] The latter, owing their success to perversion or lack of conscientiousness, derived their principal title from their vigorous fists and a fixed determination to hold on to their places as they had obtained them, that is to say by main force and by the murder or exile of their rivals. - Evidently, the staff of officials which the Declaration of Human Rights had promised was not the staff on duty ten years later there was a lack of experience. In 1789, careers were open to every ambition; down to 1799, the rivalry of ambitions had simply produced a wild uproar and a brutal conquest. The great modern difficulty remained: how to discipline the competition and to find an impartial judge, an undisputed arbitrator of the competition.

IV. Napoleon, Judge-Arbitrator-Ruler.

Napoleon as judge of competition. - Security of his seat. -
Independence of his decisions. - Suppression of former influences
and end of monarchical or democratic intrigues. - Other influences
against which he is on guard. - His favorite rule. - Estimate of
candidates according to the kind and amount of their useful labor. -
His own competency. - His perspicacity. - His vigilance. - Zeal and
labor of his functionaries. - Result of competition thus viewed and of
functions thus exercised. - Talents utilized and jealousies disarmed.

Behold him, at last, this judge-arbitrator. On the 8th November, 1799,
he appears and takes his seat, and that very evening he goes to work,
makes his selections among the competitors and gives them their
commissions. He is a military chieftain and has installed himself;
consequently he is not dependent on a parliamentary majority, and
any insurrection or gathering of a mob is at once rendered abortive
by his troops before it is born. Street sovereignty is at an end;
Parisians are long to remember the 13th of Vendémaire and the way
General Bonaparte shot them down on the steps of Saint-Roch. All
his precautions against them are taken the first day and against all
agitators whatever, against all opponents disposed to dispute his
jurisdiction. His arm-chair as first Consul and afterwards his throne
as Emperor are firmly fixed; nobody but himself can undermine
them; he is seated definitively and will stay there. Profound silence
reigns in the public crowd around him; some among them dare
whisper, but his police has its eye on them. Instead of conforming to
opinion he rules it, masters it and, if need be, he manufactures it.
Alone by himself from his seat on high, in perfect independence and
security, he announces the verdicts of distributive justice.
Nevertheless he is on his guard against the temptations and
influences which have warped the decisions of his predecessors; in
his tribunal, the schemes and intrigues which formerly obtained
credit with the people, or with the king, are no longer in vogue; from
now on, the profession of courtier or of demagogue is a poor one. -
On the one hand, there is no success, as formerly under the
monarchy, through the attentions of the ante- chamber, through
elegant manners, delicate flattery, fashionable drawing-rooms, or
valets and women on an intimate footing; mistresses here enjoy no
credit and there are neither favorites nor the favored; a valet is
regarded as a useful implement; great personages are not considered
as extra-ornamental and human furniture for the palace. Not one

among them dare ask for a place for a protégé which he is incapable of filling, an advancement which would derange the lists of promotions, a pass over the heads of others; if they obtain any favors, these are insignificant or political; the master grants them as an after-thought, to rally somebody, or a party, to his side; they personally, their ornamental culture, their high-bred tone, their wit, their conversational powers, their smiles and bows - all this is lost on him, or charged to account. He has no liking for their insinuating and discreet ways; [26] he regards them as merely good domestics for parade; all he esteems in them is their ceremonial significance, that innate suppleness which permits them to be at once servile and dignified, the hereditary tact which teaches them how to present a letter, not from hand to hand, but on the rim of a hat, or on a silver plate, and these faculties he estimates at their true worth. - On the other hand, nobody succeeds, as lately under the Republic, through tribunal or club verbosity, through appeals to principles, through eloquent or declamatory tirades; "glittering generalities, " hollow abstractions and phrases made to produce an impression have no effect; and what is better, political ideology, with a solicitor or pleader, is a bad note. The positive, practical mind of the judge has taken in at a glance and penetrated to the bottom of arguments, means and valid pretensions; he submits impatiently to metaphysics and pettifoggery, to the argumentative force and mendacity of words. - This goes so far that he distrusts oratorical or literary talent; in any event when he entrusts active positions or a part in public business then he takes no note of it. According to him, "the men who write well and are eloquent have no solidity of judgment; they are illogical and very poor in discussion, "[27] they are mere artists like others, so many word-musicians, a kind of special, narrow-minded instrument, some of them good solo players, like Fontanes, and who the head of a State can use, but only in official music for grand cantatas and the decoration of his reign. Wit in itself, not alone the wit which gives birth to brilliant expressions and which was considered a prime accomplishment under the old regime, but general intelligence, has for him only a semi-value. [28] "I am more brilliant[29], you may say? Eh, what do I care for your intelligence? What I care for is the essence of the matter. There is nobody so foolish that is not good for something - there is no intelligence equal to everything. " In fact, on bestowing an office it is the function which delegates; the proper execution of the function is the prime motive in determining his choice; the candidate appointed is always the one who will best do the work assigned him. No factitious, party popularity or unpopularity, no superficial admiration or disparagement of a clique, of a salon, or of a bureau, makes him swerve from his standard of preference. [30] He values men according to the quality and quantity of their work, according to their net returns, and he estimates them directly, personally, with superior perspicacity and universal competency. He is special in all branches of civil or military activity, and even in technical detail; his memory for facts, actions, antecedence and circumstances, is prodigious; his discernment, his critical analysis, his calculating insight into the resources and shortcomings of a mind or of a soul, his faculty for gauging men, is extraordinary; through constant verifications and rectifications his internal repertory, his biographical and moral dictionary, is kept daily posted; his attention never flags; he works eighteen hours a day; his personal intervention and his hand are visible even in the appointment of subordinates. "Every man called to take part in affairs was selected by him; "[31] it is through him that they retain their place; he controls their promotion and by sponsors whom he knows. "A minister could not have dismissed a functionary without consulting the emperor, while the ministers could all change without bringing about two secondary changes throughout the empire. A minister did not appoint even a second-class clerk without presenting a list of several candidates to the emperor and, opposite to it, the name of the person recommending him. " All, even at a distance, felt that the master's eyes were on them. "I worked, " says Beugnot, [32] "from night to morning, with singular ardor; I astonished the natives of the country who did not know that the emperor exercised over his servitors, however far from him they might be, the miracle of the real presence. I thought I saw him standing over me as I worked shut up in my cabinet. " - "Under him, " writes Roederer, "there is no man of any merit who, as a reward for long and difficult labor, does not feel himself better compensated by a new task than by the most honorable leisure. " Never did positions less resemble sinecures. Never was the happiness of successful candidates or the misery of unsuccessful candidates better justified. Never the compliance, the difficulty, the risks of a required task have been compensated more fairly by the enjoyment of the allocated rewards nor moderated the bitterness of the frustrated pretensions. [33] Never were public functions assigned or fulfilled in a way to better satisfy the legitimate craving for advancement, the dominant desire of democracy and of the century, and in a way to better disarm the bad passions of democracy and of the century, consisting of an envious leveling, anti-social rancor and the inconsolable regrets of the man who has failed. Never did human competition encounter a similar judge, so constant, so expert and so justified. - He is himself conscious of the unique part he plays. His own ambition, the highest and most insatiate of all, enables him to comprehend the ambition of others; to place everywhere the man who suits the post in the post which suits the man - this is what he has done for himself and what he does for others. He knows that in this lies his power, his deep-seated popularity, his social utility.

"Nobody, " says Napoleon, [34] "is interested in overthrowing a government in

which all the deserving are employed. "

Then, again, comes his significant exclamation at the end, his summary of modern society, a solemn grandiose figure of speech found in the legendary souvenirs of a glorious antiquity, a classic reminiscence of the noble Olympian games,

"Henceforth, all careers are open to talent! "

IV. The Struggle for Office and Title.

Competition and prizes. - Multitude of offices. - How their number is increased by the extension of central patronage and of the French territory. - Situation of a Frenchman abroad. - It gives him rank. - Rapidity of promotion. - Constant elimination and multiplicity of vacancies in the army. - Preliminary elimination in the civil service. - Proscription of cultivated men and interruption of education during the Revolution. - General or special instruction rare in 1800. - Small number of competent candidates. - Easy promotion due to the lack of competitors. - Importance and attraction the prizes offered. - The Legion of Honor. - The imperial nobility. - Dotations and majorities. - Emulation.

Let us now consider the career which he thus opens to them and the prizes he offers. These prizes are in full view, ranged along each racecourse, graduated according to distances and more and more striking and magnificent. Every ambition is provided for, the highest as well as the lowest, and these are countless; for they consist of offices of every grade in the civil and military hierarchies of a great centralized State whose intervention is universal, under a government which systematically tolerates no authority or influence outside of itself and which monopolizes every species of social importance for its own functionaries. [35] - All these prizes, even the smallest and most insignificant, are awarded by it. In the first place, Napoleon has two or three times as many offices to bestow, on the soil of old France alone, as the former kings; for, even in the choice of their staff of officials, the latter were not always free; in many places they did not have, or no longer had the right of appointment. At one time, this right be longed from time immemorial to provincial or municipal corporations, laic or ecclesiastic, to a certain chapter, abbey or collegiate church, to a bishop in his diocese, to the seignior in his seignory. At another time the king, once possessing the right, had surrendered or alienated it, in whole or in part through gratuitous favor and the concession of a survivorship or for money and through the sale of an office; in brief, his hands were tied fast by hereditary or acquired privileges There are no privileges now to fetter the hands of the First Consul. The entire civil organization dates from him. The whole body of officials is thus of his own selection, and under him it is much more numerous than that of the ancient Régime; for he has extended the attributions of the State beyond all former bounds. Directly or indirectly, he appoints by hundreds of thousands the mayors and councilors of municipalities and the members of general councils, the entire staff of the administration, of the finances, of the judicature, of the clergy, of the University, of public works and of public charity. Besides all this, myriads of ministerial and notarial officials lawyers, ushers, auctioneers, and by way of surplus, or as a natural result, the members of every great private association since no collective enterprise, from the Bank of France and the press to stage lines and tontines, may be established without his permission, nor exist without his tolerance. Not counting the latter, and after deducting likewise the military or active duty and the functionaries who draw pay, the prefect from the earliest years report that, since 1789, the number of people "employed or under government pay" has more than doubled: In Doubs, in the year IX, instead of 916 there are 1820; in Meurthe in the year XIII, instead of 1828 there are 3091; in Ain, in 1806 instead of 955 there are 1771[36]. As to the army, it has tripled, and according to the First Consul's own calculations, instead of 9,000 or 10,000 officers as in 1789, there are more than 20,000. - These figures go on increasing on the old territory through the very development of the new organization, through the enormous increase of the army, through the re-establishment of religious worship, through the installation of droits réunis, through the institution of the University, owing to the increasing number of officials, curés and assistant-priests, of professors and school-teachers, and of retired and pensioned invalids. [37]

And these figures, which already swell of themselves, are to swell an additional half through the extension of the ancient territory. Instead of 86 departments with a population of 26 millions, France ends in comprising 130 departments with 42 million inhabitants - Belgium and Piedmont, then Hanover, Tuscany, Central Italy, Illyria, Holland and the Hanseatic provinces, that is to say 44 departments and 16 millions of annexed Frenchmen; [38] affording another large outlet for little and big ambitions. - Add still another, as a surplus and not less extensive outlet, outside of France: for the subject princes and the vassal kings, Eugène, Louis, Jerome, Murat, and Joseph, each with their governments, import into their realms a more or less numerous body of French officials, familiars, court dignitaries, generals, ministers, administrators, even clerks and other indispensable subalterns, if for no other purpose than to bring the natives within the military and civil compartments of the new Régime and teach them on the spot the conscription, the administration, the civil code, and systems of accounts like those of

Paris. Even in the independent or allied States, in Prussia, in Poland, in the confederation of the Rhine, there are, at intervals or permanently, Frenchmen in position and in authority to command contingent forces, to garrison fortresses, to receive supplies and secure the payment of war contributions. Even with the corporal and custom-house inspector on duty on coast at Dantzig and at Reggio, the sentiment of victorious priority equals the possession of rank; in their eyes the natives of the country are semi-barbarians or semi-savages, a backward or prejudiced lot, not even knowing how to speak their language; they feel themselves superior, as formerly the señor soldado of the sixteenth century, or the civis romanus. Never since the great Spanish monarchy and the Old Roman empire has a conquering State and propagator of a new régime afforded its subjects such gratifications of self-esteem, nor opened so vast a career to their ambitions.

For, having once adopted their career, they know better than the Spaniards under Charles V. or the Romans under Augustus, how far they can go and how fast they can get ahead. No obstacle impedes them; nobody feels himself confined his post; each considers the one he occupies as provisional, each takes it only to await a better one, anticipating another at a very early date; he dashes onward, springs aloft and occupies in advance the superior post which he means to secure on the first vacancy, and, under this Régime, the vacancies are numerous. - These vacancies, in the military service and in the grade of officers, may be estimated at nearly four thousand per annum; [39] after 1808 and 1809, but especially after the disaster of 1812 and 1813, places are no longer lacking but subjects fill them; Napoleon is obliged to accept youths for officers as beardless as his conscripts, eighteen-year-old apprentices who, after a year or six months in the military academy, might finish their apprenticeship on the battle-field, pupils taken from the philosophy or rhetoric classes, willing children (de bonne volonté): On the 13th of December 1808, he draws 50 from his lycées, who don the gold-lace of under-officers at once; in 1809, he calls out 250, to serve in the depot battalions; in 1810, he calls out 150 of the age of nineteen who "know the drill, " and who are to be sent on distant expeditions with the commission of second-lieutenant; in 1811, 400 for the school of noncommissioned officers at Fontainebleau, 20 for the Ile-de-Ré and 84 who are to be quartermasters; and, in 1812, 112 more and so on. Naturally, thanks to annually increasing gaps made by cannon and bayonet, the survivors in this body of youth mount the faster; in 1813 and 1814, there are colonels and lieutenant-colonels of the age of twenty-five.

In the civil service, if fewer are killed everybody is almost equally over tasked. Under this reign one is soon used up, physically and morally, even in pacific employments, and this also supplies vacancies. Besides, in default of deaths, wounds and violent elimination, there is another elimination, not less efficacious, operating in this direction, and for a long time, in favor of men of ability, preparing places for them and accelerating their advancement. Napoleon accepts none but competent candidates; now, in 1800, there is a dearth of acceptable candidates for places in the civil service and not, as in 1789, or at the present time, a superabundance and even too great a crowd. - In the military service especially, capacity is innate; natural endowments, courage, coolness, quick perception, physical activity, moral ascendancy, topographical imagination form its principal elements; men just able to read, write and cipher became, in three or four years, during the Revolution, admirable officers and conquering generals. - It is not the same in relation to civil capacity; this requires long and continuous study. To become a priest, magistrate, engineer, professor, prefect or school-teacher, one must have studied theology or law, mathematics or Latin, administration or the finances. If not, the functionary is not qualified to serve: he must, at the very least, know how to spell, be able to write French, examine a law-case, draw up a report, keep accounts, and if needs be, comprehend a plan, make an estimate and read off a map. Men of this stamp are rare at the beginning of the Consulate. As notables, [40] the Revolution mowed them down first. Among all their sons and so many well-bred youth who have become soldiers through patriotism, or who have left their families to prevent these from becoming suspect, one half repose on the battlefield or have left the hospital only for the cemetery; "the muscadin[41] died from the first campaign. " In any event, for them and their younger brothers, for the children beginning to learn Latin and mathematics, for all who hoped to pursue liberal professions, for the entire generation about to receive either a superior, a common, or even a primary instruction, and hence to furnish brains prepared for intellectual work, there was a lack of this for ten years. Not only were the endowments which provided for instruction confiscated but the educational staff, nearly all ecclesiastic, was one of the most proscribed among those proscribed. Whilst military requisition and the closing of the schools suppressed the pupils, massacres, banishment, imprisonment, destitution and the scaffold suppressed the teachers. Whilst the ruin of universities and colleges did away with theoretical apprenticeship, the ruin of manufactures and of trade abolished practical apprenticeship. Through the long interruption of all studies, general instruction as well as special competency became rare product in the market. - Hence it is that, in 1800, and during the three or four following years, whoever brought to market either one the other of these commodities was certain of a quick sale; [42] the new government needed them more than anybody. The moment the seller made up his mind, he was bought, and, whatever he may be, a former Jacobin or a former émigré; he is employed. If he brings both commodities and is zealous, he is promptly promoted; if, on trial, he is found of superior capacity, he will, like Mollien, Gaudin, Tronchet, Pasquier and Molé, attain to the highest posts, for he finds scarcely any competitors. These he would have had had things followed their usual course; it is the Revolution which has cleared the ground around him; without that the road would have been obstructed; competent candidates would have swarmed. Reckon, if possible, how many men of talent who were destroyed, royalists, monarchists, feuillants, Girondists and even Jacobins. They were the élite of the noblesse, of the clergy, of the bourgeoisie, of the youth and those of riper age. Thus rid of their most formidable rivals the survivors pursue their way at top speed; the guillotine has wrought for them in advance; it has effected openings in their own ranks, made by bullets in every battle in the ranks of the army, and, in the civil hierarchy as in the military hierarchy, merit, if demonstrated by services, or not arrested by death, reaches the highest summit in very few years.

The prizes offered on these summits are splendid; no attraction is lacking. The great trainer who displays them has omitted none of the seductions which excite and stimulate an ordinary mind. He has associated with the positive values of power and wealth every value incident to imagination and opinion; hence his institution of decorations and the Legion of Honor. [43]

"They call it a toy, "[44] said he, " but men are led by toys. .. Frenchmen are not changed by ten years of revolution. . .. See how the people prostrate themselves before foreign decorations: they have been surprised by them and accordingly do not fail to wear them. . .. The French cherish but one sentiment, honor: that sentiment, then, requires nourishing - they must have honors. "

A very few are satisfied with their own achievements; ordinary men are not even content with the approbation they perceive in the eyes of others: it is too intermittent, too reserved, too mute; they need fame that is brilliant and noisy; they want to hear the constant hum of admiration and respect whenever they appear or whenever their name is mentioned. Even this does not suffice; they are unwilling that their merit should rest in men's minds in the vague state of undefined greatness, but that it should be publicly estimated, have its current value, enjoy undisputed and measured rank on the scale above all other lesser merits. - The new institution affords complete satisfaction to all these exigencies of human and French nature. On the 14th of July, 1804, [45] the anniversary of the taking of the Bastille, Napoleon administers the oath to the legionaries and, after a solemn mass, distributes the insignia under the dome of the Invalides in the presence of the empress and the court; and again one month later, August 16, 1804, on the anniversary of the Emperor's birth, in the camp at Boulogne, facing the ocean and in full view of the flotilla assembled to conquer England, before one hundred thousand spectators and the entire army, to the roll of eighteen hundred drums. No ceremony, probably, was ever more exciting. The eminent surgeon, Larrey, then decorated, a man of austere virtue, spoke of it with emotion to the end of his life and never alluded that unique day but with a trembling voice. On that day, nearly all the men of superior and tried merit and talent in France[46] are proclaimed, each with the title proportionate his degree of eminence - chevaliers, officers, commanders, grand-officers, and, later on, grand-eagles; each on the same plane with his equals of a different class, ecclesiastics alongside of laymen, civilians alongside of soldiers; each honored by the company of his peers, Berthollet, Laplace and Lagrange alongside of Kellermann, Jourdan and Lefebvre, Otto and Tronchet alongside of Masséna, Augereau, Ney, Lannes, Soult and Davout; four cardinals side by side with eighteen marshals, and likewise even down to corporal, and to Egyptian veterans blinded by ophthalmia on the banks of the Nile, comprising common soldiers who, through some brilliant achievement, had won a sword or a gun of honor, as, for instance, Coignet, [47] who, dashing ahead with fixed bayonet, kills five Austrian artillerymen and takes their cannon himself alone. Six years before this he was a stable-boy on a farm and could neither read nor write; he is now mentioned among the first of those promoted, a colleague and almost a comrade of Monge, the inventor of descriptive geometry, of de Fontanes, grand-master of the university, of marshals, admirals, and the highest dignitaries, all sharing in common an inestimable treasure, the legitimate heirs of twelve years' accumulated glory by the sacrifice of so many heroic lives and all the more glorified because so few, and because, in these days, a man did not obtain the cross by twenty years of plodding in a bureau, on account of routine punctuality, but by wonderful strokes of energy and audacity, by wounds, by braving death a hundred times and looking it in the face daily.

Henceforth, legally as well as in public opinion, they form the staff of the new society, its declared, verified notables, enjoying precedences and even privileges. On passing along the street the sentinel presents arms; a company of twenty-five soldiers attends their funeral procession; in the electoral colleges of the department or arrondissement they are electors by right and without being balloted for, simply by virtue of their rank. Their sons are entitled to scholarships in La Fléche, at Saint-Cyr, and in the lycées, and their daughters at Ecouen or Saint-Denis. With the exception of a title, as formerly, they lack nothing for filling the place of the old nobility, and Napoleon re-creates this title for their benefit. The title itself of chevalier, count, duke or prince carries along with an idea of social superiority; when announced in a drawing room, when it precedes the first sentence of an address, those who are present do not remain inattentive; an immemorial prejudice inclines them to award consideration or even deference. The Revolution tried in vain to destroy this power of words and of history; Napoleon does better: he confiscates it; he arrogates to himself the monopoly of it, he steals the trade-mark from the ancient Régime; he himself creates 48,000 chevaliers, 1000t barons, 388 counts, 31 dukes and 4 princes. Furthermore, he stamps with his own mark the old nobles whom he introduces into his nobility: he coins them anew and often with an inferior title; this or that duke is lowered a notch and becomes simply a count: taken at par or at a discount the feudal coin must, in order to pass, receive the imperial stamp which gives it its recognized value in modern figures.

But, let the old-fashioned metal be what it may, whether gold, silver or copper, even crude and plebeian, the new coin is of good alloy and very handsome. Frequently, like the old currency, it displays coats of arms in high relief, a heraldic crown and the name of a locality; it no longer bears the name of territory, and it does not call to mind a primitive sovereignty. On the contrary, it bears the name of a victory or of a conquest and reminds one of recent exploits. Duc de Montebello or a Prince de la Moskowa is equivalent in the imagination contemporaries to a Duc de Montmorency or a Prince de Rohan; for, if the prince or duke of the empire is without ancestors, he is or will be an ancestor himself. To these prizes coveted by vanity Napoleon tacks on every substantial and pecuniary advantage, in ready money or landed property, not alone large salaries, adjunctive sénatoreries, occasional munificent gifts,

* a million at one time to General Lasalle, but likewise vast revenues from the extraordinary domain[49],
* 32,463,817 francs a year divided amongst 4970 persons,
* pensions from 250 to 5000 francs for all legionaries,
* villas, large estates, private incomes, distinct and superb endowments for those of the highest rank, a fortune of 100,000 livres income and more to 34 of these,
* a fortune of 450,000 livres in the public funds to Cambacérès, of 683,000 livres in the public funds to Masséna, of 728,000 livres in the public funds to Ney, of 910,000 livres in the public funds to Davout, of 1,354,000 livres in the public funds to Berthier,
* and besides all this, three "sovereign principalities, " Neufchatel to Berthier, Benevento to Talleyrand, and Ponte-Corvo to Bernadotte. -

This last attraction which, in these times of violent and premature death, is of no little account. Napoleon opens out hereditary and undefined prospects beyond the perspectives of life and of inferior interests. Each of the titles conferred by him, that of prince, duke, count, baron, and even that of chevalier, is transmissible in direct descent, according to primogeniture from father to son, and sometimes from uncle to nephew, under specified conditions which are very acceptable, and of which the first is the institution of an inalienable majority, inattackable, consisting of this or that income or real property, of bank stock or state securities, from 3000 francs for common chevaliers up to 200,000 francs for the dukes, that is to say, a certain fortune in perpetuity due to the sovereign's liberality, or to the prudence of the founder, and intended to support the dignity of the title from male to male and from link to link throughout the future chain of successive inheritors. Through this supreme reward, the subtle tempter has a hold on the men who care not alone for themselves but for their family: henceforth, the work as he does, eighteen hours a day, stand fire, and say to themselves, while sinking at their desks or facing cannon-ball that their pre-eminence survives them in their posterity:

"In any event my son will succeed me and even become greater by my death. "

All the temptations which serve to overcome the natural lethargy of human matter are simultaneously united and; with the exception of personal conscience and the desire for personal independence, all other internal springs are strained to the utmost. One unusual circumstance gives to eager ambitions a further increase of energy, impulse and enthusiasm. - All these successful or parvenu men are contemporaries: all have started alike on the same line and from the same average or low condition in life; each sees old comrades superior to himself on the upper steps; he considers himself as good they are, suffers because he is not on their level, and strives and takes risks so as to mount up to them. But, however high he mounts, he still sees higher yet others who were formerly his equals; consequently, no rank obtained by them seems to him above his deserts, and no rank that he obtains suffices for his pretensions.

"See that Masséna, " exclaimed Napoleon, [50] a few days before the battle of Wagram; "he has honors and fame enough, but he is not satisfied; he wants be a prince like Murat and Bernadotte: he will risk getting shot to-morrow simply to be a prince. " -

Above these princes who have only the rank, the title and the money, come the grand-dukes and reigning viceroys like Murat, grand-duke of Berg, and Eugene, viceroy of Italy. Above Eugene and Murat are the vassal-kings, Louis, Joseph, Jerome, then Murat himself, who, among these, is in a better place, and Bernadotte, the only sovereign that is independent; all more or less envied by the marshals, all more or less rivals of each other, the inferior aspiring to the superior throne, Murat inconsolable at being sent to Naples and not to Spain, and at having only five millions of subjects instead of thirteen millions. From top to bottom of the hierarchy and even to the loftiest places, comprising thrones, the steps rise regularly above each other in continuous file, so that each leads to the following one, with nothing to hinder the first-comer, provided he is lucky, has good legs and does not fall on the way, from reaching the top of the staircase in twenty or thirty years. "It was commonly reported in the army - he has been promoted king of Naples, of Holland, of Spain, of Sweden, as formerly was said of the same sort of man, who had been promoted sergeant in this or that company. " - Such is the total and final impression which lingers on in all imaginations; it is in this sense that the people interpret the new Régime, and Napoleon devotes himself to confirming the popular interpretation. Accordingly, the first duchy he creates is for Marshal Lefebvre "purposely, " as he says, [51] because "this marshal had been a private and everybody in Paris had known him as a sergeant in the French guards. "

- With such an example before them, and so many others like it, not less striking, there is no ambition that does not become exalted, and often to delirium.

"At this time, " says Stendhal, who seized the master-idea of the reign, "there was no apothecary's apprentice in his back shop, surrounded by his drugs and bottles, filtering and pounding away in his mortar, who did not say to himself that, if he chanced to make some great discovery, he would be made a count with fifty thousand francs a year. "

In those days there was no under-clerk who, in his labored penmanship, inscribed names on a piece of parchment, that did not imagine his own name appearing some day on a senatorial or ministerial diploma. At this time the youthful corporal who dons his first stripes of gold braid already fancies that he hears the beating of the drums, the blast of the trumpet, and the salvos of artillery which proclaim him marshal of the Empire. [52]

V. Self-esteem and a good Reputation.

The inward spring from 1789 to 1815. - Its force. - Its decline. - How it ends in breaking the machine down.

A new force, extraordinary, is just apparent in history, a spiritual force analogous to that which formerly stimulated souls in Spain in the sixteenth century, in European the time of the crusades, and in Arabia in the time of Mahomet. It stimulates the faculties to excess, increases energy tenfold, transports man beyond or above himself, creates enthusiasts and heroes, blinding or rendering men crazy, and hence the irresistible conquerors and rulers. It stamps its imprint and leaves its memorials in ineffaceable characters on men and things from Cadiz to Moscow. It overrides all natural barriers and transcends all ordinary limits. "The French soldier, " writes a Prussian officer after Jena, [53] "are small and puny. One of our Germans could whip any four of them. But, under fire, they become supernatural beings. They are swept along by an indescribable ardor of which there is not a trace among our soldiers. . .. What can you do with peasants whom nobles lead into battle, but whose danger they share without any interest in their passions or recompenses! " - Coupled with the physical needs which requires a certain amount of ease and of daily food, and which, if too strenuously opposed, produces passing jacqueries, there is a still more potent longing which, on suddenly encountering its object, seizes on it, clings to it, gorges it, and produces revolutions that last: this longing is the desire to contemplate one-self with satisfaction and complacency, forming of one's self a pleasing, flattering image, and of trying to impress and plant this image in the minds of others; in short, the ambition for a great self-esteem and of becoming greatly esteemed by others. [54] This sentiment, according to the quality of the person and according to circumstances, gives birth sometimes to the noblest virtues and the most sublime devotion, and at other times to the worst misdeeds and the most dangerous delirium: the man becomes transfigured, the sleeping god or demon which both live within him is suddenly aroused. After 1789, both appear and both together; from this date onward, says an eye-witness, [55] and, during one quarter of a century, "for most Frenchmen and in whatever class, " the object of life is displaced; each has put it outside of himself; from now on, the essential thing for everybody is "to have lived, " or "to have died for something, " for an idea. A man becomes the slave of his idea, gives himself up to it; consequently, he has experienced the intense satisfaction of considering himself a noble being, of superior essence, foremost among the first, and of seeing himself regarded in that light and proclaimed and glorified as such. - This keen, profound and intense pleasure was first enjoyed by the French on listening to the Declaration of the Rights of Man; from then, and in good faith, they felt themselves citizens, philosophers, the destroyers of prejudices and wrongs, zealots in behalf of truth, liberty and equality, and then, when the war of 1792 came, the defenders of the country, missionaries and propagators of every grand principle. [56] - Towards 1796, principles began to recede in the background; [57] in the ideal portrait which man makes of himself the liberator and benefactor of mankind gradually gives way to the admirable and admired hero capable of great achievements. This inner portrait of himself suffices for his happiness for some years to come: vanity[58] properly so called and a calculating ambition are not the incentives of action; if he obtains promotion it is without asking for it; his aspiration is simply to display himself, to be lavish of himself and live or die courageously and gaily[59] along with his comrade; to be considered, outside the service, the equal, friend and brother of his subordinates and of his chiefs. [60] Pillage, nevertheless, has begun; for, a long continuance of war depraves the conqueror; brutality, indifference to property and to life grows on him; if callous, or he wishes to become so, he eats, drinks and enjoys the passing hour; if provident and wary, he scrapes together what he can or levies contributions and hoards money. - Under the Empire, and especially towards 1808 and 1809, the ideal figure degenerates still more; from now on, it is the successful or the coming officer, with his rank and its accouterments, his gold- embroidered uniform and badges, exercising authority over so many hundreds and thousands of men and enjoying a certain notable sum of regular salaries, besides other gratifications bestowed on him by the master, along with the profits he can make out of the vanquished. [61] All that he now cares for is rapid promotion, and in any way, noble or ignoble, at first, of course, on the main road, that is in straining himself and risking his life, but likewise on a new road, in an affectation of zeal, in practicing and professing blind obedience, in abandoning all political ideas, in devoting himself no longer to France, but to the sovereign: sympathy for his comrades gives way to harsh rivalry; soldierly friendships, under the anticipation of advancement, die out. A vacancy due to death is for the benefit of survivors and they know it. "At Talavera, " says Stendhal, "two officers stood together at their battery, while a ball comes and the captain falls. 'Good, ' says the lieutenant, 'now François is dead and I shall be captain. ' 'Not yet, ' says François, who was only stunned and who gets up on his feet. These two men were neither unfriendly nor inimical, only the lieutenant wanted to rise a step higher in rank. " And this shrewd observer adds: "Such was the furious egoism then styled love of glory and which, under this title, the Emperor had communicated to the French. "

On this slope the slide is rapid and abject. Each, at first, thinks of himself; the individual makes of himself a center. The example, moreover, comes from above. Is it for France or for himself that Napoleon works? [62] So many immense enterprises, the conquest of Spain, the expedition into Russia, the installation of his brothers and relations on new thrones, the constant partition and rearrangement of Europe, all those incessant and more and more distant wars, is it for the public good and common safety that he accumulates them? What does he himself desire if not to push his fortunes still farther? - He is too much ambitious (trop ambitionnaire), say his own soldiers; [63] and yet they follow him to the last. "We have always marched along with him, " replied the old grenadiers, [64] who had traversed Poland to penetrate into Russia; "we couldn't abandon him this time and leave him alone by himself. " - But others who see him nearer by, those who stand first and next to him, do as he does; and, however high these have mounted, they want to mount still higher, or, otherwise, to keep their places, or, at least, provide for themselves and hold on to something substantial. Masséna has accumulated forty millions and Talleyrand sixty; [65] in case of a political crash the money remains. Soult tried to have himself elected king of Portugal, [66] and Bernadotte finds means to have himself elected king of Sweden. After Leipsic, Murat bargains with the allies, and, to retain his Neapolitan kingdom, he agrees to furnish a contingent against France; before the battle of Leipsic, Bernadotte is with the allies and fights with them against France. In 1814, Bernadotte and Joseph, each caring for himself, the former by intrigues and with the intriguers of the interior, also by feeling his way with the foreign sovereigns while the latter, in the absence of Napoleon, by "singular efforts" and "assiduities" beforehand with Marie Louise thinks of taking the place of the falling emperor. [67] Prince Eugene alone, or almost alone, among the great personalities of the reign, is really loyal, his loyalty remaining always intact exempt from concealed motives and above suspicion. Everywhere else, the coming crash or sinister rumors are heard or anticipated; alarm descends from high places, spreads through the army and echoes along the lines of the lowest ranks. In 1815, the soldier has full confidence in himself and in Napoleon; "but he is moody, distrustful of his other leaders. . ..

Every march incomprehensible to him makes him uneasy and he thinks himself betrayed. "[68] At Waterloo, dragoons that pass him with their swords drawn and old corporals shout to the Emperor that Soult and Vandamme, who are at this moment about going into battle, are haranguing their troops against him or deserting him; that General Dhénin, who has repulsed a charge of the enemy and whose thigh is fractured by a cannon-ball, has just passed over to the enemy. The mechanism which, for fifteen years, has worked so well, breaks down of itself through its own action; its cog-wheels have got out of gear; cracks show themselves in the metal which seemed so sound; the divinations of popular instinct verify this; the exaggerations of the popular imagination expand it and suddenly the whole machine rattles down to the ground.

All this is due to Napoleon having introduced into it the craving for success as central motor, as the universal main-spring, unscrupulous ambition, in short, a crude egoism, and in the first place his own egoism, and this incentive, strained to excess, [70] puts the machine out of order and then ruins it. After him, under his successors, the same machinery is to work in the same manner, and break down in the same way, at the expiration of a more or less extensive period. Thus far, the longest of these periods has lasted less than twenty years.

Notes:

[1] Most of the French provinces down to the time of Richelieu still possessed a special representative body which consented to and levied the taxes; most of these bodies were supported by the all-powerful minister and replaced by intendants who, from that time on, administered, or rather exhausted, the country, divided into thirty- two generalities. A few provinces, however, Brittany, Burgundy, Languedoc, a part of Provence, Flanders, Artois, and some small districts in the Pyrenees kept their old representative body and were called pays d'état, whilst other provinces were designated, by a strange abuse of language, under the name of pays d'élection. " (Translated from" Madame de Staël et son Temps, " vol. I., p. 38.) TR.

[2] Cf. on the antiquity of this sort of mind, evident from the beginning of society and of French literature, my "History of English Literature, " vol. I., and "La Fontaine et ses fables, " pp. 10 to 13.

[3] In relation to this sentiment, read La Fontaine's fable of "The Rat and the Elephant. " La Fontaine fully comprehended its social and psychological bearing. "To believe one's self an important personage is very common in France. . .. A childish vanity is peculiar to us. The Spaniards are vain, but in another way. It is specially a French weakness. "

[4] Beugnot, "Mémoires, " I., 317. "This equality which is now our dominant passion is not the noble kindly sentiment that affords delight by honoring one's self in honoring one's fellow, and in feeling at ease in all social relationships; no, it is an aversion to every kind of superiority, a fear lest a prominent position may be lost; this equality tends in no way to raise up what is kept down, but to prevent any elevation whatever. "

[5] D'Haussonville, "l'Église romaine et le Premier Empire, " I., chs X. and XI.

[6] Decree of March 17, 1808, on the organization of the Israelite cult. The members of the Israelite consistories and the rabbis must be accepted by the government the same as the ministers of the other cults; but their salary, which is fixed, must be provided by the Israelites of the conscription; the State does not pay this, the same as with curés or pastors. This is not done until under the monarchy of July, when the assimilation of the Israelite with the other Christian cults is effected.

[7] "Travels in France during the years 1814 and 1815 "(Edinburgh, 1806) I., 176. "The nobility, the great landed proprietors, the yeomanry, the lesser farmers, all of the intermediate ranks who might oppose a check to the power of a tyrannical prince, are nearly annihilated. " - Ibid., 236. "Scarcely an intermediate rank was to be found in the nation between the sovereign and the peasant. " - Ibid., II. 239. "The better class of the inhabitants of the cities, whether traders and manufacturers or the bourgeoisie of France, are those who were the most decided enemies of Bonaparte. "

[8] Napoleon, desirous of forming an opinion of him, said to Roederer, "Send me his books. " "But, " said Roederer, "he is only a translator. " "No matter, " replied Napoleon, "I will read his prefaces, "

[9] Cf. the "Dictionnaire biographique, " published at Leipsic, 1806-1808 (by Eymory) 4 vols., and the "Almanach impérial" for 1807 to 1812; many other historic names are found there, and among these the ladies of the palace. In 1810, Comte de la Rochefoucauld is ambassador to Holland and Comte de Mercy-Argenteau ambassador to Bavaria.

[10] The Revolution, " II., 323. (Ed. Laffont I. 773, note 1)

[11] "The Revolution, " vol. III., PP. 318~322. (Ed. Laff. II. pp. 237-240.)-

[12] "The Ancient Régime, " pp. 116-119, 128. (Ed. Laff. I. pp. 90-92, 100-101.)

[13] De Tilly, "Mémoires, " I., 153. "The difference between the tone and language of the court and that of the city was about as great as that between Paris and the provinces. "

[14] Hence the lack of success of the Maupeou parliament.

[15] See the collections of songs previous to the Revolution, especially military songs such as " Malgré la bataille, " - "Dans les gardes françaises, " etc. - At the time of the Restoration, the pastoral or gallant songs of Florian, Bouffiers and Berquin were still sung in bourgeois families, each person, young or old, man or woman, singing one at the dessert. This undercurrent of gayety, geniality and amiability lasted throughout the Revolution and the Empire. ("Travels through the South of France, 1807 and 1808, " p. 132, by Lieutenant- Colonel Pinkney, of the United States.) "I must once for all say that the Memoirs of Marmontel are founded in nature. " He cites a great many facts in proof of this, and testifies in all classes to a prompt and social nature, a natural benevolence or habitual civility which leads them instinctively, and not unfrequently impertinently, into acts of kindness and consideration. " - The same impression is produced on comparing the engravings, fashion-plates, light subjects and caricatures of this period with those of the present epoch. The malicious sentiment begins only with Béranger; and yet his early pieces ("Le Roi d'Yvetot, " "le Sénateur") display the light air, accent and happy, instead of venomous, malice of the old song. Nobody now sings in the lower bourgeoisie or in gatherings of clerks or students, while, along with the song, we have seen the other traits which impressed foreigners disappear, the gallantry, the jesting

humor, the determination to regard life as so many hours (une serie de quarts d'heures, each of which may be separated from the others, be ample in themselves and agreeable to him who talks and to him or her who listens.

[16] Read the novels of Pigault-Lebrun: books of the epoch the best adapted to the men of the epoch, to the military parvenus, swift, frank, lusty and narrow-minded.

[17] Candide (Récit de la Vieille).

[18] "Souvenirs", by PASQUIER (Etienne-Dennis, duc), chancelier de France, Librarie Plon, Paris 1893. "I am sure that his imagination was more taken with Ghengis-Khan than with Caesar. "

[19] "The Revolution, " II., 12, 22. (Laff. I. pp. 574, 582.) (Articles by Mailet-Dupan, "Mercure de France, " Dec. 30, 1791, and April 7, 1792.) - Napoleon, "Mémorial" (Sept. 3, 1816), thinks so too and states the essential characteristic of the Revolution. This consisted in "telling everybody who held office, every one who had a place or a fortune: 'Get out. '"

[20] Roederer, III., 534 (January 1809, on Normandy), "Children in every situation think of becoming soldiers to get the cross (legion of honor), and the cross secures the chevalier. The desire of distinction, of passing ahead of some one else, is a national sentiment. "

[21] "The Revolution, " II., 248. (Laff. I. p. 747.)

[22] Napoleon, "Mémoires "(edited by M. de Montholon, III., 11-19), on the extraordinary ignorance of Cartaux. - Ibid., 23, on Doppet's incapacity, the successor of Cartaux.

[23] "The Revolution, " III., 310. (Laff. II. pp. 178-179.)

[24] They called themselves exclusives under the Directory. - Cf. "The Revolution, II., 23, 187, 196, 245, 297-303, 340-351, 354; book III., ch, 2 and 3, and book IV. (Ed. Laff. I. pp. 582, 701, pp. 709-710, 745, 782-787, 821-823 and in Vol. II. pp. 131-167, pp. 167-215 and pp 311-357.)

[26] Madame de Rémusat, passim. - Roederer, III., 538 (January 1809). (Words of Napoleon) "I took a few of the old court into my

household. They remained two years without speaking to me and six months without seeing me . .. I don't like them - they are no good for anything - their conversation is disagreeable to me. "

[27] Napoléon, "Mémoires. "

[28] Roederer, "Mémoires. "

[29] Taine uses the French expression "esprit" which might both mean spirit, wit, mind or sense.

[30] Roederer, "Mémoires, "III., 281. "Men, under his government, who had hitherto been considered incapable are made useful; men hitherto considered distinguished found themselves mixed in with the crowd; men hitherto regarded as the pillars of the State found themselves useless . .. An ass or a knave need never be ambitious to approach Bonaparte, they will make nothing out of him. "

[31] Fiévée, "Correspondance, " III., 33. - Roederer, III., 381.

[32] Beugnot, "Mémoires, " II., 372.

[33] Lefebvre, a former sergeant in the French guards, who became marshal of the empire and Duc de Dantzig, with 150,000 francs a year, received the visit of a comrade who, instead of having mounted the ladder as he had done, had remained at the bottom of it. The marshal, a fine fellow, welcomed his comrade heartily, and showed him over his hotel. The visitor's face gradually grew somber, and bitter words escaped from his lips; he often murmured, "Ah, how lucky you are! " - At last, the marshal, impatient, said to him, "Well, I will make all this over to you on one condition. " - "What is it? " - "You must go down into the court. I will post two grenadiers at the window with their guns, and they shall fire at you. If they miss, you shall have the hotel and everything in it. " - "Ah, no, thanks! " - "My friend, more shots than these have been fired at me and nearer by! "

[34] Roederer, III., 332 (Aug. 2, 1800).

[35] Papers of Maine de Biran. (Note communicated by M. Naville.) Letter of Baron Maurice, prefect of Dordogne, to M. Maine de Biran, sub-prefect of Bergerac, transmitting to him by order of the minister of the interior a blank form to be filled up by him presenting the "Statistics of young ladies belonging to the most notable families of

the arrondissement. " The form annexed contained several columns, one for names and given names, others for the future inheritance of real and personal estate, etc. A clever or energetic prefect, provided with this list, was able and was expected to take an active part in marriages and see that all the large dowries were appropriated on the right side. - "Memoires de Madame de — — —-, " part 3rd, ch. VIII., p. 154. (These very instructive memoirs by a very sincere and judicious person are still unpublished. I am not authorized to give the name of the author.) "It was at this time that the emperor took it into his head to marry as he saw fit the young girls who had more than 50,000 livres rental. " A rich heiress of Lyons, intended for M. Jules de Polignac, is thus wedded to M. de Marbœuf. M. d'Aligre, by dint of address and celerity, evades for his daughter first M. de Caulaincourt and then M. de Faudoas, brother-in-law to Savary, and in stead weds her to M. de Pommereu. - Baron de Vitrolles, Mémoires, I. 19. (His daughter was designated by the prefect of the Basses-Alpes.) - Comte Joseph d'Estourmel, "Souvenirs de France et d'Italie, " 239. (Details of this description of the young ladies to be married and the circular from the duke de Rovigo, minister of police.) the eight column of the form was "reserved to describe the physical charms and deformities, the talents, the conduct and the religious principles of each of the young ladies. "

[36] "Statistiques des Préfets. " (Doubs, by Debry, p. 60; Meurthe, by Marquis, p. 115, Ain, by Bossi, p. 240.)

[37] "Statistique de l'Ain, " by Bossi, p. 1808. From 1140 in 1801, the number of employees and others under state pay amounts to 1771 in 1806. This increase is attributed by the prefect to causes just stated.

[38] Napoleon, "Correspondance. " (Note of April 11, 1811.) "There will always be at Hamburg, Bremen and Lubeck from 8,000 to 10,000 French, either employees or gendarmes, in the customs and depots. "

[39] One officer may be counted to every 50 men in the infantry; in the cavalry 1 officer to every 25 or 30 men, - This ratio of one officer to every fifty men indicates that, among the 1,700,000 men who perished between 1804 and 1815, there were 24,000 officers, which gives about 3,000 vacancies per annum, to which must be added the vacancies due to the wounded, disabled and and retired. It must be noted, moreover, that the death or retirement of an officer above the grade of second-lieutenant makes several vacancies, vacancies which

are more numerous the higher the rank. When a captain is killed there are three promotions and so on.

[40] "The Revolution" III., 335. (Laff. II. p. 250) - Already, in 1795, the need of competent and specialized men was so great that the government sought, even among royalists, for financial and diplomatic heads of these services; it made offers to M. Dufresne and to M. de Rayneval. -Ib. 406. - (Cf. "Mémoires" by Gaudin, Miot de Melito and Mollien.)

[41] Words of Bouquier, reporter of the law on education (session of the Convention, Frimaire 22, year II).

[42] The reader is recommended to do as I have done and consult biographies on point, also the souvenirs of his grandparents. (H. A.Taine.)

[43] Thibaudeau, "Mémoires sur la Consulat, " p. 88. (Exposition of motives by Roederer to the corps Législatif, Floréal 25, year X.) "After all, it is the creation of a new currency of quite different value from that which issues from the public treasury, a currency of unchangeable worth and of an inexhaustible mine, since it lies in French honor; a currency which can solely reward actions regarded as above any recompense. "

[44] Thibaudeau, ibid., 83. (Address by the First Consul to the council of State, Floréal 14, year X.) - Also "Mémorial": "Old and corrupt nations are not governed the same as young and virtuous ones; sacrifices have to be made to interest, to enjoyments, to vanity. This is the secret of the return to monarchical forms, to titles. crosses, ribbons, harmless baubles suited to exciting the respect of the multitude while at the same time enforcing self-respect. "

[45] "La Légion d'honneur, " by M. Mazas, passim. Details on the nomination ceremonials. "The veritable date was July 15th, as the 14th was Sunday. Augereau and about sixty officers, "bad fellows" who disliked the mass, refused to go into the chapel and remained outside in the court.

[46] Several generals, Lecourbe, Souham, etc., were excluded as being too republican or suspect and hostile. Lemercier, Ducis, Delille, and Lafayette refused. Admiral Truguet, through pique and discontent, had at first declined the grade of grand-officer, but finally

changed his mind and became at first commander and then grand-officer.

[47] "Les Cahiers du capitaine Coignet, " passim and pp. 95, 145. "When the ceremony was over, handsome women who could get at me to examine my cross, asked me if they might give me a kiss. " - At the Palais Royal the proprietor of a café says to him: "Order whatever you want, the Legion of Honor is welcome to anything. "

[49] Edmond Blanc, ibid., 276-299, 325 and 326. (List of titles of prince and duke conferred by the emperor, and of gifts of 100,000 francs rental or of above that sum.)

[50] Mathieu Dumas, "Mémoires, " III., 363.

[51] Napoleon, "Mémoires. "

[52] Compare with the Brothers Grimm's fairytale: "The Fisherman and his Wife. "

[53] Thiers, "Histoire du Consulat et de l'Empire, " V. III., p. 210.

[54] Thiers, ibid., p. 195 (October 1806). Napoleon, in one of his bulletins, had mentioned Murat's cavalry alone, omitting to mention the infantry of Lannes, which behaved as well. Lannes, disappointed, did not dare read this bulletin to his men, and spoke to the emperor about it. 'What reward can they look for if they don't find their names published by the hundred-tongued voice of Fame which is under your control! " Napoleon replies: "You and your men are children - glory enough for all! . .. One of these days your turn will come in the bulletins of the grand army. " Lannes reads this to his troops on the great square of Stettin and it is received with outbursts of enthusiasm.

[55] Madame de Rémusat. III., 129.

[56] The Revolution, " pp. 356-358. (Laff. I. pp. 825-826.) - Marmont, "Mémoires, " I. 122. (Letter to his mother, January 12, 1795.) "Behold your son zealously fulfilling his duties, deserving of his country and serving the republic. . .. We should not be worthy of liberty if we did nothing to obtain it. "

[57] Compare the "Journal du sergent Fricasse, " and "les Cahiers du capitaine Coignet. " Fricasse is a volunteer who enlists in the defence of the country; Coignet is a conscript ambitious of distinguishing himself, and he says to his masters: "I promise to come back with the fusil d'honneur or I shall be dead. "

[58] Marmont, I., 186, 282, 296. (In Italy, 1796.) "At this epoch, our ambition was quite secondary; we were solely concerned about our duties and amusements. The frankest and most cordial union existed amongst us all. . .. No sentiment of envy, no low passion found room in our breasts. (Then) what excitement, what grandeur, what hopes and what gayety! . .. Each had a presentiment of an illimitable future and yet entertained no idea of personal ambition or calculation. " - George Sand, "Histoire de ma vie. " (Correspondence of her father, Commander Dupin.) - Stendhal, "Vie de Napoléon. " "At this epoch (1796), nobody in the army had any ambition. I have known officers to refuse promotion so as not to quit their regiment or their mistress.

[59] Roederer, III., 556. (Burgos, April 9, 1809, conversation with General Lasalle written down the same evening.) " You pass through Paris? " "Yes, it's the shortest way. I shall get there at five in the morning; I shall order a pair of boots, get my wife with child and then leave for Germany. " - Roederer remarks to him that one risks one's life and fights for the sake of promotion and to profit by rising in the world. "No, not at all. One takes pleasure in it. One enjoys fighting; it is pleasure enough in itself to fight! You are in the midst of the uproar, of the action, of the smoke. And then, on acquiring reputation you have had the fun of making it. When you have got your fortune you know that your wife and children won't suffer. That is enough. As for myself, I could die to-morrow. " (The details of this conversation are admirable; no document gives a better idea of the officer of the epoch.)

[60] Compare with the idea of an ideal Chaver (kibbutznik). : Melford E. Spiro, wrote "Kibbutz. Venture in Utopia. " 60 and described how the Israeli kibbutzim as early as 1917 wanted the ideal kibbutzim to be:

> Loyal to his people
> A brother to his fellows
> A man of truth
> A helpful and dependable brother
> A lover of nature

Obedient to the orders of his leaders

Joyful and gay

Economical and generous

A man of courage

Pure in thoughts, words, and deeds (opposition to drinking, smoking and sexual relationships).

[61] Balzac has closely studied and admirably portrayed this type in a "Ménage de Garçon. " - See other similar characters in Mérimée ("Les Mécontens, " and "les Espagnols en Danemark"); in Stendhal ("le Chasseur vert"). I knew five or six of them in my youth.

[62] Words of Marshal Marmont: "So long as he declared 'Everything for France, ' I served him enthusiastically; when he said, 'France and myself' I served him zealously; when he said, 'myself and France, ' I served him with devotion. It is only when he said, 'Myself without France, ' that I left him. "

[63] An expression found by Joseph de Maistre.

[64] An expression heard by Mickiewicz in his childhood.

[65] These sums are given, the former by Mérimée and the latter by Sainte- Beuve.

[66] M. de Champagny "Souvenirs, " III., 183. Napoleon, passing his marshals in review, said to him (1811): "None of them can take my place in the command of my armies; some are without the talent, and others would carry on war for their own benefit. Didn't that burly Soult want to be king of Portugal? " "Well, sire, war need not be carried on any longer. " "Yes, but how maintain my army? And I must have an army. "

[67] "Souvenirs", by PASQUIER (Etienne-Dennis, duc), chancelier de France. in VI volumes, Librarie Plon, Paris 1893. IV., 112. (According to the papers of Savary, many of Napoleon's letters and statements by M. de Saint-Aignan.)

[68] "Mémorial, " Aug. 26, 1816.

[70] "Travels in France during the years 1814 and 1815. " (Edinburgh, 1816, 2 vols.) - The author, a very good observer, thus sums up the principle of the system: "To give active employment to all men of

talent and enterprise. " There is no other condition: "Birth, education, moral character were completely set aside. " - Hence the general defect of the system. "The French have literally no idea of any duties which they must voluntarily, without the prospect of reward, undertake for their country. It never enters their heads that a man may be responsible for the neglect of those public duties for the performance of which he receives no regular salary. "

BOOK FOURTH. Defect and Effects of the System.

CHAPTER I. Local Society.

I. Human Incentives.

The two Stimuli of human action. - The egoistic instinct and the social instinct. - Motives for not weakening the social instinct. - Influence on society of the law it prescribes. - The clauses of a statute depend on the legislator who adopts or imposes them. - Conditions of a good statute. - It favors the social instinct. - Different for different societies. - Determined by the peculiar and permanent traits of the society it governs. - Capital defect of the statute under the new régime.

So long as a man takes an interest only in himself, in his own fortune, in his own advancement, in his own success, his interests are trivial: all that is, like himself, of little importance and of short duration. Alongside of the small boat which he steers so carefully there are thousands and millions of others of like it; none of them are worth much, and his own is not worth more. However well he may have provisioned and sailed it, it will always remain what it is, slight and fragile; in vain will he hoist his flags, decorate it, and shove ahead to get the first place; in three steps he has reached its length. However well he handles and maintains it, in a few years it leaks; sooner or later it crumbles and sinks, and with it goes all his effort. Is it reasonable to work so hard for this, and is so slight an object worth so great an effort?

Fortunately, man has, for a better placement of his effort, other aims, more vast and more substantial: a family, a commune, a church, a country, all the associations of which he is or becomes a member, all the collective undertakings in behalf of science, education, and charity, of local or general utility, most of them provided with legal statutes and organized as corporations or even as a legal entity. They are as well defined and protected as he is, but more precious and more viable: for they are of service to a large number of men and last for ever. Some, even, have a secular history, and their age predicts their longevity. In the countless fleet of boats which so constantly sink, and which are so constantly replaced by others, they last like top rated liners. The men from the flotilla now and then sign on these large vessels, and the result of their labor is not, as it is at home, futile or short-lived; it will remain above the surface after he and his boat have disappeared. It has entered into the common mass of work which owes its protection to its mass; undoubtedly the portion he contributes may be worked over again later on; but its substance remains, and often also its form:

* like a precept of Jesus,
* like Archimedes' theorem

which rests a definite acquisition, intact and permanently fixed for two thousand years, immortal from the first day. - Consequently, the individual may take an interest, no longer merely in his own boat, but again in some ship, in this or that particular one, in this or that association or community, according to his preferences and his aptitudes, according to attractiveness, proximity, and convenience of access, all of which is a new motivation for his activities, opposing his egoism, which, powerful as it may be, may still be overcome, since a soul might be very generous or qualified by long and special discipline. Out of this issues every sacrifice, the surrender of one's-self to one's work or to a cause,

* the devotion of the sister of charity or of the missionary,
* the abnegation of the scientist who buries himself for twenty years in the minutia of a thankless task,
* the heroism of the explorer who risks himself on a desert or among savages,
* the courage of the soldier who stakes his life in defense of his flag.

But these cases are rare; with the mass of men, and in most of their actions, personal interest prevails against common interest, while against the egoistic instinct the social instinct is feeble. Hence the danger of weakening this. The temptation of the individual to prefer his own boat to the large ship is only too great; if it is desirable for him to go aboard and work there, he must be provided with the facilities and motives which prompt him to go aboard and do the work; at the very least, he must not be deprived of them. Now, that depends on the State, a sort of central flag-ship, the only one that is armed, and which has all subordinate vessels under its guns; for, whatever the society may be, provincial or municipal, educational or charitable, religious or laic, it is the State which sanctions or adopts its statues, good or bad, and which, by its laws, tribunals, and police, insures their execution, whether rigidly or carelessly. Therefore, on this point, it is responsible; it must adopt or impose the proper statute, the most suitable social form for strengthening the social instinct, for maintaining disinterested zeal, for the encouragement of voluntary and gratuitous labor.

This form, of course, differs according to different societies; the same charter or constitution is not proper for a church system and a commune, nor for a Protestant church and a Catholic church, nor for a town of one hundred thousand inhabitants and a village of five hundred. Each association has its own peculiar and distinctive features, which grade it according to its kind, according to its spiritual or temporal aims, according to its liberal or authoritative spirit, according to is small or large dimensions, according to the simplicity or complexity of its affairs, according to the capacity or incapacity of its members: features which within it are both efficient and permanent; whatever the legislator may do, these will remain and will regulate all activity. Thus let him, in each case, keep this in mind. But in all cases his office is the same; always, on drawing up and countersigning a statute, he intervenes in the coming conflict between the social instinct and the egoistic instinct; every provision which he enacts will contribute, nearby or at a distance, to the final ascendancy of the former or of the latter. Now, the legislator the natural ally of the former, for the former is his indispensable auxiliary. In every work or enterprise of public utility, if the legislator is the external promoter, social instinct is the internal promoter; and on the inner spring becoming weak or breaking, the impulsion from outside remains without effect. Hence it is that, if the legislator would accomplish anything, otherwise than on paper, he must, before any object or interest, concern himself with the social instinct; thus preserving and humoring it; find room for it and its usefulness; let it have full play; getting all the service it is capable of rendering, and especially not twist or release it. - In this respect, any blunder might prove disastrous; and in every statute for each society, for each of the human vessels which gather together and serve as a retinue of individual vessels, there are two capital errors. On the one hand, if the statute, in fact and practically, is or becomes too grossly unjust, if the rights and benefits which it confers are not compensated by the duties and obligations it imposes; if it multiplies excessive burdens for some and sinecures for others; if, at last, the exploited individual discovers that he is overcharged beyond his due, - thereafter he refuses on his own to add voluntarily to his load. Let others, let the favored and the privileged bear the gratuitous, extra weight. Far from stepping forward and offering his shoulders, he gets out of the way, hides himself, and lightens his load as much as he can; he even rebels when he has a chance, and violently casts off every legal burden, be it tax or due of any kind. Thus did the ancient régime perish. - On the other hand, if the statute withdraws the management of the ship from those who are concerned; if, on this vessel, which belongs to them, it permanently installs a foreign crew, which assumes and exercises all command, then the owner of the vessel, reduced to the humble condition of a mere subject and quiescent taxpayer, will no longer feel concerned. Since the intruders exercise all authority, let them have all the trouble; the working of the ship concerns them and not him; he looks on as a spectator, without any idea of lending a hand; he folds his arms, remains idle, and becomes critical. - Against the first defect, the new régime is on its guard: there must be neither the preferred nor the disgraced, neither favors nor exemptions, neither exclusions nor releases, no more misappropriation, embezzlement, or robbery, not alone in the State, but elsewhere in any direction, - in the department, in the commune, in the Church, or in educational and benevolent institutions. It excels in practicing distributive justice. The second defect is its hidden flaw: the legislator having introduced this into all local and special statutes, its effects differ according to different societies; but all these effects converge, paralyzing in the nation the best half of the soul, and, worse still, to leading the will astray and perverting the public mind, transforming generous impulses into evil outbursts, and organizing lasting inertia, ennui, discontent, discord, feebleness, and sterility. [2]

II. Local Community.

Local societies. - Their principal and distinctive character. - Their type on a small scale. - A dwelling-house in Annecy or Grenoble. - Compulsory association of its inmates. - Its object and limits. - Private in character.

Let us first consider local society whether a province, a department, or a county. For the past ten years (1789-99), the legislator has unceasingly deformed and assaulted. On his side, he refuses to open his eyes; preoccupied with theories, he will not recognize it for what it is in reality, a society of a distinct species, different from the State, with its own peculiar aims, its limits marked out, its members prescribed, its statutes drawn up, everything formed and defined beforehand. As it is local, it is founded on the greater or less proximity of its habitations. Thus, to comprehend it, we must take a case in which this proximity is greatest that of certain houses in some of our southeastern towns, as, for example, Grenoble and Annecy. Here, a house often belongs to several distinct owners, each possessing his story, or apartment on a story, one owning the cellar and another the attic, each enjoying all the rights of property over his portion, the right of renting it, selling it, bequeathing it, and mortgaging it, but all holding it in common for the maintenance of the roof and the main walls. - Evidently, their association is not a free one; willingly or not, each forms a member of it, for, willingly or not, each benefits or suffers through the good or bad state of the roof and the principal walls: therefore, all must furnish their quota of the indispensable expenses; even a majority of votes would not rid them of these; one claimant alone would suffice to hold them responsible; they have no right to impose on him the danger which they accept for themselves, nor to shirk expenses by which they profit as well as himself. Consequently, on the report of an expert, the magistrate interferes, and, willingly or not, the repairs are made; then, willingly or not, both by custom and in law, each pays his quote, calculated according to the locative value of the portion belonging to him. - But here his obligations cease. In fact as in law, the community (of property) is restricted; the associates take good care not to extend this, not to pursue other aims at the same time, not to add to their primitive and natural purpose a different and supplementary purpose, not to devote one room to a Christian chapel for the residents of the house, another room for a kindergarten for the children that live in it, and a side room to a small hospital for those who fall ill; especially, they do not admit that a tax may be imposed for these purposes and each of them be subject to a proportional increase of assessment at so many additional centimes per franc. [3] For, if the proprietor of the ground-floor is an Israelite, the proprietor of a room on the second story is a bachelor, the proprietor of the fine suite of rooms on the first story is rich, and has a doctor visit him at the house, these must pay for a service for which they get no return. - For the same reason, their association remains private; it does not form part of the public domain; they alone are interested in it; if the State let us use its tribunals and officials, it is the same as it is with ordinary private individuals. It would be unjust both against it and against itself if it would exclude or exempting it from common right, if it put it on its administrative rolls. It would deform and disrupt its work if it interfered with its independence, if added to its functions or to its obligations. It is not under its tutelage, obliged to submit its accounts to the prefect; it delegates no powers and confers no right of justice, or police; in short, it is neither its pupil nor its agent. Such is the lien which permanent proximity establishes between men; we see that it is of a singular species: neither in fact, nor in law, can the associates free themselves from it; solely because they are neighbors, they form a community for certain indivisible or jointly owned things, an involuntary and obligatory community. To make amends, and even owing to this, I mean through institution and in the natural order of things, their community is limited, and limited in two ways, restricted to its object and restricted to its members, reduced to matters of which proprietorship or enjoyment is forcibly in common, and reserved to inhabitants who, on account of situation and fixed residence, possess this enjoyment or this property. i

III. Essential Public Local Works.

Analysis of other local societies, commune, department, or province. - Common interests which necessitate local action. - Two objects in view: care of public roads and means of protection against spreading calamities. - Why collaboration is an obligation. - Neighbors involuntarily subject to a common bond on account of proximity. - Willingly or not each shares in its benefits. - What portion of the expense belongs to each. - Equal advantages for each. - The unequal and proportionate advantages for each in his private expenses, industrial or commercial gains, and in the locative value of his real estate. - Each person's quota of expense according to his equal and proportionate share in advantages.

All local societies are of this kind, each limited to a certain territory and included with others like it inside a larger area, each possessing two budgets depending on whether it is a distinct body or member of a larger corporation, each, from the commune to the department or province, instituted on a basis of interests which make them jointly but involuntarily liable. - There are two of these important interests which, as in the Annecy building, elude human arbitrariness, which demand common action and distribution of the expense, because, as in the Annecy building, they are the inevitable results of physical proximity:

First, comes care for the public highways, by land or by water, river navigation, canals, towing-paths, bridges, streets, public squares, by-roads, along with the more or less optional and gradual improvements which public roads demand or prescribe, such as their laying-out, sidewalks, paving, sweeping, lighting, drainage, sewers, rolling, ditches, leveling, embankments, and other engineering works, which establish or increase safety and convenience in circulation, with facilities for and dispatch in transportation.

Next, comes protection against the spread of calamities, such as fires, inundations, contagious diseases, epidemics, along with the more or less optional and remote precautions which this protection exacts or recommends, night watchers in Russia, dikes in Holland, levees in the valleys of the Po and the Loire, cemeteries and regulations for interment, cleanliness of the streets, ventilation of holes and corners, drainage of marshes, hydrants, and supplies of drinkable water, disinfecting of contaminated areas, and other preventive or necessary hygienic measures which remove or prevent insalubrities growing out of neighborhood or contact.

All this has to be provided for, and the enterprise, if not wholly and in its developments, at least in itself and in what is necessary, imposes itself, collectively, on all the inhabitants of the conscription, from the highest to the lowest. For, in the absence of a public road, none of them can do his daily work, travel about, or even leave his premises; while transportation ceases and trade is suspended; hence, commerce and other pursuits languish, industry is arrested, agriculture becomes impracticable or fruitless; the fields are no longer cultivated; while provisions, food, including bread, [4] everything is wanting; the dwellings becoming uninhabitable, more so than the Annecy houses when the roofs fall in and let in the rain. - On the other hand, for lack of protection against calamities, these get a free rein: the day arrives when an equinoctial tide submerges the flat coastal area, when the river overflows and devastates the countryside, when the conflagration spreads, when small-pox and the cholera reach a contagious point, and life is in danger, far more seriously imperiled than when, in the Annecy domicile, the main walls threaten to tumble down. [5]

Undoubtedly, I can personally accept this miserable condition of things, resign myself to it, and consent, as far as I am concerned, to shut myself up within my own walls, to fast there, and run the risk, more or less imminent, of being drowned, burnt, or poisoned; but I have no right to condemn another to do this, nor to refuse my contribution to a protection by which I am to profit. As to my share of the expense it is fixed beforehand, and fixed through my share in the benefit:

Whoever receives, owes, and in proportion to what he receives;

such is an equitable exchange; no society is prosperous and healthy without this; it is essential that, for each member of it, the duties should exactly compensate the advantages, and that the two sides of the scale should balance. In the local community, the care taken of public roads and the precautions taken against natural calamities are useful in two ways: one, which especially improves the condition of persons, and the other, which especially improves the condition of things. The first is equal and the same for all. The poor man, quite as much as the rich one, needs to go and come and to look after his affairs; he uses the street, pavement, sidewalks, bridges, highways, and public fountains quite as much; he equally benefits by the sweeping and lighting of the public gardens. It may be claimed that, in certain respects, he derives more benefits from all this; for he suffers sooner and more keenly when bad roads stop transportation, arrest labor, and increase the cost of food; he is more subject to contagion, to epidemics, to all physical ills; in case of a fire, the risks of a workman in his garret, at the top of steep, narrow stairs, are greater than those of the opulent proprietor on the first story, in a mansion provided with a broad range of steps. In case of inundation, the danger is more suddenly mortal for the humble villager, in his fragile tenement, than for the gentleman farmer in his massive constructions. Accordingly, under this heading, the poor man owes as much as the rich one; the rich man, at least, owes no more than the poor one; if, each year, the poor man cannot pay but one franc, the rich one, each year, should not pay more than that sum likewise. - The second advantage, on the contrary, is not equal for all, but more or less great for each, according to what he spends on the spot, according to his industrial or commercial gains, and according to his local income. Indeed, the more perfect the public highway is, the more are the necessities and conveniences of life; whatever is agreeable and useful, even distant and remote, more within reach, and at my disposition, in my very hands, I enjoy it to the utmost, the measure of my enjoyment of it being the importance of my purchases, everything I consume, in short, my home expenditure. [6] If I am, besides, industrial or in commerce, the state of the public highway affects me even more; for my transportation, more or less costly, difficult and slow, depends on that, and next, the receipt of my raw materials and goods, the sale of my manufactures, the dispatch of my merchandise, bought and sold, while the measure of this special interest, so direct and so intense, is the annual sum-total of my business, or, more strictly speaking, the probable sum of my profits. [7] If, finally, I own real estate, a house or land, its locative value increases or diminishes according to the salubrity and convenience of its site, together with its facilities for cultivating, selling, and distributing its crops, for its various outlets, for its security against floods and fires, and, after this, to improvements in public transit, and to the collective works which protect both soil and buildings against natural calamities. [8] It follows that the inhabitant who benefits from these services, owes a second contribution, greater or lesser according to the greater or lesser advantage which he derives from them.

IV. Local associations.

Local society, thus constituted, is a collective legal entity. - The sphere of its initiation and action. - Its relation to the State. - Distinction between the private and the public domain.

Such is in itself local society and, with or without the legislator's permission, we find it to be a private syndicate, analogous to many others. [10] Whether communal or departmental, it concerns, combines, and serves none but the inhabitants of one circumscription; its success or failure does not interest the nation, unless indirectly, and through a remote reaction, similar to the slight effect which, for good or ill, the health or sickness of one Frenchman produces on the mass of Frenchmen. That which directly and fully affects a local society is felt only by that society, the same as that which affects a private individual is felt only by him; it is a close corporation, and belongs to itself within its physical limits, the same as he, in his, belongs to himself; like him, then, it is an individual, less simple, but no less real, a human combination, endowed with reason and will, responsible for its acts, capable of wronging and being wronged; in brief, a legal entity. Such, in fact, it is, and, through the explicit declaration of the legislator, who constitutes it a legal entity, capable of possessing, acquiring, and contracting, and of prosecuting in the courts of law: he likewise confers on the eighty-six departments and on the thirty-six thousand communes all the legal capacities and obligations of an ordinary individual. The State, consequently, in relationship to them and to all collective persons, is what it is with respect to a private individual, neither more nor less; its title to intervene between them is not different. As justiciary, it owes them justice the same as to private persons, nothing more or less; only to render this to them, it has more to do, for they are composite and complex. By virtue even of its mandate, it is bound to enter their domiciles in the performance of its duty, to maintain probity and to prevent disorder, to protect there not alone the governed against the governors and the governors against the governed, but again the community, which is lasting, against its directors, who are temporary, to assign to each member his quota of dues or of charges, and his quote of influence or of authority, to regulate the way in which the society shall support and govern itself, to decide upon and sanction the equitable statute, to oversee and impose its execution, that is to say, in sum to maintain the right of each person and oblige each to pay what he owes. - This is difficult and delicate. But, being done, the collective personality is, as much as any individual, complete and defined, independent and distinct from the State; by the same title as that of the individual, it has its own circle of initiation and of action, its separate domain, which is its private affair. The State, on its side, has its own affairs too, which are those of the public; and thus, in the nature of things, both circles are distinct; neither of them should prey upon or encroach on the other. - Undoubtedly, local societies and the State may help each other, lend each other their agents, and thus avoid employing two for one; may reduce their official staff, diminish their expenses, and, through this interchange of secondary offices, do their work better and more economically. For example, the commune and the department may let the State collect and deposit their "additional centimes, " borrow from it for this purpose its assessors and other accountants, and thus receive their revenues with no drawback, almost gratis, on the appointed day. In the like manner, the State has very good reason for entrusting the departmental council with the re-distribution of its direct taxes among the districts, and the district council with the same re-distribution among the communes: in this way it saves trouble for itself, and there is no other more effective mode of ensuring an equitable allocation. It will similarly be preferable to have the mayor, rather than anybody else, handle petty public undertakings, which nobody else could do as readily and as surely, with less trouble, expense, and mistakes, with fewer legal document, registers of civil status, advertisements of laws and regulations, transmissions by the orders of public authorities to interested parties, and of local information to the public authorities which they need, the preparation and revision of the electoral lists and of conscripts, and co-operation in measures of general security. Similar collaboration is imposed on the captain of a merchant vessel, on the administrators of a railway, on the director of a hotel or even of a factory, and this does not prevent the company which runs the ship, the railway, the hotel, or the factory, from enjoying full ownership and the free disposition of its capital; from holding meetings, passing resolutions, electing directors, appointing its managers, and regulating its own affairs, preserving intact that precious faculty of possessing, of willing and of acting, which cannot be lost or alienated without ceasing to be a personality. To remain a personality (i. e. a legal entity), such is the main interest and right of all persons, singly or collectively, and therefore of local communities and of the State itself; it must be careful not to abdicate and be careful not to usurp. - It renounces in favor of local societies when, through optimism or weakness, it hands a part of the public domain over to them; when it gives them the responsibility for the collection of its taxes, the appointment of its judges and police- commissioners, the employment of its armed forces, when it delegates local functions to them which it should exercise itself, because it is the special and responsible director, the only one who is in a suitable position, competent, well provided, and qualified to carry them out. On the other side, it causes prejudice to the local societies, when it appropriates to itself a portion of their private domain, when it confiscates their possessions, when it disposes of their capital or income arbitrarily, when it imposes on them excessive expenses for worship, charity, education, and any other service which properly belongs to a different association; when it refuses to recognize in the mayor the representative of the commune and the government official, when it subordinates the first of these two titles to the second, when it claims the right of giving or taking away, through with the second which belongs to it, the first which does not belong to it, when in practice and in its grasp the commune and department cease to be private companies in order to become administrative compartments. - According to the opportunity and the temptation, it glides downhill, now toward the surrender of its duty, and now toward the meddlesome interference of an intruder.

V. Local versus State authority.

Case in which the State abdicates. - Anarchy during the Revolution. - Case in which the State usurps. - Regime of the year VIII. - Remains of local independence under the ancient regime. - Destroyed under the new regime. - Local society after 1800.

From and after 1789, the State, passing through intermittent fits and starts of brutal despotism, had resigned its commission. Under its almost nominal sovereignty, there were in France forty-four thousand small States enjoying nearly sovereign power, and, most frequently, sovereignty in reality. [11] Not only did the local community manage its private affairs, but again, in the circumscription, each exercised the highest public functions, disposed of the national guard, of the police force, and even of the army, appointed civil and criminal judges, police commissioners, [12] the assessors and collectors of taxes. In brief, the central State handed over, or allowed the seizure of the powers of which it ought never to deprive itself, the last of its means by which alone it acts effectively and on the spot,

* its sword, which it alone should wield,
* its scales of justice, which it alone should hold,
* its purse, for it to fill,

and we have seen with what harm to individuals, to the communes, and to itself, with what a lamentable series of disastrous results:

* universal, incurable, persistent anarchy,
* impotence of the government,
* violation of the laws,
* complete stoppage of revenue, an empty treasury,
* despotism of the strong, oppression of the weak,
* street riots,
* rural brigandage,
* extortions and waste at the town halls,
* municipal usurpations and abdications,
* ruin of the highways, and all useful public works and buildings, and
* the ruin and distress of the communes. [13]

In contrast with this, and through disgust, the new Régime takes the other side, and even goes to the other extreme; the central State, in 1800, no longer a party that has resigned, as formerly, becomes the interloper. Not only does it take back from local communities the portion of the public domain which had been imprudently conceded to them, but, again, it lays its hand on their private domain; it attaches them to it by way of appendices, while its systematic, uniform usurpation, accomplished at one blow, spread over the whole territory, again plunges them all, communes and departments alike, into a chaos in which, under the old monarchy, they would never have fallen.

Before 1789, collective legal entities (persons), provincial and communal, still existed. On the one hand, five or six great local bodies, represented by elective assemblies, full of life and spontaneously active, among others those of Languedoc and Brittany, still provided for and governed themselves. The other provinces, which the central power had reduced to administrative districts, retained, at least, their historic cohesion, their time-honored name, the lament for, or at least the souvenir of, their former autonomy, and, here and there, a few vestiges or fragments of their lost independence; and, better yet, these old, paralyzed, but not mutilated bodies, had just assumed new life, and under their renewed organism were striving to give the blood in their veins a fresh start. Twenty-one provincial assemblies, instituted over the entire territory, between 1778 and 1787, and provided with powers of considerable importance, undertook, each in its own sphere, to direct provincial interests. Communal interest, also, had its representatives in the urban or rural communes. In the towns, a deliberative assembly, composed of the leading notables and of delegates elected by all the corporations and communities in the place, formed an intermittent municipal council the same as to-day, but much more ample, which voted and passed resolutions on important occasions; there was a board of management at the head of it, "the town corps, " comprising the various municipal officials, the mayor, his lieutenant, sheriffs, prosecuting attorney, treasurer, and clerk, [14] now elected by the deliberative assembly, now the legal purchasers, heirs, and proprietors of their office, the same as a notary or advocate of to-day owns his office, protected against administrative caprices by a royal acquittance, and, for a money consideration, titular in their towns, the same as a parliamentarian in his parliament, and hence planted in, or grafted upon, the commune like a parliamentarian among his peers, and, like him, defenders of local interests against the central power. - In the village, the heads of families met together on the public square, deliberated in common over common affairs, elected the syndic, likewise the collectors of the taille, and deputies to the intendant; of their own accord, but with his approval, they taxed themselves for the support of the school, for repairs to the church or fountain, and for beginning or carrying on a suit in court. - All these remains of the ancient provincial and communal initiative, respected or tolerated by monarchical centralization, are crushed out and extinguished. The First Consul very soon falls upon these local societies and seizes them in his claws; in the eyes of the new legislator they scarcely seem to exist; there must not be any local personalities for him. The commune and department, in his eyes, are merely territorial districts, physical portions of the public domain, provincial workshops to which the central State transfers and uses its tools, in order to work effectively and on the spot. Here, as elsewhere, he takes the business entirely in his own hands; if he employs interested parties it is only as auxiliaries, at odd times, for a few days, to operate with more discernment and more economy, to listen to complaints and promises, to become better informed and the better to apportion changes; but, except this occasional and subordinate help, the members of the local society must remain passive in the local society; they are to pay and obey, and nothing more. Their community no longer belongs to them, but to the government; its chiefs are functionaries who depend on him, and not on it; it no longer issues its mandate; all its legal mandatories, all its representatives and directors, municipal or general councilors, mayors, sub-prefects or prefects, are imposed on it from above, by a foreign hand, and, willingly or not, instead of choosing them, it has to put up with them.

VI. Local Elections under the First Consul.

Lists of notables. - Sénatus-consultes of the year X. - Liberal
institution becomes a reigning instrument. - Mechanism of the
system of appointments and candidatures. - Decree of 1806 and
suppression of candidatures.

At the beginning, an effort was made to put in practice the
constitutional principle proposed by Sieyès: Power in future,
according the accepted formula, must come from above and
confidence from below. To this end, in the year IX, the assembled
citizens appointed one-tenth of their number, about 500,000
communal notables, and these, likewise assembled, appointed also
one-tenth of their number, about 50,000 departmental notables. The
government selected from this list the municipal councilors of each
commune, and, from this second list, the general councilors of each
department. - The machine, however, is clumsy, difficult to set
going, still more difficult to manage, and too unreliable in its
operation. According to the First Consul, it is an absurd system, "a
childish piece of ideology; a great nation should not be organized in
this way. "[15] At bottom, [16] "he does not want notables accepted
by the nation. In his system, he is to declare who the notables of the
nation shall be and stamp them with the seal of the State; it is not for
the nation to present them to the head of the State stamped with the
national seal. " Consequently, at the end of a year, he becomes,
through the establishment of electoral colleges, the veritable grand-
elector of all the notables; he has transformed, with his usual
address, a liberal institution into a reigning instrumentality.
Provisionally, he holds on to the list of communal notables, "because
it is the work of the people, the result of a grand movement which
must not prove useless, and because, moreover, it contains a large
number of names. . .. offering a wide margin from which to make
good selections. [18] He brings together these notables in each
canton, and invites them to designate their trusty men, the
candidates from which he will choose municipal councilors. But, as
there are very few cultivated men in the rural districts, "nearly
always it is the old seignior who would get himself designated"; [19]
it is essential that the hand of the government should not be forced,
that its faculty of choosing should not be restricted. Thus, the
presentation of municipal councilors of that category must cease,
there must no longer be any preliminary candidates. Now, according
the sénatus-consulte, this category is a large one, for it comprises all

communes of less than 5000 souls, and therefore over 35,000 municipal councils out of 36,000, whose members are appointed arbitrarily, without the citizens whom they represent taking any part in their nomination. - Four or five hundred average or large communes still remain, in which for each municipal post, the cantonal assembly designates two candidates between whom the government chooses. Let us see this assembly duly installed and at work.

Its president, as a precautionary step, is imposed upon it. He is appointed in advance by the government, and is well informed as to what the government wants. He alone controls the police of the chamber and the order of all deliberations. On opening the session, he draws a list from his pocket, which list, furnished by the government, contains the names of one hundred of the heaviest taxpayers of the canton, from whom the assembly must select its candidates. The lists lies spread out on the table, and the electors advance in turn, spell the names, and try to read it over. The president would not be very adroit and show but little zeal did he not help them in reading it, and if he did not point out by some sign, a tone of the voice, or even a direct word, what names were agreeable to the government. Now, this government, which has five hundred thousand bayonets at command, dislikes opposition: the electors know it, and look twice before expressing any counter opinion; it is very probable that most of the names suggested by the government are found on their ballots; were only one-half of them there, these would suffice; of the two candidates proposed for each place, if one is acceptable this one will be elected; after making him a candidate the government makes sure that he will become titular. The first act of the electoral comedy is played, and it is not long before no trouble whatever is taken to play it. After January, 1806, by virtue of a decree which has passed himself, Napoleon is the only one[20] who will directly fill every vacancy in the municipal councils; from now on these councils are to owe their existence wholly to him. The two qualities which constitute them, and which, according to Sieyès, are derived from two distinct sources, are now derived from only one source. Only the Emperor can confer upon them both public confidence and legal power.

The second act of the comedy begins; this act is more complicated, and comprises several scenes which end, some of them, in the appointment of the arrondissement councils, and others in that of the council- general of the department. We will take only the latter, the most important; [21] there are two, one following the other, and in different places. - The first one[22] is played in the cantonal assembly above described; the president, who has just directed the choice of municipal candidates, draws from his portfolio another list, likewise furnished to him by the prefect, and on which six hundred names of those who pay the heaviest taxes in the department are printed. It is from among these six hundred that the cantonal assembly must elect ten or twelve members who, with their fellows, chosen in the same way by the other cantonal assemblies, will form the electoral college of the department, and take their seats at the chief town of the prefecture. This time again, the president, who is the responsible leader of the cantonal flock, takes care to conduct it; his finger on the list indicates to the electors which names the government prefers; if need be, he adds a word to the sign he makes, and, probably, the voters will be as docile as before; and all the more because the composition of the electoral college only half interests them. This college, unlike the municipal council, does not touch or hold any of them on their sensitive side; it is not obliged to tighten or loosen their purse-strings; it does not vote the "additional centimes"; it does not meddle with their business; it there only for show, to simulate the absent people, to present candidates, and thus perform the second electoral scene in the same way as the first one, but at the chief town of the prefecture and by new actors. These extras are also led by a head conductor, appointed by the government, and who is responsible for their behavior, "a president who has in sole charge the police of their assembled college, " and must direct their voting. For each vacancy in the council-general of the department, they are to present two names; certainly, almost without any help, and with only a discrete hint, they will guess the suitable names. For they are smarter, more open-minded, than the backward and rural members of a cantonal assembly; they are better informed and better "posted," they have visited the prefect and know his opinion, the opinion of the government, and they vote accordingly. It is certain that one-half, at least, of the candidates whom they present on the list are good, and that suffices, since twice the required number of candidates have to be nominated. And yet, in Napoleon's eye, this is not sufficient. For the nomination of general councilors, [23] as well as that of municipal councilors, he suppresses preliminary candidature, the last remnant of popular representation or delegation. According to his theory, he is himself the sole representative and delegate of the people, invested with full powers, not alone in the State, but again in the department and commune, the prime and the universal motor of the entire machine, not merely at the center, but again at the extremities, dispenser of all public employments, not merely to suggest the candidate for these and make him titular, but again to create directly and at once, both titular and candidate.

VII. Municipal and general councillors under the Empire.

Quality of municipal and general councilors under the Consulate and the Empire. - Object of their meetings. - Limits of their power. - Their real role. - Role of the prefect and of the government.

Observe the selections which he imposes on himself beforehand; these selections are those to which he has tied down the electoral bodies. Being the substitute of these bodies, he takes, as they do, general councilors from those in the department who pay the most taxes, and municipal councilors from those most taxed in the canton. One the other hand, by virtue of the municipal law, it is from the municipal councilors that he chooses the mayor. Thus the local auxiliaries and agents he employs are all notables of the place, the leading landowners and largest manufacturers and merchants. He systematically enrolls the distributors of labor on his side, all who, through their wealth and residence, through their enterprises and expenditure on the spot, exercise local influence and authority. In order not to omit any of these, and be able to introduce into the general council this or that rich veteran of the old régime, or this or that parvenu of the new régime who is not rich, he has reserved to himself the right of adding twenty eligible members to the list, "ten of which must be taken from among citizens belonging to the Legion of Honor, or having rendered important services, and ten taken from among the thirty in the department who pay the most taxes. " In this way none of the notables escape him; he recuits them as he pleases and according to his needs, now among men of the revolution who he does not want to see discredited or isolated, [24] now among men of the old monarchy whom he wants to rally to himself by favor or by force. Such is the Baron de Vitrolles, [25] who, without asking for the place, becomes mayor of Versailles and councilor-general in Basses-Alps, and then, a little later, at his peril, inspector of the imperial sheepfolds. Such is the Count de Villèle, who, on returning to his estate of Morville, after an absence of fourteen years, suddenly, "before having determined where he would live, either in town or in the country, " finds himself mayor of Morville. To make room for him, his predecessor is removed and the latter, "who, since the commencement of the Revolution, has performed the functions of mayor, " is let down to the post of assistant. Shortly after this the government appoints M. de Villèle president of the cantonal assembly. Naturally the assembly, advised underhandedly, presents him as a candidate for the general council of Haute-Garonne, and the government places him in that office. -"All the notable land-owners of the department formed part of this council, and the Restoration still found us there seven years afterwards. General orders evidently existed, enjoining the prefects to give preference in their choice to the most important land-owners in the country. " Likewise, Napoleon everywhere selects the mayors from the rich and well-to-do class"; in the large towns he appoints only "people with carriages. "[26] Many of them in the country and several in the towns are legitimists, at least at heart, and Napoleon knows it; but, as he says; "these folks do not want the earthquake"; they are too much interested, and too personally, in the maintenance of order. [28] Moreover, to represent his government, he needs decorative people; and it is only these who can be so gratis, be themselves, look well, at their own expense, and on the spot. Besides, they are the most informed, the best able to supervise accounts, to examine article by article the budgets of the department and commune, to comprehend the necessity of a road and the utility of a canal, to offer pertinent observations, to proclaim wise decisions, to obey orders as discreet and useful collaborators. All this they will not refuse to do if they are sensible people. In every form of government, it is better to be with the governors than with the governed, and in this case, when the broom is wielded from above and applied so vigorously and with such meticulousness to everybody and everything, it is well to be as near the handle as possible.

And what is still better, they will volunteer, especially at the beginning, if they are good people. For, at least during the first years, one great object of the new government is the re-establishment of order in the local as well as in the general administration. It is well-disposed and desires to mend matters; it undertakes the suppression of robbery, theft, embezzlement, waste, premeditated or unintentional arrogation of authority, extravagance, negligence and failure.

"Since 1790, "[29] says the First Consul to the minister of the interior, "the 36,000 communes represent, in France, 36,000 orphans . ... girls abandoned or plundered during ten years by their municipal guardians, appointed by the Convention and the Directory. In changing the mayors, assistants, and councilors of the commune, scarcely more has been done than to change the mode of stealing; they have stolen the communal highway, the by-roads, the trees, and have robbed the Church; [30] they have stolen the furniture belonging to the commune and are still stealing under the spineless municipal system of year VIII. "

All these abuses are investigated and punished; [31] he thieves are obliged to restore and will steal no more. The county budget, like of the State, must now be prepared every year, [32] with the same method, precision, and clearness, receipts on one side and expenses on the other, each section divided into chapters and each chapter into articles, the state of the liabilities, each debt, the state of the assets and a tabular enumeration of distinct resources, available capital and unpaid claims, fixed income and variable income, certain revenue and possible revenue. In no case must "the calculation of presumable expenditure exceed the amount of presumable income. " In no case must "the commune demand or obtain an extra tax for its ordinary expenses. " Exact accounts and rigid economy, such are everywhere indispensable, as well as preliminary reforms, when a badly kept house has to be transformed into one which is kept in good order. The First Consul has at heart these two reforms and he adheres to them. Above all there must be no more indebtedness; now, more than one-half of the communes are in debt. "Under penalty of dismissal, the prefect is to visit the communes at least twice a year, and the sub-prefect four times a year. [33] A reward must be given to mayors who free their commune of debt in two years, and the government will appoint a special commissioner to take charge of the administration of a commune which, after a delay of five years, shall not be liberated. The fifty mayors who, each year, shall have most contributed to unencumber their commune and assure that is has resources available, shall be summoned to Paris at the expense of the State, and presented in solemn session to the three consuls. A column, raised at the expense of the government and placed at the principal entrance of the town or village, will transmit to posterity the mayor's name, and, besides, this inscription: 'To the guardian of the commune, a grateful country. ' "

Instead of these semi-poetic honors adapted to the imaginations of the year VIII, take the positive honors adapted to the imaginations of the year XII, and the following years, brevets and grades, decorations of the Legion d'Honneur, the titles of chevalier, baron, and count, [34] presents and endowments, - the rewards offered to the representatives of local society, the same as to the other functionaries, but on the same condition that they will likewise be functionaries, that is to say, tools in the hands of the government. In this respect, every precaution is taken, especially against those who, forming a collective body, may be tempted to consider themselves a deliberative assembly, such as municipal and general councils, less easily handled than single individuals and, at times, capable of not being quite so docile. None of these can hold sessions of more than fifteen days in the year; each must accept its budget of receipts and expenses, almost complete and ready made, from the prefecture. In the way of receipts, its powers consist wholly in voting certain additional and optional centimes, more or less numerous, at will, "within the limits established by law"; [35] again, even within these limits, its decision can be carried out only after an examination and approval at the prefecture. There is the same regulation in regard to expenses; the council, indeed, municipal or general, is simply consultative; the government delegates the mayor, sub-prefect, or prefect, who prescribes what must be done. As the preliminary steps are taken by him, and he has constant direction of the local council for two weeks, and finally the right of confirmation, he controls it, and then for eleven months and a half, having sole charge of the daily and consecutive execution of its acts, he reigns in the local community. Undoubtedly, having received and expended money for the community, he is accountable and will present his yearly accounts at the following session; the law says[36] that in the commune, "the municipal council shall listen to and may discuss the account of municipal receipts and expenses. " But read the text through to the end, and note the part which the law, in this case, assigns to the municipal council. It plays the part of the chorus in the antique tragedy: it attends, listens, approves, or disapproves, in the background and subordinate, approved or rebuked, the principal actors remain in charge and do as they please; they grant or dispute over its head, independently, just as it suits them. In effect, it is not to the municipal council that the mayor renders his accounts, but "to the sub-prefect, who finally passes them, " and gives him his discharge. Whatever the council may say, the approval is valid; for greater security, the prefect, if any councilor proves refractory, "may suspend from his functions" a stubborn fellow like him, and restore in the council the unanimity which has been partially disturbed. - In the department, the council- general must likewise "listen" to the accounts for the year; the law, owing to a significant omission, does not say that is may discuss them. Nevertheless, a circular of the year IX requests it to "make every observation on the use of the additional centimes" which the importance of the subject demands, to verify whether each sum debited to expenses has been used for the purpose assigned to it, and even "to reject expenses, stating the reasons for this decision, which have not been sufficiently justified. " And better still, the minister, who is a liberal, addresses a systematic series of questions to the general councils, on all important matters, [37] "agriculture, commerce, and manufactures, asylums and public charities, public roads and other works, public instruction, administration properly so called, state of the number of population, public spirit and opinions, " collecting and printing their observations and desires. After the year IX, however, this publication stops; it renders the general councils too important; it might rally the entire population of the department to them and even of all France that could read; it might hamper the prefect and diminish his ascendancy. From now on, it is the prefect alone who replies to these questions, and of which the government gives an analysis or tables of statistics; [38] then, the publication of these ceases; decidedly, printing always has its drawbacks - manuscript reports are much better; local affairs are no longer transacted outside the bureaus, and are managed with closed doors; any report that might spread outside the prefect's cabinet or that of the minister, is carefully toned down or purposely stifled, and, under the prefect's thumb, the general council becomes an automaton.

In private, dealing directly with the Emperor's representative, it appears as if one is dealing directly with the Emperor. Consider these few words - in the presence of the Emperor; they carry an immeasurable weight in the scales of contemporaries. For them, he has every attribute of Divinity, not only omnipotence and omnipresence, but again omniscience, and, if he speaks to them, what they feel far surpasses what they imagine. When he visits a town and confers with the authorities of the place on the interests of the commune or department, his interlocutors are bewildered; they find him as well informed as themselves, and more clear-sighted; it is he who explains their affairs to them. On arriving the evening before, he calls for the summaries of facts and figures, every positive and technical detail of information, reduced and classified according to the method taught by himself and prescribed to his administrators. [39] During the night he has read all this over and mastered it; in the morning, at dawn, he has taken his ride on horseback; with extraordinary promptness and accuracy, his topographical glance has discerned "the best direction for the projected canal, the best site for the construction of a factory, a harbor, or a dike. "[40] To the difficulties which confuse the best brains in the country, to much debated, seemingly insoluble, questions, he at once presents the sole practical solution; there it is, ready at hand, and the members of the local council had not seen it;

he makes them touch it with their fingers. They stand confounded and agape before the universal competence of this wonder genius. "He's more than a man" exclaimed the administrators of Dusseldorf to Beugnot. [41] "Yes, " replied Beugnot, "he's the devil! " In effect, he adds to mental ascendancy the ascendancy of force; we always see beyond the great man in him the terror-striking dominator; admiration begins or ends in fear; the soul is completely subjugated; enthusiasm and servility, under his eye, melt together into one sentiment of impassioned obedience and unreserved submission. [42] Voluntarily and involuntarily, through conviction, trembling, and fascinated, men abdicate their freedom of will to his advantage. The magical impression remains in their minds after he has departed. Even absent, even with those who have never seen him, he maintains his prestige and communicates it to all who command in his name. Before the prefect, the baron, the count, the councilor of state, the senator in embroidered uniform, gilded and garnished with decorations, every municipal or general council loses his free will and becomes incapable of saying no, only too glad if not obliged to say yes "inopportunely, " to enter upon odious and disagreeable undertakings, to simulate at one's own expense, and that of others, excessive zeal and voluntary self-sacrifice, to vote for and hurrah at patriotic subscriptions of which it must contribute the greatest portion and for supplementary conscriptions[43] which seize their sons that are except or bought out of service. [44] It allows itself to be managed; it is simply one of the many wheels of our immense machine, one which receives its impulsion elsewhere, and from above, through the interposition of the prefect. - But, except in rare cases, when the interference of the government applies it to violent and oppressive schemes, it is serviceable; fixed in position, and confining itself to turning regularly and noiselessly in its little circle, it may, in general, still render the double service demanded of it in the year IX, by a patriotic minister. According to the definition which Chaptal then gave the general councils, fixing their powers and competence, they exist for two purposes and only two: [45] they must first "insure to the governed impartiality in the assessment of taxes along with the verification of the use of the latest levies in the payment of local expenses, " and next, they must, with discretion and modesty, "obtain for the government the information which alone enables it to provide for the necessities of each department and improve the entire working of the public administration. "

VIII. Excellence of Local Government after Napoleon.

The institution remains intact under the Restoration. - Motives of the governors. - Excellence of the machine. - Abdication of the administrator.

Such is the spirit of the institution and such is its form. After 1814 and 1815, after the fall of the Empire and the Restoration, the institution subsists and remains as it was before in form and in spirit: it is always the government which appoints and directs all the representatives of local society, in the department, in the commune, and in the intermediate circumscriptions, the prefect, sub-prefects, mayors and assistants, the councilors of the department, of the arrondissement and of the commune. Whatever the ruling power may be it is repugnant to any change; never does it voluntarily restrict itself in its faculty of bestowing or withholding offices, authority, consideration, influence, or salaries, every desirable and every desired good thing; as far as it can, it retains these in its own hands to distribute them as it pleases, and in its own interest to bestow them on its partisans and to deprive its adversaries of them, to attract clients and create minions. The four thousand offices of prefect, sub-prefect, and councilors of the prefecture, department, and arrondissement, the four hundred thousand offices of mayor, assistants, and municipal councilors, and added to these, the innumerable salaried employments of auxiliary or secondary agents, from the secretary-general of the prefecture down to the secretary of the mayor, from the scribes and clerks of the prefecture and sub-prefecture down to the staff of the municipal police and of the octroi in the towns, from the city or department architect down to the lowest road-surveyor, from the watchmen and superintendents of a canal or harbor down to the field-guards and stone-breakers or the highway, directly or indirectly, the constitutional government disposes of them in the same fashion as the imperial government, with the same interference in the most trifling details and in the most trifling affair. Commune or department, such local society remains under the second Régime what it was under the first one, an extension of the central society, an appendix of the State, an adjunct of the great establishment of which the seat is at Paris. In these adjuncts, controlled from above, nothing is changed, neither the extent and limits of the circumscription, nor the source and hierarchy of powers, nor the theoretic framework, nor the practical mechanism, not even the names. [46] After the prefects of Empire come the prefects of the Restoration, the same in title and uniform, installed in the same mansion, to do the same work, with equal zeal, that is to say, with dangerous zeal, to such an extent that, on taking leave of their final audience, on setting out for their department, M. de Talleyrand, who knows men and institutions profoundly, gives them, as his last injunction, the following admirable order: "And, especially, no zeal! " - According to the recommendation of Fouché, "the Bourbons slept in the bed of Napoleon, " which was the bed of Louis XIV., but larger and more comfortable, widened by the Revolution and the Empire, adapted to the figure of its latest occupant, and enlarged by him so as to spread over the whole of France. When, after twenty-five years of exile, one returns home, it is pleasant to find such a bed in the house ready made, taking down and remaking the old one would give double trouble; moreover, in the old one, one was less at his ease; let us profit by all that rebels and the usurper have done that was good. In this particular, not alone the king, but again the most antiquated of the Bourbons are revolutionaries and Bonapartists; despotic traditionally, and monopolists through their situation, they accept with no regrets the systematic demolition effected by the Constituent Assembly, and the systematic centralization instituted by the First Consul. The Duc d'Angoulême, when, in 1815, he was paraded about the country, among the bridges, canals, and splendid roads of Languedoc, on being reminded that these fine works were formerly executed by the "Ètats" of the province, dryly replied "We prefer the departments to the provinces. "[47]

With the exception of a few antiquarian and half-rustic royalists, nobody objects; there is no thought of reconstructing the machine on another plan; in sum, nobody is dissatisfied with the way it works. It works well, most effectively; under the Restoration as under the Empire, it renders to those who are interested the service demanded of it; it goes on providing better and better for the two grand objects of local society, care for the public highways and protection against natural calamities. In 1814, its net results are already admirable and do it credit - reparation of the ruins accumulated by the Revolution, [48] the continuation and completion of former projects, new and striking enterprises, dikes against the sea and the rivers, basins, moles, and jetties in the harbors, quays, and bridges, locks and canals, public edifices, 27,200 kilometers of national roads and 18,600 kilometers of departmental roads, [49] without counting the district roads just laid out; all this done regularly, exactly, and economically, Charles Nicolas, "Les Budgets de la France depuis le commencement du XIXe siècle. " In 1816, the four direct contributions returned, in principal, 249 millions, and, in additional centimes, 89 millions only. For a long time the additional centimes applied to the local service and voted by the department or by the commune are not many and do not exceed 5 %. of the principal. by competent functionaries, employed and superintended, who at first through fear are compelled to be prudent, and then through habit and honor have become honest accountants; there is no waste, no underhand stealing, no arbitrary charges; no sum is turned aside between receipts and expenses to disappear and be lost on the road, or flow out of its channel in another direction. The sensitive taxpayer, large or small, no longer smarts under the painful goad which formerly pricked him and made him jump. Local taxation, annexed to the general tax, is found to be reformed, lightened, and duly proportioned. Like the principal, the "additional centimes" are an equitable charge, graduated according to the sum of net revenue; like the principal, they are assessed according to the assumed sum of this net revenue by the councils of the arondissements among the communes, and by the communal assessors among the inhabitants. They are collected by the same collector, with the same formalities, and every taxpayer who thinks himself taxed too heavily finds a court of appeal in the council of the prefecture, before which he can make his claim and obtain the release or reduction of his quota. - Thus no crying iniquity exists, nor keen suffering; on the other hand, there are the infinite conveniences and daily enjoyment of possessions, the privation of which, to the modern man, is equal to the lack of fresh, pure air, physical security and protection against contagion, facilities for circulation and transport, pavements, light, the salubrity of healthy streets purged of their filth, and the presence and vigilance of the municipal and rural police. All these benefits, the objects of local society, are due to the machine which works with little cost, without breaking down or stopping for any long time, as lately under the Republic, and without any extortion and clashing, as in the times of the ancient Régime. It works by itself, almost without the help of the parties interested, and which, in their eyes, is not its least merit; with it, there is no bother, no responsibility, no elections to attend to, no discussions to maintain, no resolutions to pass. There is only one bill to be settled, not even a specified bill, but a surplus of centimes added to each franc, and included with the principal in the annual quota. Just like an owner who, by his correct, exact, and somewhat slow although punctual and capable supervisors, are relieved of the care of his property. He may dismiss the head steward of his domain in a fit of ill-humor, but, if he changes his stewards, he does not change the system; he is too accustomed to it, and his indolence demands it; he is not tempted to take care and trouble on himself, nor is he qualified to become his own intendant.

And what is worse, in the present case the master has forgotten that he is the owner of his domain, he hardly remembers that he is a personality. Whether large or small, department or commune, local society has no longer the consciousness of being a natural body, composed of involuntarily united members with common interests; this sentiment, already weakened and drooping at the end of the ancient régime, lost under the multiplied attacks of the Revolution and under the prolonged compression of the Empire. During twenty-five years it has suffered too much; it has been too arbitrarily manufactured or mutilated, too frequently recast, and made and unmade. - In the commune, everything has been upset over and over again, the territorial circumscription, the internal and external system, all collective property. To the 44,000 municipalities improvised by the Constituent Assembly, there succeeded under the Directory 6000 or 7000 cantonal municipalities, a sort of local syndicate, represented in each commune by a subaltern agent, and then, under the Consulate, 36,000 distinct and permanent communes. Sovereign at the start, through the improvidence and abdication of the Constituent Assembly, the communes become, in the hands of the Convention, so many timorous subjects surrendered to the brutality of perambulating pashas and resident agas, imposed upon them by Jacobin tyranny; then under the Empire, a docile herd governed in a correct way from above, but possessing no authority of their own, and therefore indifferent to their own affairs and utterly wanting in public spirit. Other more serious blows affect of the them still more deeply and acutely. Through a decree of the Legislative Assembly, in every commune where a third of the inhabitants demand a partition of the communal property, the commune is stripped, and its time-honored patrimony is set off in equal lots, in portions according to families or per head, and converted into small private holdings. (Page 319/584)Through a decree of the Convention, the whole of the communal fortune, its debts and assets, are swallowed up by the public fortune and engulfed along with that in the sale of real property, in the discredit of the assignats, and in the final bankruptcy. After this prolonged process, communal property, even when disgorged and restored by the exchequer, is not what it was before; once out of the monster's stomach, the remains of it, dismembered, spoilt, half-digested, are no longer held sacred and inviolable; a settlement of accounts intervenes; "there are a good many communes, " says Napoleon[50] "whose debts have been paid and whose property was not sold; there are many others whose property has been sold and whose debts are not paid . . .. The result is that many pieces of property in certain communes are not considered reputable. " Consequently, he first deprives these of one-tenth of their income from land, and then one-quarter of the produce of their extra cuttings of timber, [51] and finally, their capital. the whole of their real property, [52] estimated at 370 millions; in exchange, he gives them 138 millions in the rentes; the loss to them as well as the gain to him, is thus 232 millions, while the sale of communal properties at auction, begun in 1813, continues under the Restoration in 1814, 1815, and even in 1816. A human community treated in this way for one quarter of a century, ceases to be a personality, and becomes a mere material object; as far as this is concerned, its members have come to believe, that it is and must be so and cannot be otherwise.

Above the commune, nearly dead, is the department, completely dead; here local patriotism is stamped out at the beginning by the destruction of the provinces. Among so many political crimes and other outrages committed by the Revolution against France, this is one of the worst. The Constituent Assembly has dismantled long-established associations, the accumulated work of ten centuries, historic and powerful names, each of which aroused enthusiasm in thousands of breasts and cemented together thousands of wills, centers of spontaneous co-operation, firesides warm with generous feeling, zeal, and devotion, a practical school of high political education, an admirable theater for available talent, noble careers open to legitimate ambition, in short, the small patrimony whose instinctive cult forms the first step out of egoism and a march onward toward thoughtful devotion to the large patrimony. Cut apart by geometrical shears, and designated by an entirely new geographical term, small sections of the province became so many factitious agglomerations of juxtaposed inhabitants, human assemblages without any soul; and, for twenty years, the legislator fails to communicate to them that semblance of spirit, the judicial quality of which it disposes; it is only after 1811 that the departments arrive at civil proprietorship and personality: this dignity, besides, the State confers only to disburden itself and to burden them, to impose expenses on them which hardly concern them but which do concern it, to compel them in its place to support the costly maintenance of its prisons, police quarters, courts of justice, and prefectorial mansions; even at this late date, they are not yet, in the eyes of jurisconsults or before the Council of State, incontestable proprietors and complete personalities; [53] they are not to be fully qualified in this sense until the law of 1838.

Local society, accordingly, proves abortive over the whole 27,000 square leagues of territory; it is simply a legal figment, an artificial grouping together of neighbors who do not find themselves bound and incorporated together by neighborhood; in order that their society might become viable and stimulating would require both commune and department to have in mind and at heart the following idea, which they no longer entertained:

"We are all aboard the same ship, it is ours and we are its crew. We are here to manage it ourselves, with our own hands, each according to his rank and position, each taking his part, little or big, in doing his own work. "

Notes:

[2] That is what has happened during communism where men worked as little as possible since the principle of equality made most effort rest without reward.

[3] The so-called "Centimes additionels" was an increase in certain taxes to be paid to the communes and departments.

[4] Rocquain, "L'État de la France au 18 Brumaire" (report by Fourcroy)": A sack of wheat worth 18 francs at Nantes costs an equal sum for its cartage to Brest. I have seen carters plodding along, seven or eight in a line, each with six or eight strong horses dragging their vehicles and alternately helping each other, their horses hauling their carts out of ruts into which they had got stuck . .. In many places, I was grieved to see carts and wagons leaving the high-road and traversing, in spaces from 100 to 200 yards wide, the plowed ground, when each made his own road . . .. The carters sometimes make only three or four leagues from morning to night. " - Hence, a dearth of provisions at Brest. "We are assured that the people have long been on half-rations, or even quarter rations. " - And yet, " There is now in the river, at Nantes, from four to five hundred boats loaded with grain; they have been there for months, and their number increases daily. Their cargoes are deteriorating and becoming damaged. "

[5] Ibid., preface and summary,(on the dikes and works of protection against inundations at Dol in Brittany, at Fréjus, in Camargue, in Lower Rhine, in Nord, in Pas-de-Calais, at Ostende and Blankenberg, at Rochefort, at La Rochelle, etc.). At Blankenberg, a gale sufficed to carry away the dike and let in the sea. "The dread of some disaster which would ruin a large portion of the departments of the Lys and of the Escaut kept the inhabitants constantly in a state of frightful anxiety. "

[6] Hence the additional centimes to the tax on doors and windows, the number of which indicates approximately the value of the rent. Hence also the additional centimes to the personal tax, which is proportionate to the rent, this being considered as the most exact indication of domestic expenditure.

[7] Hence the communal "additional centimes" to the tax on business licenses.

[8] Hence the " additional centimes" to the land tax.

[10] Syndicates of this kind are instituted by the law of June 25, 1865, "between proprietors interested in the execution and maintenance of public works: 1st, Protection against the sea, inundations, torrents, and navigable or non-navigable rivers; 2d, Works in deepening, repairing, and regulating canals and non-navigable water- courses, and ditches for draining and irrigation; 3d, Works for the drainage of marshes; 4th, Locks and other provisions necessary in working salt marshes; 5th, Drainage of wet and unhealthy ground. " - "Proprietors interested in the execution of the above-mentioned works may unite in an authorized syndical company, either on the demand of one or of several among them, or on the initiative of the prefect. " - (Instead of authorized, we must read forced, and we then find that the association may be imposed on all interested parties, on the demand of one alone, or even without any one's demand.) - Like the Annecy building, these syndicates enable one to reach the fundamental element of local society. Cf. the law of September 26, 1807 (on the drainage of marshes), and the law of April 21, 1810 (on mines and the two owners of the mine, one of the surface and the other of the subsoil, both likewise partners, and no less forcibly so through physical solidarity.)

[11] See "The Revolution, " vol. I., passim. (Ed. Laff. I).

[12] Two kinds of police must be distinguished one from the other. The first is general and belongs to the State: its business is to repress and prevent, outside and inside, all aggression against private and public property. The second is municipal, and belongs to the local society: its business is to see to the proper use of the public roads, and other matters, which, like water, air, and light, are enjoyed in common; it undertakes, also, to forestall the risks and dangers of imprudence, negligence, and filth, which any aggregation of men never fails to engender. The provinces of these two police forces join and penetrate each other at many points; hence, each of the two is the auxiliary, and, if need be, the substitute of the other.

[13] Rocquain, "l'État de la France au 18 Brumaire, " passim.

[14] Raynouard, "Histoire du droit municipal, "II., 356, and Dareste, "Histoire de l'administration en France, " I., 209, 222. (Creation of the posts of municipal mayor and assessors by the king, in 1692, for a money consideration.) "These offices were obtained by individuals, along with hereditary title, now attached to communities, that is to say, bought in by these, " which put in their possession the right of election. - The king frequently took back these offices which he had sold, and sold them over again. In 1771, especially, he takes them back, and, it seems, to keep them forever; but he always reserves the right of alienating them for money. For example (Augustin Thierry, "Documens sur l'histoire du tiers État, " III., 319), an act of the royal council, dated October 1, 1772, accepts 70,000 francs from the town of Amiens for the repurchase of the installment of its magistracies, and defining these magistracies, as well as the mode of election according to which the future incumbents shall be appointed. Provence frequently bought back its municipal liberties in the same fashion, and, for a hundred years, expended for this purpose 12,500,000 livres. In 1772, the king once more established the venality of the municipal offices: but, on the Parliament of Aix remonstrating, in 1774, he returned their old rights and franchises to the communities. - Cf. Guyot, "Répertoire de jurisprudence" (1784), articles, Echevins, Capitouls, Conseillers.

[15] Thibaudeau, p. 72 (words of the First Consul at a meeting of the Council of State, Pluvi'se 14, year X).

[16] Roederer, III., 439 (Note of Pluvi'se 28, year VIII), ib., 443 "The pretended organic sénatus-consulte of Aug. 4, 1802, put an end to

notability by instituting electoral colleges. ... The First Consul was really recognized as the grand-elector of the notability, "

[18] Thibaudeau, 72, 289 (words of the First Consul at a meeting of the Council of State, Thermidor 16, year X).

[19] Ibid., Sénatus-consulte of Thermidor 16, year X, and of Fructidor 19, year X.

[20] Decree of January 17, 1806, article 40.

[21] Aucoc, " Conférence sur l'administration et le droit administratif, " §§ 101, 162, 165. In our legislative system the council of the arrondissement has not become a civil personality, while it has scarcely any other object than to apportion direct taxes among the communes of the arrondissement

[22] Sénatus-consulte of Thermidor 16, year X.

[23] Decree of May 13, 1806, title III., article 32.

[24] Thibaudeau, ibid., 294 (Speech of the First Consul to the Council of State, Thermidor 16, year X). "What has become of the men of the Revolution? Once out of place, they have been entirely neglected: they have nothing left; they have no support, no natural refuge. Look at Barras, Reubell, etc. " The electoral colleges are to furnish them with the asylum they lack. "Now is the time to elect the largest number of men of the Revolution; the longer we wait, the fewer there will be. . .. With the exception of some of them, who have appeared on a grand stage, . .. who have signed some treaty of peace . .. the rest are all isolated and in obscurity. That is an important gap which must be filled up . . .. It is for this reason that I have instituted the Legion of Honor. "

[25] Baron de Vitrolles, "Memoires, " preface, XXI. Comte de Villèle, "Memoires et Correspondance, " I., 189 (August, 1807).

[26] Faber, "Notice sur l'intérieur de la France" (1807).

[28] The following document shows the sense and aim of the change, which goes on after the year VIII, also the contrast between both administrative staffs. (Archives Nationales, F 7, 3219; letter of M. Alquier to the First Consul, Pluviose 18, year VIII.) M. Alquier, on

his way to Madrid, stops at Toulouse and sends a report to the authorities of Haute-Garonne: "I was desirous of seeing the central administration. I found there the ideas and language of 1793. Two personages, Citizens Barreau and Desbarreaux, play an active part then. Up to 1792, the first was a shoemaker, and owed his political fortune simply to his audacity and revolutionary frenzy. The second, Desbarreaux, was a comedian of Toulouse, his principal role being that of valets. In the month of Prairial, year III, he was compelled to go down on his knees on the stage and ask pardon for having made incendiary speeches at some previous period in the decadal temple. The public, not deeming his apology sufficient, drove him out of the theater. He now combines with his function of departmental administrator the post of cashier for the actors, which thus brings him in 1200 francs . .. The municipal councilors are not charged with lack of probity: but they are derived from too law a class and have too little regard for themselves to obtain consideration from the public. .. The commune of Toulouse is very impatient at being governed by weak, ignorant men, formerly mixed in with the crowd, and whom, probably, it is urgent to send back to it. . .. It is remarkable that, in a city of such importance, which provides so large a number of worthy citizens of our sort of capacity and education, only men are selected for public duties who, with respect to instruction, attainments, and breeding, offer no guarantee whatever to the government and no inducement to win public consideration. "

[29] "Correspondance de Napoléon, " No. 4474, note dictated to Lucien, minister of the interior, year VIII.

[30] Cf. "Procés-verbaux des conseil généraux" of the year VIII, and especially of the year IX. "Many of the cross roads have entirely disappeared at the hands of the neighboring owners of the land. The paved roads are so much booty. " (for example, Vosges, p. 429, year IX.) "The roads of the department are in such a bad state that the landowners alongside carry off the stones to build their houses and wall in their inheritance. They encroach on the roads daily; the ditches are cultivated by them the same as their own property. "

[31] Laws of February 29- March 9, 1804 And February 28 - March 10, 1805.

[32] Laws of July 23, 1802, and of February 27, 1811.

[33] "Correspondance de Napoléon, " No. 4474 (note dictated to Lucien).

[34] Decree of March 1, 1808: "Are counts by right, all ministers, senators, councilors of state for life, presidents of the corps Legislatif, and archbishops. Are barons by right, all bishops. May become barons, after ten years of service, all first presidents and attorney generals, the mayors of the thirty-six principal towns. (In 1811, instead of 36, there are 52 principal towns.) May also become barons, the presidents and members of the department electoral colleges who have attended three sessions of these colleges. "

[35] Decree of Thermidor 4, year X.

[36] Law of Pluvi'se 28, year VIII.

[37] "Procés-verbaux des conseils généraux" of the years VIII and X. (The second series drawn up after those propounded by the minister Chaptal, is much more complete and furnishes an historical document of the highest importance.)

[38] " Statistiques des préfets (from the years IX to XIII, about 40 volumes).

[39] Beugnot, "Mémoires, " I., 363.

[40] Faber, ibid., 127. - Cf. Charlotte de Sohr, "Napoleon en 1811" (details and anecdotes on Napoleon's journey through Belgium and Holland).

[41] Beugnot, I., 380, 384. "He struck the good Germans dumb with admiration, unable to comprehend how it was that their interests had become so familiar to him and with what superiority he treated them. "

[42] Beugnot, ibid., I., 395. Everywhere, on the Emperor's passage (1811), the impression experienced was a kind of shock as at the sight of a wonderful apparition.

[43] Thiers, " Histoire du Consulat et l'Empire, " XVI., 246 (January, 1813). "A word to the prefect, who transmitted this to one of the municipal councilors of his town, was enough to insure an offer from some large town and have this imitated throughout the empire.

Napoleon had an idea that he could get towns and cantons to offer him troops of horse, armed and equipped. " - In fact, this offer was voted with shouts by the Paris municipal council and, through contagion, in the provinces. As to voting this freely it suffices to remark how the annexed towns voted, which, six months later, are to rebel. Their offers are not the least. For instance, Amsterdam offers 100 horsemen, Hamburg 100, Rotterdam 50, the Hague 40, Leyden 24, Utrecht 20, Dusseldorf 12. - The horsemen furnished are men enlisted for money; 16,000 are obtained, and the sum voted suffices to purchase additionally 22,000 horses and 22,000 equipments. - To obtain this money, the prefect himself apportions the requisite sum among those in his department who pay the most taxes, at the rate of from 600 to 1000 francs per head. On these arbitrary requisitions and a great many others, either in money or in produce, and on the sentiments of the farmers and landed proprietors in the South, especially after 1813, cf. the " Mémoires de M. Villèle, " vol. I., passim.

[44] Comte Joseph d'Estourmel, "Souvenirs de France et d'Italie, 240. The general council of Rouen was the first to suggest the vote for guards of honor. Assembled spontaneously (meetings are always spontaneous), its members pass an enthusiastic address. "The example was found to be excellent; the address was published in the Moniteur, and sent to all the prefects . . .. The councils were obliged to meet, which generously disposed of other people's children, and very worthy persons, myself first of all, thought that they might join in this shameful purpose, to such an extent had imperial fanaticism fascinated them and perverted consciences! "

[45] Archives nationales (state of accounts of the prefects and reports of the general police commissioners, F7, 5014 and following records. - Reports of senators on their senatoreries, AF, IV., 1051, and following records). - These papers disclose at different dates the state of minds and of things in the provinces. Of all these reports, that of Roederer on the senatorerie of Caen is the most instructive, and gives the most details on the three departments composing it. (Printed in his "Œuvres complètes, " vol. III.)

[46] The reader will find in the Archives nationales, the fullest and most precise information concerning local administration and the sentiments of the different classes of society, in the correspondence of the prefects of the first Restoration, of the hundred days, and of the second Restoration from 1814 to 1823 (Cf. especially those of

Haute-Garonne, the Rhine, C'te d'Or, Ain, Loiret, Indre-et-Loire, Indre, Loire-Inférieure and Aisne.) The letters of several prefects, M. de Chabroe, M. de Tocqueville, M. de Remusat, M. de Barante, are often worth publishing; occasionally, the minister of the interior has noted with a pencil in the margin, " To be shown to the King. "

[47] M. de Villèle, ibid., I., 248.

[48] Rocquam, "l'État de la France au 18 Brumaire, " reports of the councilors of state sent on missions, p. 40.

[49] De Feville, "La France economique, " 248 and 249.

[50] Pelet de la Lozère, "Opinions de Napoléon au conseil d'Etat, " (Session of March 15, 1806). - Decree of March 16, 1806, and of September 15, 1807.

[51] Ibid., 276. "To those who objected that a tax could only be made according to law, Napoleon replied that it was not a tax, since there were no other taxes than those which the law established, and that this one (the extra assessment of a quarter of the produce of timber) was established by decree. It is only a master, and an absolute master, who could reason in this way. "

[52] Law of March 20, 1813. (Woods, meadows, and pasture-grounds used by the population in common are excepted, also buildings devoted to public use, promenades, and public gardens.) - The law takes rural possessions, houses and factories, rented and producing an income. Thiers, XVI., 279. The five percents at this time were worth 75 francs, and 138 millions of these gave a revenue of 9 millions, about the annual income derived by the communes from their confiscated real estate.

[53] Aucoc, ibid., §§ 55 and 135.

CHAPTER II. Local society since 1830.

I. Introduction of Universal suffrage.

Local society since 1830. - Introduction of a new internal motor. - Subordinate to the external motor. - Advantageous under the system of universal suffrage.

Neither lips nor heart are capable of pronouncing the above invigorating and conclusive phrase after a silence of 30 years. That local society ought to be a private association, does not interest those who are concerned, while the legislator does not permit it. Indeed, after the year VIII (1799), the State (Napoleon) introduces into the machine the new motivation described above. After the revolution of 1830, [1] the municipal and general councilors become elective and are appointed by a limited suffrage; after the revolution of 1848, they are elected by universal suffrage. [2] After the revolution of 1870, [3] each municipal council elects its own mayor, while the council-general, whose powers are enlarged, leaves in its place, during its vacations, a standing committee who arrange with, and govern along with, the prefect. Here, in local society, is a superadded internal motor, working from below, whilst the first one is external and works from above; from now on, both are to work together and in accord. - But, in reality, the second (the council-general) remains subordinate; moreover, it does not suit the machine[4] and the machine does not suit it; it is only a superfluity, an inconvenient and cumbersome intruder, nearly always useless, and often mischievous. Its influence is feeble and of little effect; too many brakes are attached to it; its force diminishes through the complexity of its numerous wheels; it fails in giving action; it cannot but little more than impede or moderate other impulses, those of the external motor, sometimes as it should, and sometimes the contrary. Most frequently, even nowadays (1889), it is of no efficiency whatever. Three-quarters of the municipal councils, for three-fourths of their business, hold sessions only to give signatures. Their pretended deliberations are simply a parade formality; the incentive and direction continue to come from without, and from above; under the third Republic, as under the Restoration and the first Empire, it is always the central State which governs the local society; amid all the wrangling and disputes, in spite of passing conflicts it is, and remains, the initiator, mover, leader, controller, accountant, and executor of every undertaking, the preponderating power in the department as well as in the commune, and with what deplorable results we all know. - There is still another and more serious result. Nowadays, its interference is an advantage, for should it renounce its preponderance this would pass over to the other power which, since this has become vested in a numerical majority, is mere blind and brutal force; abandoned to itself and without any counter-weight, its ascendancy would be disastrous, we would see reappearing along with the blunders of 1789, the outrages, usurpations, and distress of 1790, 1791 and 1792. [5] - In any event, there is this advantage in despotic centralization, that it still preserves us from democratic autonomy. In the present state of institutions and minds, the former system, objectionable as it may be, is our last retreat against the greater evil of the latter.

II. Universal suffrage.

Application of universal suffrage to local society. - Two assessments for the expenses of local society. - The fixed amount of one should in equity be equal to the average sum of the other. - Practically, the sum of one is kept too low. - How the new régime provides for local expenditure. - The "additional centimes. " - How the small taxpayer is relieved in town and country. - His quota in local expenditure reduced to the minimum. - His quota of local benefits remains intact. - Hence the large or average taxpayer bears, beside his own burden, that of the relieved small taxpayer. - Number of those relieved. - The extra burden of the large and average taxpayer is alms-giving. - The relief of the small taxpayer is a levy of alms.

In effect, direct universal suffrage, counted by heads, is in local society a discordant element, a monstrous system, to which it is adverse. Constituted as this is, not by human judgment, but by the preponderance of numbers and their force, its mechanism is determined beforehand; it excludes certain wheels and connections. That is why the legislator must write laws which reflect the nature of our existence, or, at least, translate this as closely as he can, without any gross contradiction. Nature herself presents him with ready-made statutes. His business is to read these properly; he has already transcribed the apportionment of burdens; he can now transcribe the apportionment of rights.

So, we have seen, local society renders two distinct services[8], which, that the expenses of both may be met, require two distinct assessments, one personal and the other real, one levied on everybody and of which the amount is alike for all, and the other levied only on those whose amount is based on what he spends, on the importance of his business, and on the income from his real estate. - In strict equity, the amount of the former should be equal to the average amount of the latter; in effect, as has been shown, the services defrayed by the former are as many, as diverse, and as precious, still more vital, and not less costly than those of which the latter is the price. Of the two interests which they represent, each, did it stand alone, would be obliged to secure the same services, to take upon itself the whole of the work; neither would obtain more in the dividend, and each would have to pay the whole of the expense. Accordingly, each gains as much as the other in the physical solidarity which binds them together. Hence, in the legal bond which unites them they enter into it on an equal footing, on condition that each is burdened or relived as much as the other, on condition that if the latter assumes one-half of the expense the former shall assume the other half, on condition that if the latter quota on each one hundred francs expended against calamities and for public roads is 50 francs, the former quota shall also be 50 francs. - Practically, however, this is impossible. Three times out of four the former levy with this apportionment would not be returned; through prudence as well as humanity, the legislator is bound not to overburden the poor. Recently, in organizing the general tax and the revenue of the State, he has looked out for them; now, in organizing the local tax and the revenue of the department or of the commune, he looks out for them to a still greater extent.

In the new financial scheme, so many centimes, added to each franc of direct tax, form the principal resource of the department and commune, and it is through this extra charge that each taxpayer pays his quota of local expenditure. Now, there is no surcharge on the personal tax, no additional centimes. Under this heading, the laborer without any property or income, the workman who lives in lodgings, on his wages, and from day to day, contributes nothing to the expenses of his commune or department. In vain do "additional centimes" pour down on other branches of direct taxation; they are not grafted on this one, and do not suck away the substance of the poor. [9] - There is the same regard for the half poor, in relation to the artisan who furnishes his own room, but who lodges in an upper story, and in relation to the peasant whose hovel or cottage has but one door and one window. [10] Their rate of taxation on doors and windows is very low, purposely reduced, kept below one franc a year, while the rate of their personal tax is scarcely higher. "Additional centimes" may be imposed on so small a principal and be multiplied in vain, never will they reach more than an insignificant amount. -Not only are the destitute relieved of both principal and "additional centimes, " the verified poor, those who are registered and are helped, or should be, that is to say 2,470,000 persons; [11] but, again, others, by hundreds of thousands, whom the municipal council judges incapable of paying. - Even when people possess but a small piece of land, they are also relieved of the land tax and of the numerous additional centimes which increase it. Such is the case with those who are infirm or burdened with a family. The exchequer, so as not to convert them into beggars and vagabonds, avoids expropriation, selling out their concrete hovel, vegetable garden, and small field of potatoes or cabbages; it gives them receipts gratis, or, at least, refrains from prosecuting them. [12] In this way the poor peasant, although a land-owner, again exempts himself, or is exempted from his local indebtedness. In truth, he pays nothing, or nearly nothing, otherwise than by prestations (payments) in money or in kind; that is to say, by three days' work on the district roads, which, if he pays in kind, are not worth more than 50 sous. [13] Add to this his portion, very small and often null, of the additional centimes on the tax on doors and windows, on the personal tax, and on the tax on real estate, in all 4 or 5 francs a year. Such is the amount by which the poor or half-poor taxpayer in the villages liberates himself toward his department and commune. -In the towns, he apparently pays more, owing to the octroi. But, at first, there are only 1525 communes out of 36,000 in which the octroi[14] has been established; while in the beginning, under the Directory and Consulate, it was revived only on his account, for his benefit, in behalf of public charity, to defray the expenses of asylums and hospitals ruined by revolutionary confiscation. It was then "an octroi for charity, " in fact as well as in name, like the surplus tax on theater seats and tickets, established at the same time and for the same purpose; it still to-day preserves the stamp of its first institution. Bread, the indispensable provision for the poor, is not subjected to the octroi nor the materials for making it, either grain or flour, nor milk, fruits, vegetables, or codfish, while there is only a light tax on butcher's meat. Even on beverages, where the octroi is heavier, it remains, like all indirect taxes, nearly proportional and semi-optional. In effect, it is simply an increase of the tax on beverages, so many additional centimes per franc on the sum of indirect taxation, as warrantable as the impost itself, as tolerable, and for the same motives. [15] For the greater the sobriety of the taxpayer, the less is he affected by this tax. At Paris, where the increase is excessive, and adds to the 6 centimes paid to the state, on each quart of wine, 12 centimes paid to the city; if he drinks but one quart a day, he pays, under this heading, into the city treasury 43 francs 80 centimes per annum: but, as compensation for this, he is free of personal tax of 11 3/4 %, which this adds to the amount of each rental of the 11 3/4 %, whereby this would have added to his rent, and therefore 47 francs per annum as a rent of 400 francs. Thus what he has paid with one hand he gets back with the other. Now, at Paris, all rentals under 400 francs[16] are thus free of any personal tax; all rentals between 400 and 1000 francs are more or less free, and, in the other octroi towns, an analogous discharge reimburses to the small taxpayers a portion more or less great of the sum they pay to the octroi. - Accordingly, in the towns as in the country, they are favored at one time through fiscal relief and at another through administrative favor, now through compulsory deduction and now through total or partial reimbursement. Always, and very wisely, the legislator apportions the burden according to the strength of the shoulders; he relieves them as much as he can, at first, of the general tax, and next, which is still better, of the local tax. Hence, in local expenditure, their quota diminishes out of all proportion and is reduced to the minimum. Nevertheless, their quota of local benefit remains full and entire; at this insignificant price they enjoy the public highways and profit by all the precautions taken against physical ills; each profits by this personally, equally with any millionaire. Each personally receives as much in the great dividend of security, health, and convenience, in the fruit of the vast works of utility and enjoyment due to improved communications, which preserve health, assist traffic, and beautify the locality, and without which, in town as well as in the country, life would be impossible or intolerable.

But these works which cost so much, these defensive operations and apparatus against inundations, fires, epidemics, and contagions, these 500,000 kilometers of district and department roads, these dikes, quays, bridges, public gardens, and promenades, this paving, drainage, sweeping and lighting, these aqueducts and supplies of drinkable water, all this is paid for by somebody, and, since it is not done by the small taxpayer, it is the large or average taxpayer who pays for it. The latter then, bears, besides his obligatory weight, a gratuitous surplus burden, consisting of the weight of which the other is relieved.

Evidently the greater the number of the relieved, the heavier will be this overweight, and the relieved count by millions. Two millions and a half of declared poor[17] are relieved of any direct tax, and, therefore, of all the centimes which have just increased the burden. Out of 8 millions of real-estate owners, [18] 3 millions, considered as insolvent, pay neither the real estate tax nor the centimes which it comprises. In the octroi towns, it is not the minority but the majority of the inhabitants who are relieved in the way just described; in Paris, [19] out of 685,000 rentals, 625,000, in other terms twelve out of thirteen lodgings, are exempt, wholly or in part, from the personal tax, the principal and "additional centimes. " On each franc of this principal there are 96 of these superadded centimes for the benefit of the town and department and because the department and the town expend a good deal, and because receipts are essential for the settlement of these accounts, this or that sum is noted beforehand in every chapter of receipts, and the main thing now is to have this paid in, and it must be paid by somebody; it matters little whether the peasants are few or numerous; if among thirteen taxable persons there is only one that pays, so much the worse for him, for he must pay for himself and the other twelve. Such is the case in Paris, which accounts for the "additional centimes" here being so numerous, [20] owing to there being less than 60,000 rentals for the acquittance of the entire tax, and, besides paying their own debt, they must discharge the indebtedness of 625,000 other rentals, the tax on which is reduced or null. - Frequently, before the Revolution, some rich convent or philanthropic seignior would pay the taxes of his poor neighbors out of his own pocket; willingly or not, 60,000 Parisians, more or less well lodged, now hand over the same sum, bestow the same charity, on 625,000 thousand badly or only tolerably lodged Parisians; among these 60,000 benefactors whom the exchequer obliges to be benevolent, 34,800 who pay from 1000 to 3000 francs rent, bestow, under this heading, a pretty large sum for charitable purposes, while 14,800, who pay more than 3000 francs rent, pay a very large one. Other branches of direct taxation, in the country as well as in the city, present the same spectacle: it is always the rich or the well- to-do taxpayers who, through their over-tax, more or less completely relieve the poor or straitened taxpayers; it is always the owners of large or small properties, those who pay heavy or average licenses, the occupants of lodgings with more than five openings, [21] and whose locative value surpasses 1000 francs, who in local expenditure pay besides their own dues the dues of others and, through their additional centimes, almost entirely defray the expenses of the department and commune. —This is nearly always the case in a local society, except when it chances to possess an abundant income, arising from productive real estate, and is able to provide for its wants without taxing its members; apart from this rare exception, it is forced to tax some in order to relieve others. In other words, the same as with other enterprises, it manufactures and sells its product but, just the reverse of other enterprises, it sells the product, an equal quantity of the same product, that is to say, equal protection against the same calamities, and the equal enjoyment of the same public highway, at unequal prices, very dear to a few, moderately dear to many, at cost price to a large number, and with a discount to the mass; to this last class of consumers the discount goes on increasing like the emptiness of their purse; to the last of all, extremely numerous, the goods are delivered almost gratis, or even for nothing.

But to this inequality of prices may correspond the inequality of rights, and compensation will come, the balance may be restored, distributive justice may be applied, if, in the government of the enterprise, the parts assigned are not equal, if each member sees his portion of influence growing or diminishing along with the weight of his charge, if the regulations, graduating authority according to the scale of the levies, assigns few votes to those who pay the lowest quotas of expense and receive alms, and many votes to those who give alms and pay the largest quotas of the expenditure.

III. Equity in taxation.

Possible compensation in the other side of the scale. - What the distribution of rights should be according to the principle of distributive justice. - In every association of stock-owners. - In local society confined to its natural object. - In local society charged with supplementary functions. - The local statue in England and Prussia. - The exchange equitable when burdens are compensated by rights.

Such is the rule in every association of interests, even in stock companies in which the distribution of charges allows of no favor or disfavor to any associate. It must be noted that, in these companies, co-operation is not compulsory, but voluntary; the associates are not, as in the local society, conscripts enlisted under the constraint of physical solidarity, but subscribers bound together under the impulsion of a deliberate preference, each remaining in its of his own free will just as he entered it; if he wishes to leave it he has only to sell his stock; the fact of his keeping this confirms his subscription, and, thus holding on to it, he daily subscribes anew to the statute. Here, then, is a perfectly free association; its is accordingly perfectly equitable, and its statute serves as a model for others.

Now this statute always makes a distinction between the small and the large stockholders; it always attributes a greater share of authority and influence to those who share most largely in the risks and expenses; in principle, the number of votes in confers on each associate is proportionate to the number of shares of which he is the owner or bearer. - All the stronger is the reason why this principle should be embodied in the statutes of a society which, like the local community, diminishes the burden of the small taxpayer through its reductions, and increases by its extra taxation the burden of the large or average taxpayer; when the appointment of managers is handed over to universal suffrage, counted by heads, the large and average taxpayers are defrauded of their dues and deprived of their rights, more so by far and more deeply wronged than the bearer or owner of a thousand shares in an omnibus or gas company if, on voting at a meeting of stockholders, his vote did not count for more than that of the owner or bearer of a single share. -

How is it then when a local society adds to its natural and unavoidable purpose an optional and supplementary purpose;

* when, increasing its load, it undertakes to defray the cost of public charity and of primary education;

* when, to support this additional cost, it multiplies the additional centimes;

* when the large or average taxpayer pays alone, or nearly alone, for this benevolent work by which he does not benefit;

* when the small taxpayer pays nothing, or next to nothing, to this benevolent work by which he does benefit;

* when, in voting for the expense thus apportioned, each taxpayer, whatever the amount of his contribution, has one vote and only one?

In this case, powers, benefits, reductions, and exemptions, all the advantages are on one side, that of the poor and half-poor forming the majority and who if not restrained from above, will persistently abuse their numerical force to augment their advantages, at the increasing expense of the rich or well-do-do minority. In the future, in the local society, the average or large taxpayer is no longer an associate but a victim; were he free to choose he would not enter into it; he would like to go away and establish himself elsewhere; but were he to enter others, near or remote, his condition would be no better. He remains, accordingly, where he is, physically present, but absent in feeling; he takes no part in deliberate meetings; his zeal has died out; he withholds from public affairs that surplus of vigilant attention, that spontaneous and ready collaboration which he would have contributed gratis; he lets matters go along without him, just as it happens; he remains there just what he is, a workable, taxable individual in capricious hands, in short, a passive subject who gives and has become resigned. - For this reason, in countries where an encroaching democracy has not yet abolished or perverted the notion of equity, the local statute applies the fundamental rule of an equitable exchange; it lays down the principle that

he who pays commands, and in proportion to the sum he pays. [22]

In England, a surplus of votes is awarded to those most heavily taxed, even six votes to one voter; in Prussia, local taxation is divided into thirds, and, accordingly, the taxpayers into three groups, the first one composed of heavy taxpayers, few in number, and who pay the first third, the second composed of average taxpayers, average in number, and who pay the second third, and the third composed of the great number of small taxpayers, who pay the last third. [23] To each of these groups is assigned the same number of suffrages in the commune election, or the same number of representatives in the commune representation. Through this approximate balance of legal burdens and of legal rights, the two sides of the scales are nearly level, the level which distributive justice demands, and the level which the state, special interpreter, sole arbiter and universal minister of distributive justice, should establish when, in the local community, it imposes, rectifies, or maintains the articles in accordance with which it derives its income and governs.

IV. On unlimited universal suffrage.

How unlimited universal suffrage found its way into local society. -
Object and mode of the French legislator.

If the government, in France, does just the opposite, it is at the height
of a violent and sudden revolution, forced by the party in power and
by popular prejudice, through deductive reasoning, and through
contagion. According to revolutionary and French usage, the
legislator was bound to institute uniformity and to make things
symmetrical; having placed universal suffrage in political society, he
was likewise determined to place it in local society. He had been
ordered to apply an abstract principle, that is to say, to legislate
according to a summary, superficial, and verbal notion which,
purposely curtailed and simplified to excess, did not correspond
with its aim. He obeyed and did nothing more; he made no effort
outside of his instructions. He did not propose to himself to restore
local society to its members, to revive it, to make it a living body,
capable of spontaneous, co-ordinate, voluntary action, and, to this
end, provided with indispensable organs. He did not even take the
trouble to imagine, how it really is, I mean by this, complex and
diverse and inversely to legislators before 1789, and adversely to
legislators before and after 1789 outside of France, against all the
teachings of experience, against the evidence of nature, he refused to
recognize the fact that, in France, mankind are of two species, the
people of the towns and the people of the country, and that,
therefore, there are two types of local society, the urban commune
and the rural commune. He was not disposed to take this capital
difference into consideration; he issued decrees for the Frenchman in
general, for the citizen in himself, for fictive men, so reduced that the
statute which suits them can nowhere suit the actual and complete
man. At one stroke, the legislative shears cut out of the same stuff,
according to the same pattern, thirty-six thousand examples of the
same coat, one coat indifferently for every commune, whatever its
shape, a coat too small for the city and too large for the village,
disproportionate in both cases, and useless beforehand, because it
could not fit very large bodies, nor very small ones. Nevertheless,
once dispatched from Paris, people had to put the coat on and wear
it; it must answer for good or for ill, each donning his own for lack of
another better adjusted; hence the strangest attitudes for each, and,
in the long run, a combination of consequences which neither
governors nor the governed had foreseen.

V. Rural or urban communes.

No distinction between the rural and the urban commune. - Effects
of the law on the rural commune. - Disproportion between the
intelligence of its elected representatives and the work imposed
upon them. - The mayor and the municipal council. - Lack of
qualified members. - The secretary of the mayoralty. - The chief or
under chief of the prefectorial bureau.

Let us consider these results in turn in the small and in the great
communes; clear enough and distinct at the two extremities of the
scale, they blend into each other at intermediate degrees, because
here they combine together, but in different proportions, according
as the commune, higher or lower in the scale, comes nearer to the
village or to the city. - On this territory, too, subdivided since 1789,
and, so to say, crumbled to pieces by the Constituent Assembly, the
small communes are enormous in number; among the 36,000, more
than 27,000 have less than 1000 inhabitants, and of these, more than
16,000 have less than 500 inhabitants. [24] Whoever has traveled over
France, or lived in this country, sees at once what sort of men
compose such purely rural groups; he has only to recall
physiognomies and attitudes to know to what extent in these rude
brains, rendered torpid by the routine of manual labor and
oppressed by the cares of daily life, how narrow and obstructed are
the inlets to the mind; how limited is their information in the way of
facts; how, in the way of ideas, the acquisition of them is slow; what
hereditary distrust separates the illiterate mass from the lettered
class; what an almost insurmountable wall the difference of
education, of habits, and of manners interposes in France between
the blouse and the dress-coat; why, if each commune contains a few
cultivated individuals and a few notable proprietors, universal
suffrage sets them aside, or at least does not seek them out for the
municipal council or the mayoralty. - Before 1830, when the prefect
appointed the municipal councilors and the mayor, these were
always on hand; under the monarchy of July and a limited suffrage,
they were still on hand, at least for the most part; under the second
Empire, whatever the elected municipal council might be, the mayor,
who was appointed by the prefect, and even outside of this council,
might be one of the least ignorant and least stupid even in the
commune. At the present day (1889), it is only accidentally and by
chance that a noble or bourgeois, in a few provinces and in certain
communes, may become mayor or municipal councilor; it is,

however, essential that he should be born on the soil, long established there, resident and popular. Everywhere else the numerical majority, being sovereign, tends to select its candidates from among the average people: in the village, he is a man of average rural intelligence, and, mostly, in the village a municipal council which, as narrow- minded as its electors, elects a mayor equally as narrow-minded as itself Such are, from now on, the representatives and directors of communal interests; except when they themselves are affected by personal interests to which they are sensitive, their inertia is only equaled by their incapacity[25]

Four times a year a bundle of elaborately drawn papers, prepared by the prefecture, are submitted to these innately blind paralytics, large sheets divided into columns from top to bottom, with tabular headings from right to left, and covered with printed texts and figures in writing - details of receipts and expenses, general centimes, special centimes, obligatory centimes, optional centimes, ordinary centimes, extra centimes, with their sources and employment; preliminary budget, final budget, corrected budget, along with legal references, regulations, and decisions bearing on each article. In short, a methodical table as specific as possible and highly instructive to a jurist or accountant, but perfect jargon to peasants, most of whom can scarcely write their name and who, on Sundays, are seen standing before the advertisement board[26] trying to spell out the Journal Officiel, whose abstract phrases, beyond their reach, pass over their heads in aerial and transient flight, like some confused rustling of vague and unknown forms. To guide them in political life, much more difficult than in private life, they require a similar guide to the one they take in the difficult matters of their individual life, a legal or business adviser, one that is qualified and competent, able to understand the prefecture documents, sitting alongside of them to explain their budget, rights and limits of their rights, the financial resources, legal expedients, and consequences of a law; one who can arrange their debates, make up their accounts, watch daily files of bills, attend to their business at the county town, throughout the entire series of legal formalities and attendance on the bureaus, - in short, some trusty person, familiar with technicalities, who they might choose to select. - Such a person was found in Savoy, before the annexation to France, a notary or lawyer who, practicing in the neighborhood or at the principal town, and with five or six communes for clients, visited them in turn, helped them with his knowledge and intelligence, attended their meetings and, besides, served them as scribe, like the present secretary of the mayoralty, for about the same pay, amounting in all to about the same total of fees or salaries. [27] - At the present time, there is nobody in the municipal council to advise and give information to its members; the schoolmaster is their secretary, and he cannot be, and should not be, other than a scribe. He reads in a monotonous tone of voice the long financial enigma which French public book-keeping, too perfect, offers to their divination, and which nobody, save one who is educated to it, can clearly comprehend until after weeks of study. They listen all agog. Some, adjusting their spectacles, try to pick out among so many articles the one they want, the amount of taxes they have to pay. The sum is too large, the assessments are excessive; it is important that the number of additional centimes should be reduced, and therefore that less money should be expended. Hence, if there is any special item of expense which can be got rid of by a refusal, they set it aside by voting No, until some new law or decree from above obliges them to say Yes. But, as things go, nearly all the expenses designated on the paper are obligatory; willingly or not, these must be met, and there is no way to pay them outside of the additional centimes; however numerous these are, vote them they must and sanction the centimes inscribed. They accordingly affix their signatures, not with trust but with mistrust, with resignation, and out of pure necessity. Abandoned to their natural ignorance, the twenty-seven thousand petty municipal councilors of the country are no more passive, more inert, more constrained than ever; deprived of the light which, formerly, the choice of the prefect or a restricted suffrage could still throw into the darkness around them, there remains to them only one safe tutor or conductor; and this final guide is the official of the bureaus, especially this or that old, permanent chief, or under clerk, who is perfectly familiar with his files of papers. With about four hundred municipal councils to lead, one may imagine what he will do with them: nothing except to drive them like a flock of sheep into a pen of printed regulations, or urge them on mechanically, in lots, according to his instructions, he himself being as automatic and as much in a rut as they are.

VI. The larger Communes.

Effects of the law on the urban commune. - Disproportion between the administrative capacity of its elected representatives and the work imposed on them. - Lack of a special and permanent manager. - The municipal council and the mayor. - The general council and the intermediary committee. - The prefect. - His dominant rule. - His obligatory concessions. - His principal aim. - Bargains between the central authority and the local Jacobins. - Effect on this on local government, on the officials, and in local finances.

Let us now look at the other side of the scale, on the side of the large urban communes, of which there are 223, with above 10,000 inhabitants, 90 of these above 20,000 inhabitants, 9 of the latter above 100,000 inhabitants, and Paris, which has 2,300,000. [28] We see at the first glance cast upon an average specimen of these human anthills, a town containing from 40,000 to 50,000 souls, how vast and complex the collective undertaking becomes, how many principal and accessory services the communal society must co-ordinate and unite together in order to secure to its members the advantages of public roads and insure their protection against spreading calamities:

* Maintenance and repairs of these roads, the straightening, laying-out, paving, and drainage, the constructions and expense for sewers, quays, and rivers, and often for a commercial harbor;

* the negotiations and arrangements with departments and with the state for this or that harbor, canal, dike, or insane asylum; the contracts with cab, omnibus, and tramway companies and with telephone and house-lighting companies; the street-lighting, artesian wells and aqueducts;

* the city police, supervision and rules for using public highways, and orders and agents for preventing men from injuring each other when collected together in large assemblies in the streets, in the markets, at the theater, in any public place, whether coffee-houses or taverns;

* the firemen and machinery for conflagrations; the sanitary measures against contagion, and precautions, long beforehand to insure hygiene during epidemics;

* and, as extra burdens and abuses, the establishment, direction and support of primary schools, colleges, public lectures, libraries, theaters, hospitals, and other institutions which should be supported and governed by different associations; at the very least, the appropriations to these establishments and therefore a more or less legitimate and more or less imperative intervention in their internal management.

Such are the great undertakings which form a whole, which bear alike on the present, past, and future budget of the commune, and which, as so many distinct branches of every considerable enterprise, require, for proper execution, to have their continuity and connection always present in the thoughtful and directing mind which has them in charge. [29] Experience shows that, in the great industrial or financial companies, in the Bank of France, in the Crédit Lyonnais, and in the insurance, navigation, and railroad companies, the best way to accomplish this end is a permanent manager or director, always present, engaged or accepted by the administrative board on understood conditions, a special, tried man who, sure of his place for a long period, and with a reputation to maintain, gives his whole time, faculties, and zeal to the work, and who, alone, possessing at every moment a coherent and detailed conception of the entire undertaking, can alone give it the proper stimulus, and bring to bear the most economical and the most perfect practical improvements. Such is also the municipal administration in the Prussian towns on the Rhine. Then, in Bonn, for instance, [30] the municipal council, elected by the inhabitants "goes in quest" of some eminent specialist whose ability is well known. It must be noted that he is taken wherever he can be found, outside the city, in some remote province; they bargain with him, the same as with some famous musician, for the management of a series of concerts. Under the title of burgomaster, with a salary of 10,000 francs per annum, he becomes for twelve years the director of all municipal services, leader of the civic orchestra, solely entrusted with executive power, wielding the magisterial baton which the various instruments obey, many of these being salaried functionaries and others benevolent amateurs, [31] all in harmony and through him, because they know that he is watchful, competent, and top quality, constantly occupied with am overall view, responsible, and in his own interest, as a point of honor, wholly devoted to his work which is likewise their work, that is to say, to the complete success of the concert.

Nothing in a French town corresponds to this admirable type of a municipal institution. Here, also, and to a much greater extent in the village, the effect of universal suffrage has been to discredit the true notables and to incite the abdication or insure the exclusion of men who, by their education, the large proportion of the taxes they pay, and still greater influence or production on labor and on business, are social authorities, and who should become legal authorities. In every country where conditions are unequal, the preponderance of a numerical majority necessarily ends in the nearly general abstention or almost certain defeat of the candidates most deserving of election. But here the case is different; the elected, being towns-people (citadins) and not rural, are not of the species as in the village. They read a daily newspaper, and believe that they understand not only local matters but all subjects of national and general importance, that is to say, high level economy, philosophy and law; somewhat resembling the schoolmaster who, being familiar with the rules of arithmetic, thinks that he can teach the differential calculus, and the theory of functions. At any rate, they talk loud and argue on every subject with confidence, according to Jacobin traditions, being, indeed, so many budding Jacobins. They are the heirs and successors of the old sectarians, issuing from the same stock and of the same stamp, a few in good faith, but mainly narrow- minded, excited, and bewildered by the smoke of the glittering generalities they utter. Most of them are mere politicians, charlatans, and intriguers, third-class lawyers and doctors, literary failures, semi-educated stump-speakers, bar-room, club, or clique orators, and vulgar climbers. Left behind in private careers, in which one is closely watched and accepted for what he is worth, they launch out on a public career because, in this business, popular suffrage at once ignorant, indifferent, is a badly informed, prejudiced and passionate judge and prefers a moralist of easy conscience, instead of demanding unsullied integrity and proven competency. Nothing more is demanded from candidates but witty speech-making, assertiveness and showing off in public, gross flattery, a display of enthusiasm and promises to place the power about to be conferred on them by the people in the hands of those who will serve its antipathies and prejudices. Thus introduced into the municipal council, they constitute its majority and appoint a mayor who is their figurehead or creature, now the bold leader and again the docile instrument of their spite, their favors, and their headlong action, of their blunders and presumption, and of their meddlesome disposition and encroachments. - In the department, the council general, also elected by universal suffrage, also bears the marks of its origin; its quality, without falling so low, still descends in a certain degree, and through changes which keep on increasing: politicians install themselves there and make use of their place as a stepping-stone to mount higher; it also, with larger powers and prolonged during its vacations by its committee, is tempted to regard itself as the legitimate sovereign of the extensive and scattered community which it represents. - Thus recruited and composed, enlarged and deteriorated, the local authorities become difficult to manage, and from now on, to carry on the administration, the prefect must come to some understanding with them.

VII. Local society in 1880.

Present state of local society. - Considered as an organism, it is
stillborn. - Considered as a mechanism, it gets out of order. - Two
successive and false conceptions of local government. - In theory,
one excludes the other. - Practically, their union ends in the actual
system. - Powers of the prefect. - Restrictions on these through
subsequent changes. - Give and take. - Bargaining. - Supported by
the government and cost to the State.

Before 1870, when he appointed the mayors and when the council
general held its sessions only fifteen days in the year, the prefect was
almost omnipotent; still, at the present day, (1889), "his powers are
immense, "[32] and his power remains preponderant. He has the
right to suspend the municipal council and the mayor, and to
propose their dismissal to the head of the state. Without resorting to
this extremity, he holds them with a strong hand, and always
uplifted over the commune, for he can veto the acts of the municipal
police and of the road committee, annul the regulations of the
mayor, and, through a skillful use of his prerogative, impose his
own. He holds in hand, removes, appoints or helps appoint, not
alone the clerks in his office, but likewise every kind and degree of
clerk who, outside his office, serves the commune or department,
[33] from the archivist, keeper of the museum, architect, director,
and teachers of the municipal drawing-schools, from the directors
and collectors of charity establishments, directors and accountants of
almshouses, doctors of the mineral springs, doctors and accountants
of the insane asylums and for epidemics, head-overseers of octrois,
wolf-bounty guards, commissioners of the urban police, inspectors
of weights and measures, town collectors, whose receipts do not
exceed thirty thousand francs, down to and comprising the lowest
employees, such as forest guards of the department and commune,
lock-keepers and navigation guards, overseers of the quays and of
commercial ports, toll-gatherers on bridges and highways, field-
guards of the smallest village, policemen posted on the corner of a
street, and stone- breakers on the public highway. When things and
not persons are concerned, it is he, again, who, in every project,
enterprise, or proceeding, is charged with the preliminary
examination and final execution of it, who proposes the department
budget and presents it, regularly drawn up, to the council general,
who draws up the communal budget and presents that to the
municipal council, and who, after the council general or municipal

council have voted on it, remains on the spot the sole executor, director, and master of the operation to which they have assented. Their total, effective part in this operation is very insignificant, it being reduced to a bare act of the will; in reaching a vote they have had in their hands scarcely any other documents than those furnished and arranged by him; in gradually reaching their decision step by step, they have had no help but his, that of an independent collaborator who, governed by his own views and interests, never becomes the mere instrument. They lack for their decision direct, personal, and full information, and, beyond this, complete, efficient power; it is simply a dry Yes, interposed between insufficient resources, or else cut off, and the fruit of which is abortive or only half ripens. The persistent will of the prefect alone, informed, and who acts, must and does generally prevail against this ill-supported and ill-furnished will. At bottom, and as he stands, he is, in his mental and official capacity, always the prefect of the year VIII.

Nevertheless, after the laws lately passed, his hands are not so free. The competency of local assemblies is extended and comprises not only new cases but, again, of a new species, while the number of their executive decisions has increased five-fold. The municipal council, instead of holding one session a year, holds four, and of longer duration. The council general, instead of one session a year, holds two, and maintains itself in the interim by its delegation which meets every month. With these increased authorities and generally present, the prefect has to reckon, and what is still more serious, he must reckon with local opinion; he can no longer rule with closed doors; the proceedings of the municipal council, the smallest one, are duly posted; in the towns, they are published and commented on by the newspapers of the locality; the general council furnishes reports of its deliberations. - Thus, behind elected powers, and weighing with these on the same side of the scales, here is a new power, opinion, as this grows in a country leveled by equalized centralization, in heaving or stagnant crowd of disintegrated individuals lacking any spontaneous, central, rallying point, and who, failing natural leaders, simply push and jostle each other or stand still, each according to personal, blind, and haphazard impressions - a hasty, improvident, inconsistent, superficial opinion, caught on the wing, based on vague rumors, on four or five minutes of attention given each week, and chiefly to big words imperfectly understood, two or three sonorous, commonplace phrases, of which the listeners fail to catch the sense, but the sound which, by din of frequent repetition, becomes for them a recognized signal, the blast of a horn or a shrieking whistle which assembles the herd and arrests or drives it on. No opposition can make head against this herd as it rushes along in too compact and too heavy masses. - The prefect, on the contrary, is obliged to cajole it, yield to it, and satisfy it; for under the system of universal suffrage, this same herd, besides local representatives, elects the central powers, the deputies, the government; and when the government sends a prefect from Paris into the provinces, it is after the fashion of a large commercial establishment, with a view to keep and increase the number of its customers, to stay there, maintain its credit, and act permanently as its traveling-clerk, or, in other terms, as its electoral agent, and, still more precisely, as the campaign manager of coming elections for the dominant party and for the ministers in office who have commissioned and appointed him, and who, from top to bottom, constantly stimulate him to hold on to the voters already secured and to gain fresh ones. - Undoubtedly, the interests of the state, department, and commune must be seriously considered, but, first and above all, he is the recruiting officer for voters. By virtue of this position and on this he treats with the council general and the standing committee, with the municipal councilors and mayors, with influential electors, but especially with the small active committee which, in each commune, supports the prevailing policy and offers its zeal to the government.

Give and take. These indispensable auxiliaries must obtain nearly all they ask for, and they ask a great deal. Instinctively, as well as by doctrine and tradition, the Jacobins are exacting, disposed to regard themselves as the representatives of the real and the ideal people, that is to say, as sovereigns by right, above the law, entitled to make it and therefore to unmake it, or, at least, strain it and interpret it as they please. Always in the general council, in the municipal council, and in the mayoralty, they are tempted to usurp it; the prefect has as much as he can do to keep them within the local bounds, to keep them from meddling with state matters and the general policy; he is often obliged to accept their lack of consideration, to be patient with them, to talk to them mildly; for they talk and want the administration to reckon with them as a clerk with his master; if they vote money for any service it is on condition that they take part in the use of the funds and in the details of the service, in the choice of contractors and in hiring the workmen; on condition that their authority be extended and their hands applied to the consecutive execution of what does not belong to them but which belongs to the prefect. [34] Bargaining, consequently, goes on between them incessantly and they come to terms. - The prefect, it must be noted, who is bound to pay, can do so without violating the letter of the law. The stern page on which the legislator has printed his imperative text is always provided with an ample margin where the administrator, charged with its execution, can write down the decisions that he is free to make. In relation to each departmental or communal affair, the prefect can with his own hand write out what suits him on the white margin, which, as we have already seen, is ample enough; but the margin at his disposition is wider still and continues, beyond anything we have seen, on other pages; he is chargé d'affaires not only of the department and commune, but again of the State. Titular conductor or overseer of all general services, he is, in his circumscription, head inquisitor of the republican faith, even in relation to private life and inner sentiments, the responsible director of orthodox or heretical acts or opinions, which are laudable or blamable in the innumerably army of functionaries by which the central state now undertakes the complete mastery of human life, the twenty distinct regiments of its vast hierarchy - with the staff of the clergy, of the magistracy, of the preventive and repressive police, of the customs; with the officials of bridges and highways, forest domains, stock-breeding establishments, postal and telegraph departments, tobacco and other monopolies; with those of every national enterprise which ought to be private, Sévres and Gobelins, deaf and dumb and blind asylums, and every auxiliary and special workshop for war and navigation purposes, which the state supports and manages. I pass some of them and all too many. Only remark this, that the indulgence or severity of the prefecture in the way of fiscal violations or irregularities is an advantage or danger of the highest importance to 377,000 dealers in wines and liquors; that an accusation brought before and admitted in the prefecture may deprive 38,000 clergymen of their bread, [36] 43,000 letter-carriers and telegraph messengers, 45,000 sellers of tobacco and collecting-clerks, 75,000 stone-breakers, and 120,000 male and female teachers; [37] directly or indirectly, the good or ill favor of the prefecture is of consequence, since recent military laws, to all adults between 20 and 45 years, and, since recent school laws, to all children between 6 and 13 years of age. According to these figures, which go on increasing from year to, calculate the breadth of the margin on which, alongside of the legal text which states the law for persons and things in general, the prefect in his turn gives the law for persons and things in particular. On this margin, which belongs to him, he writes what he pleases, at one time permissions and favors, exemptions, dispensations, leaves of absence, relief of taxes or discharges, help and subventions, preferences and gratuities, appointments and promotions, and at another time disgrace, hardship, legal proceedings, dismissals, and special favors. To guide his hand in each case, that is to say, to spread all the favors on one side and all the disfavors on the other, he has, among the local Jacobins, special informers and important applicants. If not restrained by a very strong sentiment of distributive justice and very great solicitude for the public good he can hardly resist them, and in general when he takes up his pen it is to write under the dictation of his Jacobin collaborators.

Democracy in France in 1889, Summary.

Thus has the institution of the year VIII deviated (The France of the revolution corrected and decreed by Napoleon), no longer attaining its object. The prefects, formerly appointed to a department, like a pacier of the Middle Ages, imposed on it from above, ignorant of local passions, independent, qualified and fitted for the office, was, during fifty years, in general, able to remain the impartial minister of the law and of equity, maintaining the rights of each, and exacting from each his due, without heeding opinions and without respect to persons. Now he is obliged to become an accomplice of the ruling faction, govern for the advantage of some to the detriment of others, and to put into his scales, as a preponderating weight, every time he weighs judgment, a consideration for persons and opinions. At the same time, the entire administrative staff in his hands, and under his eye, deteriorates; each year, on the recommendation of a senator or deputy, he adds to it, or sees, intruders there, whose previous services are null, feeble in capacity and of weak integrity who do poor work or none at all, and who, to hold their post or get promoted, count not on their merits but on their sponsors. The rest, able and faithful functionaries of the old school, who are poor and to whom no path is open, become weary and lose their energy; they are no longer even certain of keeping their place; if they stay, it is for the dispatch of current business and because they cannot be dispensed with; perhaps to-morrow, however, they will cease to be considered indispensable; some political denunciation, or to give a political favorite a place, will put them by anticipation on the retired list. From now on they have two powers to consult, one, legitimate and natural, the authority of their administrative chiefs, and the other illegitimate and parasite, consisting of democratic influence from both above and below. For them, as for the prefect, public welfare descends to the second rank and the electoral interest mounts upward to the first rank. With them as with him self-respect, professional honor, the conscientious performance of duty, reciprocal loyalty go down; discipline relaxes, punctuality falters, and, as the saying goes, the great administrative edifice is no longer a well-kept house, but a barracks.

Naturally, under the democratic regime, the maintenance and service of this house becomes more and more costly; [38] for, owing to the additional centimes, it is the rich and well-to-do minority which defrays the larger portion of the expense. Owing to universal suffrage, the poor or half-poor majority which dominate the elections so that the large majority with impunity can overtax the minority. At Paris, the parliament and the government, elected by this numerical majority, contrive demands in its behalf, force expenditure, augment public works, schools, endowments, gratuities, prizes, a multiplication of offices to increase the number of their clients, while it never tires in decreeing, in the name of principles, works for show, theatrical, ruinous, and dangerous, the cost of which they do not care to know, and of which the social import escapes them. Democracy, above as well as below, is short-sighted; it seizes whatever food it comes across, like an animal, with open jaws and head down; it refuses to anticipate and to calculate; it burdens the future and wastes every fortune it undertakes to manage, not alone that of the central state, but, again, those of all local societies. Up to the advent of universal suffrage, the administrators appointed above or elected below, in the department or in the commune, kept tight hold of the purse-strings; since 1848, especially since 1870, and still later, since the passage of the laws of 1882, which, in suppressing the obligatory consent of the heaviest taxed, let slip the last of these strings, this purse, wide open, is emptied in the street. - In 1851, [39] the departments, all together, expended 97 millions; in 1869, 192 millions; in 1881, 314 millions. In 1836, the communes, all together, save Paris, expended 117 millions, in 1862, 450 millions, in 1877, 676 millions. If we examine the receipts covering this expenditure, we find that the additional centimes which supplied the local budgets, in 1820, with 80 millions, and, in 1850, with 131 millions, supplied them, in 1870, with 249 millions, in 1880, with 318 millions, and, in 1887, with 364 millions. The annual increase, therefore, of these superadded centimes to the principal of the direct taxes is enormous, and finally ends in an overflow. In 1874, [40] there were already 24 departments in which the sum of additional centimes reached or surpassed the sum of the principal. "In a very few years, " says an eminent economist, [41] "it is probable that, for nearly all of the departments, " the overcharge will be similar. Already, for a long time, in the total of personal taxation, [42] the local budgets raised more than the state, and, in 1888, the principal of the tax real property, 183 millions, is less than the total of centimes joined with it, 196 millions. Coming generations are burdened over and beyond the present generation, while the sum of loans constantly increases, like that of taxation. The indebted communes, except Paris, owed, altogether, in 1868, 524 millions francs[43], in 1871, 711 millions, and in 1878, 1322 millions francs. [44] Paris, in 1868, already owed 1326 millions, March 30, 1878, it owed 1988 millions. In this same Paris, the annual contribution of each inhabitant for local expenses was, at the end of the first Empire, in 1813, 37 francs per head, at the end of the Restoration, [45] francs, after the July monarchy, in 1848, 43 francs, and, at the end of the second Empire, in 1869, 94 francs. In 1887,45 it is 110 francs per head.

VIII. Final result in a tendency to bankruptcy.

Such, in brief, is the history of local society from 1789 down to 1889. After the philosophic demolition of the Revolution and the practical constructions of the Consulate, it could no longer be a small patrimony, something to take pride in, an object of affection and devotion to its inhabitants. The departments and communes have become more or less vast lodging-houses, all built on the same plan and managed according to the same regulations one as passable as the other, with apartments in them which, more or less good, are more or less dear, but at rates which, higher or lower, are fixed at a uniform tariff over the entire territory, so that the 36,000 communal buildings and the 86 department hotels are about equal, it making but little difference whether one lodges in the latter rather than in the former. The permanent taxpayers of both sexes who have made these premises their home, have not obtained recognition for what they are, invincibly and by nature, a syndicate of neighbors, an involuntary, obligatory and private association, in which physical solidarity engenders moral solidarity, a natural, limited society whose members own the building in common, and each possesses a property right more or less great, according to the greater or lesser contribution he makes to the expenses of the establishment. Up to this time no room has yet been found, either in the law or in minds, for this very plain truth; its place is taken and occupied in advance by the two errors which, in turn or both at once, have led the legislator and opinion astray.

Taking things as a whole, it is admitted up to 1830 that the legitimate proprietor of the local building is the central state, that it may install its delegate therein, the prefect, with full powers; that, for better government, he consents to be instructed by the leading interested and most capable parties on the spot; that he should fix the petty rights he concedes to them within the narrowest limits; that he should appoint them; that, if he calls them together for consultation, it is from time to time and generally for form's sake, to add the authority of their assent to the authority of his omnipotence, on the implied condition that he shall not give heed to their objections if he does not like them, and not follow their advice if he does not choose to accept it. - Taking things as a whole, it is admitted that, since 1848, the legitimate proprietors of the building are its adult male inhabitants, counted by heads, all equal and all with an equal part in the common property, comprising those who contribute nothing or nearly nothing to the common expenditure of the house, the numerous body of semi-poor who lodge in it at half price, and the not less numerous body to whom administrative charity furnishes house comforts, shelter, light, and frequently provisions, gratuitously. - Between both these contradictory and false conceptions, between the prefect of the year VIII, and the democracy of 1792, a compromise has been effected; undoubtedly, the prefect, sent from Paris, is and remains the titular director, the active and responsible manager of the departmental or communal building; but, in his management of it he is bound to keep in view the coming elections, and in such a way as will maintain the parliamentary majority in the seats they occupy in parliament; consequently, he must conciliate the local leaders of universal suffrage, rule with their help, put up with the intrusion of their bias and cupidity, take their advice daily, follow it often, even in small matters, even in payments day by day of sums already voted, in appointing an office-clerk, in the appointment of an unpaid underling, who may some day or other take this clerk's place. [47] - Hence the spectacle before our eyes: a badly kept establishment in which profusion and waste render each other worse and worse, where sinecures multiply and where corruption enters in; a staff of officials becoming more and more numerous and less and less serviceable, harassed between two different authorities, obliged to possess or to simulate political zeal and to neutralize an impartial law by partiality, and, besides performing their regular duties, to do dirty work; in this staff, there are two sorts of employees, the new- comers who are greedy and who, through favor, get the best places, and the old ones who are patient and pretend no more, but who suffer and grow disheartened; in the building itself, there is great demolition and reconstruction, architectural fronts in monumental style for parade and to excite attention, entirely new decorative and extremely tiresome structures at extravagant cost; consequently, loans and debts, heavier bills at the end of each year for each occupant, low rents, but still high, for favorites in the small rooms and garrets, and extravagant rents for the larger and more sumptuous apartments; in sum, forced receipts which do not offset the expenses; liabilities which exceed assets; a budget which shows only a stable balance on paper, - in short, an establishment with which the public is not content, and which is on the road to bankruptcy.

Notes:

[1] Laws of March 21, 1831, and July 18, 1837, June 22, 1833, and May 10, 1838. The municipal electors number about 2,250,000 and form the superior third of the adult masculine population; in the choice of its notables and semi-notables, the law takes into account not only wealth and direct taxation but likewise education and services rendered to the public. - The department electors number about 200,000, about as many as the political electors. The reporter observes that "an almost complete analogy exists between the choice of a deputy and the choice of a department councilor, and that it is natural to confide the election to the same electoral body otherwise divided, since the object is to afford representation to another order of interests. "

[2] Laws of July 3, 1848.

[3] Laws of Aug. 12, 1876, March 28, 1882, and April 5, 1884; law of Aug. 10, 1871.

[4] The prefect, who is directed and posted by the minister of the Interior in Paris.

[5] "The Revolution, " vol. I., book VIII. (Laff. I)

[8] Construction of roads, canals, sewers, highways etc and protection against calamities.

[9] Paul Leroy-Beaulieu, "Traité de la science des finances, " 4th edition, I., p. 303: "The personal tax, levied only as principal, oscillates between the minimum of 1 fr. 50 and the maximum of 4 fr. 50 per annum, according to the communes. - Ibid., 304: "In 1806 the personal tax produced in France about sixteen millions of francs, a little less than o fr. 50 per head of the inhabitants. "

[10] Ibid., I., 367 (on the tax on doors and windows). According to the population of the commune, this is from 0 fr. 30 to 1 fr. for each opening, from 0 fr. 45 to 1 fr. 50 for two openings, from 0 fr. 90 to 4 fr. 50 for three openings, from 1 fr. 60 to 6 fr. 40 for four openings, and from 2 fr. 50 to 8 fr. 50 for five openings. The first of these rates is applied to all communes of less than 5000 souls. We see that the poor man, especially the poor peasant, is considered; the tax on him is progressive in an inverse sense.

[11] De Foville, "La France Economique" (1887): "Our 14,500 charity bureaux gave assistance in 1883 to 1,405,500 persons; . . .. as, in reality, the population of the communes aided (by them) is only 22,000,000, the proportion of the registered poor amounts to over six per cent. "

[12] Paul Leroy-Beaulieu, " Essai sur la répartition des richesses, " p. 174, et seq. - In 1851, the number of land-owners in France was estimated at 7,800,000. Out of these, three millions were relieved of the land tax, as indigent, and their quotas were considered as irrecoverable.

[13] Paul Leroy-Beaulieu, "Traité de la science des finances, ".

[14] De Foville,(In 1889.)

[15] Cf ante, on the characteristics of indirect taxation.

[16] Here it is the estimated rent, which stands to the real rent as four to five; an estimated rent of 400 francs indicates a real rent of 500 francs.

[17] De Foville.

[18] Paul Leroy-Beaulieu, " Essai sur la répartition de richesses, " p. 174.

[19] Ibid.: In 1878, in Paris, 74,000 houses with 1,022,539 rentals, 337,587 being for trade and commerce, and 684,952 for dwelling purposes. Among the latter, 468,641 have a locative value inferior to 300 francs a year; 74,360 are between 500 and 750 francs; 21,147 are between 750 and 1000 francs. All these lodgings are more or less exempt from the personal tax: those between 1000 and 400 francs pay it with a more or less great reduction: those under 400 francs pay nothing. Above 1000 francs, we find 17,202 apartments from between 1000 and 1250 francs; 6198 from between 1250 and 1500 francs; 21,453 from 1500 to 3000 francs. These apartments are occupied by more or less well-to-do people. - 14,858 apartments above 3000 francs are occupied by the richer or the wealthy class. Among the latter 9985 are from 3000 to 6000; 3040 are from 6000 to 10,000; 1443 are from 10,000 to 20,000; 421 are above 20,000 francs. These two latter categories are occupied by the really opulent class. - According to the latest statistics, instead of 684,952 dwelling rentals there are 806,187,

of which 727,419 are wholly or partly free of the personal tax. ("Situation au 1ère Janvier, 1888, " report by M. Lamouroux, conseiller-municipal.)

[20] The following appropriations for 1889 are printed on my tax-bill:"To the State, 51 %. ; to the Department, 21 %; to the commune, 25 %. " On business permits: "To the State, 64 %. ; to the Department, 12 %. ; to the commune, 20 %. The surplus of taxes is appropriated to the benevolent fund and for remission of taxes. "

[21] Paul Leroy-Beaulieu, "Traité de la science des finances, " I., pp. 367-368: "In communes under 5000 inhabitants the principal of the tax on doors and windows is, for houses with one opening, 0 fr. 30 per annum; for those with four openings, 1 fr. 60. " Now, "a house with five openings pays nearly nine times as much as a house with one opening. " The small taxpayers are accordingly largely relieved at the expense of those who pay heavy and average taxes, the magnitude of this relief being appreciable by the following figures: In 1885, out of 8,975,166 houses, 248,352 had one opening, 1,827,104 two openings, 1,624,516 three openings, and 1,165,902 four openings. More than one- half of the houses, all of those belonging to the poor or straitened, are thus relieved, while the other half, since the tax is an impost, not a quota, but an apportionment, is overcharged as much.

[22] One result of this principle is, that the poor who are exempt from taxation or who are on the poor list have no vote, which is the case in England and in Prussia. - Through another result of the same principle, the law of May 15, 1818, in France, summoned the heaviest taxpayers, in equal number with the members of the municipal council, to deliberate with it every time that "a really urgent expenditure" obliged the commune to raise extra additional centimes beyond the usual 0 fr. 05. "Thus, " says Henrion de Pancey ("Du pouvoir municipal, " p. 109), "the members of the municipal councils belong to the class of small land-owners, at least in a large number of communes, voted the charges without examination which only affected them insensibly. " - This last refuge of distributive justice was abolished by the law of April 5, 1882.

[23] Max Leclerc, "Le Vie municipale en Prusse. " (Extrait des "Annales de l'Ecole libre des sciences politique, " 1889, a study on the town of Bonn.) At Bonn, which has a population of 35,810 inhabitants, the first group is composed of 167 electors: the second,

of 471; the third, of 2607, each group elects 8 municipal councilors out of 24.

[24] De Foville, "La France économique, " p. 16 (census of 1881). - Number of communes, 36,097; number below 1000 inhabitants, 27,503; number below 500 inhabitants, 16,870. - What is stated applies partly to the two following categories: 1st, communes from 1000 to 1500 inhabitants, 2982; 2nd, communes from 1500 to 2000 inhabitants, 1917. - All the communes below 2000 inhabitants are counted as rural in the statistics of population, and they number 33,402.

[25] See Paul Leroy-Beaulieu, "L'État moderne et ses fonctions, " p. 169. "The various groups of inhabitants, especially in the country, do not know how to undertake or agree upon anything of themselves. I have seen villages of two or three hundred people belonging to a large scattered commune wait patiently for years and humbly petition for aid in constructing an indispensable fountain, which required only a contribution of 200 or 300 francs, 5 francs per head, to put up. I have seen others possessing only one road on which to send off their produce and unable to act in concert, when, with an outlay of 2000 francs, and 200 or 300 francs a year to keep it in order, it would easily suffice for all their requirements. I speak of regions relatively rich, much better off than the majority of communes in France. "

[26] In French villages, on one of the walls of a public building on the square are notices of all kinds, of interest to the inhabitants, and among these, in a frame behind a wire netting, the latest copy of the government official newspaper, giving authentic political items, those which it thinks best for the people to read. (Tr.)

[27] On the communal system in France, and on the reforms which, following the example of other nations, might be introduced into it, cf. Joseph Ferrand (formerly a prefect), "Les Institutions administratives en France et à l'étranger"; Rudolph Gneist, "Les Réformes administratives en Prusse accomplies par la legislation de 1872, " (especially the institution of Amtsvorsteher, for the union of communes or circumscriptions of about 1500 souls); the Duc de Broglie, "Vues sur le gouvernement de la France" (especially on the reforms that should be made in the administration of the commune and canton), p. 21. - "Deprive communal magistrates of their quality as government agents; separate the two orders of functions; have the

public functionary whose duty it is to see that the laws are executed in the communes, the execution of general laws and the decisions of the superior authority carried out, placed at the county town. "

[28] De Foville, ibid., p. 16. - The remarks here made apply to towns of the foregoing category (from 5000 to 10,000 souls), numbering 312. A last category comprises towns from 2000 to 5000 souls, numbering 2160, and forming the last class of urban populations; these, through their mixed character, assimilate to the 1817 communes containing from 1500 to 2000 inhabitants, forming the first category of the rural populations.

[29] Max Leclerc, "La Vie municipale en Prusse, " p 17. - In Prussia, this directing mind is called "the magistrate, " as in our northern and northeastern communes. In eastern Prussia, the "magistrate" is a collective body; for example, at Berlin, it comprises 34 persons, of which 17 are specialists, paid and engaged for twelve years, and 17 without pay. In western Prussia, the municipal management consists generally of an individual, the burgomaster, salaried and engaged for twelve years.

[30] Max Leclerc, ibid., p. 20. - "The present burgomaster in Bonn was burgomaster at Münchens-Gladbach, before being called to Bonn. The present burgomaster of Crefeld came from Silesia . . .. A lawyer, well known for his works on public law, occupying a government position at Magdeburg, " was recently called "to the lucrative position of burgomaster " in the town of Münster. At Bonn, a town of 30,000 inhabitants, "everything rests on his shoulders he exercises a great many of the functions which, with us, belong to the prefect. "

[31] Max Leclerc, ibid., p. 25. - Alongside of the paid town officers and the municipal councilors, there are special committees composed of benevolent members and electors "either to administer or superintend some branch of communal business, or to study some particular question. " "These committees, subject, moreover, in all respects to the burgomaster, are elected by the municipal council. " - There are twelve of these in Bonn and over a hundred in Berlin. This institution serves admirably for rendering those who are well disposed useful, as well as for the development of local patriotism, a practical sense and public spirit.

[32] Aucoc, p. 283.

[33] Paul Leroy-Beaulieu, "L'administrateur locale en France et en Angleterre, " pp. 26, 28, 92. (Decrees of March 25, 1852, and April 13, 1861.)

[349 J. Ferrand, ibid., p. 169, 170 (Paris, 1879): "In many cases, general tutelage and local tutelage are paralyzed . . .. Since 1870-1876 the mayors, to lessen the difficulties of their task, are frequently forced to abandon any rightful authority; the prefects are induced to tolerate, to approve of these infractions of the law. . .. For many years one cannot read the minutes of a session of the council general or of the municipal council without finding numerous examples of the illegality we report . . .. In another order of facts, for example in that which relates to the official staff, do we not see every day agents of the state, even conscientious, yield to the will of all-powerful political notabilities and entirely abandon the interests of the service?" - These abuses have largely increased within the past ten years.

[36] Ibid., p. 105: "Each cantonal chief town has its office of informers. The Minister of Public Worship has himself told that on the first of January, 1890, there were 300 curés deprived of their salary, about three or four times as many as on the first of January, 1889. "

[37] These figures are taken from the latest statistical reports. Some of them are furnished by the chief or directors of special services.

[38] Taine could hardly have imagined how costly the modern democracy would, 100 years later, become. How could he have imaged that the "Human Rights" should become the right to live comfortably and well at the expense of an ever more productive society.

[39] DeFoville, pp. 412, 416, 425, 455; Paul Leroy-Beaulieu, "Traité de la science des finances, " I., p. 717.

[40] "Statistiques financières des communes en 1889": - 3539 communes pay less than 15 common centimes; 2597 pay from 0 fr. 15 to 0 fr. 30; 9652 pay from 0 fr. 31 to 0 fr. 50; 11,095 from 0 fr. 51 to 1 franc, and 4248 over 1 franc. - Here this relates only to the common centimes; to have the sum total of the additional local centimes of each commune would require the addition of the department centimes, which the statistics do not furnish.

[41] Paul Leroy-Beaulieu, ibid., I.

[42] Ibid. : "If the personal tax were deducted from the amount of personal and house tax combined we would find that the assessment of the state in the product of the house tax, that is to say the product of the tax on rentals, amounts to 41 or 42 millions, and that the share of localities in the product of this tax surpasses that of the state by 8 or 9 millions (Year 1877.)

[43] Between 1805 and 1900 the French franc was tied to the gold standard. A 20 francs coin thus weighed 7,21 grams. Its price is today in 1998 1933. - francs. Taine's figures have to be multiplied by app. ten in order to compare with today's prices. No real comparison can, however, be made since production per capita has multiplied by a large factor and so have taxes.

[44] "Situation financière des department et des communes, " published in 1889 by the Minister of the Interior. Loans and indebtedness of the departments at the end of the fiscal year in 1886, 630,066,102 francs. Loans and indebtedness of the communes Dec. 30, 1886, 3,020,450,528 francs.

[45] De Foville, p. 148; Paul Leroy-Beaulieu, " L'État moderne et ses fonctions, " p. 21.

[47] Paul Leroy-Beaulieu, "L'Administration locale en France et en Angleterre, " p. 28. (Decrees of March 25, 1852, and April 13, 1861.) List of offices directly appointed by the prefect and on the recommendation of the heads of the service, among others the supernumeraries of telegraph lines and of the tax offices.

End of The Modern Regime, Volume 1 [Napoleon]

Lightning Source UK Ltd.
Milton Keynes UK
UKHW042152100223
416857UK00006BA/41